APR   2004

Big Sky Rivers

Robert Kelley Schneiders

Big Sky
Rivers

The Yellowstone & Upper Missouri

 University Press of Kansas

Published by the University Press of Kansas (Lawrence, Kansas 66049), which was organized by the Kansas Board of Regents and is operated and funded by Emporia State University, Fort Hays State University, Kansas State University, Pittsburg State University, the University of Kansas, and Wichita State University

Library of Congress Cataloging-in-Publication Data

Schneiders, Robert Kelley, 1965–

   Big sky rivers : the Yellowstone and Upper Missouri / Robert Kelley Schneiders.

     p. cm.

Includes bibliographical references (p.   ) and index.

   ISBN 0-7006-1264-5 (cloth : alk. paper)

   1. Yellowstone River—History. 2. Yellowstone River Valley—History. 3. Missouri River—History. 4. Missouri River Valley—History. 5. Yellowstone River Valley—Environmental conditions. 6. Missouri River Valley—Environmental conditions. 7. Indians of North America—Yellowstone River Valley—History. 8. Indians of North America—Missouri River Valley—History. 9. Natural history—Yellowstone River Valley. 10. Natural history—Missouri River Valley. I. Title.

   F737.Y4S37 2003

   978—dc21   2003006867

British Library Cataloguing in Publication Data is available.

Printed in the United States of America

10 9 8 7 6 5 4 3 2 1

The paper used in this publication meets the minimum requirements of the American National Standard for Permanence of Paper for Printed Library Materials Z39.48-1984.

To Elizabeth Ann Wieling,
for all she has given to the Missouri River

To my father, Robert Joseph Schneiders,
for pointing me toward the Mighty Missouri

To my mother, Mary Jean (Lang) Schneiders,
for raising me as an Upper Missourian

Contents

Maps and Figures

Preface

There is no "other world."

I only know what I've experienced.

You must be hallucinating.

—Jelaluddin Balkhi, Rumi, thirteenth-century Afghan poet

The experience that inspired the writing of this book began in September 1995. In the second week of that month, my brother Tom and I drove west from Sioux City, Iowa, through the sagebrush plains of Nebraska, South Dakota, and Montana; our ultimate objective was Wolf Creek, Montana, and the trout swimming in the Missouri River below Holter Dam. In midafternoon of the second day of road travel, we descended from the hills of southeast Montana toward Billings and the Yellowstone Valley. Just before we entered the metropolis of Billings, we passed over the Interstate 90 bridge, which spans the Yellowstone two miles east of the city's center. At that moment I looked out of the driver's-side window, toward the west, and in a blur of motion, I eyed the fabled river. In a brief, seventy-mile-per-hour glimpse, I viewed the Yellowstone's inexorable power. The river moved with celerity, jumping over boulders, ramming into the rim rocks on its south, and swirling as it pushed hard against its riprapped north bank.

Later that same afternoon, we drove on toward Columbus, Montana, passing Youngs Point—a mammoth block of sandstone along the south flank of the Yellowstone—along the way. This impressive mountain extends thousands of feet from west to east, and its crest is poised hundreds of feet above the waterline. The Yellowstone cuts into the edge of this stone mass, rubbing its lowest layer spherical and smooth and simultaneously removing any prop for the rock above. The river bores deep into the mountain, forcing the upper strata to shift and then skid into the Yellowstone below. Foaming rapids churn at the base of Youngs Point. Tom and I saw the mountain, and the river at its feet, just as the sky darkened its blues and remnant fingers of soft light refracted off golden sandstone. In a matter of hours I witnessed the Yellowstone's power and splendor.

I saw the Yellowstone River again in September 1996, but like the year before, only from a fast-moving automobile. By then I had started to ask questions, two of which piqued my interest more than any others. Why did this river appear so wild, so untamed, so unlike the Missouri that I knew? Second, why did the Yellowstone remain the longest, largest unregulated river in the contiguous United States? Upon those two questions rested much of my subsequent research into the Yellowstone's history.

I did not see the Yellowstone in 1997. That summer my wife and I graduated from Iowa State University and moved to West Texas, a land without rivers or much water at all. West Texas possesses few wild spaces and even fewer streams of liquid wonder. Atop the flat, dry plateau known as the Llano Estacado, I felt as though I had been thrown out with the bathwater. In June 1998 I had the good fortune and, more important, the time, to travel and camp along the Yellowstone for four weeks. I drove from the river's mouth to Livingston, Montana, and then on to Bozeman and Helena. I visited the libraries, museums, and/or archival collections located at Sidney, Glendive, Terry, Miles City, Huntley, Billings, Livingston, Bozeman, and Helena. I took hundreds of photographs not only of the river but also of the cultural constructs located on its banks and of the vegetation and wildlife living within its valley.

After returning to Lubbock, Texas, in July 1998, I decided that another extended trip to Colorado, Wyoming, and Montana would be necessary to complete the research for a comprehensive history of the Yellowstone River. I convinced myself I had to make this additional foray into the land of research, knowing full well that it would also give me another opportunity to leave the overdeveloped Llano Estacado. I hoped to conduct research at the National Archives in Denver and Mammoth Hot Springs, as well as at the Montana Historical Society archives in Helena. What is more, I wanted to gain a first-hand knowledge of the entire river system by hiking through the Yellowstone's headwaters district and canoeing the reach from Livingston to the mouth. This scheme did not even appear possible until March 1999, when We no nah Canoe Company of Winona, Minnesota, donated a canoe and paddling gear for the river journey. Cabela's Corporation and Coleman Corporation provided camping equipment. By this time I referred to the enterprise as the Yellowstone Expedition. Only one glitch remained before this grand plan became a reality. I needed a partner, someone with the time and enthusiasm to endure miles of hiking and hundreds of miles of canoeing. I tried to recruit friends, family, and acquaintances, but to no avail. No one could get away from his job or spouse for the estimated five or six weeks required to travel the length of the river. More than one friend flat out refused to go along with what appeared to him to be a rather outrageous idea. Luckily, Todd Siefker, who refers to himself as an itinerant poet and occasional meatpacker, told me that he would be "in between jobs" (a softer definition of unemployed) during the coming summer and would have the time to serve as cocaptain of the Yellowstone Expedition. Planning for the trip moved ahead.

In late June and early July 1999, I went to Colorado and Montana to conduct research at the National Records Center in Denver and the Montana Historical Society archives in Helena. In the middle of July, Todd took a bus from Sioux City, Iowa, to Livingston, Montana. I met him at the bus depot in that openly blue-collar western town. Within days, he and I donned backpacks and hiked through the little-known but spectacular Black Canyon of the Yellowstone. Later in July, we hiked along the eastern shore of Yellowstone Lake and into the valley of the far Upper Yellowstone. During both of those excursions, Todd and I took copious notes on the observed land, water, flora, and fauna. After battering our feet into red, mushy pulp, we gladly boarded the canoe and pushed into the Yellowstone's current east of the Ninth Street Bridge at Livingston. Out on the river, Todd and I took photographs and wrote hundreds of pages of notes on the Yellowstone's biohydrology and the valley's geography. At the end of fifteen days of steady canoeing, we reached the Yellowstone's mouth. By then, I felt quite close to the Yellowstone River.

In fall 1999, I finished the research necessary to write a Yellowstone River history. But just as I began to wrap up the preliminary work, I realized that I could no longer ignore the multiple links between the Yellowstone River and the Upper Missouri River. To write a history of the Yellowstone exclusive of the Upper Missouri would not be accurate, and certainly would not do either river justice. The Yellowstone River could not be separated from the Upper Missouri or vice versa. These two tremendous hydraulic systems and their histories had undeniably been tied together. I could not write a history that decoupled the two streams; it would not be true to their pasts.

Therefore, in spring 2000, I decided to research and write a broader history, one that included the Upper Missouri main stem, the Yellowstone main stem, and the drainage basins of both rivers. This larger history had a strong foundation in the geographic past and possessed a cohesion and comprehensibility that was lacking from the earlier Yellowstone history. I convinced myself and, more important, my wife that with this shift in focus I needed to make yet another research trip to the last best place—Montana.

In the hot, smoky, drought-stricken month of August 2000, I plopped my six-foot, seven-inch frame down into my tiny 1991 Toyota Corolla and drove a thousand miles to the southern fringe of the Yellowstone basin. Once along the South Fork of the Powder River, north of Casper, Wyoming, I began looking for the ancient bison roads that traversed the territory. I spent weeks cruising around northern Wyoming and eastern Montana, guzzling water from plastic gallon jugs, listening to the transcendental music of Dead Can Dance, and scanning the horizon for old, worn trail ruts. The drought, devastating for the people and wildlife of Montana, aided my research tremendously. Since the land turned dusty brown and most streams vanished into a cloudless sky, only the most persistent perennial streams maintained their flows. In several instances, I only had to find water and a scattering of green to locate the prehistoric routes of travel for bison and Indians alike. It became apparent that in the semiarid environment of the Upper Missouri, climate pushed Indians and bison toward the perennial creeks and rivers. In August 2000, the climate had forced Montanans to do the same: everywhere water flowed, there lay cattle, crops, and conservatives.

I came back from this field trip and wrote, until the charms of the Upper Missouri called me forth again. Todd Siefker and I made a trip through the Upper Missouri in the globally warm winter of 2002. In the first two weeks of January, with daytime temperatures in the seventies, Todd and I visited the Fort Niobrara National Wildlife Refuge near Valentine, Nebraska; the White River bottom at Fort Robinson, Nebraska; the valley of Wounded Knee Creek, South Dakota; Badlands National Park, South Dakota; Bear Butte State Park, South Dakota; and the Missouri Valley in south central South Dakota. The trip, especially the four days spent hiking in Badlands National Park, confirmed earlier conclusions about the Upper Missouri's bison road network and the import of timbered bottoms to the region's ecology. A final trip to the Yellowstone plateau in June 2002 did the same, reinforcing judgments made from years of book study and field research.

The present book differs substantially from my first book on the Missouri River, *Unruly River*, published by the University Press of Kansas in 1999. Although *Big Sky Rivers* deals with some of the same topics examined in *Unruly River*, the two books cover different water. *Unruly River* focused on the Lower Missouri Valley and the efforts of its Euro-American inhabitants to channelize and dam the stream. *Big Sky Rivers* remains firmly set in the

Upper Missouri, with only cursory coverage of the Lower Missouri. Although some of the subjects addressed here also appeared in the earlier book, I have meticulously sought to avoid any redundancy in presented material. I finished the research for *Unruly River* in late 1996. I spent the past six years, up to November 2002, conducting full-time research for this second book on the Missouri and Yellowstone. *Big Sky Rivers* incorporates the information and interpretations learned during those additional six years.

Acknowledgments

My experiences with the Yellowstone River and Upper Missouri territory would not have been possible without the assistance of a multitude of individuals and organizations. Their efforts, sacrifice, and imagination helped make this book a reality. I firmly believe in the efficacy of fieldwork as a learning tool. To achieve an awareness of the Upper Missouri, I needed to get off the page and onto the land and into the water. My fieldwork could not have been done without Todd Siefker. I want to thank Todd for possessing as much fanaticism for the rivers and region of the Upper Missouri as myself. He and I shared all the laughs, adventures, and fears entailed in hiking nearly 150 miles through grizzly habitat inside Yellowstone National Park, canoeing hundreds of miles down the riotous Yellowstone River, and spending days among the bison and their old roads in Badlands National Park. Over the years Todd and I have talked much about the many Wests that course through American culture. Todd's Western and non-Western ideas have been indispensable in the creation of this work.

I want to thank Jordan Messerer, who taught me how to kayak along the San Marcos River near Austin, Texas. Jordan, who embodies the essence of the river rat, knows the behavior of water better than anyone I have ever met. I have seen him flit about on the water in his kayak with the ease of a merganser. Jordan, and his knowledge of kayaking, brought me closer to water. This means of travel has allowed me to feel the push, pull, downward tug, and upward shove of rivers. When I ride a river on a kayak, I am as close to water as I can possibly be without being flung beneath its surface.

Bill and Sybol Srigley, of Columbus, Montana, deserve thanks for their unwavering faith that two men who lacked canoeing experience could actually reach the Yellowstone's mouth alive. Bill's and Sybol's spirits rode down the Yellowstone with us. Rob Linden of We no nah Canoe, of Winona, Minnesota, provided the logistical support necessary for Todd and me to complete the Yellowstone River trip. A sincere thank-you to Mike Cichanowski, president of We no nah Canoe, for donating the "Spirit II" canoe, along with gear, that made the 1999 canoe trip possible in the first place. Coleman Corporation and Cabela's Corporation also donated equipment needed to complete the fieldwork. Norma Cunningham, of Lubbock, Texas, possesses loads of compassionate buffalo medicine. She walked with me through the bleakest of deserts, and for that I give her thanks. My mother and father, Mary Jean (Lang) Schneiders and Robert Joseph Schneiders, helped this project in many ways. Over the years, I have launched several expeditions into the Upper Missouri from their big, sturdy kitchen table. I am grateful for their willingness to let me transform their domicile into a boisterous base camp. William Lang provided excellent suggestions for the improvement of the manuscript. I thank him for his diligent editorial efforts on my behalf. The faith of Editor Nancy Scott Jackson at the University Press of Kansas in this book and in my abilities came at a time when I needed it most. Nancy served as midwife to this book just as she was about to give birth to her own child. I owe a thank-you to the copy editor, Susan Ecklund, for cleaning up my prose.

I thank Bob Clark and Angela Murray at the Montana Historical Society archives in Helena, Montana, for assistance in finding and retrieving archival materials. They made visiting the archives productive and enjoyable. A thank-you is extended to the staffs of the National Archives and Records Center, Denver, Colorado, and the National Archives and Records Center, Mammoth Hot Springs. Carol Edwards, United States Geological Survey Library, Denver, Colorado, spent hours copying the original journals of A. C. Peale. Dolores Drennan at the Miles City Public Library believed in this project and its import to Montana. She readily assisted me when I requested information. I also want to thank the staffs of the following organizations: Livingston Public Library, Billings Public Library, Miles City Public Library, Denver Public Library, and Sioux City Public Library.

I owe an intellectual debt to four men I have never met, historians Dan Flores, Elliot West, and Howard Zinn and geographer D. W. Meinig. Flores, in both *Horizontal Yellow* and *The Natural West*, led me toward a bioregional approach to the study of the Upper Missouri's history. West, in his book *Contested Plains*, highlighted the crucial historical and ecological importance of bottomland sanctuaries in a semiarid environment. Zinn, in *On War* and *On History*, moved me toward a more activist approach to the writing and practice of history. Meinig, who wrote *The Great Columbia Plain,* helped me delineate the Upper Missouri as a distinct watershed, separate in so many ways from the Lower Missouri basin. Three others, through their life stories, have had a positive influence on my thinking about the Upper Missouri. Buffalo Bird Woman in *Buffalo Bird Woman's Garden*, White Bull in *Lakota Warrior*, and Black Elk in *The Sacred Pipe* and *Black Elk Speaks* revealed to me the depth, vitality, and richness of the Upper Missouri's indigenous cultures, ecology, geography, and history.

Introduction

May they always remember their relatives at the four

quarters, and may they know that they are related to all that

moves upon the universe, and especially the buffalo, who is the

chief of the four-leggeds, and who helps to raise the people.

—Black Elk, Oglala Sioux

All things are related. Bioregional history provides a theoretical and historical framework for presenting connections. *Big Sky Rivers* is a bioregional history, or an examination of a biotic community, defined in broad terms. In this case, the biotic community includes the Upper Missouri watershed and its flora and fauna, including *Homo sapiens*. *Big Sky Rivers* pays particular attention to four entities within the Upper Missouri bioregion: the Missouri River Valley, the Yellowstone River Valley, *Homo sapiens,* and bison. The study focuses on these four components acting in concert, since that interaction has been, and will continue to be, the most ecologically, geographically, and historically significant for the Upper Missouri bioregion.

This book focuses on the Missouri and Yellowstone, which are the two biggest rivers in the Upper Missouri bioregion and have had a decided influence on the territory's history. The unifying theme of *Big Sky Rivers* is that the Missouri and Yellowstone Rivers once represented, and continue to represent (although in a substantially diminished capacity), the center of a tremendous living system. The Upper Missouri basin is a living organism. The Missouri River long served as the heart of a vast areal body, while the Yellowstone River functioned as an aorta. Throughout the nineteenth and into the early twentieth century, the two great rivers were intimately linked through hydrology, ecology, geography, and history. Yet in the twentieth century, Euro-Americans dismantled many of those connections, attempted to decouple the streams, and worked to sever the multiple ties that bound them to each other. Euro-American geographic constructs tore the Missouri from the Yellowstone perceptually, physically, geographically, and ecologically.

This book is a history of one of the world's most majestic rivers, the Missouri, and how it was once wedded to the Yellowstone. To a lesser extent, the book explores the connections between the Missouri and its other, smaller tributaries. These other streams receive less textual coverage because the Yellowstone-Missouri relationship has been so dominant. *Big Sky Rivers* also explains how the histories, geographies, and ecologies of the Missouri and its largest tributary diverged in the twentieth century. The book addresses why the Yellowstone and Missouri are so unalike today—one unregulated, with a semblance of wildness, and the other dammed into reservoirs. *Big Sky Rivers* tacitly asserts that ecological understanding and a reading of history present contemporary society with a blueprint for restoring the Upper Missouri's ecological health and economic sustainability, and concomitantly the bioregion's economic independence and political autonomy. The story of the Upper Missouri also suggests a model for restoration of other bioregions within the United States and around the globe.

Throughout the text, and for several reasons, I deploy the word "Sioux" to identify the members of the Lakota, Dakota, and Nakota tribes. First, the name was used by nineteenth-century Euro-Americans, French Canadians, and English who lived and traveled throughout the Upper Missouri; as a result, it has a historical foundation. Second, many contemporary Lakota, Dakota, and Nakota Indians refer to themselves as Sioux. It is a word that remains incarnate in the Upper Missouri. Third, the word "Sioux" is inclusive. Since members of the Lakota, Dakota, and Nakota tribes continually mixed and migrated together, I found it impossible, after reading numerous journal accounts from the eighteenth and nineteenth centuries, to confidently claim that only one grouping or another exclusively occupied particular regions of the Upper Missouri. Diaries and secondary sources indicate that the borders between the three Sioux tribes disintegrated on contact.[1] Hard borders did not exist across the Upper Missouri. For example, Santee, Yanktonai, Yankton, Brule, Oglala, and Hunkpapa frequently occupied the same territory along the Missouri River either simultaneously or at different times. The term "Sioux" acknowledges that convoluted reality and bows respectfully to the fluidity of both Indian life and geography across the Upper Missouri. Nonetheless, the focus of this study is on a group known in the early nineteenth century as the western Sioux or Teton Sioux, who lived along the westernmost fringe of the Sioux empire. Why do I place special

emphasis on this group? First and foremost, in the eighteenth and nineteenth centuries it played important political, economic, and military roles
throughout the Upper Missouri territory and along the Upper Missouri and
Yellowstone main stems. Moreover, the Teton Sioux experience in the
Upper Missouri offers an excellent example of how river systems and bison
influenced Indian geography and history. Finally, the Teton Sioux's relationship to bison offers the present occupants of the Upper Missouri lessons in
human-bison interactions and bison conservation.

A brief note is in order on the historiography of the Upper Missouri territory, the northern Great Plains, and the states of Montana, North Dakota,
South Dakota, and Nebraska, and *Big Sky Rivers'* place in it. The historical
literature of this region is replete with four notable themes: region as last
best place, place as plundered province, land of redemption, and/or desert of
damnation. Joseph Kinsey Howard's *Montana: High, Wide, and Handsome*
describes Montana as plundered province, ruthlessly exploited by Euro-
Americans possessing a philosophy of "git and git out." In Howard's interpretation, successive waves of white folk got Montana's riches and then got
the hell out of the state, leaving behind a ravaged rape victim. Robert
Athearn in *High Country Empire,* Michael Malone in *The Battle for Butte,*
and William Lang and Michael Malone in *Montana* reinforce Howard's thesis. Recently, Jonathan Raban's *Bad Land: An American Romance* presents
Montana as worked-over wasteland. Raban asserts that the plains damn
rather than redeem. According to him, a parochial, mutated, and maladapted Euro-American culture survives today on the grassland. In contrast,
Kathleen Norris's *Dakota: A Spiritual Geography* contends that the grassland environment offers its inhabitants spiritual and cultural redemption,
and even community. Stephen R. Jones in *The Last Prairie: A Sandhills
Journal* argues that the Nebraska Sandhills are a transcendental landscape
of human hope in a nation of increasing urbanization. To Jones, the Sandhills are one of the last best places. Where does *Big Sky Rivers* fit into the
existing literature? It asserts that the Upper Missouri (especially the Yellowstone Valley) is a last best place because it was one of the final, and one of the
more environmentally problematic, provinces plundered by Euro-America.
What is more, the Euro-American position in the Upper Missouri is rapidly
washing away, melting with the rivers into silt. Euro-American culture in the
Upper Missouri is maladapted to the bioregion's environment because Euro-
American geographic constructs are out of sync with the bioregion's ecology.
If redemption exists, and I am not sure that it does, it lies not in heaven but
on earth. Spiritual, economic, and cultural revival is attainable through the

deconstruction of contemporary extractive geography and the reconstruction of ancient bison and Indian geography.

The Upper Missouri territory existed as a Euro-American perceptual reality and folk geography from 1804 into the 1870s. From the actual transfer by Spain of its Upper Louisiana Territory to the United States in 1804 to the U.S. Army campaigns against the Sioux in 1876 and 1877, Euro-Americans referred to the Upper Missouri as a regional entity, a hydrologic entity, or both. As a regional cognomen, the Upper Missouri contained discernible borders, although by no means universally recognized ones. The majority of French Canadians, English, and Euro-Americans believed that the Upper Missouri country began where the broad, winding, rapid Platte River poured its waters into the slower, darker Missouri. North, west, and slightly east of the mouth of the Platte, all the lands drained by the Missouri and its thousands of feeder streams belonged within the dominion of the Upper Missouri.

Euro-Americans also knew the Upper Missouri as a distinct river, separate from the Lower Missouri. Above the Platte, the Missouri main stem became the Upper Missouri, stretching all the way to the juncture of the Jefferson, Madison, and Gallatin at Three Forks. The Upper Missouri far surpassed the Lower Missouri in length. A degree of confusion surrounds the former length of the Missouri. In 1952, before the completion of the Dakota dams and the channelization project south of Sioux City, the river measured 2,466 miles from head to mouth. Today it runs 2,341 miles. Because of changes in the channel of the Missouri over the past two centuries from both natural and human causes, it is impossible to calculate with absolute accuracy the river's length in the early nineteenth century. Yet from numerous journal accounts, including those of the Lewis and Clark expedition, the entire Missouri main stem likely flowed 200 miles farther than it does today, making its length approximately 2,541 miles. Roughly 1,911 miles of river flowed between the Platte and the Three Forks. The most significant shortening of the Upper Missouri occurred between the Calumet Bluffs (at today's Gavin's Point Dam) and the mouth of the Platte. Clark in 1804 to 1805 estimated the length between those two points at 354 river miles. Today the Corps of Engineers measures the distance between those same two points at roughly 214 miles. In that reach alone, hydrologic and human forces have shortened the river by 140 miles. At the time of Lewis and Clark, the Upper Missouri River was over three times longer than the Lower Missouri.

The most inclusive definition of the Upper Missouri insisted that it encompassed both the Missouri main-stem north of the Platte, along with all the main-stem tributaries, and all the lands drained by the upper basin. But not everyone in nineteenth-century America agreed on even those parameters. For instance, by the 1860s, steamboat company executives designated the Upper Missouri main stem as the river north and west of the Big Sioux River confluence. Sometime in the late 1870s or early 1880s, the Corps of Engineers added further credibility to this demarcation line when it, too, named the Upper Missouri the river northwest of the Big Sioux confluence. Steamboat companies and the Corps of Engineers, because of their water-bound activities, considered the Upper Missouri strictly as a hydrologic unit, a river reach from the Three Forks to the Big Sioux.

By labeling the Big Sioux River as the line between the Upper and Lower Missouri, the Corps of Engineers and the steamboat companies overturned a long-established boundary. From at least the 1790s until the late 1850s, the majority of Euro-Americans believed the Upper Missouri main stem began at the Platte River confluence, not the Big Sioux. Why did the Corps of Engineers and the steamboat company executives arbitrarily designate the Big Sioux as the demarcation line? Maybe because no academic or government experts told them that they could not create their own geography. Another explanation may be that steamer companies operating in the Dakotas jumped off to the upper river from Sioux City. In other words, alterations in steamboat company economics and operations explain the alteration in the Upper Missouri's southeastern border. A third possible reason for the shift northward in the boundary between the Upper and Lower Missouri was related to environmental change.

Modifications in vegetation in the Missouri Valley may explain the re-drawing of the Upper Missouri's southeastern boundary. By 1856 the line of Euro-American agricultural settlement reached the Big Sioux River and the small, rough-and-tumble frontier community of Sioux City, Iowa. Below Sioux City, thousands of Euro-American settlers busily converted the Missouri Valley bottoms, and the Loess Hills, to fields, forests, and farms. Euro-Americans diligently suppressed fire to protect their recently erected and/or claimed buildings, crops, stock animals, and timber reserves. Once white settlers arrived in an area, the centuries-old Indian practice of setting the bottomland grasses ablaze each autumn and spring came to an end.

That Euro-Americans induced significant environmental change as they advanced up the Missouri Valley is evident from several nineteenth-century journal accounts. In April 1811, Scottish naturalist John Bradbury claimed that Indian fire contributed to an absence of trees in the Missouri bottoms north and west of the Platte-Missouri confluence. Bradbury wrote the following after hiking through the valley lowlands near present-day Council Bluffs, Iowa: "[I] traveled nearly a mile on a low piece of ground, covered with long grass: at its termination we ascended a small elevation and entered on a plain of about eight miles in length, and from two and a half to three miles in breadth. As the old grass had been burned in the autumn, it was now covered with the most beautiful verdure, intermixed with flowers. It was also adorned with clumps of trees, sufficient for ornament, but too few to intercept the sight."[2] In 1823, Paul Wilhelm, the duke of Württemberg, a German principality, provided an eloquent description of a prairie fire in the Missouri Valley:

> Both banks of the Missouri soon became the scene of an enormous struggle of the elements, which man had loosened for the destruction of organic matter. It was truly horrifying but at the same time a magnificent sight, as we drifted along in the middle of the river, and watched the banks of the giant Missouri as it appeared for miles a sea of flames. At night the spectacle defied description. . . . It is true that prairie fires make the grass more luxuriant in the following spring. The forests, however, are in part wholly destroyed. In many places in the western territory one now sees only stunted bushes and the charred stumps of former forest giants, where earlier virgin forest stood."[3]

A decade after Prince Wilhelm made this observation, another German prince, Maximilian of Wied, noticed how Indian fire prevented the spread of forestland in the river bottoms. Near Bellevue, Nebraska, Maximilian remarked, "On the left bank [of the Missouri] there were whole tracts covered with dead poplars [cottonwood], which had been killed by the fires caused by the Indians in the forest and prairie."[4]

By the mid-1850s, Euro-American agriculturalists had moved beyond the Platte. Cleansing burns ceased to sweep through the Missouri Valley. Without those fires, trees, especially cottonwoods, flourished across the moist, fertile valley floor. Proof of that fact comes from another Missouri River travel journal. In 1862, James Harkness, floating up the river from St. Joseph, Missouri, found an abundance of trees in the Missouri Valley north of the Platte. Not until Harkness approached Sioux City, Iowa, did he notice "the character of the country changing, timber very scarce."[5] As a result, by

1862, the grassland, so long associated with the Upper Missouri, did not begin until one approached the Big Sioux River. Thus, the public, and possibly the Corps of Engineers and steamboat company executives, redrew the Upper Missouri's southernmost boundary to reflect the retreat of the grassland northward up the Missouri Valley. The geography of the Upper Missouri fluctuated with changes in ecology.

This example illustrates the fickleness of geography. The presence or absence of a single vegetative type, the cottonwood tree, may have affected Euro-American geographic perceptions and boundaries. In this case, the spread of timber northward in the 1850s may have caused the contraction of the geographic entity known as the Upper Missouri. A second conclusion that can be drawn from this example is that changes in ecology forced changes in geography. The Upper Missouri represented a dynamic geography; it never remained static because ecology does not remain static. The history of the Upper Missouri provides numerous examples of the linkages between ecology and geography.

One of the difficulties of defining the Upper Missouri's boundaries stems from the character of United States society in the early and middle nineteenth century. Dispersed, individualistic, laissez-faire, and grassroots-democratic (at least for propertied Euro-American males), with a supposed minimum of state interference in private affairs, individuals and private corporations freely defined their own geographic entities, giving places their own meanings, borders, and names. As a result, the public, steamboat companies, and the Corps of Engineers could freely alter the boundary of the Upper Missouri without receiving criticism from any other institutions or individuals.

In the early and middle nineteenth century, no government agency with socially sanctioned experts named a land area as the Upper Missouri. As a result, the Upper Missouri never appeared as an official territory within the United States; it never gained that level of legitimacy. But that fact does not mean the Upper Missouri did not exist. It remained confined to the minds of trappers, traders, steamboat pilots, settlers, and free-spirited individuals unconcerned with geographic objectivity. Lacking maps depicting the region, some might question whether the Upper Missouri existed at all. But from the available documentation, particularly the journals in archives in Montana and the Dakotas, compelling evidence suggests that a distinct region known as the Upper Missouri did in fact exist, only to be subsumed by new geographies in the late nineteenth century.

Only when the railroad crisscrossed the Upper Missouri Valley and the grassland we now call the northern plains in the late 1870s and 1880s did the designation of the region change. The unofficial, individualistic, and largely indigenous Upper Missouri dissolved as a geographic unit. By that late date the federal government had taken firm control of the territory and officially renamed much of it the states of Montana, North and South Dakota, Nebraska, and Wyoming. In the late nineteenth century and throughout the twentieth century, Euro-American constructs further severed the multiple associations between the Missouri and its tributaries. An imperial order and official sanction, along with territorial, state, and federal political borders, replaced the nebulous Upper Missouri. By the middle of the twentieth century, geography reflected the region's thorough integration into the Euro-American empire.

The definition presented in these pages adheres to the broadest delineation of the Upper Missouri. It includes the Upper Missouri main stem and the entire drainage basin of the Missouri River above the Platte River confluence. Furthermore, I argue that the Upper Missouri represented more than a hydrologic or geographic unit. The Upper Missouri territory functioned as a living system, with the Missouri River main stem operating as the center or core of a larger landscape and waterscape. The Upper Missouri ecological system depended on hydrology and the energy that flowed unimpeded up and down the river's main stem and its tributaries. This idea does not have a nineteenth-century equivalent. Euro-Americans, although familiar with the land- and waterscape of the Upper Missouri and the myriad creatures and plants that lived there, did not consider the region as a living system. Indian peoples, on the other hand, may have contemplated the Upper Missouri basin and its tributary basins as living systems.

Rails, roads, reservoirs, bridges, and buildings eventually covered the Upper Missouri. The region now lies silently under layers of Euro-American geography. But it is still there, dormant, waiting for rebirth, eager for the gift of human touch. If a person is quiet and stares long enough across plain or valley, he or she can see the beautiful shape of the Upper Missouri beneath a thin linen veil of white clouds. The gentle curves of the Upper Missouri are visible in the graceful erosion lines passing through the sides of the Bighorn Mountains, in the serpentine trails cutting through the Dakota Badlands, and in the lively, thrashing current of the unregulated Yellowstone River. Atop the altar of the great grassland, the Upper Missouri awaits our return.

The Upper Missouri

Character and Ecology in
the Early Nineteenth Century

This immence river so far as we have yet ascended, waters

one of the fairest portions of the globe, nor do I believe that there

is in the universe a similar extent of country, equally fertile, well

watered, and intersected by such a number of navigable streams.

—Meriwether Lewis

The Upper Missouri enclosed a vast and varied land- and water-scape. The entire Missouri basin encompasses 529,350 square miles, or one-sixth the land area of the contiguous United States. Roughly 350,000 square miles of the Missouri basin lie north and west of the Platte confluence. Three geographic features delineated the Upper Missouri's eastern border: the sculpted Loess Hills of western Iowa, formed during the last glaciation episode from dried Missouri River silt; the once-sparkling Big Sioux River; and the upper reaches of the cottonwood-encased James River. The Upper Missouri's northern border fanned out from the James watershed across the flat, pothole-dotted lands of present-day North Dakota, to the White Earth River, and thence on to the Milk River and the grassy plains surrounding its erratic course.

The region's boundary followed the Milk to its source in the Rocky Mountains. The dramatic peaks of the Rockies announced the western edge of the Upper Missouri. Tracing the fractured ridges of the Continental Divide, the

Upper Missouri's western boundary drew southeastward. Below the high alpine spine of North America lay such notable landmarks as the Gates of the
Mountains, the spongy pastures surrounding the Three Forks of the Missouri, and the frigid waters of Yellowstone Lake. Farther south and east into
modern Wyoming, the Continental Divide nears the Sweetwater River and
then the North Platte. Once at the North Platte, the boundary of the Upper
Missouri turned east, following the north side of the Platte Valley until its
termination at the Missouri, nearly 600 miles away (fig. 1.1).

The distance as the crow flies between the Upper Missouri's southern
roots at the Platte's mouth to its far northwestern terminus at the headwaters of the Milk River is roughly 950 miles. In this automobile age, it takes a
person averaging 60 miles per hour, cruising over linear, north-south, and
east-west highways, close to twenty-four driving hours to get from Platts-
mouth, Nebraska, to Kiowa, Montana, near the head of the Milk River.

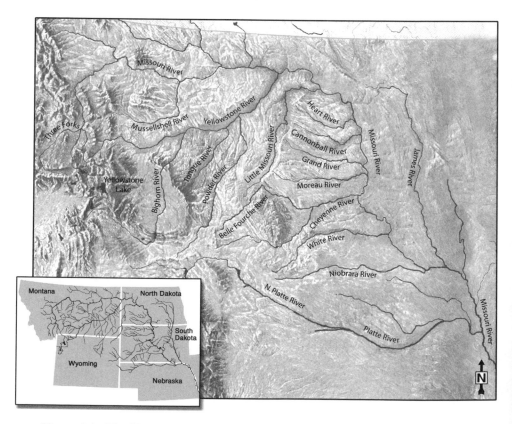

Figure 1.1. The Upper Missouri bioregion. (Paul Davidson, South Plains
College, Levelland, Texas)

The elevation of the region tips from west to east. The highest mountains in the Upper Missouri easily exceed 12,000 feet in elevation. From these snow-topped heights, the Upper Missouri slides downward, descending over 2 miles as it lunges eastward toward the Missouri River trough, eventually culminating at an elevation of 975 feet above sea level where the Platte comes to an end. In the intervening spaces exist a number of noteworthy subregions and rivers. An ancient outcropping of the Rocky Mountains, the Black Hills, is situated in the south central Upper Missouri. The Bighorn Mountain range, dark green even in the heat and sun of August, power skyward 130 miles west of the Black Hills. North of the Bighorn Mountains flows the Yellowstone—the Missouri's strongest and most voluminous tributary. Born high in the hidden peaks of the Teton National Forest of northwestern Wyoming, the Yellowstone dashes 671 miles before casting its snowmelt, sand, and gravel into the Missouri 20 miles west of Williston, North Dakota.

All the major tributaries of the Yellowstone, including the Clarks Fork, Bighorn, Tongue, and Powder Rivers, originate to its south, in either the Absaroka or the Bighorn mountain range. These tributaries flow north through foothills and knotted sagebrush plains before falling into the Yellowstone. The majority of the Upper Missouri main stem's plains tributaries flow from west to east. The Knife, Heart, Cannonball, Grand, Moreau, Cheyenne, Bad, White, Niobrara, and Platte Rivers originate in mountains or hills and descend toward the sunrise. East of the Upper Missouri main stem, two sizable prairie rivers join it, the James and the Big Sioux.

Of all the physical features present in the Upper Missouri territory, one stood apart, dominating all others, and that was the Missouri River itself. The Missouri River held this entire region tightly in its grasp, stretching out its arms and fingers up its tributaries, sinking its tentacles into the soil, then firmly pulling the earth toward its bosom. The Missouri River bound mountain to plain, sky to land, clay to loess, and bison to grass. It unified the land and brought order to its ecology.

North of the Platte confluence, Euro-Americans entered another world, one removed from anything they had previously experienced in their brief time on the continent. The Platte River confluence became the door into a dissimilar reality. Euro-Americans left the shaded forest, humid climate, and big, deep midcontinental rivers and entered a place startlingly exotic. Beyond the Platte, they found rolling plains enveloped by orbital sky; intense, illuminating, even painful sunlight; tall, billowing thunderclouds that hurled hail, rain, and lighting upon their crouched shoulders; heavy, shallow, tawny rivers; wind, incessant, howling, and strong enough to stop boats dead in their tracks; and hundreds of thousands of statuesque bison and their well-worn roads and traces. Above the Platte, they also encountered Indians who displayed confidence, power, and speed. Indians there, unlike those defeated or denigrated in the East, did not defer to the Euro-Americans or show them the requisite degree of respect. The Upper Missouri and its indigenous peoples shocked Euro-American sensibilities, challenged Euro-American identities, and weakened Euro-American notions of cultural, technological, and racial superiority.

Nineteenth-century Europeans or Euro-Americans who traveled up the Missouri River noticed that above the Platte they entered a new place, where the Missouri became a different river and the land shed its trees. Pierre Antoine Tabeau, one of the most geographically knowledgeable traders on the Upper Missouri in the first decade of the 1800s, provided a summation of the Missouri basin north and west of the Platte: "The two banks of the Missouri are well wooded as far as the approaches to the River Platte. . . . Then vast and high prairies, separated from the river by low and humid plains, present to the eye a monotonous expanse."[1] In July 1804, as the men of the Lewis and Clark expedition neared the Platte River, Patrick Gass expressed surprise: "This is the most open country I ever beheld, almost one continued prairie."[2] Once the explorers went past the Platte, they recognized the stark difference between the Lower and Upper Missouri. Meriwether Lewis recollected, "The country as high up this river as the Mouth of the river Platte, a distance of 630 miles is generally well timbered; at some little distance above this river the open or prarie [sic] country commences."[3]

Henry Brackenridge, a lawyer by training and an adventurer at heart who went up the Missouri on board a keelboat (at the time referred to simply as a keel) in 1811 with the famous fur trader Manuel Lisa, wrote, "The river Platte is regarded by the navigators of the Missouri as a point of as much importance, as the equinoctial line amongst mariners. All those who had not passed it before, were required to be shaved, unless they could compromise the matter by treat. Much merriment was indulged on the occasion. From this we enter what is called the Upper Missouri. Indeed the change is perceptible and great, for the open bare plains now prevail."[4] At the Platte, the Upper Missouri grassland began to unfold.

In the early and middle nineteenth century, the majority of Euro-Americans saw the Upper Missouri main stem and the Upper Missouri region from the deck of a boat. Few whites ventured far from the river. To leave the Missouri Valley meant the loss of contact with the outside world and the Euro-American civilization and cities in the southeast and east. The Missouri Valley offered Euro-Americans a security blanket, a buffer against ambivalent nature. The Missouri River and its valley served as a lifeline, route of supply, and mode of communication. To abandon that route and its multiple connections meant uncertainty, the absence of necessities, and possibly death.

Euro-Americans stayed close to the Missouri for a host of reasons. The river valley and its respective resources offered protection against a frequently rancorous Upper Missouri environment and potentially hostile indigenes. The timber, water, and grass in the bottoms ensured the survival of stock animals crucial for human transport, while the edible creatures and vegetation concentrated in the lowlands provided the food to combat famine. The river valley offered Euro-Americans solid defensive and offensive military positions against Indian peoples who stood in the way of their advance. Most important, the river carried keels and steamers. Watercraft hauled the supplies, arms, and ammunition vital for Euro-American defense and offense.

The valley's timbered bottoms presented cover in case of attack from Indians. When Euro-Americans came under assault from an indigenous force, they moved into the trees to shield themselves from lead balls and flint arrows.[5] They also sought the forests because they knew that to engage an Indian in combat out in the open atop a horse increased the odds of death for themselves. Indians, especially the Sioux, excelled at hand-to-hand and equestrian combat. Euro-Americans much preferred to fight the Sioux and the other tribes of the Upper Missouri from a distance, plinking off warriors from hundreds of feet, rather than attempting to take Indians down through direct physical contact. Euro-American frontiersmen understood that trees forced the equestrian nomads to dismount to engage in close-quarters combat. A dismounted Indian leveled the playing field, increasing the chances of victory for Euro-Americans with lackluster equestrian skills.

To Euro-Americans, the open plains entailed risk. There always existed the danger of losing one's bearings in an apparently featureless land. In contrast to the plains above, the Missouri River Valley provided recognizable features, direction markers, and a sense of safety. Travel across the expansive plains carried the very real possibility of disorientation, starvation, thirst, and a horrible death. Consequently, Euro-Americans held firmly to the valley of the Missouri.

Because Euro-Americans stayed so close to the Missouri, the river influenced their perceptions of the entire Upper Missouri. Euro-Americans saw the region through a watery lens. A big, rowdy river shaped their impressions of the land and its indigenes. The wild river produced a perception of the Upper Missouri as a brutal, barely comprehensible place. The Missouri—its variable movements, seemingly destructive propensities, and obvious, readily apparent power—had a profound influence on Euro-American thought. A rambunctious river appropriately flowed through a wild, uncivilized land. The nomadic Missouri mirrored the nomadic Indians and their world.

In the nineteenth century, the Corps of Engineers divided the Upper Missouri main stem into two sections to denote the different character of the river's bed material. The Rocky River flowed from the Three Forks to the Yellowstone confluence. This section of river channel resembled a mountain stream, with a steep slope, a bed lined with boulders and cobbles, a swift current, and bluish green water. But as the Rocky River approached the Yellowstone confluence, it flattened out, slowed down, and picked up sediment. As the Missouri decelerated, it lost the momentum to push large boulders or cobbles along its bottom. Gradually, the Rocky River's bed shifted from boulders to cobbles to gravel to sand. The surface of the river reflected the changes occurring below. The Missouri appeared smooth, glassy, even tranquil the closer it came to the Yellowstone. The rolling, tumbling, white-water river visible above the Gates of the Mountains or at the Great Falls disappeared before arriving at the Yellowstone's mouth.

From the Yellowstone to the Platte, the corps referred to the Upper Missouri as the Sandy River because its bed consisted predominantly of coarse and fine sediments that poured into the river from plains and badlands. The sediments consisted of klinker, powdered clay, and minute fragments of milled stone, which either floated down the Missouri or tumbled along its bed. The Sandy River resembled all other plains rivers—warm in summer, shallow by September, swift through narrow chutes, slow across open flats, and yellowish brown when the sun struck it. One nineteenth-century traveler, north of Fort Randall, recalled the Sandy River's appearance: "The river very rapid and so very muddy looks more like clay than water. Its seems to boil from the bottom."[6] Edward Harris, who accompanied ornithologist John James Audubon up the Missouri in 1843, did not think highly of the Sandy River's appearance: "No otters, beavers, muskrats, or even minks, are found in or about the turbid waters of this almighty stream, the water of which looks more like that of a hog puddle than any thing else I can compare it to."[7]

The Upper Missouri's sediment load gave the river its color. That load did not move downstream in a solid mass. Instead, like the water that carried it, the silt moved in all directions, with the finest, or tiniest, particles near the surface and the heaviest, or coarsest, particles near the bed itself. On bright blue days, the Missouri's yellowish brown surface resembled greasy, bubbling gravy—veins of fatty broth circling around and around, percolating up from below, or trailing downstream in thin streaks.

The Lower Missouri, called the Muddy River, earned its name because it hauled copious amounts of prairie topsoil and alluvium. In 1850, Thaddeaus Culbertson, on his way to the Dakota Badlands via the Missouri River, re-marked, "The banks of the [Lower] Missouri, except where there are bluffs, present an alluvial appearance and are constantly washing away; the water is therefore discolored presenting the appearance of water mixed with ashes.[8] In the early and middle nineteenth century, the majority of Euro-Americans who traveled in the region encountered the Muddy River and the Sandy River. Few had any reason to travel as far as the Rocky River. Only after the commencement of gold mining in western Montana in 1862, and the use of the Rocky River as a route to the gold fields, did significant num-bers of Euro-Americans view the far Upper Missouri. But before that late date, the bulk of Euro-Americans equated the Sandy River with the Upper Missouri.

The silt spinning in the Sandy River consisted of organic substances, minerals, clays, and worn stones. After a freshet, the Missouri spread its pea-nut-buttery silt across its valley floor. That silt provided the pabulum neces-sary for the growth of plant life, including cottonwood trees, willows, big bluestem, slough grass, chokecherry bushes, and buffalo berry bushes. In the form of silt, the mountains and plains fed milky detritus to vegetative offspring.

Nineteenth-century Euro-Americans and Indians bathed and drank di-rectly out of the Missouri. Nineteenth-century Missouri Valley residents bathed on a regular basis. That silt sloshing through a washbasin or floating downstream on the current acted like a scrub brush, scouring dirt, dead in-sects, and sweat from rank flesh. Prince Maximilian of Wied wrote of Man-dan hygienic practices, "Many of them [the Indians] are particularly cleanly in their persons, and bathe daily, both in winter and summer." He contin-ued, "The rude inhabitants of the prairies are extremely agile and hardy;

they bathe, in the depth of the winter, in the half frozen rivers."[9] Maximilian's observations challenge the stereotype of the filthy Indian so prevalent among nineteenth-century Euro-Americans.

Besides using the Missouri for bathing, Indians and Euro-Americans drank the river's water. One journalist wrote while on the Rocky River, "We have a fine deep river and are making a steady run—the river of late has been becoming clearer until now it is quite clear enough to drink without settling though it has a yellowish tinge."[10] Dr. Elias Marsh wrote of the Upper Missouri's water in his 1859 journal: "As we began to feel considerably thirsty, the sight of the water was very grateful, and after climbing several other hills, we soon descended to the bank of the river, and quenched our thirst."[11] Maximilian summed up the high quality of Missouri River water: "There are no endemic disorders [among the Mandan], and the fine water of the Missouri, which, notwithstanding the sand mixed with it, is light and cold, does not a little contribute to make the inhabitants attain an advanced age."[12] Like their human counterparts, the Upper Missouri's birds, bison, coyotes, wolves, and deer (to name just a few species) swallowed the river's moisture.

Across the wide valley that lies between the James River and the Platte, the Missouri poured out its waters, gouging sweeping bends. The winding Upper Missouri frustrated prairie sailors (the name given to those who worked as crewmen on keelboats or steamboats that plied the Missouri) because the bends added distance and toil to their upriver journeys. A straighter river meant a more direct route to the north and west. Cartographer Joseph Nicollet wrote in the first week of May, 1839, while close to present-day Onawa, Iowa, "The bends of the river increase in scale also and come so closely one after the other that the shortest distances between two points are tripled or quadrupled."[13] Above the James River, the Missouri did not burrow such long, graceful bends. The narrower valley and the impermeable Pierre shale and Niobrara chalk that bolster the valley walls reined in the river. Those bends that navigators found so annoying contributed to the valley's biological diversity. Bends and the river's lateral movements created riparian habitat, including point bars, sand flats, and willow shorelines, all vital to birds such as the least tern and piping plover.

Since the Missouri's channel underwent frequent change, the bends did not remain for long. Erosive floods, an annual occurrence on the Upper Missouri each spring and summer, slashed away at the necks of the bends, squeezing the peninsulas until they collapsed and fell into the water. Once the river sliced through a bend, the full fury of the Mighty Mo pushed through the opening. Water gushed through these recently dug apertures with terrifying force. Steamboat pilots and prairie sailors called these breaches "cutoffs" because the Missouri cut off and abandoned a bend once it plowed across the neck. The water racing through a recently opened cutoff reached high speeds and displayed incredible puissance. The reason the Missouri became so ferocious through these clefts is that in cutting off a bend, the river increased its slope or gradient. Before the cutoff took place, the Missouri wound around a bend, dropping an average of a foot and a half in elevation each mile. Along a bend of eighteen miles, which has been documented on the Missouri north of the Platte, the river fell roughly twenty-seven feet from the upstream commencement of the bend to its downstream end. Once the river cut off that eighteen-mile bend, it fell twenty-seven feet in less than a hundred yards. Rushing through these punctures, the Missouri became a raging torrent.

A keelboat or steamboat crew confronting the Missouri as it tore through a cutoff faced the river at its navigational worst. John Luttig, who accompanied a fur trading expedition to the Upper Missouri, ran into a cutoff on July 5, 1812, north of Blackbird's Hill. Luttig fearfully remembered, "Came to a Channel which we entered, in hopes to go through, to cut off 6 Leagues [eighteen miles] of the River, but were disappointed, having ascended within 150 yards toward the head of it, the Water became so rapid as to endanger our Boats to sink, we returned with Difficulty."[14] Brackenridge refers to a reach of the Missouri known as "la coupe a L'Oiselle. This name originated in the circumstance of a trader having made a narrow escape, being in the river at the very moment that this cut-off was forming. It had been a bend of fifteen miles round, and perhaps not more than a few hundred yards across; the gorge, which was suddenly cut through by the river, became the main channel. This was affected in a few hours."[15]

When the Missouri made dramatic shifts in channel direction, it abandoned its previous course, leaving behind either a dry riverbed or an oxbow lake. John Ordway, of the Lewis and Clark expedition, wrote in his journal on August 9, 1804, while in Monona County, Iowa: "Capt. Clark and Sgt. Floyd went out hunting on S.S. [starboard side or right side of the river] came 11 miles by 12 o.C. where the River had formerly Cut across a bend Said to be 15 mes. [miles] Round & a very Short distance a cross where it had Broke through a narrow Stripe [sic] of woods on each side of the River, the old Channel in the above mentioned bend is ponds & Islands."[16] The river planted oxbow lakes across its valley floor from the Platte confluence to the Three Forks. Euro-Americans discovered the greatest concentration of oxbows in the valley between the Platte and the James. The calmer, clearer water of the lakes and their edge habitat offered high-quality living quarters for a variety of species, including bluegill, northern pike, perch, bullhead, Canadian geese, mallards, wood ducks, and bald eagles.

The Missouri did more than abandon channels. The river's thalweg (its deepest, fastest channel) could instantly change its direction, slam straight into a sandbar, island, or bank, and move terra firma off to the Gulf of Mexico. Culbertson wrote of a phenomenon known as "rapicages," which according to him "are fearfully rapid flows of the water as it rises over sand bars and moving them off. The water rushes over [the bar], roars like a cataract and runs in high waves so that if a small boat be struck, it is swallowed up at once. When the bar has been swept away and the full rise has been attained these Rapicages subside."[17] Prince Wilhelm recalled seeing rapicages: "The Missouri makes a great bend here. This place is very dangerous because of some shallow places over which the water rushes like rapids."[18]

As just noted, the Missouri's thalweg could quickly alter its direction, tearing at bars or banks. Tabeau wrote about the dangers navigators faced when confronted with a sudden shift in the course of the thalweg. He recounted, "It has often happened that travelers, camped on a bank, have suddenly discovered that it was sinking and, allowing them barely time to jump into their boat, it has disappeared before their eyes. This misfortune happened to me myself the 19th of May, 1804."[19] Henry Boller, a trader at Fort Berthold in the late 1850s and early 1860s, described how at night he heard few sounds except the infrequent thud as the Missouri ate at its sides: "The perfect stillness that reigns over everything is broken only by the sullen, ceaseless roar of the Missouri, or the occasional whistle of an elk, borne faintly on the evening breeze. Now and then a crash tells of some portion of the river's bank, undermined by the rushing of the current, crumbling."[20] The Missouri possessed a huge appetite for alluvium, sands, and gravels.

The Missouri never looked the same. It changed its appearance from day to day. After returning from the Pacific Ocean in 1806, William Clark commented on just how much the Missouri had changed in the past two years. He wrote on August 20, 1806, south of the Cannonball River: "I observe a great alteration in the Corrent course and appearance of the pt. Of the Missouri. In places where there was Sand bars in the fall 1804 at this time the main Current passes, and where the current then passed is now a Sand bar—Sand bars which were then naked are now covered with willow Several feet high. The enteranc of Some of the Rivers & Creeks Changed owing to the mud thrown into them, and a layor of mud over Some of the bottoms of 8 inches thick."[21] Crashing banks denoted the movement of the Missouri across its valley floor. Channel changes meant habitat variability. What appeared violent and dangerous to *Homo sapiens* navigating the river actually fostered biodiversity. Rapicages or slower channel shifts resculpted the valley's habitat types. More habitat types meant greater species diversity. The Missouri Valley contained a medley of species precisely because of the river's malleability.

Human constructions in the valley lowlands faced either eventual destruction by the wandering Missouri or the possibility of being left high and dry without a riverfront as the Muddy Mo veered off to the other side of the valley. But early nineteenth-century Euro-Americans took their chances with the Missouri, believing the benefits of remaining in the valley bottoms close to the river offset the dangers of having forts or farmsteads cast aside or washed away. Writing in 1820 from Cantonment, Missouri (a post built to house U.S. soldiers north of today's Omaha), Surgeon John Gale observed how the Missouri encroached upon the fort: "The bank has fallen in to such an extent that we have been compelled to take away the Sutlers Store, Blacksmith Shop and several other out houses to prevent their falling into the River."[22] Marsh commented on the Missouri's migrations: "The channel of the river as you have probably heard, varies its position from year to year, as the banks wash away on one side and sand bars form on the other, or islands in the middle of the river. We frequently pass fields which were planted last season, and this year are falling into the river."[23] Culbertson noted the dilemma Euro-Americans encountered in their relationship to this shifting river: "Every few miles places can be seen where the river has changed its channel, sometimes in one year moving off a mile or two from a place where a good channel had been; it is said that at Old Council Bluffs the river flows three miles from where it did when the Fort was first built. All along its course they [the valley residents] calculate for these changes and don't put substantial buildings where there is danger of the bank moving away."[24]

Each spring and summer, the Missouri went over its banks, covering the valley floor with a slow-moving sheet of dazzling, wave-tossed water. Charles Larpenteur, a longtime trader at Fort Union who eventually settled near the mouth of the Little Sioux River, remembered that in May 1851 "the Missouri, as well as all other streams, had overflowed their banks, and the bottoms were all inundated. I had to remain about 15 days at Sergeant's Bluffs, waiting for the roads to become practicable. . . . [I] hired a guide, at $2 a day, to pilot me through the water, for there was very little dry land to be seen between this [Sergeant Bluff, Iowa] and my place [on the Little Sioux River, a distance of fifty miles]."[25]

Water that sat atop the valley floor for month after month gradually rose into the clouds. Any remaining water cleared as its sediments fell on top of the valley floor. Those sediments, in conjunction with that water, ignited an explosion of plant growth. By late June and early July, slough grass, receiving injections of water and nutrients, began to break through the oceanic expanses, blanketing acre after acre of the valley. From atop the Loess Hills and looking west, Euro-Americans viewed a green flag of slough grass flapping above the azure waterline.

The Upper Missouri experienced two major flood events each year. The first flood, called by navigators and settlers a "rise" or "fresh" ("fresh" was an abbreviated version of "freshet"), occurred during the longer, warmer days of late March and early April. Euro-Americans called this flood the April rise, spring rise, or spring fresh. The spring rise did not last long, in some years only a couple of days, in other years a week or two at the most. The spring rise's duration depended on the severity of the preceding winter and the amount of snow covering the plains and tall grass prairies to the west, east, and north of the Missouri main stem. An insignificant snow cover meant a short, small rise. A heavy snowpack contributed to a long, higher rise. The spring rise began with ice-out.

Euro-Americans who lived, worked, and played along the Missouri River in the nineteenth and early twentieth centuries, remembered ice-out. To pale-faced, sun-deprived, grimy, and cabin-bound Missouri Valley residents, ice-out meant one thing—spring had finally come to the Upper Missouri. Ice-out was a time for celebration, signaling an end to cabin fever, months without a dip in the river to bathe, and night after monotonous night indoors with a family that had become all too intimate. Ice-out also meant an end to isolation and the lack of news. Once the river broke up, navigation of the Missouri began anew. Visitors arrived from above or below aboard keels, pirogues, bullboats, mackinaws, and steamers, bringing the latest happenings from back in the states or the upriver posts.

Ice-out, like the spring rise itself, symbolized the harshness or mildness of the preceding winter. When ice went out of the Missouri early, in February or the first weeks of March, it signaled a mild winter. When the ice shat-

tered and paraded downstream in April or as late as May, everyone
understood just how long and hard the preceding winter had been. Missouri
Valley residents could also predict how severe the spring rise would actually
be based on the date of ice-out. When the ice broke up late, say in April, they
expected a higher spring rise because more snow likely fell on the short-
grass plains and mountains of the Upper Missouri. Ice-out represented a
bellwether. Euro-Americans who traveled through, or inhabited, the Missouri Valley observed the date of its occurrence, much like they would record
major holidays such as Christmas, New Year's, and the Fourth of July. Boller
fondly remembered ice-out at Fort Berthold: "Everybody had been watching
for its [the ice's] first movement and when the dull, crushing sound that accompanied it struck the ear the excitement and joy were universal. The men
in the fort dropped their work and rushed to the river's brink, along with
hundreds of Indians, while the tops of the [earth] lodges were crowded with
eager, excited groups, and the dogs, of course, testified their entire approba-
tion by prolonged and vigorous howls."[26] American Fur Company trader
Francis Chardon at Fort Clark near the mouth of the Knife River wrote on
April 11, 1837, "Ice Not yet started, although it has the appearance of a
Move." The next day he reminisced, "The ice broke up to day at 1 P.M.—in
fine stile. The Mandans are in high spirits, anxiously waiting for the drown-
ded Buffaloe to Pass."[27]

Ice-out began when southerly winds and extended hours of sunshine
warmed the land. The winter snow cover, which by March appeared
smeared brown and gray with wind-borne dust, lay in piles around the buffalo grass and in drifted gullies. As daytime temperatures pushed into the
forties and fifties Fahrenheit, the snow melted and dripped down into creeks
and rivers, where it then slid toward the Missouri. On March 24, 1836,
Chardon watched the first awakenings of spring and recorded, "Great
change in the weather—a warm South wind has prevailed during the day—
the Snow has disappeared from the prairies as if by Magic, each ravine or
gully has become a roaring torrent."[28]

The first meltwater of spring flowed out on to the Missouri's ice sheet,
creating a river on top of a river. Within days, several feet of frigid water
might be flowing upon the Missouri's icy sheath. Luttig, at Fort Manuel near
today's South Dakota–North Dakota state line, wrote on February 4, 1813:
"Fine weather and warm. . . . [Missouri] thawed very much and plenty of
water on the Ice."[29] This exterior river bore into the ice beneath it. Water
drilled down into small fissures, widening tiny cracks into crevices. After a

succession of sunny days, the ice became pockmarked with holes, where water pushed up from the river below or forced its way down from the river above. At a climactic moment, the contrary moving water blew the ice sheet into pieces.

The actual breakup of ice and subsequent spring rise happened very fast, often preceded by thunderous booms, a series of rolling dull thuds, or an intense crackling. Maximilian remarked on the speed of the breakup and the resultant rise on April 3, 1834: "The ice broke up so rapidly in the river, that it was necessary to set a watch over our boats during the night, lest the rising water should carry them away."[30] Francis Chardon noted that the breakup occurred in just hours on March 18, 1838: "Since eight Oclock this Morning, the Water commenced riseing—at 10 A.M. the ice broke up."[31] Because of the strength and rapidity of the spring rise, Indians who lived in the valley, including the Sioux, Mandan, Arikara, and Hidatsa, feared the river as the day of ice-out approached. They worried about being caught near the river at the moment the ice moved downstream. Maximilian recalled, "On the 9th of February the inhabitants of Ruhptare [the Mandan village] had all moved from their winter to their summer quarters; they were evidently afraid that the ice would break up early, and the water of the Missouri rise considerably."[32]

At the instant of ice-out, the Missouri behaved like a caged beast just set free. Once the ice shattered, tattered icebergs and black slush rushed downriver. Blocks of ice knocked down bankside saplings or sheered the bark and low branches from larger cottonwoods. On the outside edge of tight bends, the Missouri piled its waters, throwing ice over the banks into the forests. The moving water and the projectiles pulverized forest tracts. Traveler Rudolph Friederich Kurz, at the mouth of the Little Cheyenne in 1852, remarked, "We find here also great blocks of ice caught in the boughs of trees along the shore; they were deposited there upon the outbreak of the high waters. They melt slowly on account of their great size."[33] Maximilian noted, "We observed that the stems of the poplars [cottonwoods], to the height of five feet, or fifteen feet above the present level of the river, had the bark rubbed off by the ice."[34] In clear-cutting forests, the ice opened up the woodlands to a new growth of grass and trees. Additionally, the ice mulched the timber while running water put the splintered organic material into the river. Consequently, scouring ice increased the volume of leaves, bark, and wood in the Missouri, which aided microorganisms and the fish that foraged on them.

Frequently, the floating debris came up against an immovable object, where it stopped dead. Subsequent ice chunks crowded on top of one another to create a makeshift dam. Ice jams formed in narrow, hairpin turns in the channel, on the upstream end of islands or bars, or in tight channel chutes. Wherever the Missouri pinched into a narrow slot, there an ice jam potentially could occur. Ice jams and their temporary reservoirs brought on the first flooding of the year on the Upper Missouri. A high, strong ice jam might hurl ten feet of water over the Missouri's immediate banks. Below the jam, the river's flow might dwindle to a trickle. Larpenteur, in a canoe traveling downstream from Fort Union (near the mouth of the Yellowstone) to Fort Clark in March 1838, recounted an incident that illustrates the nature of the spring rise and its relation to ice jams: "The next day we found but little current [in the Missouri], and had to paddle hard to make much headway. We went on thus until about three in the afternoon, when we found the river nearly blocked by large dykes, which had formed across it and caused the slowness of the current; but we forced our way through a narrow channel, and kept on by hard paddling. By the time we were about 10 miles from Fort Clark the dyke broke loose and the ice came down upon us with such a rush, and tossing our canoe like an old log at such a rate, that we thought ourselves in greater danger of our lives than we had been from the Indians."[35] Chardon commented on the formation of ice jams and their relation to flooding. On March 18, 1838, he wrote, "At 3 P.M. the ice stopped running occassioned by a bridge of ice formeing a few miles below—since Morning the water has rose 12 feet."[36] Thus, ice jams quickly raised the Missouri's water level on their upstream sides, forming miniature reservoirs. An ice jam held firm for minutes, hours, or even days. Eventually, excessive water pressure tore the dam apart. The wall of water released by the jam sent a surge of sludge downriver, causing more lowland flooding. Once the ice cleared from the river, the Missouri remained high for only a few days longer. In 1838, the Missouri ran high for five days after ice-out, then experienced a precipitous decline.

Ice-out meant something entirely different to some of the Indian inhabitants of the valley. It signaled a feast not of freshly killed game but of long-dead bison or elk. In the winter and spring, when the Missouri glided under ice, thousands of heavy mammals crossed it to reach prime feeding areas or the shelter of timber. Countless animals fell through thin ice, splashing down into cold, ebony waters, where the current hurried them off downstream, drowning them as they bounced along the underside of the icy cover. Audubon wrote of this occurrence: "It happens not infrequently, when the river is entirely closed in with ice, that some hundreds of Buffaloes attempt to cross; their aggregate enormous weight forces the ice to break, and the whole of the gang [herd] are drowned, as it is impossible for these animals to climb over the surrounding sharp edges of ice."[37] These soggy, lifeless creatures lodged against snags and shoals until the water became tepid. Eventually the carcasses ballooned with gas and decay. Once the river's ice broke apart, bison bobbed to the surface. In the days immediately after ice-out, the Missouri carried the animals downstream along with all the other flotsam. After weeks, or sometimes months, in the river, the meat greened with putrefaction. The Mandan Indians considered this rancid meat a delicacy. Young men made Herculean efforts to retrieve pungent bison carcasses from the Missouri, often risking their lives by skipping and hopping from one ice cake to the next to reach a dead animal in midriver. A misstep meant a fall into the Missouri, where the frigid waters induced hypothermia, dizziness, and death in minutes. If lucky enough, a Mandan captured one of these prizes, pulled its wet, hairy body onto the bank, cut it open, and feasted on the flesh.[38] Ice-out was a time of celebration for the Indians, and a time of nausea for those who did not enjoy the delights of green bison meat.

Following the April rise, the Missouri became more docile, usually dropping back below bank full through the rest of April and for much of May. In drought years, which came with regular frequency to the Upper Missouri, the April rise might be minimal, imperceptible, or nonexistent. During those years, the Missouri dropped in late April and May to levels usually not seen until August and September. Little moisture fell across the Upper Missouri during the fall, winter, and spring of 1832–1833, so Maximilian and Swiss artist Karl Bodmer on board the steamboat *Yellow Stone* experienced an exceptionally low Missouri in May 1833. On May 18, 1833, Maximilian stated, "The river being so shallow, we were not able to proceed on the following day [May 19] and continued our excursions on shore."[39] Nicollet endured the Missouri at low stage in May 1839. His steamer, the *Antelope,* remained stuck for nine days on a sandbar at Dixon's Bluff, within the boundaries of today's Ponca State Park.[40]

The diary of Emma Slack Dickinson expresses her angst with the shallow waters found in the Missouri in the interim between the April and June rise. In 1869, while traveling on board the *Mollie Ebert* through Nebraska and Dakota, Dickinson wrote on May 7, "We did not travel far before we struck a sand bar and was seven hours working to get off it." Later that same day she sardonically remarked, "Six O'clock and stuck again." On the next day, she noted that her boat "got along a great deal better today only stuck once and then not very long." Her frustration worsened, though, on May 11: "We started off early this morning but before breakfast got stuck so badly we did not get off until after two o'clock." And then the next day: "I thought yesterday we were making slow progress but today we have been in one place all day." At the pinnacle of her anxiety on May 14 she jotted, "There was four steamers all got on a sand bar together [including her own]."[41] The Missouri River fell to low levels in May, a month that late twentieth-century and early twenty-first-century Missouri Valley residents normally associated with high flows released from the Dakota and Montana dams. After this springtime dip in the Missouri, the river witnessed its great June rise.

The start of the June rise depended on when the mountain snows drained away. A warm April and May might cause the June rise to actually be a May rise. A cold May and June might turn the June rise into a July or even an August rise. But in a normal year, something that was, and remains, rare in the Upper Missouri, the rise started in the first week of June, and it came on fast. Consider what nineteenth-century observers recorded about the advent of the June rise. John Bradbury wrote, "We found that the river was rising rapidly; it rose during this day more than three feet: we therefore concluded that this was the commencement of the annual flood of the Missouri, occasioned by the melting of the snow on the Rocky Mountains."[42] Maximilian penned on June 14, 1833, "The Missouri had risen considerably; and, during the night, our people were obliged to keep off, with long poles, the trunks of trees that came floating down the river, without being able to prevent our receiving shocks which made the whole vessel tremble."[43] Chardon knew just how expeditiously the June rise came down the river. He chronicled on June 7, "The water rose last night 2 feet[.] Sunday [June] 8—The water rose last night 3 feet[.] Thursday [June] 11—The water continues riseing—it is much higher at present—than it was at the spring rise, March 26th."[44]

In June the Missouri displayed its grandeur. The summer rise lasted weeks and hauled far more water than the April rise. It reached truly impressive levels. Throughout much of the year, the Upper Missouri carried approximately thirty thousand cubic feet per second down to the Platte. But in June, the Missouri might move ten times that amount past the mouth of the Platte. Nothing stood in the way of this heaving juggernaut. Mammals, birds, and reptiles fled from the rising water. The Missouri uprooted thousands of cottonwood trees or bowled over entire forests. Bluff sides of shale, clay, or loess, undermined by hard-running water, fell into the channel, putting suds into the stream and adding tons of sediment to an already overloaded river. At the height of the June rise, the river covered its islands, sandbars, high banks, and valley bottoms. The June rise demanded the respect of Euro-Americans. Boller recalled, "The Missouri commenced to feel the melting of the snows in its mountain tributaries and its swollen and turbid waters rushed and foamed wildly."[45] The June rise earned the river its nickname, the Mighty Missouri.

The June rise usually passed on down to the Lower Missouri by the middle of July, but before it did, it remade the river's morphology. The floodwaters, with their weight, speed, and force, washed away old sand and gravel bars, dug cavernous holes, excavated new channel chutes through alluvium, sawed down cottonwoods, cut off bends, abandoned long-held channels, put islands squarely ashore, and deposited millions of tons of gooey, yellow silt on top of the valley floor. The June rise was the most important biohydrologic event of the year. It rearranged the valley's habitat mosaic and offered up volumes of water, silt, and organic refuse for the continued sustenance of flora and fauna.

By the third week of July, the Upper Missouri dropped sharply, once more exposing sandbars and sand flats to view. Deprived of rainwater and snowmelt, the Missouri dipped even lower in August and early September. Maximilian noted how different the river appeared during the low stages of September. At Fort Union the German monarch stated, "The appearance of the country about Fort Union had much changed since our visit in the month of July. . . . the river was shallow, narrow, and full of sandbanks."[46]

Cool fall rains threw an autumn rise down the river in late September and October. During November and December, as drizzle congealed into snow and cold temperatures locked away moisture in the land, the Missouri retreated again behind sandbars and islands. In the months of January and February, when the river flowed under a blanket of white, the Missouri shrank, withdrawing to its lowest stage. But it would bounce back again in March and April with the advent of the spring rise.

Although the Missouri exhibited a discernible and predictable pattern of high and low flows throughout the year, the river still underwent great variation within those supposed norms. The Missouri's flow regime underwent daily or weekly fluctuations. Small, erratic rises resulted from tributary inflows. Tributaries occasionally drained large quantities of water into the Missouri, causing a miniature flood in the main stem below their mouths. These minifloods occurred even when the Missouri as a whole ran low. Bradbury mentioned several small rises in the river that his crew experienced as they pulled and prodded their keel upstream through today's central South Dakota. He remarked, "The river had risen considerably during the night, and we were now convinced that the floods we had before encountered, and which were of short duration, were only partial, and caused by the rising of the tributary streams that have their sources in the lower regions."[47]

The Missouri's haphazard flow regime also resulted from the soil types prevalent throughout the Upper Missouri basin. Impermeable clays are widespread across the region, especially throughout the badlands of western North and South Dakota and eastern Montana. When rain strikes these clays, the water does not soak into the soil; instead, it runs down into the Missouri or one of its branches. During a downpour, a gully or creek can be transformed in minutes from a parched arroyo to a cataract. The consequent sheet runoff passes from the badlands into the big river, causing a crest of high water to descend the Missouri. Brief, intense thunderstorms and the resultant runoff contributed to the Missouri's frequent ups and downs.

Variability in flow was the name of the game along the Missouri. Chardon kept one of the best journals of the unevenness in the river's flows. He wrote in May 1837, "Monday 22—Water commenced riseing—Tuesday 23—the water continues riseing—Tuesday 30—The water since 3 or 4 days has been falling, to day it has began to rise."[48] The river eternally rose and fell, never maintaining a steady, uniform depth. Variability in flow, like channel changes, played an important role in creating and sustaining habitat diversity; the two went hand in hand. Variable flows equaled variable habitat and therefore greater species abundance.

The Missouri's rises and falls also reflected the climatic cycle prevalent across its basin. By late July, August, and September, the skies cleared, the humidity dropped, high-pressure systems dominated the atmosphere, and the rains altogether ceased. The land emerged shriveled, brown, and brittle. With nothing falling from above, creeks and rivers shrank, some disappearing entirely into salt-stained sand or clay. The dry season affected the Missouri and Yellowstone main stems the least, but lesser tributaries lost volumes. The White, Bad, Cheyenne, Moreau, Grand, Knife, Little Missouri, Poplar, Milk, Musselshell, and Judith Rivers faded to strips of brackish liquid or recoiled into intermittent pools of warm, bacterial water. Gouverneur K. Warren, a lieutenant in the U.S. Army, reported in 1855, "Besides a deficiency of forest trees [in the Upper Missouri territory], there is a great want of water, and in the dry season of autumn and winter, in all the small tributaries of the Missouri, the water is either entirely absent, or so impregnated with saline matter as to be unfit for use."[49] Maximilian wrote in July 1833 near the mouth of the Milk River, "It was now the dry season, which, in these parts continues from the middle of July to the end of autumn. The whole prairie was dry and yellow; the least motion, even of a wolf crossing it, raised the dust. . . . All the small rivers were completely dried up. Even the Missouri was very shallow, which it always is in summer and autumn."[50]

Yet, unlike smaller streams, the Missouri and Yellowstone kept water in their channels year-round, never going dry. The size and topographic irregularity of each of these drainage basins ensured against total water depletion. Somewhere in the Upper Missouri, natural springs, thunderstorms, or snowbanks fed water into either one or both of these two rivers. As further insurance against an absolute diminishment of flows, the Yellowstone and far Upper Missouri received the bulk of their inflows from snowmelt. Snow amounts in the northern Rockies have been more consistent through the years than rain amounts on the plains to the east. Thus, if the plains ran dry, mountain snows still nursed the two dominant rivers. Severe drought struck the Upper Missouri at various times in the nineteenth century, but the Yellowstone and Missouri stayed afloat.[51]

From the time of the Lewis and Clark expedition until at least the mid-1840s and possibly the mid-1850s, the channel of the Upper Missouri wound its way to the Mississippi in long bends. Channels of this sort—labeled sinuous by hydrologists—have few islands, sandbars, and side channels. The water flows through a single channel instead of through numerous chutes. The width of the Upper Missouri in the first decades of the nineteenth century varied considerably from place to place, with the widest sections in the extensive alluvial valley between the James and Platte. Here the Missouri opened its arms, in certain locations attaining a width of ten thousand feet or more. Nicollet wrote of the Missouri's girth above the Platte: "Sometimes the river bed narrows to 1/5 of a mile, but usually it is 1, 1½, or 2 miles wide."[52] Observers unanimously agreed that the Missouri maintained its characteristic width up to the Mandan villages, and from there to the Yellowstone it began to gradually taper until beyond the Yellowstone the shrinkage in the Missouri became readily apparent.[53]

The Missouri's waters flowed in different directions and at different speeds. The nineteenth-century Missouri had no consistent velocity, as it does today in the channelized reach south of Sioux City. Water scraping against banks flowed slower than water at midchannel. Water tumbling along the river's bed and rubbing against gravel, sand, and clay flowed slower than water at middepth. Water on the surface did not run as fast as water beneath the surface because wind put the brakes on its forward thrust. Water at middepth in the thalweg flowed the fastest because it encountered the least resistance. During floods, water massed in the thalweg, brought there by gravity to its steeper slope and greater depth. Consequently, during the spring and summer rises the thalweg flowed several feet higher than the water moving through side channels.

It is hard to gauge the average current velocity of the Upper Missouri in the early and middle nineteenth century because the thalweg's velocity differed from place to place. To complicate matters, the Missouri flowed at different speeds simultaneously. Off the end of a sandbar, the current might shoot along at six or seven miles per hour. But as the thalweg moved through a flat, it might run at only two miles per hour. The journalistic evidence indicates that the Upper Missouri's thalweg averaged between four and five miles per hour during the early decades of the nineteenth century when the river coursed through a sinuous channel. Once the river became braided after the mid-1850s, the thalweg's velocity slowed down to a mere two miles per hour (a wet precipitation cycle and higher runoff braided the Missouri's channel). A sinuous channel, with its concentrated water volumes, has greater gravitational momentum, less bank and bed resistance, and therefore a higher rate of descent. A braided river that is wide and shallow rubs against more bars, shoals, islands, river-edge vegetation, and bank lines, and this excessive resistance causes braided rivers to slow down. Culbertson, writing in 1850, before major changes in the Missouri's channel morphology, estimated the river's current velocity at "from four to seven miles per hour, depending upon the stage of water."[54] Marsh admitted the pitfalls of trying to gauge the Missouri's rate of descent: "The current is very strong in the river and washes strongly along the bank. It is difficult to describe the current of the Missouri, and to understand it, it is necessary to see it."[55] Irregular current velocities fostered diverse fish habitat. Certain fish need fast water, others slow. In the erratic Missouri, fish found the current velocity to suit their evolutionary needs.

As Clark and others noted, the Upper Missouri possessed more sandbars and gravel bars than the Lower Missouri. Although sandbars provided wonderful habitat for a host of birds, keelboat and steamboat travelers abhorred them because watercraft frequently ran aground on their soft shores. A preponderance of sandbars lay in front of, or directly below, the mouths of the Upper Missouri's tributaries. River travelers found sandy deltas at the mouths of the Platte, Niobrara, White, Bad, Cheyenne, Little Missouri, and Yellowstone. The bars crept across the Missouri's channel at these places because the tributaries possessed steeper slopes than the Missouri, and thus their currents moved faster than the Missouri River's current. Hence, the tributaries hurled klinker, clay, and gravel off the plains and shuffled them out into the Missouri. The slower, flatter Missouri, lacking the propulsion of the tributaries, could not cart away all of the silt, so the silt and sandbars piled up in the vicinity of these tributary embouchements. Bars, although a nuisance to navigators, aided flora and fauna. Birds, bison, and *Homo sapiens* used them for protection from enemies on the river's banks.

According to navigators, the Missouri demonstrated a nasty habit of shoaling. Shoals are underwater ridges of sand, gravel, or clay erected by crosscurrents. When the channel of the Missouri wound its way down to the Mississippi, the thalweg wound though the channel area, a river inside a river. Currents flowed back and forth across the riverbed. When currents moved in opposite directions, the thalweg constructed ridgelines in the calm water that sat between the two contrary currents. The majority of shoals in the Upper Missouri consisted of sand or fine sediments. However, the Missouri also dug out clay ridges in its bed. Clay ridges formed when contrary currents burrowed into the riverbed and tore away the uppermost layers of sand and gravel, leaving only the rock-hard, impermeable clay still standing. Clay shoals could damage or destroy vessels. If a steamer rammed a clay shoal at full speed, the boat's hull might warp or break into pieces. A sand shoal usually gave way when a steamer struck it. More often than not, the boats slid atop the sand shoals and fell into the water on the other side; the weight of the boat, along with the undercutting current, caused the shoal to collapse beneath the hull.

On the Upper Missouri, shoals crisscrossed the channel. Some ran alongside the thalweg; others, the ones that perplexed and haunted steamboat pilots, ran perpendicular to the thalweg's apparent direction. Nicollet watched the Missouri, in its dizzying movements, diligently building ridgelines of sand, clay, and gravel. To his amazement, these shoals did not run analogous to the direction of the river's flow. Rather, the Missouri built shoals out from its banks. The river's bed resembled an accordion, with one ridge of sand or clay after another. Nicollet wrote, "The substances which form the bed of the river are so mobile that they settle almost parallel to the undulations of the water's surface, forming thus waves of moving sand, mud, and diluted soil. One moment they take a certain shape and then at the next they take another."[56] The problem with Missouri River shoals was that steamboat and keelboat pilots could not always discern their position, since they lay hidden under inches of plains syrup. Shoaling on the Upper Missouri caused steamboat and keelboat pilots to go up or down a channel only to reach a point where shoals prevented further advance. In other words, the boats went into dead ends.[57] From a biological perspective, shoals served fish as spawning sites and feeding lies. The mounds of sand and silt deflected or decelerated the current, providing fish calm water in which to lay eggs or lie in wait for prey.

The reach below the James River held a plethora of sandbars but almost no islands. Here the Missouri's volatility prevented the accretion of sediments necessary for island formation. But north and west of the James, where the Missouri River trench narrowed and the river's course became less haphazard, luxuriant islands sprawled out in the river channel. Certain islands gained popularity among keelboat and steamboat passengers for their breathtaking beauty. Bon Homme Island was well known for its scenery. A jade meadow cushioned the interior of the island, while a green carpet grew in the shade of the tall trees on its banks. Bon Homme Island is now immersed by Lewis and Clark Lake.

Another very popular island in the nineteenth century protruded from the Missouri River channel near today's Lake Andes, South Dakota—its name, Little Cedar Island. Maximilian provided a description of Little Cedar Island:

On the following morning, the 16th of May, having passed a village of prairie dogs, we reached, at nine o'clock, the [Little] Cedar Island, which is said to be 1,075 miles from the mouth of the Missouri. On the steep banks of this long narrow island, which lies near the south-west bank, there were thickets of poplars [cottonwoods], willows, and buffalo berry; the rest of the island is covered with a dark forest of red cedars. . . . The notes of numerous birds were heard in the gloom of this cedar forest, into which no ray of the sun could penetrate. Here, too, we found everywhere traces of the elks and stags, and saw where they rubbed off the bark with their antlers.[58]

Steamers frequently docked at Little Cedar Island to gather cedar wood. Steamboat crews preferred to burn dead, dry cedar in the boats' boilers, rather than the softer cottonwood. Cedar burned hotter than cottonwood, and the added heat translated into a greater head of steam to thwart the Missouri's onrushing current. Little Cedar Island is now snug inside the bowels of Lake Francis Case.

Bradbury, in 1811, described an island that sat directly opposite present-day Chamberlain, South Dakota: "The island is about three quarters of a mile in length, and five hundred yards in width. The middle part is covered with the finest cedar, round which there is a border from sixty to eighty yards in width, in which were innumerable clumps of rose and currant bushes, mixed with grape vines, all in flower, and extremely fragrant. . . . Betwixt the clumps and amongst the cedars, the buffaloes, elks, and antelopes had made paths, which were covered with grass and flowers. I have never seen a place, however embellished by art, equal to this in beauty."[59] The island, which would later be named American Island, was drowned by a Corps of Engineers dam at Fort Randall in 1953–1954.

A few days later, Bradbury's keel sailed up to Great Cedar Island, once located thirty miles below Pierre but now fermenting underneath Lake Sharpe. "This island is about two miles in length, and chiefly covered with very fine cedar, and some rose and currant bushes, considerably overrun with vines, on which some of the grapes were already changing colour."[60] Steamboat traveler Daniel Weston described a piece of land known as Blue Blanket Island (Blue Blanket being an Indian who may have died nearby), situated in the vicinity of the Cannonball River's juncture with the Missouri. "Yesterday we lay all day at Blue Blanket Island—Read a good deal and walked far and long upon the charming island. Birds of rare song flocked the trees and flowers filling the eye with beauty and the air with perfume shone in great beds over the grassy knolls."[61] This island is now under Oahe Reservoir. Islands, in a manner similar to sandbars, offered prey species protection from predators located on the river's main banks. Islands acted as safe zones in dangerous territory. The *Homo sapiens* of the Lewis and Clark expedition camped on Missouri River islands when passing through areas occupied by the Sioux and Blackfeet. The leaders of the exploring party wanted to put distance and water between themselves and their potential enemies.

As noted earlier, the Missouri and Yellowstone Valleys became dumping grounds for materials hauled in from distant lands. When detritus-laden flows hit the slower-moving Missouri, the coagulating sediment settled on top of its bed. Through the centuries, tablelands of accumulated muck arose above and below the mouths of the Missouri's largest tributaries. Tablelands also formed out of the Missouri's erosion processes. Since the Wisconsin glaciation, the Missouri had incised its channel, leaving in its wake a series of terraces on either bank. These terraces marked the former high-flow line of the river.

Tributary deposition and terracing formed extensive tablelands at certain locations within the river valley. These tablelands differed from a simple, low-lying point. Tablelands rested higher above the floodplain, more secure from the Missouri's average annual inundations. Tablelands might stand ten or twenty feet above the waterworn valley floor. Certain tablelands, the ones referred to as "bottoms" by nineteenth-century Euro-Americans, possessed more wood, grass, and brush than mere points, and their areal coverage surpassed that of lowland forests or meadows.

The bottoms resembled oases, pockets of extreme fertility in the Upper Missouri, and held the greatest degree of biodiversity in the Upper Missouri region. A motley crew of plants, animals, and birds lived, mated, and died in these loud, cackling environments. Edward Harris noted the connection between the bottoms and the presence of wildlife. He wrote the following passage while steaming upstream in the vicinity of today's Garrison Dam: "A white frost this morning was followed by a beautiful day, saw a good deal of game today—the bottom lands are now much better covered with timber than they have been for some hundreds of miles, and we are told that the balance of the route is pretty well timbered. Saw a good many elk to-day, they are fond of timbered bottoms."[62]

A significant bottom, in both size and ecological import, lay on the Upper Missouri's west bank from old Council Bluffs (directly across from the Boyer-Missouri confluence) to the Omaha village (near present-day Homer, Nebraska). Euro-Americans knew this as the Sixty-Mile Bottom, in reference to its length.[63] Another bottom, which covered the Missouri–Vermillion River confluence, was spotted by Maximilian in 1833: "We continued our voyage, but soon lay to at the prairie, on the right bank, because Mr. McKenzie wished to form a plantation at this place. The whole plain [bottom] was covered with high, dry grass. On the bank of the river there was a fine border of tall timber trees, in which the turtle-dove cooed, and flocks of blackbirds were flying about. . . . At the spot where we now were, it is said that large herds of buffaloes are seen in the winter."[64]

A third bottom, known for its grove of soaring cottonwoods, straddled the Missouri Valley at the James-Missouri juncture. From the James to the Yellowstone every major bottom occupied the Missouri's right bank (steamboat pilots designated left or right bank as they looked downstream). Through this reach, the Missouri's biggest tributaries enter the main stem from the west. This hydrologic, geologic, and ecological fact explains why the Missouri River tribes (such as the Mandan) and the equestrian nomads (including the Sioux) maintained the bulk of their villages or temporary hunting camps on the Missouri's western shore rather than its eastern side. Productive bottoms meant improved hunting and berry picking and more cottonwood trees for fuel and horse feed.

A small bottom blanketed the Missouri Valley just below the mouth of the Niobrara (where Old Niobrara once stood). Prince Wilhelm laid eyes on this refuge in 1823 and recalled, "The southern bank near the mouth of the stream [Niobrara] expands into a beautiful prairie region with tall grass. The northern bank is covered with tall timber."[65] A bottom sprawled on the Missouri's western bank from the White River northward for three miles. Clark predicted that one day this bottom would be the site of a city. Today it is the site of a mudflat, formed from the gunk dropping into Lake Francis Case from the White River (fig. 1.2).

Only nine miles upstream, another bottom jutted its steep banks into the Missouri at the mouth of today's American Crow Creek, at Oacoma, South Dakota. Clark's journal states, "The deer very gentle and in great numbers on this bottom which had more timber on it than any part of the river we had seen for many days past, consisting of Cottonwood Elm, some indifferent ash and a considerable quanty of a small species of white oak which is loaded with acorns of an excellent flavor. . . . the acorns were now falling, and we concluded that the number of deer which we saw here had been induced thither by the acorns of which they are remarkably fond."[66] North and west of American Crow Creek, fertile tablelands thinned out until the Big Bend. Known as the Grand Detour to eighteenth-century French traders on the Missouri, the Big Bend (a twenty-six-mile loop in the Missouri channel in central South Dakota) did not possess notable bottomland in the river channel itself. Rather, a large corral of bottomland filled the entire southern interior of the bend. From Big Bend northwestward, large, well-timbered bottoms did not exist in the Missouri Valley.

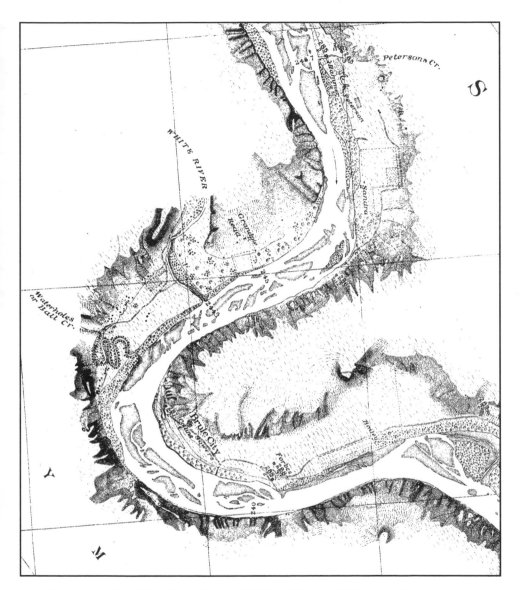

Figure 1.2. The White River bottom. William Clark in 1804 noted the presence of tablelands at the White–Missouri River confluence. He predicted that in the future the bottom would be the site of a settlement. Today, the bottom lies under the water and sediment stored behind Fort Randall Dam. (Missouri River Commission Map, 1894)

Not until the Bad River–Missouri confluence, roughly eighty river miles from the Grand Detour, did long swaths of cottonwood trees make their reappearance. A high, flat bottom began two miles southeast of the Bad River on the Missouri's west bank and extended to a point five miles north of the Bad's mouth. Thirty miles away in a straight line from the Bad River bottoms rested the Cheyenne bottom, which reached from the mouth of the Cheyenne seven miles down the Missouri's western shore. Brackenridge wrote the following about this location: "This morning, passed a large and handsome river, called the Chienne [Cheyenne], S.W. side. It appears as large as the Cumberland or Tennessee. Saw at this place, the ruins of an old village and fortification. The country hereabouts is fine, and better wooded than any I have seen for the last three hundred miles. A tolerable settlement might be supported here. Game is very abundant—elk, deer, and buffaloe without number."[67]

North of the Cheyenne River, the Missouri passed through a narrow, comparatively barren valley for a distance of ninety miles. Notable bottoms remained absent. Not until the vicinity of the Cannonball River did significant numbers of trees reappear. Six miles north of the Cannonball, at the site of historic Fort Rice, began one of the greatest tracts of bottomland in the Upper Missouri. This bottom extended upstream for nearly eighty miles, culminating at the Missouri's Great Bend (not to be confused with the Big Bend in South Dakota). The Great Bend is the modern location of the Big Dam: Garrison. This large bottom lay astride both banks of the Missouri, but more bottomland rested on the west bank than on the east. To this bottom poured the waters of the Heart River, Square Butte Creek, and the Knife River from the west and Turtle and Apple creeks from the east. Once in the lowlands, the waters of these streams pooled, giving rise to thick meadows and cottonwood forests.

Upstream from the Great Bend, the Missouri Valley wall opened to let in the Little Missouri River, which headed in the rough-and-tumble badlands to the south and west. At the mouth of the Little Missouri sat a bottom of some repute. Maximilian wrote, "At noon we passed the Little Missouri, at the mouth of which there were now extensive sand banks; we stopped a little below it, and found a spot very favourable for the chase, in a forest alternating with morass, high grass, and various plants."[68]

An enormous bottom extended from where the blurred waters of the Yellowstone mingled with the more lucent Missouri, stretching from the confluence up the Yellowstone to O'Fallon Creek (fig. 1.3). Game abounded in

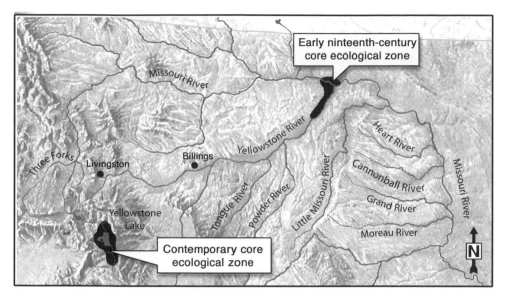

Figure 1.3. Yellowstone River Valley. The Lower Yellowstone River and Valley held a high concentration of biological diversity in the early years of the nineteenth century. Today the highest degree of biological diversity in the contiguous United States is found in Yellowstone National Park and the Greater Yellowstone Ecosystem at the headwaters of the Yellowstone River. (Paul Davidson, South Plains College, Levelland, Texas)

this far northern province. Bison, elk, and grizzly bears tore through shrubbery and timber. Maximilian saw this area and remarked, "We reached at seven o'clock in the evening, the mouth of the Yellow Stone, a fine river, hardly inferior in breadth to the Missouri at this part. It issues below the high chain of hills, and its mouth is bordered with a fine wood of tall poplars, with willow thickets."[69]

Other bottomland sanctuaries existed along the Missouri main stem to the west of the Yellowstone-Missouri confluence. Predictably, these bottoms formed where perennial streams came into the Missouri. Euro-Americans found bottoms where the Redwater-Poplar, the Big Dry–Milk, and the Musselshell-Valentine tributaries joined the Missouri (fig. 1.4). Still more bottomland laid down at the mouths of the Judith and Marias Rivers to the west. The Judith bottom, and its striking good looks, captured the attention of many. One chronicler remembered, "Yesterday morning we wooded at the mouth of the Judith in a most charming spot amid so much desolation—it was a green grove of cottonwoods whose floor was green with grass

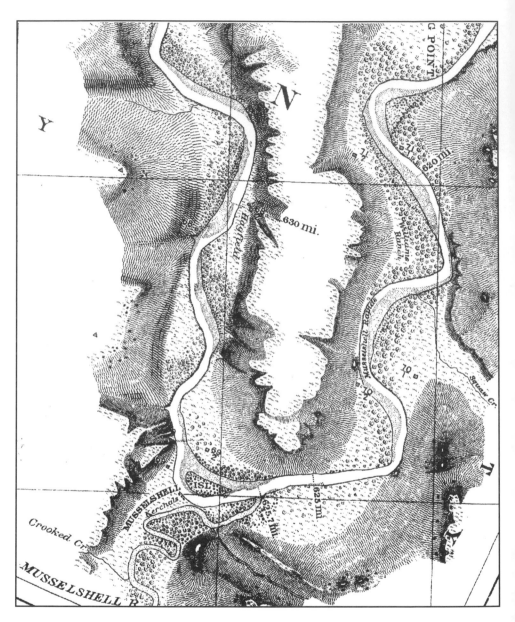

Figure 1.4. The Musselshell River bottom. Located along the far Upper Missouri, the Musselshell bottom represented a vital oasis in a semiarid environment. Nineteenth-century European and Euro-American travelers remarked on the beauty of this bottomland sanctuary. (Missouri River Commission Map, 1894)

and fragrant with acres of wild roses. I wandered along in the grateful shade and balmy bracing air—gathering at times wild strawberries. I found the remains of many Indian camps and it seems a favorite haunt of the red man. They show their good taste to frequent such a lovely spot."[70] Euro-Americans found the last bottom on the Missouri at the Three Forks, where meadows blended into bogs.

Besides the bottom northeast of O'Fallon Creek, the Yellowstone Valley possessed several other biological havens. Paradise Valley, south of Livingston, Montana, served as a winter retreat for creatures that summered in the higher elevations of today's Yellowstone National Park. At Youngs Point began a broad, level, treeless plain, bordered on the north by golden, vertical rock and on the south by white, thrashing water. Where the Clarks Fork enters the Yellowstone, this plain opened on the north shore, with six miles of grass from river to rimrocks. Clarks Fork Bottom narrowed to a pinhead a few miles northeast of modern Billings. At the point where Clarks Fork Bottom came to an end, another bottom commenced on the south shore. This bottom reached from Huntley, Montana, to Pompey's Pillar, roughly twenty miles to the east, northeast. A further piece of tableland extended on the Yellowstone's south bank from present-day Myers, Montana, to the vicinity of Sanders, Montana. Hysham, Montana, is platted squarely in the center of what nineteenth-century Euro-Americans knew as the Sarpy Bottom or Great Bottom. Where the Big Porcupine met the Yellowstone, a bottom covered the later valley. Finally, Euro-Americans discovered elevated tablelands of trees and grass where the Little Porcupine–Rosebud, Tongue-Sunday, and Powder-Cedar tributaries touched the Yellowstone. When Clark passed the Powder River bottom in 1806, he wrote, "In the evening below the enterance [sic] of redstone river [Powder] I observed great numbers of Buffalow feeding on the plains, elk on the points and antilopes."[71]

Other bottoms flanked the higher reaches of tributary streams, including the Big Horn, Little Horn (today's Little Bighorn), Rosebud, Tongue, Powder, North Platte, White, Cheyenne, and Little Missouri. The ultimate tributary oasis surrounded the flat, damp headwaters of the Tongue and Powder Rivers (in the vicinity of Sheridan, Wyoming). A confusing mixture of creeks and meadows entwined the heads of these two rivers. Here, at the height of summer, blasphemous numbers of bison passed hot days, feeding, mating, and fending off biting flies. An army officer who trekked through this area in 1859 wrote:

The country passed through is the best seen on our whole route. The hills are high and rugged; but the soil is good, and both hills and valleys are covered with a luxuriant growth of bunch grass. . . . A large portion of the grass has just been burned over, and the surface of the country is therefore black and forbidding; but it is evident that, in the spring, the prospect is most beautiful from the exuberance of verdure and foliage. The close proximity of the mountains not only adds beauty to the landscape, but they are the sources of numerous brooks of clear running water that fertilize the soil and teem with mountain trout. Bears are very numerous, more than a dozen having been seen in the course of the day's march, and one, a yearling cub, was brought down by Bridger's rifle. Elk, deer, and antelope have also been seen in abundance, and we can now understand why the Indians cling with such tenacity to their country. No buffalo have been seen today, but the number of skeletons visible upon all sides show that at times they are to be found here in large numbers.[72]

The refuge at the head of the Tongue and Powder represented an exception, rather than the rule, to the location of sanctuaries in the Upper Missouri. For the most part, the largest oases embraced the tablelands of the two big rivers, while the smaller bottoms clung to the tributaries (fig. 1.5).

The bottoms along the Missouri from the Platte to the Musselshell and adjacent to the Yellowstone from its mouth to the Clarks Fork enclosed big cottonwood trees, their roots hungrily slurping up minerals and organic matter from an alluvial malt. Cottonwoods grew fat and tall in these riverside resorts, attaining heights of eighty feet or more. Cottonwoods, because of their prevalence and size, garnered a lot of attention from river passengers and valley residents. A. H. Wilcox, who settled near the Missouri River in southeast Dakota Territory in the early 1860s, fondly recalled the appearance of bottomland cottonwoods: "[My] most westerly forty [acres of land] lay in a beautiful grove of Cottonwood trees near the Missouri river. The Cottonwood groves in that vicinity while in a state of nature were beautiful in the extreme, resembling the artificial parks belonging to some of our eastern cities, no underbrush, no stumps or decaying tree tops."[73]

Tracts of cottonwood could be found throughout the Missouri Valley and inside the gullies and tributary valleys entering the Missouri River trench. Gigantic trees normally grew on the outside edge of bends, where cut banks threatened to undermine the forests. The inside of bends invariably contained willows and small cottonwood saplings. Missouri River cottonwoods

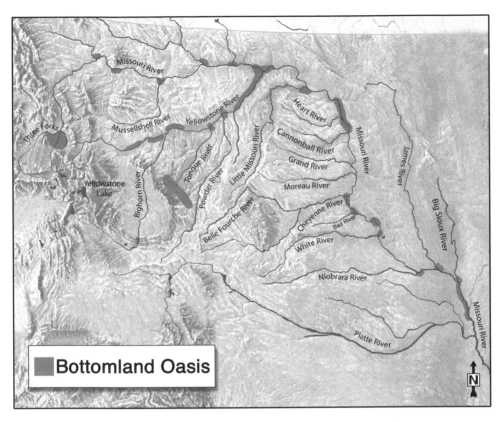

Figure 1.5. Bottomland sanctuaries throughout the Upper Missouri bioregion. Biologically diverse zones, referred to by nineteenth-century Euro-American travelers as "bottoms," interlaced the Upper Missouri. The majority of the bottoms existed immediately above or below where perennial tributaries entered the Missouri or Yellowstone trenches. The most notable bottoms sat at the Three Forks and Tongue River headwaters, the Yellowstone River–Missouri River confluence, the Heart River region, and the Cheyenne River–Missouri River confluence, and on the Missouri River's west bank between the Omaha village (near today's Homer, Nebraska) and the old Council Bluffs (on the Missouri's west bank across from the mouth of the Boyer River). (Paul Davidson, South Plains College, Levelland, Texas)

lived approximately one hundred years, a life cycle that corresponded to the river's hundred-year meander pattern, or its back-and-forth movement across the floodplain. Accordingly, in any hundred-year period, the Missouri occupied a portion of its floodplain. But that occupancy did not last long. Since the Missouri persistently shifted course, it abandoned old channels while simultaneously boring new ones. While the river creeped sideways, it deposited sediments on top of its former river channel until the imprint of the earlier channel disappeared under several feet of alluvium. But the river would eventually return to its past haunts. It might take thirty, forty, fifty, or one hundred years, but the Missouri would find its way back to a portion of its former bed and plow open another channel.

Cottonwoods adorning the river evolved with that meander pattern. In a remarkable convergence of ecology and hydrology, the Missouri returned in time to destroy the high, whitening cottonwoods as they approached the end of their life cycle. It took their lives in an act of mercy killing, undermining their roots and dispatching them before they succumbed to disease and decay. It was as if the river harvested the trees at the moment they ripened. All along the Upper Missouri, the connection between river and cottonwoods was visible, nowhere more so than along the cut banks. Here the river ripped and slashed through mature forest tracts. After a big tree was undercut and killed, it fell into the river; each year, thousands of cottonwoods found their way into the Missouri. Audubon viewed the Missouri gnawing away at the cottonwoods along its banks: "We saw several trees falling in, and beautiful, though painful, was the sight. As they fell, the spray which rose along their whole length was exquisite."[74] Once a tree dipped into the Missouri, its roots settled to the riverbed and received a hurried burial, while the stem and branches stood upright. Meriwether Lewis recalled, "The timber thus precipitated into the water with large masses of earth about their roots, are seen drifting with the stream, their points above the water, while the roots more heavy are dragged along the bottom until they become firmly fixed in the quicksands which form the bed of the river, where they remain for many years, forming an irregular, tho' dangerous chevauxdefrise to oppose the navigator."[75]

Inside a sharp bend, the river resembled an elephant bone yard—a place where the Missouri brought its dead. Stark white trunks lay on top of one another or inches apart, cluttering the channel with their lifeless forms. Nineteenth-century Euro-Americans named these dead trees "snags." Navigators agreed that the river reach between the Platte and the James held the most snags. As Culbertson approached the mouth of the James River from the north in 1850, he remarked, "We are again getting into the region of snags, but we have made fine running yesterday and today."[76] Brackenridge also experienced the Missouri's snag-filled channel while navigating from the James to the Platte. Near the Omaha village he stated, "It was dangerous to proceed after night on account of the number of trees fixed in the bottom of the river, and besides in almost every bend there were a number which had fallen in: even in the day time there was frequently great difficulty in passing along, we several times narrowly escaped being dashed to pieces. The arks, or flat boats, in use on the Ohio and Mississippi, could not possibly navigate this river."[77]

A "snag" referred to a dead tree that rose above the surface of the water. Euro-Americans called trees that remained entirely submerged "breaks," "sawyers," or "planters." Unseen and often unperceived (even to the trained eyes of veteran pilots), planters induced great fear. Pilots knew that thousands of them gripped the river's bed, yet they could do nothing about that reality; they had to pass over those torpedoes, or skirt around them, to avert disaster and deliver their passengers and cargo to the far corners of the Euro-American empire. Pilots also knew that at any moment their boat might be impaled on a planter, the hull quickly filled with sandy water, and the cargo and boat lost to the river. Steamer pilots played Russian roulette on the Missouri, gingerly snaking their way over the river's surface, hoping against hope to miss the giants lying in wait at their feet.

Before a tree fell into the Missouri, it leaned far out over the water, eventually becoming horizontal. Prairie sailors named these faltering trees "sweepers" because the trees and their foliage swept the water passing through their branches. Sweepers, like planters, made life unpleasant for Missouri River navigators, especially those manning the keels or towing mackinaws upstream. Time after time, keels passing under an overhanging sweeper broke their center mast. To navigate the Missouri properly and safely, boats risked losing their masts; it was the price they paid for working the river.

Keelboatmen on the Missouri (the written record does not include any keelboatwomen) tried as much as possible to hug the shoreline. The shore meant safety. If anything went wrong, if the boat abutted a shoal, struck a planter, or suddenly turned sideways in the thalweg, crews onshore or in the shallows, who held the cordell attached to the bow, possessed better odds of righting the craft or salvaging it if it went down. A keelboat in trouble in deep water in the middle of the river was a boat more likely to be lost. Lacking any support from a shore crew and in water too deep for the men to set their feet, midriver accidents turned disastrous in an instant. Prairie sailors hated sweepers because the trees forced them to abandon their beloved shoreline and push their boats out into deeper, faster, more dangerous water beyond the end of the hanging tree. In the water shooting past a sweeper, boats became unwieldy and occasionally untenable.

Crews dreaded sweepers for other reasons. An overhanging tree meant more work for the men. Cordelling, oaring, or poling the boat past the fast water running off the end of the sweeper took tremendous strength, endurance, and courage. The cordell might become entangled in the sweeper's billowing branches, and in oaring or poling, the crews had to muster the muscle power to push the boat past the sweeper. Some keelboat crews, not wanting to risk all the hazards of outflanking the sweepers, just sawed them in half and pushed the severed trunk and branches into the river, where the current carried them away. Sometimes the time and energy required to cut down a sweeper were preferable to the risk of attempting to stem the river's thalweg off the end of it.

Mary Cook's boat, the *Henry Adkins,* took several hits from sweepers. She wrote, "We had a little smash-up this afternoon, caused by running too near the bank where some fallen trees projected out into the river, and came in contact with the side of the boat at the cook room on the lower deck; I don't know the exact amount of damage done, but was aroused from my afternoon nap by the sound of crashing timbers and broken glass directly under me."[78] Tabeau described a close encounter with a sweeper: "A tree about thirty feet high and from nine to ten inches in diameter was uprooted directly in front of the barge [keel], but, as we were passing very near to it, it rested gently upon the loaded barge just as it started to lean and we escaped except for a scratch on the shoulder of one of our men."[79] From a navigational point of view, snags and sweepers created all sorts of problems. Yet, from an ecological perspective, they dropped important organic matter into the Missouri, providing the base for the riverine environment's food chain. Additionally, the Missouri's current hollowed out idyllic nesting sites for blue catfish on the downstream side of snags and planters.

After a hard rain or during one of its flood episodes, the Missouri filled with ruins. Downed trees, bunches of grass, shredded bark, branches, berry bushes, beetles, ants, feathers, mosquitoes, caddis flies, pumice stone, foam from dissolved loess, and bloated bison all found their way into the river, where the current propelled them aloft. Brackenridge saw batches of dead bison float past his keelboat, drifting with the current on their way to who knows where. Audubon described a time when his steamboat, the *Omega,* took several direct hits from floating trees: "The wind continued an irregular gale the whole of the night, and the frequent logs that struck our weather side kept me awake until nearly daybreak."[80] Audubon saw the Missouri as a mammalian goulash: "We have seen floating eight Buffaloes, one Antelope, and one Deer; how great the destruction of these animals must be during high freshets!"[81] All this refuse fed fish and fertilized the lowlands with its gooey affluence. The ingredients in this buoyant mush alighted on everything it touched. Driftwood, fly-coated bison, and stacks of fluffy tan foam amassed at the heads of islands, sandbars, and point bars or on top of sweepers and snags. After the passage of the two freshets, midchannel sandbars resembled modern city dumps, with dirt blowing high into the air, compacted garbage in long stacks, and circling gulls. Woodpiles atop some sandbars might exceed ten feet in height, fifty yards in width, and a hundred yards in length. By midsummer these mounds of wood turned bright white under the drying sun and appeared as imposing trash heaps.

Sand flats followed the whole course of the Upper Missouri. Boatmen, explorers, fur trappers, traders, and soldiers enjoyed sleeping on the flats during cool, windless spring or fall evenings. During the nighttime hours, the stored heat of the day escaped through the sand and warmed the bodies of the weary. Sand made a comfortable, if messy, body-molding bed for the voyager. The men of the Lewis and Clark expedition preferred to sleep on the soft surface of sand flats rather than the buggy meadows beyond the high banks.[82]

In late July, August, and September, moisture sank away from the sand flats. Strong southerly winds then lifted tiny, dehydrated particles from the beaches into the sky, spawning tumultuous sandstorms. Dense clouds of sand floated over the river and lowlands, completely obscuring both from view and whitewashing everything in their path. Any person unlucky enough to experience a Missouri Valley sandstorm did not soon forget it. The worst sandstorms blitzed their way across the valley floor only a mile northwest of the mouth of the Big Sioux River. Here, on the Missouri's east bank, dunes mounted one another in wave after wave. Henry Brackenridge wrote the following as he and his colleagues passed the great dunes northwest of the Big Sioux: "We ascended along the sand bars with difficulty on account of the wind, which blew the sand in our faces, and our men suffered much from fatigue."[83] Maximilian, at the same location, wrote, "At noon, with a temperature of 75, there was such a violent wind, that the fine sand from the banks penetrated into the innermost parts of our vessel; the broad river was so agitated by the wind, that the pilot could not distinguish the sand banks, and we were obliged to lie to."[84]

Sandstorms erected hillocks among the willows, cottonwoods, and prairie grasses. Besides the great dunes near the Big Sioux, a notable high dune formation sat on the Missouri's west bank across from Bon Homme Island. Nicollet described these dunes in 1839: "The ancient deposit on the bottom of the Missouri Valley forms banks on occasion 12 to 20 feet high, topped with unified magnificent prairies alternating on both sides of the river. Over these prairies are scattered mounds, 6 to 8 feet tall, resembling redoubt constructions. There are some, for example, near Bon Homme Island which Lewis and Clark thought were ancient fortifications but that, in my opinion, are the results of the work of the river in past times."[85] Sandstorms and the sight of tall dunes added one more element of the alien to the experience of Missouri River travelers.

The same winds that blew sand into the eyes of navigators also drove the Missouri into a frenzy. Throughout the year, powerful winds poured over the short-grass plains before sliding down into the Missouri River Valley. Once there, the valley walls compressed and funneled the air currents. The strongest winds blew directly above the water, where few, if any, obstacles blocked or deflected the onrushing airstreams. With little to stand in its way, the wind followed the Missouri's winding course. Edward Harris commented on this meteorologic anomaly: "The wind has just commenced blowing violently directly up the river and I know the *Omega* well enough to be satisfied that she will not stand driving."[86] Harris continued, "The wind blew so strong up stream that the boat would not steer, we had to lie until nearly night—we lost by the sand-bar and the wind just 24 hours."[87] Luttig, tugging a keel upriver, wrote with exasperation on August 4, 1812, "Headwind as usual."[88]

On excessively windy days, which occurred frequently, navigation on the Missouri came to a standstill. Nothing but wind and waves moved on the water. With monotonous regularity, navigators had to "lie by" and wait until the river became less agitated. In April 1805, after leaving the Mandan villages for the Pacific, the Lewis and Clark expedition confronted strong winds blowing straight into their faces from the west. Repeatedly, the men of the expedition had to take to the shore or risk losing their vessels and lives. Mary Cook penned in her journal for May 5, 1868, "Passed the mouth of the big Cheyenne; went three of [or] four miles and laid by all day for the wind."[89]

If crews chanced navigating the river on windy days, they often bore the brunt of the Missouri's power. High winds and the accompanying waves threw mackinaws, keels, and even steamboats into the bank or onto sandbars and snags. Navigators witnessed three- and four-foot high swells racing across the Upper Missouri. Tsunamis of brown water swamped small craft such as canoes, dugouts, and pirogues and damaged larger boats. Amazingly, winds and waves easily jostled boats weighing over fifteen tons. Maximilian explained in horrific detail just what the winds could do to a steamboat on the Upper Missouri. Near the Big Bend the prince chronicled: "The current of the swollen river was so strong that we long contended against it to no purpose, in order to turn a certain point of land, while, at the same time, the high west wind was against us, and both together threw the vessel back three times on the south coast. The first shock was so violent, that the lower deck gallery was broken to pieces. Our second attempt succeeded no better; part of the paddle-box was broken, and carried away by the current.[90] The strength of the wind and waves reached their utmost along wide-open stretches of river where neither trees nor islands or bars dissipated the force of the wind or turbulent water. After passing the mouth of the Niobrara, Bradbury's keel encountered a particularly tough section of water: "As the river is in this place nearly a mile in breadth, and being on the lee shore, the waves were of considerable magnitude, and frequently broke over the boats."[91]

The Missouri behaved oddly at times, especially during flood events, when high, fast water did strange things. Brackenridge in 1811 saw the Missouri overtop its banks on the upstream end of its bends, while remaining within its banks on the downstream side. The water dashing across each bend's neck fell off the banks on the lower side. As water slid over the cut bank, it took on the appearance of a long, even waterfall. Brackenridge stated it best: "The water rushed into the woods with great velocity, and in bends it poured over the gorge into the river again; a sheet of water sometimes for a mile, flowed over the bank, forming singular cascades of eighteen inches in height."[92]

The Upper Missouri distorted human perception. On the river, Euro-Americans witnessed optical illusions. Luttig saw an illusion in 1812. He recounted that the river to his front appeared to end abruptly, simply stopping against a tree line several hundred yards ahead of him. This illusion occurred during windless days while sailors traversed the Missouri's straight channel reaches. Atop the calm flats, sailors could not see approaching bends. As a result, the Missouri looked as though it just stopped against the concave bank to the front. Flats distorted perception in another way. Crews riding a boat down the center of a flat gained the very real sense that the river protruded at its center and sloped down at its edges. Prairie sailors felt as though they floated precariously atop a big, round balloon and might at any moment slide off to one side or the other and smack into the banks. Moreover, through the river's flats, navigators might look ahead of them and see a waterfall. But the waterfall did not fall away from them; instead, it appeared to fall toward them. These waterfalls spilled their waters upstream. This illusion gave prairie sailors the impression that they might flow under the waterfall rather than over it. The distortion appeared where the Missouri flowed along a flat and then into a sharp bend. Witnesses saw the concave bank to their front, water splashing into the cut bank, and concluded that the excited water resembled a waterfall cascading toward them.

When the Missouri crashed into a limestone or shale bluff, its waters bounced off the rock back upstream. Strong eddies spun beneath steep bluff faces. The Missouri held whirlpools that took human life and impeded steamboat navigation. In 1862, just above the Milk River–Missouri confluence, Lewis Henry Morgan chronicled what might have been the largest whirlpool witnessed on the Missouri River: "This morning at a sharp bend in the river we were detained by a remarkable whirlpool which we had some difficulty in passing without being drawn in. . . . The river at the eddy was about half a mile wide or near that, and the diameter of the whirl was more than half the width of the river. The current moved in the direction of the arrows, and was a mass of flood wood. The appearance of the wood as it coursed around in a great circle was quite remarkable. F. De Smet [Father Peter John De Smet] pronounced it the most remarkable sight he had ever seen on the river."[93] Eddies added one more element of the mysterious and dangerous to a Euro-American voyage on the Missouri.

Other anomalies on the river included deep depressions of surface water. A boat traveling through the river might dip down into one of these pockets and emerge on the other side without its passengers perceiving the drop in elevation. These surface dimples, some several feet deep, marked the locations of cavernous holes in the riverbed. Holes pockmarked the Missouri's bed, and anyone wading the river or pulling a boat through the water had to be aware of their presence. To ignore their existence might result in a dunking or drowning. Bubbles of high water, inches or feet above the surrounding surface water, occurred when water bounced up from the riverbed, deflected off of large stones or hidden shoals. The Missouri's surface waters did not present a singular level expanse. Rather, the river rode a roller coaster from the mountains to the Mississippi, rising and falling with the contours of its bed.

Many nineteenth-century Euro-Americans viewed the Missouri's caving banks, ice jams, floods, rapicages, inundated valley bottoms, snags, and spiraling eddies as destructive forces, all proof of the perfidy of nature. Few of them saw the Missouri as a creative force. Rather, the majority of nineteenth-century chroniclers perceived the river in a negative light; those perceptions stemmed from how most Euro-Americans related to the river, which was as a navigation route. Since the navigation of the Missouri with heavily laden keels, steamboats, and mackinaws was fraught with danger and presented the traveler with countless difficulties, the river was perceived as a hindrance to the advance of Euro-American civilization. For example, many early nineteenth-century Euro-Americans considered the steamboat the vanguard of civilization and viewed the wild Missouri, with its snags, sweepers, and sandbars, as literally thwarting the progress of Euro-American culture by blocking the path of the steamers.

This Euro-American focus on the river's navigability or lack thereof ignored the Missouri's connections and contributions, especially to nomadic indigenes and bison. A nomadic river was vital to Indian nomadism and its biological underpinnings—bison ecology. In other words, Indian culture and its basis in bison flowed directly out of the rambling Missouri. If Euro-Americans considered the river in positive terms, it was usually as static scenery or as the home of curious creatures. Few, if any, nineteenth-century Euro-Americans made connections between the grandeur of the river valley's scenery, the variety of its creatures, the diversity and independence of its indigenous cultures, and the river's wandering, flooding, sometimes violent character. Rather, scenery, wildlife, Indian culture, and the marauding river all occupied distinct perceptual places. Many whites did recognize the ties between wildlife and Indian culture, yet none wrote of the linkages between a roaming river, migrating animals, and indigenous nomadism. This compartmentalization of the Upper Missouri, which rested on the scientific reasoning of the Enlightenment era, defied ecological realities. Such compartmentalization also enabled Euro-Americans to dismantle the Upper Missouri's ecology without awareness of ecological consequences.

Bison World

Migration Routes and the Missouri and Yellowstone Main Stems

The Indians say, however, that in traveling over a country with which they are unacquainted they always follow a buffalo trail, for this animal always selects the most practicable route for his road.
—Gouverneur K. Warren, lieutenant, U.S. Army

Up to the middle of the nineteenth century, bison epitomized the Upper Missouri. The animal dominated the region. Upper Missouri hydrology, ecology, geography, and history felt the imprint of this being, which represented the single greatest influence in the history of the Upper Missouri in the seventy-five years after 1804. For a historian, or anyone for that matter, to ignore bison or give the animal scant attention in a history of the Upper Missouri is to overlook this fabulous mammal's ability to affect the whole gamut of human thought, belief, and action. Bison molded and routed Indians and Euro-Americans alike. When Euro-Americans referred to the Upper Missouri as "buffalo country," they admitted a physical, ecological, and geographic reality. Bison joined geography as one.

Euro-Americans or European tourists often mentioned bison and the Upper Missouri in the same breath. Rudolph Friederich Kurz, while approaching the Upper Missouri territory aboard a keel, penned, "The consciousness of being actually on the voyage up the Missouri, drawing nearer and nearer each day to the buffaloes, deer, and bears, was intoxicating."

Henry Brackenridge gave the Upper Missouri a nickname: "I have called the region watered by the Missouri and its tributaries, THE PARADISE OF HUNTERS; it is indeed to them a paradise." Edward Harris, in the vicinity of the James River confluence, wrote to a friend, "We have got into the Buffalo Country. Yesterday we saw a small gang of 5 or 6 at a long distance, just as they were crossing one of the knolls of the prarie. This morning while I was dressing about half past 5 o'clock, I was called out to see a large gang of about 38 about a mile distant, they were feeding on a bottom prairie just under the hills and were not disturbed by the boat."[1]

Along the Missouri, the great range of the bison commenced at the Platte, where grassland first took hold of horizon. In the first two decades of the 1800s, bison trod in the valley below the Platte, but in small, dispersed herds and in numbers that did not captivate the soul. As early as 1820, Euro-Americans had blasted the bison herds north of the Platte. A combination of pressures pushed the animals out of the lower reaches of the Missouri Valley, including a succession of ponderous and ecologically disruptive U.S. military expeditions, excessive river travel, bustling trading posts, Indian hunting, and the annoying propensity of many Euro-Americans to shoot every living thing with four legs and fur. Because of the absence of bison in the Lower Missouri, the region above the Platte became more than ever synonymous with bison.

Euro-Americans expressed mixed emotions toward the bison and its world. The majority stared directly into the face of the Upper Missouri and recoiled at its perceived desolation, openness, unrestrained savagery, and violence. Very few Euro-Americans recognized its order, comprehensible patterns, complex interconnections, and communalism. Instead, they compared their heavily populated, game-depleted, domesticated, sedentary agricultural world to the fecund, nomadic, and fast-paced bison world and fell back in confusion and revulsion. Henry Brackenridge noted the differences between the Upper Missouri and the more settled eastern United States. Brackenridge, like so many others in the nineteenth century, did not see the Upper Missouri as anything more than an album of scenic vistas. He wrote the following lines while passing through the Missouri Valley a few miles north of the Cheyenne River confluence: "The country rises in steps, each step an extensive plain. Herds of buffaloe could be seen at such a distance as to appear like black spots or dots. How different are the feelings in the midst of this romantic scenery, from those experienced in the close forests of the Ohio?" He then wrote, "At four o'clock hoisted sail with a fair wind. From the moment of our departure, we were hardly ever out of sight of herds of buffaloes, feeding on the hills and in the plains, and in the course of the day saw elk and antelopes in abundance. These objects enliven the scenery, but there is something strange in thus passing day after day without meeting any human beings. A vast country inhabited only by buffaloes, deer, and wolves, has more resemblance to the fictions of the 'Arabian Nights Entertainments' than to reality."[2]

To Brackenridge, and many others who entered the Upper Missouri in succeeding years, the region represented something otherworldly, surreal, static, and ultimately illegitimate. A world dominated by Euro-American agriculturalists equaled the ultimate reality; anything else made little sense, represented a perversion of a Christian god's will, and/or lacked even an ounce of authenticity. Brackenridge summed up this idea: "Suppose for a moment, the most beautiful parts of France or Italy should at once be divested of their population, and with it their dwellings and every vestige of human existence—that nothing but the silent plains and few solitary groves and thickets should remain, there would then be some resemblance to the scenery of the Missouri; though the contemplation would produce grief instead of pleasure. Yet even here, I could not but feel as if there existed a painful void—something wanting—'a melancholy stillness reigns over the interminable waste'—no animated beings."[3] Brackenridge failed to realize that many of the region's humans had perished from Euro-American diseases or had evacuated the Missouri River trench for their annual summer migration along the river's tributaries.

Prince Maximilian of Wied, like Brackenridge, experienced loneliness and desolation rather than community while on the Upper Missouri. In the vicinity of the Milk River confluence, he mused in his journal, "While here, the silence of the bare, dead, lonely wilderness is but seldom interrupted by the howling of the wolves, the bellowing of the buffaloes, or the screaming of the crows. The vast prairie scarcely offers a living creature, except now and then, herds of buffaloes and antelopes, or a few deer and wolves. These plains, which are dry in summer, and frozen in winter, have certainly much resemblance, in many of their features, with the African deserts."[4] Thaddeus Culbertson, on his way through the Upper Missouri in the summer of 1850, expressed surprise that he did not feel lonely while passing through such a land. Culbertson's remarks indicate that the social discourse of nineteenth-century America dictated that upper-class Euro-Americans and Europeans should feel loneliness while entering the unsettled West, with its

Indians, bison, and seemingly chaotic rivers. To feel anything else, or possibly a liking for the land- and waterscape of the Upper Missouri, might indicate a reversion to a more primitive state of mind, something elite elements in nineteenth-century America feared for what it meant for their social and intellectual standing. Culbertson exclaimed, "Here we are encamped in the western wilds far from any house but I don't feel any lonliness [*sic*], or any of those feelings which we expect to experience in these circumstances."[5] Mary Cook expressed dread just moments before departing for the Upper Missouri, as though she and her travel partners were about to step off into a frightening void. She wrote, "It was with feelings of profound regret that I took the last look at the lovely town [Omaha] as I begin to realize that we are leaving home and the turbid waters of the Mo. are carrying us into strange lands, and the formidable barriers of many thousand miles would soon intervene between me and my brothers and sisters, and my dear son and his little family."[6] Brackenridge wrote how disconcerting the bison world of the Upper Missouri could be for a Euro-American: "Shortly before sun-down the air became calm, and our disturbed minds, (such is the effect upon our feelings of the objects which surround us) appeared to grow composed as the strife of the elements gave way to calmness and serenity."[7] The Upper Missouri environment had the ability to upset the Euro-American paradigm, especially notions of order founded on agriculture.

The journal entries indicate that Euro-Americans could not, and would not, absorb the bison world of the Upper Missouri into their frame of reference, so they identified it as something else, something negative, something that placed it on the other side of a perceptual line. They called the bison world wilderness, thus drawing the proverbial line in the sand, with themselves on one side (the civilized, good side) and wilderness on the other (the wild, immoral side). A Missouri River traveler commented on the region as wilderness: "For weeks we have been steaming up this great river and now though over two thousand miles from its mouth we hardly find it narrower and it is even more navigable than below—Yet what a wilderness we pass through—No human being for thousands of miles but wandering and scattered savages or a few soldiers at widely separated and solitary government posts. Wild animals roam at their own free will over the almost trackless leagues." As Euro-Americans tagged the region a wilderness, room for compromise with that world disappeared. The wilderness designation dichotomized, separated, and sundered people, places, and things.[8]

Paradoxically, bison fascinated Euro-Americans. Their endless numbers, physical size, and rapid movements caught the eye of a people accustomed to a linear landscape with melancholy cattle moving slowly across small, fenced plots. Pastoralism may have inspired patriotism and a sense of national success, but it hardly fired the nineteenth-century imagination. The bison's delicious flesh and marrowbones added an element of the exotic to the diet of a people who subsisted on corn and salt pork. And the often brutal bond between Indians and bison astounded Euro-Americans who believed the complacent, sometimes stifling life of a farmer superior to that of an equestrian nomad.

In 1804, bison rambled across the entire Upper Missouri territory from the James and Big Sioux Rivers on the east to the foothills of the Bighorn Mountains on the west and from the far Upper Missouri's Marias and Milk Rivers to the Platte Valley (fig. 2.1). The number of bison in the Upper Missouri just prior to the advent of Lewis and Clark is impossible to accurately gauge. No one knows how many bison fattened on the grasses and herbs of the Upper Missouri. One problem in estimating their numbers is that the animals never quit traipsing around; thousands moved easily from the Upper Missouri to points south of the Platte or vice versa. Furthermore, numbers fluctuated with changes in climate, disease prevalence, levels of Indian and Euro-American interference, predation, and hunting pressure. Yet historians and aficionados of bison have taken jabs at bison demographics. Several brave souls have come up with a number of estimates for how many bison roamed the Great Plains region prior to the Euro-American era. Tom McHugh estimated that the grassland supported 24 bison per square mile; Dan Flores argued that the plains likely sustained 22.75 bison per square mile; yet another study claimed that the Great Plains environment supported 22 bison per square mile. Thus, the Upper Missouri basin, enclosing close to 350,000 square miles, could have supported between 7,678,125 and 8,531,250 bison according to these calculations. Yet those numbers do not take into consideration the variability in habitat present throughout the Upper Missouri region. Undoubtedly, bison did not flourish on the steep slopes of the Absarokas or Bighorns or high in the Wind River range. Even more important, the uplands supported fewer bison than the richer lowlands in the Yellowstone and Missouri River trenches. Another factor that makes estimating the plains bison population such a precarious business is the high annual increase and decrease in animal numbers. The bison population might grow between 13.6 and 17.6 percent each year, but that increase might be nearly canceled out by an annual decrease of between 10

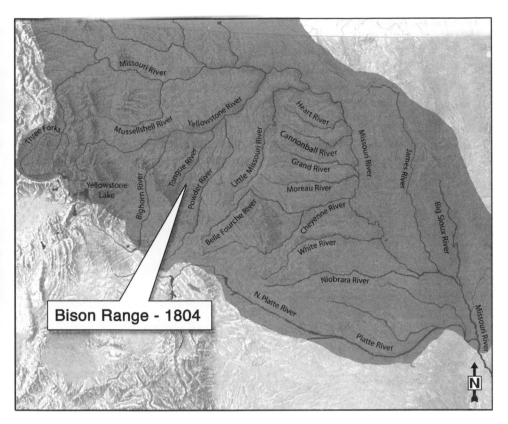

Figure 2.1. The bison range, Upper Missouri, circa 1804. At the time of Lewis and Clark, bison roamed throughout the Upper Missouri. (Paul Davidson, South Plains College, Levelland, Texas)

and 15 percent. During drought years, the annual decrease in the population likely exceeded the annual increase. The size of the population decrease during a drought year is hard to measure. One indication of how bison numbers were affected by drought is provided by what happened to the carrying capacity of the grassland (its ability to support grazers) in southeastern Montana during the drought of 1934. In that year, the carrying capacity of the land dipped 64 percent from the previous year, a decrease that would have walloped bison numbers, or so that is the immediate conclusion. Hypothetically, if 22 bison fed on a square mile of southeastern Montana in 1933, and in 1934 that square mile lost 64 percent of its carrying capacity, 14 bison would be without forage. A fair assumption would be that those 14 bison then perished from hunger. But that assumption is debatable. Such high death rates for bison during a drought would have resulted in the extirpation of the species over large areas of the Great Plains after only two or three consecutive years of drought, but that does not appear to have happened. The journal accounts show that animal abundance in the Yellowstone basin remained high even during the back-to-back drought years of the 1840s and 1850s. What appears feasible is that during drought episodes, as upland carrying capacity diminished, bison moved down into river valleys where forage still grew and the carrying capacity of the land exceeded 22 to 24 bison per square mile.[9] The river valleys acted as grassland reserves. The important question needing an answer is how many bison could a square mile of river valley support in any given year? The carrying capacity of the perennial stream valleys of the Upper Missouri to a large extent governed how low bison numbers could go in any drought year or succession of drought years, whereas the carrying capacity of the lowlands and uplands determined how high they might rise during wet years.

What all this means is that bison numbers bounced all over the place, in large part because the animals existed within a dynamic ecological system. The Upper Missouri never sat still; winter cold, summer heat, wolf packs, Indian warfare, flood events, disease, and bison themselves all shook the system, forcing it to vibrate and shudder. But it is clear that the Upper Missouri nourished an incredible number of bison in the early nineteenth century. John Bradbury wrote of the Upper Missouri and its ability to support a high concentration of biomass, "When the great extent of this plain, and its fertility in grass are considered, we cannot but admit that the number of animals it is capable of containing must be immense."[10]

The Yellowstone and far Upper Missouri (west of the Yellowstone confluence) and their tributary streams held the greatest concentrations of bison in the Upper Missouri territory. Akin to a cumbersome buffalo blanket, millions of bison rolled over a two-hundred-mile-wide swath of land that ran from the Marias River's headwaters to the Poplar River's source streams, then swept south from the Canadian plains, stampeded over the Milk, Missouri, and Musselshell Valleys, climbed atop the Yellowstone-Missouri Divide, glided down into the Yellowstone Valley, and dashed onward to the headwaters of the Bighorn, Little Bighorn, Rosebud, Tongue, and Powder Rivers.

Herds varied in size from a handful of animals to hundreds or even thousands. Bulls tended to range either individually or in small herds of from two to ten. Euro-Americans and Indians frequently saw the bulls standing alone.

Bulls caught a person's attention because of their size; a mature bull might weigh fifteen hundred pounds and stand six feet high from hoof to shoulder. The bulls most often recognized by Euro-Americans stood astride notable promontories—kings scrutinizing their domain. Brackenridge described a massive bull he saw on the hills above the James River confluence: "A huge buffaloe bull made his appearance on the top of the bluff standing almost at the edge of the precipice, and looking down upon us. It was the first we had seen. Long and matted wool hung over his head, and covered his huge shoulders, while his body was smooth, as also the tail, except a turf at the end. It was a striking and terrific object; he eyed us with the ferocity of the lion, seemed at length to 'snuff the tainted breeze': threw his head into the air, wheeled round and trotted off."[11] Although this description of a bison bull is poetic, it is unlikely the bull actually followed the progress of Brackenridge's keelboat, since the animals are notoriously nearsighted. Clark recalled seeing bulls in ones or twos. The lieutenant of the Lewis and Clark expedition also noted the absence of cows around the bulls. The larger herds, made up of hundreds and sometimes thousands of animals, consisted mostly of cows and calves or yearlings. During the rutting season the bulls did commingle with the cows, but for much of the year they preferred to remain alone. Bulls, because of their substantial size and muscular strength, could forage and rove in smaller numbers. A mature, virile fifteen-hundred-pound bull could protect itself against all comers, including a grizzly bear, the only real mammalian threat to its life. For cows and calves, strength lay in numbers. Cows and calves, which were smaller and less strong than bulls, moved in larger herds because of the protection afforded by congregating animals. When in danger of attack from marauding wolves or a grizzly, the adult cows encircled their young in a protective perimeter.

From at least 1804 to the 1830s, herd numbers across the Upper Missouri remained high. Bison numbers intensified the farther one traveled up the Missouri, reaching very dense numbers along the Yellowstone River Valley. In today's southeast South Dakota, America's most famous explorers first began to see large numbers of the animals. On August 25, 1804, Clark and several other men left the keelboat and pirogues and hiked inland to Spirit Mound, located northeast of the mouth of the Vermillion River. On top of the hillock, Clark scanned the far edges of his visible world and recollected, "From the top of this Mound we observed Several large gangus of Buffalow & Elk feeding upwards of 800 in number." Such scenes became everyday fare as the expedition proceeded up the Missouri.[12]

Others detailed their memorable encounters with bison. Along northeast Nebraska's Ponca Creek, the German prince Paul Wilhelm, in 1824, described an early encounter with one of North America's premier mammalian species: "In the night a heavy shower with thunder and lightning passed over us. The ceaseless rolling of the thunder, the sharp electric discharges and the bellowing of the bison gave this night the true character of the wilderness. The bison that had run in such great numbers to the Ponca were badly frightened. Their restlessness was still increased by the fact that this was the breeding season."[13]

Meriwether Lewis, a member of the Lewis and Clark expedition who possessed a degree of literary flair and sophistication, described the landscape surrounding modern-day Oacoma, South Dakota. On September 17, 1804, Lewis climbed to the top of a high ridgeline that overlooked the Missouri River on the east and jumbled plains to the west. Gazing to the west and north, the captain wrote, "This senery already rich pleasing and beatiful, was still farther hightened by immence herds of Buffaloe deer Elk and Antelopes which we saw in every direction feeding on the hills and plains. I do not think I exaggerate when I estimate the number of Buffaloe which could be compreed at one view to amount to 3000."[14]

William Clark wrote the following about the bison seen farther up the Missouri River at the Big Bend, describing the animals as they loitered across the great mesa that sits on the southern side of the bend: "The plain in the bend as also the two opposite Sides abov and below is delightfull plains with graduel assents from the river in which there is at this time Great number of Buffalow Elk & Goats feedg."[15]

Bison draped the Missouri Breaks, those deeply gullied hills that fall into the Missouri trench through the Dakotas and Montana. At the mouth of the Cheyenne River, in July 1811, John Bradbury marveled at the bruised green, black-brown, and deep blue canvas all around him: "The banks [of the Cheyenne River] appear to be more steep than those of the Missouri, and are clothed with trees to the water's edge. On both sides of the river we saw numberless herds of buffaloes, grazing in tranquility, some of them not a quarter of a mile from us when we pass them."[16] Francis Chardon, hunkered down in his loathsome, rat-infested Fort Clark, scratched in his gruff, succinct journal for September 4, 1837, "Report that from Grande River up, all the Country is black with Buffaloe, all comeing in this way. I am in hopes that we shall have them here soon."[17]

On a sweaty, dusty day in late July 1860, atop the height of land that separates the far Upper Missouri drainage from the Yellowstone drainage (known as the Missouri-Yellowstone Divide), and close to where the Mussel-shell River turns north to make its final run into the Missouri main stem, a U.S. Army officer, Captain John Mullan, glanced toward the southeast and the Yellowstone River. He wrote, "The country east and south of us seems very much broken, with constant appearance of pine and cedar reefs. From this point, as far as the eye could reach, the country seemed covered with immense herds of buffalo, all moving toward the valley of the Yellowstone."[18]

The Yellowstone River held a reputation among explorers, travelers, Indians, fur trappers, traders, and U.S. Army soldiers as a game preserve that possessed immeasurable numbers of bison, bears, elk, deer, wolves, and beaver. This reputation would remain in place until the 1880s and the final demise of the great bison herds. Meriwether Lewis and William Clark did much to perpetuate the Yellowstone Valley's reputation as game country. On April 26, 1805, Lewis became the first non-Indian to cast eyes upon the Yellowstone River. His description of the territory surrounding the Yellowstone's confluence with the Missouri is worthy of note: "I ascended the hills [on the south side of the Missouri] from whence I had a most pleasing view of the country, particularly of the wide and fertile vallies formed by the missouri and the yellowstone rivers, which occasionally unmasked by the wood on their borders disclose their meanderings for many miles in their passage through these delighfull tracts of country. . . . the whole face of the country was covered with herds of Buffaloe, Elk, & Antelopes; deer are also abundant, but keep themselves more concealed in the woodland."[19] From his vantage point in the hills, the captain stepped down into a bountiful bottomland that bordered the east shore of the Yellowstone River. At the base of the bluffs, Lewis stood in awe at the number of bison surrounding him, many so tame and unaccustomed to humans that they approached within feet of the captain and his small party, curious to see and smell the strange, pungent *Homo sapiens,* an animal these bison may never have laid eyes on in their brief lives.

William Clark also wrote glowingly of the wildlife present in the Yellowstone Valley. On July 24, 1806, near the Clarks Fork–Yellowstone River confluence, he commented, "For me to mention or give an estimate of the different Spcies [sic] of wild animals on this river particularly Buffalow, Elk Antelopes & Wolves would be incredidable. I shall therefore be silent on the Subject further."[20] But Clark could not keep from writing about what he witnessed along the river. The amount of wildlife continued to surprise him with its density and areal extent. Only three days after promising to stop mentioning the Yellowstone Valley's wildlife populations, he wrote the following passage while encamped near the mouth of Muggin's Creek, approximately fifteen miles below the mouth of the Bighorn River: "The Buffalow and Elk is estonishingly noumerous on the banks of the river on each Side, particularly the Elk which lay on almost every point in large gang and are So jintle that we frequently pass within 20 or 30 paces of them without their being the least alarmd. the buffalow are Generally at a greater distance from the river, and keep a continueing bellowing in every direction."[21]

Undoubtedly, bison resided across the Upper Missouri in significant numbers in the early nineteenth century. The largest concentrations roamed the grasslands along the Upper Missouri main stem between the Yellowstone River and the Great Falls and along the Yellowstone from where it exits the Rocky Mountains at present-day Livingston to its mouth. One reason journalists saw so many bison along the Missouri and Yellowstone Rivers in the early nineteenth century related to the migratory patterns of the animals and the travel schedules of Euro-American explorers, traders, and tourists. Most Missouri River travelers went upstream in March and April, during the calving season, when cows and their newborns remained close to the Missouri or Yellowstone bottoms. Thus, they recorded seeing many animals in the river bottoms. Had they traveled upstream in June, when the river's flows peaked and the Missouri swamped its valley floor with soapy water, the numbers would have been far fewer. This fact explains why Lewis, on the Yellowstone in April 1805, saw so many bison down in the bottomlands. Additionally, Missouri River travelers often left the Upper Missouri for St. Louis in August, or even September. That departure time coincided with the bison rut, when the animals again moved into the river valleys to mate. This is why William Clark and company saw so much wildlife along the Yellowstone Valley in July and August 1806. The animals had moved off the highlands into the river valley to propagate their species. Had Clark gone down the Yellowstone in June, only a few weeks earlier, he would have found far fewer animals milling about in the valley lowlands. This fact does not imply that bison numbers were substantially smaller than the journalists indicated in their papers. Rather, the perception of superabundance among Euro-Americans emerged because the animals concentrated in the valleys at certain times of the year and thus came into the line of sight of inquisitive Euro-Americans.

The extreme numbers of bison on the Upper Missouri meant that Euro-

Americans never wandered far from the creatures. Sometimes the animals came too close for comfort, actually violating personal space and forcing Euro-Americans to retreat, alter course, and/or cower in fear. In 1824, Prince Wilhelm explained that bison frequently trekked through Euro-American campsites because Euro-Americans placed their wagons, horses, and tents firmly atop, or adjacent to, bison roads:

> The great herds maintain a peculiar order on their march, and thus make broad trails, sometimes several feet wide, which are tramped out deep. Frequently several such trails run one beside the other, forming regular roads. The Creoles and the Canadians call them chemins de boeufs. Since we were obliged to ride in such trails, freshly made by the herds, we had to exercise the greatest caution in the selection of camp sites. Unless the wind apprises these creatures of the proximity of the camp, they walk right thru it, stampeding the horses and often endangering the men and the baggage. These animals, usually the old bulls and old cows, follow the trail stubbornly.[22]

Patrick Gass of the Lewis and Clark expedition recalled that on the night of May 29, 1805, only a few miles east of the Judith River, a bison bull tore through the party's campsite. This bull moved along one of the Upper Missouri's main north-south bison roads, which traced the Judith River to where it touched the Missouri and then crossed the Missouri main stem before doodling its way north up Chip Creek, Sand Creek, or Birch Creek. The members of the expedition had unfortunately camped in close proximity to this route and thus encountered one of the thousands of bison that annually moved along the road.[23]

Clark, on the expedition's return to the states in 1806, repeatedly recognized the prevalence and dominance of bison. He wrote of an encounter he and his men had with a bison on July 25, 1806, a few miles east of Pompey's Pillar: "Emence herds of Buffalow about our [camp] as it is now running time with those animals the bulls keep Such a grunting nois which is very loud and disagreeable Sound that we are compelled to Scear them away before we can Sleep. the men fire Several shot at them and Scear them away."[24] On July 31, 1806, at the mouth of Crooked Creek, Prairie County, Montana, Clark penned, "I was much disturbed last night by the noise of the buffalo which were about me. one gang Swam the river near our Camp which alarmed me a little for fear of their Crossing our Canoes and Splitting them to pieces."[25] On August 1, 1806, at today's Intake Dam, bison forced the expedition to halt while a massive herd swam the Yellowstone to their front. Farther downstream, near the modern Seven Sisters Wildlife Management Area, Clark and company again had to submit to the power of the bison. He wrote, "We were very near being detained by the Buffalow today which were Crossing the river we got through the line between 2 gangues."[26] The presence of bison demanded attention, respect, vigilance, and submission. When bison strode through an encampment and trampled camp equipage, their supremacy over the region became apparent. Bison not only roamed everywhere but also roamed at will, showing little fear for the human presence. When Lewis and Clark's men ducked and covered on the night of May 29, 1805, as a bison bull ripped through their camp, or when Clark's small entourage waited in the Yellowstone River for a herd to pass on August 1, 1806, the men grudgingly admitted that bison ruled the land and that they were at the animals' mercy. As Gass's, Wilhelm's, and Clark's comments attest, bison required humans to bend to their will. The bison of the Upper Missouri set the agenda, sculpted the land, and forced humans to respond to them. They dominated their world.

Besides their overpowering physical presence, bison asserted their dominion over the Upper Missouri through their enormous system of roads and traces. A bison road network existed across the Upper Missouri since at least the Pleistocene. In their seasonal migrations, bison did not randomly cross the landscape, lumbering from place to place without considering topography or ecology. Instead, the animals willfully followed routes of least resistance. Bison, and other large mammals, first discovered the mountain passes that incise the Upper Missouri, located the shortest, most feasible paths from one watershed to the next, and discerned practical fords across rivers. Bison built roads to connect one ecologically rich zone with another. Their roads wove the land into an interlaced web. Bison herds pounded roads into shape to facilitate their exploitation of the resource base (fig. 2.2).

Bison developed and maintained roads each year by lessening the grade through a mountain pass or grinding down a cut bank at a river crossing. Incessant hoof traffic trampled pathways through gumbo, gravel, or loam, plowing thoroughfares through mountains, hillocks, and valley lowlands, all the while creating ever-deeper, wider, and smoother gradients. Some of these roads resembled human-engineered horse and wagon roads. As Audubon observed in 1843, "The prairies are literally covered with the skulls of the victims, and the roads the Buffalo make in crossing the prairies have all

Figure 2.2. A large, complex bison road network crisscrossed the Upper Missouri territory from the Pleistocene epoch to the nineteenth century. Bison roads followed the contours of watersheds. Bison forded the Missouri where their trails touched the river's banks. In this illustration by William de la Montagne Cary, bison are shown swimming through the strong current of the Missouri, arriving on the far bank exhausted from the ordeal. (Courtesy of the Thomas Gilcrease Institute of American History, Tulsa, Oklahoma)

the appearance of heavy wagon tracks."[27] Brackenridge, at Fort Pierre in 1811, recollected, "There was something picturesque in the appearance of these herds of buffaloe, slowly winding round the sides of the distant hills, disappearing in some hollow and again emerging to view. Wide and beaten roads formed by the passing of the buffaloe, may every where be seen."[28] Patrick Gass, the enlisted man who took on the duties and responsibilities of the deceased Sergeant Charles Floyd, recounted the bison roads of the Upper Missouri: "There are Indian paths along the Missouri and some in other parts of the country. Those along that river do not generally follow its windings but cut off points of land and pursue a direct course. There are also roads and paths made by the buffaloe and other animals; some of the buffaloe roads are at least ten feet wide."[29] Edward Harris witnessed the transformative influence bison had upon the landscape: "You would be surprised to see how the whole country here is trodden up by the feet of the Buffalo, and we see their deeply worn paths in all directions, they are now shedding their coats which they leave on every bush."[30] Maximilian, just south of the Cheyenne River's mouth, added, "We found many traces of antelopes and of herds of buffaloes. The latter had everywhere trodden broad paths on their way to the river to drink."[31] Bison (in concert with other mammalian species) blazed the first roads across the Upper Missouri.

Bison roads adhered to the outlines of watersheds. Audubon alluding to the connection between bison roads and river valleys, wrote, "Notwithstanding the rough nature of the country, the Buffaloes have paths running in all directions, and leading from the prairies to the river." The widest, deepest trails skirted the major rivers of the Upper Missouri, actually running through the valleys. For example, Captain Raynolds observed the following along the Yellowstone: "It [the Yellowstone Valley] is the paradise of the Indian, and in every direction it is marked by the tracks of the vast herds of buffalo, antelope, and elk which are subsisted upon it."[32] Roads left the bottoms only when a bluff abutted a river and intercepted the lower route, or when the animals bypassed a long river bend by seeking the hills, or when the valley lowlands narrowed too precipitously for travel. Smaller, secondary roadways plowed up tributary valleys and spacious gullies. A big river with a wide, flat valley often meant a big bison road, while the smaller traces followed the minor tributaries.

Trails passing through one valley crossed over to another valley at the point where the two watersheds came closest to one another or where a gradual grade lay from one valley bottom over the dividing ridge to the next valley bottom. For example, a well-worn, easily visible bison road connected the Missouri watershed at the Three Forks with the Yellowstone watershed. A trace cut through the Three Forks from west to east and climbed the Gallatin Range, crossing to the Yellowstone watershed where Interstate 90 now oversteps Bozeman Pass.[33] Other connecting roads tied the lower Yellowstone Valley with the Missouri Valley. A bison superhighway passed up Sunday Creek (to the north and east of present-day Miles City, Montana) to North Sunday Creek, climbed the Missouri-Yellowstone Divide, and went down Red Butte Creek, Thompson Creek, and Little Dry Creek until reaching the Big Dry, where it followed that latter stream to the Missouri main stem. One of the greatest of all connecting roads linked the Missouri main stem to the Yellowstone via the Cheyenne, Belle Fouche, Little Missouri, and Powder Rivers. Bison geography equaled watershed geography. All roads, and all movements, traced the lines of watersheds. Rudolph Friederich Kurz, writing near Fort Clark, in present-day North Dakota, succinctly stated the relationship between bison geography and the stream valleys of the Upper Missouri: "On the other side of the [Missouri] river herds came continually into view, emerging from glens and valleys and descending slopes on their way to the river."[34]

Since the bison road network followed drainages, its parameters easily floated to the surface. Along the fringes and foundations of gullies, creeks, streams, and rivers, hoof prints wrote the ancient language of bison geography in curving lines on earthen parchment. The most significant bison roads followed the two great rivers, the Yellowstone and Missouri. But inland from those valleys, other roads chiseled their way through the region. In the Yellowstone basin the road network followed a decidedly north-south orientation. A still-visible migration route congealed at the north end of the Black Canyon of the Yellowstone, followed the Yellowstone River's west bank all the way to the Shield's River, where it then entered the Shield's and passed up its valley to Potter Creek and from thence on to the South Fork Smith River. Onward it went, up Beaver Creek on to Hound Creek and then back to the Smith River again until it finally landed inside the Missouri Valley. But the road did not stop there; it went on to the Sun River, where it veered toward the west and the spiked peaks of the Rocky Mountains. A spur of this road shot off to the west and crossed today's Flathead Pass to the Three Forks. Captain Raynolds viewed this pass. He may in fact be the individual responsible for its naming. Raynolds remarked, "Following the lodge trail we entered the pass by a well-defined road with evident marks of the recent passage of a large band of Indians, probably the Flatheads on their hunt."[35]

Another notable bison road headed in the watery meadows at the base of the Bighorn Mountains, near present-day Sheridan, Wyoming. The road originated in the oasis at the headwaters of the Tongue River, shot up the numerous fingers that suckle the Tongue, entered Twin Creek, East Pass Creek, or West Pass Creek, followed any one of those three routes to Pass Creek, and from there into the Little Bighorn Valley. The road then spiraled northward, staying largely on the Little Bighorn's west bank, until it entered the Bighorn Valley.[36] Three miles below the mouth of the Bighorn, the trail forded the Yellowstone, hugging the north bank of that river until it reached Alkali Creek or Muggins Creek, where it turned to the northwest. Alkali and Muggins Creeks connected the Yellowstone watershed with the Musselshell. Once on the Musselshell, the herds funneled through its valley to the Missouri, crossed it, and spread over the flats on the north side of the stream. Several journalists confirm the existence of the Musselshell thoroughfare.

One unknown chronicler wrote at the mouth of the Musselshell, "We saw a herd of Buffalo, about sixty in number, crossing the river in front of us, while several hundred more were observable from the hillsides. This must be their highway of travel north and south, for well-beaten roads could be followed by the eye for miles."[37] Maximilian remembered the Musselshell road: "Accompanied by Dreidoppel, I went two miles up the [Musselshell] river, which was narrow and shallow; its banks were thickly grown with poplars, and the bones of buffaloes and elks were everywhere scattered about. We followed a path trodden by the buffaloes along the bank of the river."[38] A member of the Northern Pacific Railroad survey, while on the Musselshell in the summer of 1873, provided further support for the Musselshell as a primary bison route. His report stated, "The Musselshell Valley is fertile, and, uninhabited by game, would furnish good grazing; but our march had been preceded by thousands of buffaloes, and the grass was completely exhausted."[39] After exiting the Musselshell, bison poured their energies northward, up Valentine Creek to Telegraph Creek, eventually driving down Beaver Creek to the wetlands adjacent to the Milk River at present-day Bowdoin, Montana. Where the Beaver approaches the Milk, the herds crossed due north to Whitewater Creek. Once astride the Whitewater, the bison bolted north over its valley to the plains of British Canada.

A third very big road began amid the boggy paddocks at the head of the Tongue and paralleled that stream until it ran within twelve miles of the headwaters of the Rosebud, where it crossed the gentle divide that is now beneath the blacktop designated Montana Highway 314. The road ran down through the Rosebud Valley until it struck the Roche Jaune. First Lieutenant H. E. Maynadier, an unwitting chronicler of bison geography, surveyed the Rosebud road in 1859. He reported, "Resting here a day, we proceeded up the Rosebud, the lodge-trail guiding us as before, and traveled by a very fine road along the valley of the stream. Our route lay along this stream until the 11th September, and I may say generally that a finer natural road cannot be found."[40] At the Yellowstone, the road made an abrupt turn to the left, trailing across the high bottom on the Yellowstone's south bank. A mere one hundred yards above the mouth of the Rosebud, the trace forded the Yellowstone River and entered the wooded bottoms on the north shore. Heading west up the Yellowstone, one spur swerved up Little Porcupine Creek. Another spur continued due west until it, too, bent northwestward up Big Porcupine Creek.[41] Diverging up the two creeks, both roads headed north over the Missouri-Yellowstone divide, with the Little Porcupine route joining the

Little Dry, and the Big Porcupine mixing with Sand Creek and the Big Dry. These two separate roads united once more on the Big Dry and then pursued it to the Missouri. The road crossed the Missouri and immediately entered the Milk Valley, tagging along its banks to the north and west or mapping one of its perennial tributaries into Canada. A nineteenth century fur trader, camped along the Big Dry–Milk River road in August 1855, recounted the prolific number of bison traveling this path: "On getting up this morning I found myself completely surrounded by Buffaloes my horses were feeding along with them. . . . Buffaloes very plenty, I should not be surprised if there is a [Indian] camp on Milk river the Buff are all traveling down [it]."[42]

The greatest of all north-south bison roads in the Upper Missouri, and not coincidentally the last to be abandoned by the Indians in the 1870s and the herds in the 1880s, originated in those same moist fields surrounding the headwaters of the Powder and Tongue, between present-day Buffalo, Wyoming, and Ranchester, Wyoming. Out of the verdure foothills, bison spilled toward the Tongue along countless creek beds. Sixmile, Fivemile, Big Goose, and Prairie Dog Creeks guided the animals toward the embracing arms of the Tongue. These converging creeks concentrated the herds upon a level valley floor where the Tongue then directed the mammals to the north and east. The Tongue Valley's quenching waters, shielding trees, and slight slope provided bison with an ideal marching route. Raynolds, who scouted the Tongue in 1859, wrote this about it: "We reached Tongue river, having a good road in its valley, only interrupted in a few instances by ravines not very difficult to cross, and with good crossings of the stream when they became necessary."[43] Bison obeyed the Tongue's contours all the way to the Yellowstone Valley. Once there, a benevolent Tongue Valley gently set the bison down in a large, opulent, timbered bottomland at its mouth. This bottom lolled seductively on the Yellowstone's south bank from the mouth of the Tongue to a collection of high cliffs twelve miles to the northeast. From here, the Yellowstone Valley acted as a conduit. Steep, pebbly, gray bluffs directly north of the Tongue-Yellowstone confluence prohibited bison from immediately crossing to the Yellowstone's north bank. The creatures had no choice but to stay on the south side of the Yellowstone.[44]

In a beautiful congruence of ecological, hydrologic, and geologic forces, the Yellowstone Valley corralled the animals, then shepherded them to an ideal ford. Bison exiting the Tongue Valley had to follow the south wall along the Yellowstone Valley to find a fording location across the big, brisk river. As the south wall gradually pinched in on the river, it nudged the herds closer and closer to the Yellowstone. Twelve miles northeast of Miles City, the south wall abuts the Yellowstone River, hindering further movement along the valley floor to the northeast. There the bottom became so narrow that the herds literally found themselves at the river's edge. At that point lay the Great Ford, a shallow riffle protruding from the bed of the Yellowstone. Here bison safely waded across the river, shook themselves clean of water, and walked up the flat, cobblestone north bank. Once firmly afoot on the northern shore, the herds passed into the grass and trees fringing Sunday Creek (fig. 2.3).

The Great Ford, denoted on modern maps as Buffalo Rapids, whispers eulogies for millions of bison. Along both the north and south banks of the Yellowstone, bison engraved a tribute to their passing. Landward of the Great Ford, the once-sharp cut banks have been dulled, perverted by pounding hooves. Since at least 11,000 B.P., innumerable bison rumbled down the south side of the Yellowstone Valley, rushed over the banks of the river, crashed into the chilly waters of the Yellowstone, struggled to the north bank, tottered out of the frigid water, and dashed into the wide valley of Sunday Creek. In a great historical irony, William Clark, on July 30, 1806, saw a

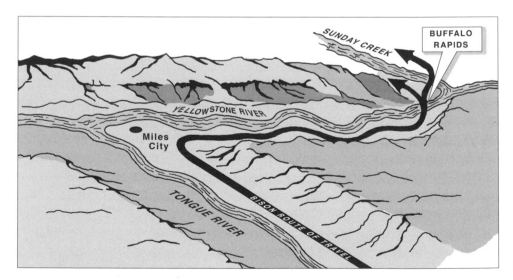

Figure 2.3 The great ford across the Yellowstone River at Buffalo Rapids. The Yellowstone Valley's south wall directed migrating bison to the crossing point and into the Sunday Creek trench. (Paul Davidson, South Plains College, Levelland, Texas)

bison standing in the middle of the Yellowstone River at this ford and named the shallows Buffalo Shoals. Clark's journal entry proclaimed, "Set out early this morning at 12 miles arived at the Commencement of Shoals the Chanel on the Stard Side near a high bluff. passed a Succession of those Shoals for 6 miles the lower of which was quit across the river and appeared to have a decent of about 3 feet. . . . I call the [shoals] Buffalow Sholes from the Circumstance of one of those animals being in them."[45] Clark did not know it at the time, but the shoals he so aptly named represented the most significant ford across the Yellowstone River and a vital choke point along the greatest of all north-south roads in the Upper Missouri territory. That bison bull Clark found standing in the middle of the Yellowstone had been a traveler on a grand mammalian highway.

Once on the north shore of the Yellowstone, and after entering Sunday Creek, the bison grazed their way up North Sunday Creek or Rock Springs Creek, over the divide to Red Butte Creek, Thompson Creek, or Uall Creek, and down to the Little Dry. Inside the Little Dry Valley, they shadowed its twists and turns to the Big Dry, negotiating it to the Missouri. Herds crossed the Missouri at the foot of the Big Dry and infiltrated the Milk River Valley, traversing it to the north and west. Thaddeaus Culbertson also provides solid support for the existence of the Milk River–Big Dry road. On June 20, 1850, near the confluence of the Milk and Missouri, Culbertson asserted, "Buffalo have been seen in great bands for several days past; last evening probably five-hundred were in sight at one time on the river banks. I have seen paths beaten by them which look like traveled roads in a thickly settled country, and paths of this kind are seen at almost every landing [bottom]."[46]

A fourth significant north-south thoroughfare over the Upper Missouri opened at present-day Casper, Wyoming. This road linked the Platte with the Yellowstone and the Missouri. It left the Platte and ran northwest along Casper Creek, eventually dispersing along the Middle Fork of Casper Creek, the North Fork of Casper Creek, or up the featureless land encircling the Teapot Creeks. From one of these routes, bison discovered the South Fork of the Powder or the Powder River proper. Embracing the Powder, the road hit the Yellowstone River at the head of a twenty-mile-long bottom that lolled on the Yellowstone's southern coast. Migrating bison piled into this bottom, sliding east until the valley walls once more elbowed them toward the Yellowstone. Without any room to maneuver, the bison crossed the Yellowstone and swam toward the mouth of another perennial stream pouring in from the north. Crashing through the bottoms of Cedar Creek, the brown and

black brutes headed northwest along Cedar Creek until reaching the Redwater drainage, where the road ran over the Redwater Valley to the Missouri.
On the north bank of the Missouri, the animals pierced the Poplar River Valley, its wide-open mouth directly opposite that of the Redwater. The bison
ran with the Poplar north to the plains of Canada.[47]

A smaller road passed down O'Fallon Creek, crossed the Yellowstone,
and entered Cedar Creek and from there went to the Redwater, Missouri,
and Poplar.[48] The other major north-south road in the Yellowstone basin remained confined to the Lower Yellowstone Valley north and east of O'Fallon
Creek. Bison lumbered down O'Fallon Creek, crossed the Yellowstone (approximately one hundred yards south of the Interstate 94 bridge at O'Fallon,
Montana), and skirted the Yellowstone's west bank until arriving at the Yellowstone-Missouri confluence. The hilly badlands on the east bank of the
Yellowstone below O'Fallon Creek precluded the use of that shore as a bison
route of travel.[49]

The Little Missouri drainage system played a pivotal role in Upper Missouri bison ecology. The Little Missouri and its principal feeders coupled the

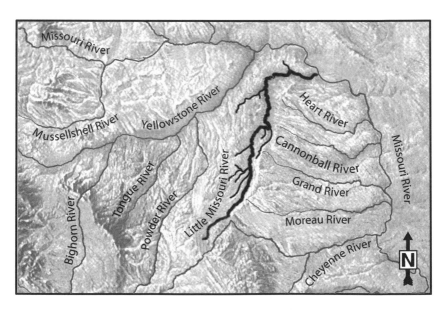

Figure 2.4. The Little Missouri basin. The Little Missouri basin served as
geographic and ecological linchpin between the Yellowstone basin to the west
and the Missouri main stem to the east. (Paul Davidson, South Plains College,
Levelland, Texas)

Big Missouri River to the Yellowstone River; it represented a linchpin in the Upper Missouri territory (fig. 2.4). Yet the Little Missouri also stood as a major north-south road in its own right. Bison found succor in the Little Missouri badlands (the area now largely within Theodore Roosevelt National Park) during inclement weather. From the gumbo hills, the animals shuffled back and forth to the Missouri main stem. The mouth of the Little Missouri contained a bulky bottom, where the Missouri Valley walls fell away to reveal a gaping hollow. Bison swam the strapping Missouri just opposite the Little Missouri's mouth. Once on the northern shoreline, the creatures entered the flat now covered by the Van Hook Arm of Lake Sakakawea. Maximilian in 1833 saw bison paths cutting in every direction as his boat passed the Little Missouri. "Continuing our voyage, we saw the buffaloes hasten away, and moored our vessel at twilight to some trees on the north bank. All over the plain [possibly the Van Hook Arm] there were deeply trodden paths of the buffaloes."[50] From the Van Hook Arm of Lake Sakakawea the animals moved up Shell Creek, the Little Knife River, or even the White Earth River off to the west. Maximilian, who saw a bison road dart up the White Earth River, commented, "A little below the mouth of this river [White Earth River], the high wind obliged us to lay to; woods and tickets, with high dry grass, and prairies, either bare or covered with artemisia [sage] formed an extensive wilderness, traversed by the paths of stags and buffaloes, where we found many deer's horns and other remains of these animals, as well as tracks of enormous bears (Ursus ferox)."[51]

The bison roads east of the Little Missouri–Big Missouri confluence shifted their axes. Rather than run north-south as did the roads in the far Upper Missouri and Yellowstone basins, the roads gouged paths along west-east axes perpendicular to the Missouri, which turns south, southeast at the Great Bend. The Missouri main stem itself served as a major north-south route of passage. Once more, Maximilian lends credence to this conclusion. He penned, "Several deep ravines, or clefts, were all dry, and opened towards the high, steep bank of the Missouri. At some accessible places these ravines were crossed by the deeply trodden paths of the herds of buffaloes, which wind through the whole prairie along the chain of hills and the bank of the [Missouri] river."[52] He continued on another page, "We proceeded by the paths trodden by the buffaloes and elks through the thick willow copses, along the [Missouri] river, and were just in sight of the keelboat."[53]

A primordial bison road paralleled today's Turtle Creek (on the Missouri's east bank) until it sluiced into the Missouri. That road crossed the main stem and stalked up the Knife River to its westernmost head, where it dropped down the Little Missouri tributary known as Whitetail Creek. The road dipped across the Little Missouri, climbed its slippery western bank, and fled southwest up Beaver Creek. Near present-day Wibaux, Montana, the road turned west and shadowed Glendive Creek to the Yellowstone River.

An additional road overtook Apple Creek (on the east side of the Missouri main stem), pierced the Missouri Valley bottoms four miles south of the city later named to honor Germany's Otto von Bismarck, dispersed over the lowlands, and then regrouped on the west bank, where converging trails funneled the animals into the Heart River Valley. Once astride the Heart River, the road rushed into the setting sun. This route straddled the Heart to its highest reaches before crossing over to the Little Missouri drainage. Once beyond the Little Missouri, the route ran up Andrews Creek, down Little Beaver Creek, up Beaver Creek, and then down Glendive Creek to its final destination, the Yellowstone River. The Heart River road served the herds and the Indians alike as a major artery, connecting the Missouri to the Yellowstone. This road also illustrates the role of the Little Missouri as an indispensable joint in the system.

South of the Heart, small, infrequently trodden trails pricked both sides of the main-stem Missouri. A relatively barren zone muffled the Missouri Valley between the Heart and the Big Cheyenne. The next sizable road to intersect the Upper Missouri tied the James River watershed to the Missouri via Okoboji Creek. Okoboji Creek comes to an end on the Missouri's east shore just south of where the Big Cheyenne ends its course on the western shore. Bison flooded down Okoboji Creek, crossed the Missouri, broke into the Cheyenne Bottoms, and moved west up the Cheyenne. Brackenridge, in 1811, confirms this pathway and the use of islands as way stations while swimming the Big Muddy: "Discovered great numbers of buffaloe; on the N.W. side, an extensive level meadow. Numbers began to swim across the river, as Hunt whose party was before us, was passing along; they waited and killed as many as they wanted; a number which were started from an island, swam towards us, and we killed several also."[54] The Cheyenne River road pointed bison toward the Black Hills, whose front range acted as one of the summer haunts of the herds.

Nineteenth-century observers, and even twentieth-century commentators, argued that bison annually left the Missouri River in the fall to winter up in the Black Hills. However, it appears that bison actually steered clear of the Black Hills between October and March/April, although some bands likely spent the winter in the rolling plains on the east side of the Black Hills. During late fall, winter, and early spring, the Black Hills can be a viciously hostile place, ravaged by winds, cold, and wet snows. In addition to bison, pronghorn also veered away from the hills during the coldest months of the year, preferring the warmer and safer river trenches to high-elevation meadows. The Black Hills, for at least half of the year, possessed a silence that is now impossible to comprehend. The sound of human voices or obstreperous bison could not be heard in winter. The tranquillity of the hills only thickened when the area's black and grizzly bears fell into hibernation. Only the gentle crunch of tiptoeing elk, the howl of sequestered coyotes or forgotten wolves, and the crackle of ravens interrupted the whining wind.

The Cheyenne road split before reaching the Black Hills. At the forks, the main trail turned into the Belle Fourche Valley, which spun its way northwestward past the sacred mound of volcanic ash known as Bear Butte. Under its conical shadow, the Belle Fourche River pulled the pressed brown earth taut into a crumpled wrinkle of green. Where the Belle Fourche does an abrupt left face, turning to the south (in present-day Wyoming), the bison road left the river and fell apart. Bison scattered over the flats west of the Belle Fourche and stumbled down into the Little Missouri Valley. Once inside the Little Missouri's walls, the bison either followed that road north or south or continued west over bumpy plains to the Little Powder River. The waters of the Belle Fourche, Little Missouri, and Little Powder flowed close to one another; six miles separated the Belle Fourche from the Little Missouri drainage, and only twelve miles of grass lay between the Little Missouri and the Little Powder. Bison that walked to the Little Powder went north or south along that trench. Those choosing the northern route eventually found the Powder River, one of those splendid north-south thoroughfares in the Yellowstone basin.

The Okoboji Creek–Cheyenne River–Belle Fourche road was the longest east-west road in the Upper Missouri territory. Since the end of the Pleistocene and the beginning of the Holocene, it carried millions of bison and hundreds of thousands of Indian foot and horse travelers on its back. This avenue quickly transported animals (including the aggressive *Homo sapiens*) from the Missouri to the Black Hills. It served as a key biological corridor across the region, tying together two rich vegetative and ecological zones (the Missouri River trench and the Black Hills) over an occasionally sparse short-grass plain.

At the forks of the Cheyenne, where the Belle Fourche headed northwest, the Cheyenne itself continued south and west around the southern border of the Black Hills. This river road entered present-day Wyoming and continued driving to the west, southwest, until its highest feeder neared the North Platte River. The Dry Fork of the Cheyenne River comes within fourteen miles of the North Platte. Thus, one great road found its way to another great road.

The Bad River (known in nineteenth-century folk geography as the Bad, Teton, or Little Missouri) is the next significant tributary to mix with the Missouri. Two roads from the east brought bison to the doorstep of the Bad. Okoboji Creek on the north and Medicine Creek on the south offered up bison to the Bad. Whichever route the animals followed out of the east, once at the Missouri they swam that stream at what had earlier been known as Bad Humor Island and Horse Island (today's La Framboise Island and Farm Island, respectively). These islands presented rest stops during the journey over the Missouri. After arriving on the western shore, the bison skipped up a high, steep bank, rattled themselves dry, and then trod along the Bad River bottom (located on both sides of the Bad confluence) before finding their way into the Bad Valley. This road, not as large as the Cheyenne River road to the north, narrowed into insignificance as it neared today's Badlands. Small shoots branched off to the north and south to join with the Cheyenne or the White River.

To the Missouri's east, roads paralleled Smith Creek and Crow Creek (both to the north of contemporary Chamberlain, South Dakota). This trail stuck its nose into the Missouri Valley at the mouth of Crow Creek and crossed the broad river directly opposite the embouchement (where an island broke the Missouri into two fordable parts). John Evans, a noted cartographer of the Missouri River in the late eighteenth century, denoted the crossing point at Crow Creek as "Sioux Pass." He named another ford higher up the Missouri where Lower Brule Island formerly sat "Portage de Sioux." The Teton Sioux and bison forded the Missouri at these two locales. Evans, who knew the Missouri well, noted these passes because they represented key junctures, or choke points, where the Teton Sioux intersected the Missouri on their annual migrations. Any entrepreneur wanting to trade with these Indians could have utilized Evans's information to his advantage.

Those choke points could be ideal trading locations. Evans's remarks also indicate that the Teton Sioux's main route of travel (at least on the Missouri's eastern shore in the 1790s) consisted of Crow Creek and Smith Creek. Ordway confirmed the mouth of Crow Creek as a point where bison crossed the Missouri. The sergeant claimed, "A large Gang of them Swam the river near the Boats we Shot a fat Cow likewise & a Small Bull. took the meat & hides on bord the pearogues. we proceeded on under a fine Sailing Breeze from E. S. E. passed 3 large Creeks (called the Sioux 3 river pass) on N.S. [north shore] which came in behind an Island."[55] It is more difficult to discern the Teton's route of travel after they passed over to the Missouri's west bank from Crow Creek. Yet the absence of perennial streams on the western shore opposite Crow Creek and the existence of rugged terrain in the Missouri breaks suggest that the Teton followed the Missouri Valley to the Big Bend bottoms and from there to the Bad River bottoms. The Missouri Valley would have also taken the Teton, and bison, to the bottoms at American Crow Creek (at Oacoma) and the White River bottom.

Roads traced the Missouri's other perennial tributaries, including the White River, Ponca Creek, and Niobrara River. Prince Wilhelm, who literally felt the indentations made by bison hooves along the floor of Ponca Creek, remarked, "The Ponca is forced into a narrow bed. The sides are for the most part wall-like, abrupt cliffs. Only here and there the banks are shaded by low trees. Deep bison trails cut up the narrow valley."[56] He went on to write, "The bison had tramped out the banks of the stream so deep in places, that it was hard to travel. They had also made deep wallows in the bed itself."[57] Bradbury in 1811 eyed the bison route that plowed through the Niobrara Valley and noted, "We this day made considerable progress, and had many fine views of the bluffs, along which, from the L'Eau qui Court [Niobrara River], we observed excellent roads made by the buffaloes. These roads I had frequent opportunities of examining, and am of the opinion that no engineer could have laid them out more judiciously."[58]

On the east, or left, bank of the Big Missouri, roads darted up the James, Vermillion, Big Sioux, Little Sioux, and Boyer Rivers. The last significant road worthy of note, and the one destined to become part of the Oregon Trail, straddled the north banks of the Platte and North Platte Rivers. The name Platte (French for "plate") accurately describes the flat topography that made this an ideal route of travel for animals. Gouverneur Warren summarized the important role that the Upper Missouri's tributaries played as routes of communication and transportation:

> The streams of the prairies of Nebraska [including the streams in the present states of North and South Dakota] below the Yellowstone, flowing into the Missouri River, are none of them navigable to any reliable extent; and as most of them run from west to east, their greatest practical value is in affording the land route of communication between our present western settlements and those to be formed in the mountains. Their valleys furnish us the only routes by which to traverse the intervening desert, for here only are such supplies of water to be found as are required, and here, too, is the only soil that can be cultivated, and such scanty supplies of wood as the region produces. Of all the valley of rivers running into the Missouri, that of the Platte furnishes the best route for any kind of a road leading to the interior.[59]

In an era before the advent of the railroad on the plains, Warren, and other Euro-American military men of like mind, saw the Upper Missouri's western tributaries as pathways to empire.

Not all bison roads followed valleys. Some did diverge from the paths swept by running water. For instance, in 1811 John Bradbury viewed a bison road on the west side of the Missouri that galloped through the roller-coaster hills between the Platte River and the Omaha villages. This trail connected the Pawnee on the Platte with the Omaha on the Missouri. This road may have been a human construct later adopted by the bison or a bison road overtaken by Indians; there is no way of knowing the road's ultimate origins. Yet the route of the road (from one Indian settlement to another) lends credence to the former theory. Other bison roads connected river basins. The road between the Three Forks and the Yellowstone joined two river systems, as did the road from the Belle Fourche to the Little Missouri, and the Little Missouri to the Powder. These intersections attached one living system to another. Rivers also connected ecosystems: a river such as the Yellowstone united alpine meadows to sagebrush mesas and lower-elevation marshland. Rivers acted as strings, binding together ecological pearls. Creatures jumped from one system to the next by moving up or down river valleys. Such ecological linkages reveal the permeability of the Upper Missouri bioregion. Firmly established boundaries did not exist in the region. Species easily moved between and within drainages within the Upper Missouri. Species also readily passed between the Upper Missouri and other large systems functioning across the central plains, northern Rocky Mountains, and prairie-pothole region. Bison roads and biological corridors beyond the valleys remained the exception rather than the rule. For most of the year, travel atop the highlands entailed uncertainty for bison as sudden storms, excessive heat, and speedy predators carried off scores of young and old. Safety lay down below, next to the water, in the high grass, under the cover of brush and branches.

Bison geography displayed a marvelous symmetry. The roads did not haphazardly weave through the Upper Missouri. Nature, especially climate, frequently restricted bison movements to the perennial streams that flowed over the country. Amazingly, the perennials joined one to another across the whole Upper Missouri basin. All the significant routes exhibited symmetry. For example, opposite the Tongue's mouth, the perennial stream known as Sunday Creek poured forth into the Yellowstone. Bison conveniently moved from the Tongue into Sunday Creek. Redwater Creek fell into the Missouri due south of the mouth of Poplar River. Bison left the always-wet Redwater and penetrated the still wetter Poplar. Bison trailing southwest down Okoboji Creek (in central South Dakota) trekked into the Missouri Valley and headed either to the nearby mouth of the Cheyenne or to the even closer Bad-Missouri juncture. What is more, the perennials in the region possess wide, level valleys, an abundance of timber and hearty grasses, and a benign slope that dipped from their headwaters to their mouths. In terms of efficiency, safety, and comfort, the perennials offered superb paths.

Bison did not have other potential routes of travel. For instance, not a single perennial stream enters the Yellowstone on its south side between Rosebud Creek and the Tongue River or between the Tongue and Powder. On the north shore of the Yellowstone the possible travel routes are just as sparse. There are no perennials between Little Porcupine Creek and Sunday Creek or between Sunday Creek and Cedar Creek. The presence, or absence, of water and the accompanying timber and grass restricted available travel routes more than any other factor.

During the wet months of April through June, bison did leave the perennials and move about with more freedom. But during the winter and at the height of summer, they massed inside the valleys of the perennials, especially the Missouri and Yellowstone main stems.[60] How did this symmetrical system come into being? It appears that climate, hydrology, and geology initially combined to sculpt spacious, slightly tilted valleys through layers of substrate. Nature placed moist valleys in close proximity to one another, along north-south or east-west axes. But climate, hydrology, and geology did not act with rhyme or reason. Inanimate force is not purposeful. The Poplar River does not enter the Missouri due north of the Redwater because the gods of earth, wind, and water willed it. Some other natural force developed the symmetry of the system, a force acting with purposeful intent.

Since 14,000 B.P., large and small mammals, including the ancient horse, musk ox, camel, sloth, mammoth, mastodon, and *Bison antiquis,* moved up and down routes such as the Musselshell–Alkali Creek–Bighorn–Little Big-horn road or the Powder–Cedar Creek–Redwater–Poplar road. The valleys through which the roads passed possessed inviting environments for mammalian life, especially as the Upper Missouri environment became pro-gressively drier with the retreat of the glaciers and the warming of the mid-continent. Water, grass, and timber lay in profusion on their valley floors. But the same resources could be found in other valleys across the Upper Missouri region at that time. Yet the creatures chose particular north-south and east-west routes over others for the purposes of resource exploitation or ease of movement. Thus, mammals chose to travel along the Powder–Cedar Creek–Redwater–Poplar road rather than attempting to traverse a different route.

For thousands of years, mammals pulverized and compacted the soil in the Powder, Cedar Creek, Redwater, and Poplar Valleys, as well as other val-leys of choice. Hoof traffic flattened the topography within these valleys, lessening their slopes and leveling their bottoms. As megafauna populations crashed in the years between 11,000 and 9,000 B.P. from Indian hunting pressure, global warming, or both, bison numbers rose. *Bison antiquis* and later *Bison bison* filled the niches created by the departure of other large mammals.[61] From 11,000 B.P. until the nineteenth century, bison pounded down the valleys, and valley floors became less and less steep, which sped the movement of the herds overland and reduced the amount of energy ex-pended in migration. The leveling of the valley trenches also meant greater water retention. Stomping bison turned valley bottomlands into bogs. A di-minished stream slope meant more water remained in the valley through the driest summer months. Bison ensured that their travel routes retained water year-round. More water attracted more grass and timber, which at-tracted more bison. The process operated as a feedback loop of complemen-tary actions. Travel routes became havens, sanctuaries developed by and for bison. The Upper Missouri was not unique in possessing a symmetrical mammalian road network. Other river basins within what is now the United States contained symmetrical trail networks, the Rio Grande and Columbia basins being two examples (fig. 2.5).

Besides displaying symmetry, the Upper Missouri vibrated with life. As mentioned earlier, from an ecological standpoint, the two great river valleys of the Upper Missouri, the Yellowstone and the Missouri, embodied the center of an immense living system. Life circulated within the entire organism,

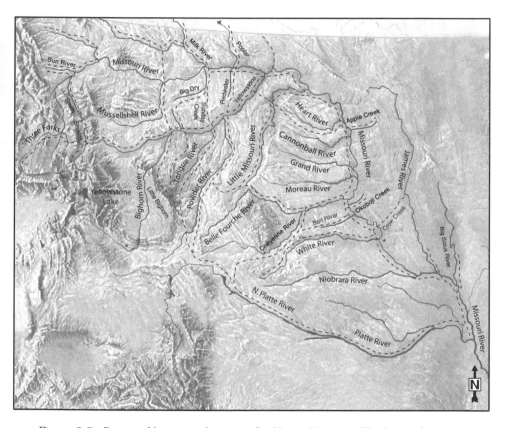

Figure 2.5. Principal bison roads across the Upper Missouri. The largest bison roads paralleled the region's perennial streams. Note the symmetry displayed in the system, especially in the far Upper Missouri and Yellowstone basins, where roads cut north and south and struck the Yellowstone and Missouri directly opposite one another. For example, just opposite from where the Poplar Road entered the Missouri Valley lay the Redwater Road; and nearly due west of Apple Creek (in today's North Dakota) sat the mouth of the Heart River Road. (Paul Davidson, South Plains College, Levelland, Texas)

surging in and out of the Upper Missouri main stem's heart, passing through hundreds of tributaries and arteries, and reaching far inland along rivulets and tiny liquid veins.

Like a living organism, the Upper Missouri system exhibited a rhythmic beat. Those erratic lines on the Missouri's nineteenth-century hydrograph illustrated the river's pulse in the same manner that a cardiogram indicates the human body's vitality. When the Missouri leaped upward in April at the commencement of the spring rise, energy shot outward from the main stem, up the tributaries and feeders. By June, and the start of the summer rise, the Missouri's energy flows penetrated the most distant creeks and gullies. In mid-July, when the river began to fall away, life abandoned the far-flung plains, dropped down into the tributary valleys, and followed the retreating water back to the Missouri main stem. In late September or early October, the rains once more fell upon the encrusted plains of the Upper Missouri and pushed the Missouri out. Life once more pressed up the tributaries, where it would remain until November or even December. When rain turned to snow and the ground sparkled silver, energy flows reversed direction, racing down toward the Missouri in advance of approaching northers. During the blistering cold months from December through February, the Missouri slid underneath a slab of ice. Beneath its winter coat, the river shrank to its lowest levels of the year. In January, it looked dead, and snow blew drifts over its still surface. Life appeared to have completely left the river, which was now motionless and eerily quiet, and its face ghostly white. But the Missouri only slept, waiting for the spring thaw to release it onto the land once more. The Yellowstone River experienced a rhythm similar to the Missouri's (figs. 2.6 and 2.7).

Indians recognized the pulse of the Missouri River. The Mandan named the juncture of the Missouri and one of its feeders the Natke-Passaha, which roughly translates as "the heart." A Mandan elder in 1833 stated, "The lord of life said, this [region] shall be the heart, the center of the world; and this river shall be the Heart River." Thus, the Mandan placed the confluence of the Missouri and the Heart River at the center of their universe. To the Mandan, all life emanated from that focal point.[62]

The Missouri's inward and outward pulsation affected the entire ecology of the Upper Missouri region. Fish, birds, vegetation, and all the large ungulates abided by the river's rhythm. Between April and early July, when the Upper Missouri often flowed at bank full or higher, fish species (including northern pike, buffalo fish, pallid sturgeon, shovelnose sturgeon, and spoon-

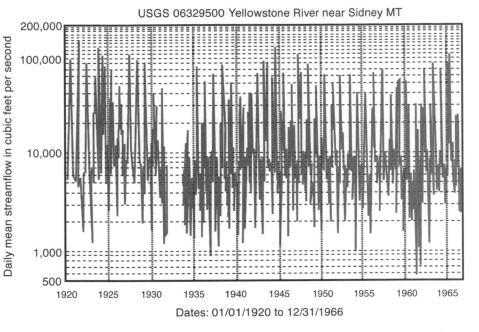

Figure 2.6. The Yellowstone River's hydrograph. In many respects a hydrograph resembles an electrocardiogram by illustrating a river's heart rate. This hydrograph of the unregulated Yellowstone's fluctuating volume between 1920 and 1966 shows the river's healthy pulse. The discernible beat and variable flows sustain biological diversity, making the Yellowstone Valley one of the most biologically diverse areas in the contiguous United States. (Courtesy of the United States Geological Survey)

bill) turned their noses toward the tributaries. Leaving the churning Missouri, with its fast, even dangerous, currents, fish sped up shallower, calmer, safer side streams or into oxbows to spawn. During the searing month of July, as the Missouri's tributaries recoiled toward the main stem, the progeny of the recent spawn arched toward home. Harried fingerlings bolted to the Missouri before drought captured them in stagnant, evaporating pools.

Birds of prey followed the annual fish migration. Bald eagles, golden eagles, and ospreys on the far Upper Missouri and Yellowstone entered tributary valleys in April and May to hunt. The hungry birds circled above the fleets of fish heading inland to spawn, diving toward sailing fins careening across the water surface. Tributaries provided birds of prey with ideal hunting. Narrower and shallower than the Big Missouri or Yellowstone, tributaries bunched fish into a few deep holes. Eagles and ospreys hungrily hung

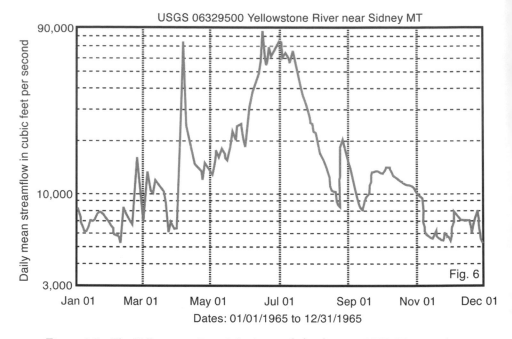

Figure 2.7. The Yellowstone River's hydrograph for the year 1965. This graph displays the Yellowstone River's rise and fall over the course of an entire year. The Yellowstone jumps dramatically upward in April and again in June, only to fall back down during the late summer months of July and August. In September or October, the river experiences another rise. Bison migration patterns mimicked the Yellowstone's and Missouri's pulses. (Courtesy of the United States Geological Survey)

over these holes or crouched in trees feet above the waterline, catching the inattentive upon their razor-tipped talons. The relative clarity of the tributaries of the far Upper Missouri and Upper Yellowstone made hunting a simple proposition. Transparent water translated into a clear line of sight, which meant fish on the skewer. Adult fish, preoccupied with the spawn and throwing caution to the wind, died in droves. Inexperienced fingerlings, without the distrust of adulthood, also fell prey to vigilant birds. In July, the birds followed the receding tributaries back to the Missouri. The constant, harassing attacks continued without letup as fish desperately tried to reach the security of the Missouri. Eagles and ospreys hounded fleeing hatchlings or dispatched hapless fish stuck in drying backwaters. The spawn and subsequent hatch represented a boon to birds of prey—a fat time before the onset of famine.[63]

Vegetation also moved from the Missouri Valley into the tributary valleys with the April and June rises. Song birds, herons, grizzly bears, and wolves carried the seeds of plants in their feathers or buried in their fur. Riding piggyback on a magpie or an elk, seeds dispersed across the Upper Missouri territory. Other varmints hauled seeds deep inside their bellies, plopping kernel and fertilizer onto the ground whenever and wherever nature called. The seeds of grasses, berry bushes, wild vegetables, and trees spread out in concert with the great out-migration of energy in the spring and early summer of each year. Maximilian indicates that birds and mammals moved as a single parade to and from the Missouri Valley. In 1833, the prince viewed an eclectic cast of characters along the Missouri: "At half past two in the afternoon, we passed the mouth of Milk River, where we remarked great numbers of bears, elks, deer, and wolves on the bank, and some wild geese and sandpipers on the strand."[64]

Elk, mule deer, eagles, and the rest of the biological community of the Upper Missouri never randomly moved into, and out of, the Missouri Valley. Instead, they followed the big roads to the Missouri and Yellowstone and went directly into the bottoms that lay astride tributary embouchements. As a result, at various times during the year, the bottoms possessed magnificent concentrations of biological diversity. Predictably, nineteenth-century Euro-American hunters and trappers on the Upper Missouri focused their efforts in the bottoms.

Bison migration patterns also mimicked the Upper Missouri's hydraulic regime. In January, February, and March, with the river at its lowest, bison clustered in the Missouri and Yellowstone River bottoms or inside the valleys of their major tributaries. They bunched together there to escape the winds, cold, and snow whipping over the hard plains. In the bottoms, bison found big bluestem, cottonwood trees, and brush to block the winds and get them through the winter. The advent of severe cold and/or storms always brought the bison into the river bottoms. Edwin Denig, an American Fur Company employee, noted the connection between cold, snow, bison, and the rivers of the Upper Missouri. He wrote, "The severe cold of the winter and deep frozen snow on the plains forces these animals to seek grazing and shelter in the woods, along streams and in broken country protected by hills from the wind, but during the summer months they remain on the plains."[65] Maximilian of Wied remarked, "In the cold snow-storms, so prevalent during the winter, these animals [bison] take refuge in the forests on the banks, when great numbers of them are killed, and it is often almost impossible to drive them out of the wood."[66]

Denig's and Maximilian's comments are instructive for a couple of reasons. First, they note the tie between cold temperatures and bison movements. Second, they illustrate the import of wooded bottoms to the animal's winter survival. Third, each man makes it plain that bison remained close to the Missouri River trench during the winter months. The herds stayed near the Missouri for protection against the elements. Chardon, who confirms that bison held near the river in the winter, wrote on March 10, 1835, "Cattle plenty in 15 Miles from the Fort."[67] Bison held within a fifteen- to thirty-mile radius of the Missouri throughout the winter—close enough to quickly retreat to the valley when cold or snow came down from the Arctic. Bison could not chance going high up the tributaries or unto the uplands, where timber and grass thinned out. The animals could not stray far from the Missouri bottoms in the unpredictable winter months; otherwise they might die if caught in the open by a blizzard. One study done on the northern plains in the late twentieth century found that an adult male bison is capable of traveling twenty-six miles in a single day. Prime bulls averaged roughly eight miles per day when moving toward rutting grounds. These statistics support the conclusion that bison held within only a day or two from the Missouri River trench and the other wooded valleys of the Upper Missouri during the winter.[68] With severe weather pending, the herds moved into the lowlands in a day or two.

Bottoms allowed the herds to ride out the little ice ages that periodically swept down from the north and froze the Upper Missouri country. A little ice age struck the Upper Missouri in the first decade of the 1800s. The herds survived those long winters by relying on the bottoms. If the bison hugged the Missouri River trench during the cold months, they remained outside of it when temperatures rose during brief winter thaws. Again, the journalists support this assertion. Chardon wrote on December 16, 1834, "The weather continues Mild, having had no snow of any consequence this season—and cattle scarce owing to the warm weather."[69]

Pregnant bison cows stayed in the bottoms through March, April, or the first weeks of May—until they calved. Cows remained in the bottoms during the calving season for numerous reasons. Luxuriant bottoms offered protection for mother and calf from the vagaries of the weather. It is an understatement to claim that the weather in March and April across the Upper Missouri is variable. It can be just crazy. A March or April day may witness the full gamut of weather phenomena, including heat, sun, wind, cloud cover, sleet, snow, and cold. Blazing snowstorms often came on the heels of a rapid drop in air temperature. Bison cows and calves lay secure in the bottoms in March and April while the Upper Missouri's temperatures jerked up and down.

Bottomland grasses and herbs offered food to allow cows to recuperate and calves to gain strength. Bottoms also secured them from marauding predators. Lying in high grass, thickets, or shaded forests, calves and cows avoided bears and wolves. If cows did not actually birth inside a bottom, they did so on the islands in the Missouri's midchannel. Islands protected newborns from predators nosing through the underbrush along the bank line.

At the termination of calving season, the Upper Missouri's snows melted, its rivers rose, and its grasses grew. In March, April, and May, millions of bison turned away from the trampled, dungy bottoms of the Missouri and Yellowstone. In an erratic, noisy procession, accompanied by loud grunts and snorts, bison dashed in short, pounding bursts out of the bottoms and into tributaries. Heads bowed low, bison ate their way up the Missouri's tributaries, into scattered gullies and creeks, eventually climbing up steep embankments. By May and early June, the animals attained the summits of the world's grandest grassland.

Europeans and Euro-Americans observed an abject lack of game along the Missouri and Yellowstone Valleys in June and early July of each year. These river valleys appeared empty, all their occupants having headed for the hills. Tabeau understood how the Missouri's flow regime influenced species migration patterns. He observed, "The dearth of hunting is another necessary result of high water. The animals, not being able to approach the Missouri, remain far away on the prairies and upon the high land along the little rivers." On the other hand, "Game is very abundant at low water."[70]

When dry, hot, sunny weather assaulted the Upper Missouri in late June and July, bison, wearing thick coats and battling clouds of insects swirling with the heat, left the uplands to seek relief from the high temperature. Shade, pasture, and fresh flowing water awaited their arrival in the valley lowlands. Since hot air rises and cold air sinks, valleys, at lower elevations than the surrounding landscape, stayed cooler during muggy summer nights. Bison preferred to stay in those air-conditioned places. Guide and hunter Luther S. Kelly remembered how the valley lowlands stayed cool even in the dead of summer: "As the darkness fell the sky became luminous with stars, and it was still and warm on the high ground. When I had descended at midnight I came into the chill air of the lowlands, and found and followed the fresh trail of the column leading down the Musselshell."[71]

A loss of herbage also set bison on the move to the river valleys. By July, bison denuded the uplands and its grasses. Henry Boller noted the voracious hunger of the bison and their influence on the grassland: "Buffaloes had recently roamed here in great numbers, for the grass was eaten quite short and other traces were everywhere visible."[72] Captain W. F. Raynolds, surveying the course of the Little Powder River, wrote on July 23, 1859, that the bison ate the grass as methodically as swarming sheep. He stated, "The grass is very scarce, the buffaloes having recently consumed very thoroughly such little as there naturally would be, and we are compelled to give our animals a wide stretch of grazing to satisfy their wants."[73] In many respects, their own appetites drove bison off the high plains. As their forage diminished, then disappeared altogether, bison had no choice but to turn their heads toward the river valleys, where herbage, especially big and little bluestem, still grew, naturally irrigated by the waters of the perennial streams.

The absence of water on the uplands, within gullies, and inside feeder creeks across the Upper Missouri territory served to further propel bison down into the Yellowstone and Missouri River trenches. Only a handful of streams in the Upper Missouri are perennial. The vast majority of Yellowstone and Missouri tributaries dripped beneath the hardpan by the middle of August, if not earlier, leaving behind only a salty, white residue to mark the passage of water. As the Upper Missouri baked, only the perennials contained water. Life drew into those last, moist bastions. Water still coursed in the Yellowstone, the Missouri, and the lower reaches of their principal branches. Bison went to that water. In July and August, millions of bison converged in the Yellowstone and Missouri troughs and in the lower extremities of such streams as the Musselshell, Marias, Milk, Poplar, Redwater, Clarks Fork, Bighorn, Rosebud, Tongue, and Powder. Several other creeks and rivers in the basin enticed bison to their banks, including Alkali, Big and Little Porcupine, Sunday, Cedar, and O'Fallon Creeks on the Yellowstone and the White Earth, Little Missouri, Knife, Heart, Apple Creek, Cannonball, Grand, Moreau, Cheyenne, Okoboji Creek, Bad, Crow Creek, White, Niobrara, James, Vermillion, and Big Sioux along the Missouri. The drier the plains, the more congested became these valleys.

Heat, loss of grass, and an absence of water drove bison to the big rivers, but the animals fled to the largest river valleys in late summer for another important reason   to mate. Throughout much of the year, bison bulls and cows stayed apart. But in July and August, and even into September, the bulls mingled among the cows to propagate the species. Bradbury described the annual rut he witnessed in late July 1811, west of the Calumet Bluffs: "This plain was literally covered with buffaloes as far as we could see, and we soon discovered that it consisted in part of females. The males were fighting in every direction, with a fury which I have never seen paralleled, each having singled out his antagonist. We judged that the number must have amounted to some thousands, and that there were many hundreds of these battles going on at the same time, some not eighty yards from us. . . . I shall only observe farther, that the noise occasioned by the trampling and bellowing was far beyond description."[74] The journal accounts provide evidence that the bison rut lasted from the middle of July to the end of August and sometimes into the middle of September.[75]

Down in the valleys in midsummer, male and female bison easily found partners. Most important, bulls found a willing entourage of cows. By timing the rut with the dry season, evolutionary ecology placed the sexes close to one another for procreation. A concentration of the animals contributed to energy efficiency. In other words, the bison expended far less energy mating in the lowlands than if they attempted to mate on the high plains. With so many cows within range, a bull can copulate with several in a matter of hours. In one study, a single bull copulated with four females during a twenty-four-hour period.[76] Trying to do the same on the high plains would not have been possible; cows would have been dispersed over larger tracts of territory, and thus bulls would have had to work much harder to find and impregnate cows there than in the lowlands. Just the act of locating mates would have meant bulls had less energy for the task of mounting and impregnating cows. For bison, and other mammals, it is crucial that as little energy as possible is expended in actually finding mates and more energy expended in the act of copulation.

Besides putting the animals together, the river valleys provided bison with plenty of food, water, and protection from the elements during the rut. River valley resources enabled bison bulls to stay strong during the mating season. With grass and water close at hand, they did not have to travel far to forage and drink. As a result, they could focus strictly on the rut.

Another reason bison bulls stayed in the valleys during and immediately after the rut is that the animals exhausted themselves from their frequent and brief trysts with the females. A bull may stay in the midst of cows for anywhere from four to thirty-three days. During that length of time, the animals spent themselves in strenuous physical activity, butting heads with competitors, mounting females, copulating, and scouting for new mates. Prime adult males (between the ages of seven and twelve years) could sire over sixteen calves in a single year.[77] Besides expending vast amounts of energy during the rut, adult males fed 80 percent less while in the presence of the females. What this information indicates is that a mature male quickly lost strength and weight during the mating season. Tabeau confirmed this conclusion: "The bull is so weakened that he cannot recover soon enough to endure the rigor of the winter and that even those that vigor and youth have sustained do not regain their weight until the middle of May."[78] In order to recharge their optimum energy levels, bison males needed the precious herbage and water of the Yellowstone and Missouri Valleys and their perennial tributaries. The food source in the valleys helped them restore stamina as quickly as possible so they could defend themselves against the many predators, including the grizzlies and wolves, roaming all around them. Being on the uplands, with their sparse, or nonexistent, vegetation, would require the bison to take longer to recover from the rut. The longer a bison remained weak, the more likely it would fall prey to wolves or bears.

In September, the rut came to an end at the same time fall rains commenced across the Upper Missouri. Cool mist dripping from low clouds turned pale yellows, dusty browns, and grays to emerald, while generating a rise in the Missouri main stem. Maximilian described those late September rains: "About eleven in the morning of the 27th of September, we reached the Prairie a la Corne de Cerf. The sky was overcast, the weather very cool, and about noon it began to rain so heavily."[79] Directed by a climatic cue, bison left the Missouri and Yellowstone and its perennial tributaries and followed their snouts back to the uplands and its reemerging greenery. Chardon, at Fort Clark, confirms that bison evacuated the Missouri River in September and October. He penned on September 25, 1834, "Cattle very scarce." He continued on October 7, 1834, "Cattle scarce."[80] Maximilian, gliding downstream from Fort Union to Fort Clark in late October and early November 1833, noticed that bison had completely abandoned the river valley at that time. He stated, "We did not encounter any buffaloes till we reached Fort Clarke; they appeared to have retired from the river; very frequently however we saw the paths and traces of other animals."[81]

With the onset of winter, bison gravitated back to the Missouri and Yellowstone and their larger tributaries, holding close to those lifelines until spring once more called them yonder. Chardon, ever alert to the movements of bison (probably because he was always so hungry), confirmed that bison came back to the Missouri in November, holding again within fifteen to thirty miles from the trench. On November 22, 1834, he chronicled, "Cattle [bison] are plenty 30 Miles from the Fort."[82] Luttig also stated that the bison came back to the Missouri in November, as did Maximilian. Maximilian stated, "Their [the Assiniboine] chief subsistence they derive from the herds of buffaloes, which they follow in the summer, generally from the rivers, to a distance in the prairie; in the winter, to the woods on the banks of the rivers, because these herds, at that time, seek for shelter and food among the thickets."[83]

Bison migration patterns indicate the life-giving role that the Missouri, Yellowstone, and their perennial tributaries played in preserving and propagating the species. Bison found succor and sanctuary in the valleys at the most stressful times of the year, the stormy winter months and the parched summer. River valleys and their bottoms, which contained reliable supplies of water, grass, and timber, evened out or moderated the environmental extremes prevalent in the Upper Missouri. The Yellowstone and Missouri kept the bison population from crashing on the heels of climatic fluctuation.

The Yellowstone, Missouri, and their perennials performed even more vital roles in years of exceptionally low moisture. During drought, bison lingered longer in the valley bottoms, consuming more of the valley's grasses and shrubs while they waited for rain. The big rivers also allowed the animals to survive superdroughts, decades-long periods of below-average moisture that struck the plains once or twice every five hundred years. Archaeologists, reading minuscule tree rings, determined that a twenty-two-year superdrought ravished the plains and the Upper Missouri from 1572 to 1593. During those years, the entire biological community of the Upper Missouri contracted in area extent. In an ecologically perilous time, bison found secure havens only in the Yellowstone and Missouri Valleys.[84]

By offering sanctuary not just to bison but to the entire biological community of the Upper Missouri, the Yellowstone and Missouri averted total ecological collapse. Once a superdrought passed, the river valleys became species banks, sending forth the species necessary to repopulate long-abandoned tributaries, creeks, and plains. Using the heartbeat analogy once more, the two big rivers prevented palpitations in the system, keeping up a continual, low pulse that sustained the larger organism.

Some nineteenth-century bison observers claimed that bison migrated between north and south. According to this thesis, bison moved from the northern Upper Missouri to the southern Upper Missouri or central plains during the fall and then returned gradually north with the sprouting grasses and budding trees, reaching the northern latitudes in May and June. John Bradbury believed this when he wrote:

> We had for some days past seen a great number of [buffalo] herds, con-
> sisting of from fifty to a hundred in each. On expressing my surprise at
> seeing so many, the hunters assured me, that so far from its being ex-
> traordinary, they had been in the expectation of seeing them in much
> greater numbers. Some of the hunters, who had been six or eight years
> about the head of the Missouri, said they had seen them during their
> annual migrations from north to south in autumn, and to the northward
> in spring; and agreed in stating, that at these times they assemble in vast
> herds, and march in regular order. Some asserted that they had been
> able to distinguish where the herds were even when beyond the bounds
> of the visible horizon, by the vapour which arose from their bodies. Oth-
> ers stated that they had seen herds extending many miles in length.[85]

Edward Harris would indicate much the same during his visit to the region in 1843: "The winter has been so very severe that buffaloes have been 3 or 400 miles lower down the river than they had been for twenty years."[86] Tabeau, that competent observer of the Upper Missouri environment, also believed bison moved from north to south and back again between the fall and the spring. He noted, "Every autumn these animals periodically pass from the north to the south, from whence they return in the springtime at the first good weather."[87]

Although a widely held belief among numerous nineteenth-century Euro-Americans, the north-south bison migration thesis possesses a number of weaknesses. Bison in the Upper Missouri did move between northern and southern locales, but not as part of some great north-south migration pattern. Bison did not behave like geese, seeking the southern latitudes at the first hint of winter. Rather, they followed the seasonal pulsations of the Upper Missouri system, moving north or south depending on climate and hydrology. Bison did move north or south through the Missouri corridor that extends in a north-south direction through present-day North and South Dakota, Nebraska, and Iowa. That corridor represented an excellent path of movement. Bison also followed the great north-south roads that cut across the far Upper Missouri and Yellowstone main stems and extended through present-day Montana and Wyoming. But there exists no evidence that these movements occurred as part of a larger north-south migration.

The north-south thesis originated in the nineteenth century among Euro-Americans who witnessed large numbers of bison or pronghorn moving in a southern direction in the fall. These Euro-American observers speculated that the animals went to warmer climes. These same theorists speculated that pronghorn or bison crossed the Missouri on their way toward the Black Hills, where they wintered in a supposedly more hospitable environment. Millions of antelope or bison in the Black Hills in the dead of winter would have overwhelmed the carrying capacity of the hills and led to massive die-offs.

Just as a Missouri–to–Black Hills migration pattern does not make ecological sense, neither does a great north-south migration pattern. Bison abandoning the rivers and moving south, over the dangerous uplands, would have confronted millions of bison already crowded into the river valleys of the central and southern plains. The addition of millions of animals from the north, in the stressful winter months when herbage shrank under snow and ice, would have overburdened the carrying capacity of the central and southern plains and led to rapid population declines.

Furthermore, the north-south thesis does not explain how those bison reached the central or southern plains and where they resided once there. Bison followed established paths across the plains. In the Dakotas, the largest north-south bison route paralleled the Missouri trench, while a smaller one pursued the Little Missouri to the south. Other significant routes in the Dakotas moved between east and west. There exists no large road in the Dakotas, other than the Missouri main stem, that might have carried the animals to the south. Additionally, there is no evidence after 1804 that bison moved in large numbers down the Missouri corridor each fall, even though that would have been the most likely corridor. Harris, in 1843, mentions bison present far lower down the Missouri than in previous years because of the severity of the winter, but that movement of animals in that year does not appear to be evidence of a larger annual pattern. From the available documentation, bison from the Dakotas and Montana did not concentrate in Iowa, Nebraska, or Wyoming during the winter months, and they surely did not pass down into the more distant central plains.

The north-south theory also does not hold up against the weight of a bison. Bison did not and could not travel hundreds of miles each fall. More-over, the animals certainly could not travel hundreds of miles in the spring, after a winter had stripped the fat from their bones. Travel cost the animals sorely needed energy stores. Not surprisingly, bison moved as little as possi-ble, preferring to eat more and walk less. Traversing such huge distances would deprive the animals of weight and thereby weaken them, increase their susceptibility to disease and predation, and seriously harm the unborn fetuses slated for birth in March and April. Bison did not make such formi-dable journeys each year; ecology kept them rooted in the river valleys of the Upper Missouri.

Additionally, the north-south exodus theory does not explain the contin-ued presence of hundreds of thousands of bison on the frigid Upper Missouri and Yellowstone in December, January, and February of each year. During several of the coldest winters in Upper Missouri history, massive numbers of bison remained in the Yellowstone and Missouri Valleys. Oscar Brackett remembered seeing plenty of bison in the Yellowstone Valley during the win-ter of 1876–1877, one the coldest winters of the nineteenth century in the Upper Missouri territory: "We went in on an Island just above mouth of Lit-tle pocupine & built us a Cabain there was no Bufaloo up to that time on the Yellow Stone the Morning after we had got our Cabbain done it had turned very Cold. I went out so I could see up & down the bottom & the Buffaloo was Coming down from the Bluffs by the hundreds & the Bottoms was cov-ered with them & from that time until Spring the Country was full of Buffa-loo."[88] Another indication that bison stayed put in the Upper Missouri's valleys during the winter months came from a market hunter based in the Miles City, Montana, area in the early 1880s. Peter Jackson recalled that "75,000 buffalo were killed on the Yellowstone River the winter of 1880–81 [a brutally cold, blustery, and wet winter that preceded the Great Flood of 1881 along the Missouri main stem]. The skin hunters took 100,000 buffalo hides from the Yellowstone River country in the winter of 1881–82. The slow disappearance of the northern herd can be seen in the winter of 1882–83 when the number of buffalo hides taken fell to 45,000."[89] Finally, James H. Chambers at Fort Sarpy, on the Yellowstone River near today's Cartersville, Montana, saw scores of animals in the dead of winter. He wrote on Decem-ber 22, 1855, "Snow during the night 30 below zero Buffaloa plenty around the Fort our hunters killed 4 cows." Two weeks later, after the passage of enough time for the bison to clear out of the area and head south, Chambers wrote on January 3, 1856, "Thermometer stood at 34 below zero Buffaloa thick close to the fort."[90] The question begs to be answered: Why hadn't any of those bison seen in the Yellowstone Valley in 1855–1856, again in 1876–1877, and throughout the early 1880s moved their stiff, frigid, rank carcasses to the sunny southern plains to soak up the sun's rays and ride out the winter? Ultimately, the answer lies in the fact that the river valleys of the Upper Missouri met their survival needs and that they had no need to risk their lives on a southern sojourn.

Some animals did move south during the autumn. Harris's comment that bison moved down the Missouri main stem to seek a warmer clime during the severe winter of 1842–1843 possesses merit. But that movement likely occurred sporadically rather than as a coordinated, ongoing, yearly, big move. Euro-American observers apparently misread these southern movements for some sort of grand parade of bison from the northern plains to the southern plains. More likely, journalists saw the animals as they left the Missouri or Yellowstone main stem after the fall rut or at the commencement of the fall rains in September and October. Consequently, animals moving up the southern tributaries of the Yellowstone appeared to be migrating south for the winter, when in actuality those animals migrated up the Bighorn, Little Bighorn, Rosebud, Tongue, and Powder for shorter distances, eventually returning to the Yellowstone main stem with the commencement of winter. The bison along the Missouri main stem did the same, only pursuing the tributaries west, east, or south, for limited distances, so they could turn back to the Missouri when the need arose.

Although bison migration patterns imitated the grand pulsation of the Upper Missouri system, there still existed variability in their movements. During the summer months, localized thundershowers influenced the whereabouts of the animals. In July and August, when available pasturage diminished with the sun, isolated storms flew over the land, dumping inches of rain on dust. The strip of foliage that burst outward attracted bison, which followed the grassy paths to their ends. Gouverneur Warren, at Bear Butte, near present-day Sturgis, South Dakota, witnessed this phenomenon in the otherwise bone-dry year of 1855. Bison approached an area that had recently received rain. The Teton Sioux, desperate for meat, also went to where the rain fell, knowing the bison would be there.[91]

Indians affected the migration of bison in many ways, most commonly through the application of fire. In March, indigenes, including the Teton Sioux, burned the plains. Why March? Because during that month strong southern winds sucked the residue of winter moisture from the grass before

April showers dampened it. The grass stood ready to burn. March fires fertilized the land with nitrogen, spurred the growth of fresh herbage, and attracted bison to the blossoming buffet. Depending on their needs, the Teton
Sioux, Crow, Mandan, Hidatsa, Arikara, Ponca, and Omaha burned the
plains again in the middle or late summer, hoping the resulting new plant
life would bring the bison close to their encampments, making the hunt easier and safer. Tribes employed this technique to avoid long-distance hunting
forays. If bison came to them, they would not have to go out on the exposed
plains and chance an encounter with an enemy tribe. The Missouri River
village tribes practiced more frequent burning of the grasses than the Teton
Sioux residing in the south and west. As Teton power and confidence increased in the 1830s, the village tribes increasingly feared venturing too far
to the west, so they attempted to bring the bison to them with fire.

Indian hunters also torched the plains to redirect bison from the path of
an enemy column. Rising flames drove the herds away from the blackened
land. All Upper Missouri Indians used fire for this purpose. Rerouting the
animals with fire represented a form of conservation. The tribe that set the
plains ablaze hoped to frighten the herds away from an enemy while con-
serving the animals for themselves. D. S. Stanley in 1872 observed that the
Indians had pushed the bison out of the path of his military escort. He wrote,
"Buffaloes were first found at Pompey's Pillar, the Indians having driven the
herds off the Yellowstone."[92]

The Teton Sioux set fire to the grassland more frequently in the 1870s
than at any previous time. During that combative decade, Teton hunters
sought to protect the dwindling herds from the guns of U.S. Army soldiers
and settlers. For instance, in 1873, George A. Custer and the Seventh Cavalry provided protection to one of the railroad survey teams working in the
Yellowstone Valley. While the column moved up the Yellowstone, the men
noticed the plains to their front ablaze. Custer rightly concluded that the
Teton had attempted to frighten the game away from American guns. In
1876, when Colonel John Gibbon led a column from Fort Ellis to the east
down the Yellowstone, one of his junior officers, Lieutenant Bradley, also
recognized the Teton Sioux practice of deploying fire to conserve bison.

Teton Sioux males used fire to keep bison from approaching too close to
Euro-American encampments and posts located on the banks of the Missouri and Yellowstone. In 1818, when Secretary of War John C. Calhoun's
Yellowstone Expedition came up the Missouri to plant the American flag in
the Upper Missouri territory, the men of that disastrous military endeavor

witnessed a series of fires to their front. Once the soldiers encamped at Engineer Cantonment, the smoke and ash blew through their post with annoying
regularity. The Oto, like the Teton Sioux to the north, wanted to keep game
animals far from the trigger-happy Euro-Americans. More often than not,
Euro-Americans had no idea that their presence precipitated the blazes that
roared all around them. Instead, they interpreted the fires as something
else—an Indian warning to friends to watch out for the Euro-Americans.
Brackenridge, near the Niobrara, concluded the same: "The plain was
strewed with the ordure of the buffaloe, which gave it the appearance of an
immense pasture field. We discovered this morning, a great deal of smoke up
the river, which we suppose to have been made by the Indians, in order to
give notice of our approach; some of their scouts having probably discovered
us. This is the usual mode of giving warning."[93] The Indians undoubtedly
started fires to warn their brethren of the presence of Euro-Americans; but
just as frequently, Indian peoples fired the grass to clear away the game, depriving the Euro-Americans of a resource while saving that resource for
themselves at a later date. Luttig, in 1812, witnessed a fire near his encampment, set by some disgruntled Arikara Indians who went home hungry after
a visit with the Euro-Americans. The Arikara, who felt slighted by the intrud-
ers who hunted and resided on their territory, burned the grass as a rebuke
to the Euro-Americans for depriving them of food. These Indians likely concluded that if they went hungry, then the Euro-Americans should, too. Luttig stated, "Thursday the 12 [November], cloudy 3 Rees which had camped
with us last night went away displeased getting not enough to eat and set the
Prairie around us a fire, Immel returned with 5 Cows."[94] Another explanation for the fires may be the Arikara desire to literally burn the Euro-
Americans out of their position.

Indian war parties affected bison migration patterns. Warriors skulking
through valley lowlands, up and down gullies, and across or along bison
roads frightened the animals from their established routes of travel. Tribes
in the Upper Missouri frequently learned of the presence of enemy warriors
or U.S. soldiers by the harried movements of bison. Frightened bison
sprinted away from *Homo sapiens*. Bradbury wrote, "Soon after we passed
the [White] river, we saw a buffalo running over the bluff towards the Missouri, which put us on our guard, as we considered it a certain indication
of Indians being near."[95] Prince Wilhelm believed the movement of people
through the Missouri River trench dramatically influenced the whereabouts
of bison: "As the result of the march of so many Indians and whites along the

banks of the river, the bison had withdrawn, and the hunt was insufficient for the needs of the people."[96] Additionally, war parties, desirous of losing a trailing enemy force, or covering their route of attack, set the plains ablaze to their rear or front. These fires, which had nothing to do with bison per se, nonetheless diverted or rerouted bison caught too close to the flames. Chardon wrote about patrolling Indians using fire to deflect an enemy. He commented on July 6, 1836, "This Morning the praries are all on fire, made by the war party of last night."[97] Two months later, on September 5, 1836, a conflagration near Fort Clark convinced Chardon that Indian warriors were using fire to cover their route of attack toward the fort. He wrote, "Strong south wind—The Praries [sic] are all on fire, impossible to see the hills, on account of the thick smoke. No doubt but the Yanctons are near at hand, as we expect an attack from them every day."[98] Finally, the trader commented, "Prairies are all on fire on the North side, lit by the War Parties of Assinniboines and Gros Ventres—that are roveing from Camp to Camp, in search of a scalp—I think there will be hard fighting in this neighborhood this summer."[99]

Battles between Indians and other Indians, and between Indians and non-Indians undoubtedly affected the bison. The firing of rifles, the whoop of warriors, the guttural bark of a sergeant, and the cries of the wounded and dying scared bison from their established paths. What is more, the smell of sweaty, dirty human flesh or that of the blood of other slain bison alerted migrating herds of danger. One other factor to consider about Indian warfare is that battles most often occurred on established bison roads. Indians walked or rode along the same roads traveled by the bison herds. Predictably, Indians, either out on a hunt or passing from one camp to another, ran into their enemies passing along the same routes. Indians on the plains, like their Euro-American counterparts, practiced the old adage "When in doubt, shoot first." Consequently, gunfire and the whirl of arrows shattered the peaceful air of the plains and tore at the earth. These quick conflicts pushed adjacent herds off the roads onto the uplands or onto another, safer roadway.

Indians did alter and willfully manipulate bison migration patterns. They affected bison ecology by scaring the herds away from a locale or by enticing those animals to a particular location. Just what the effects of these human manipulations were on bison ecology and population numbers is impossible to quantify. Any action humans took in the bison world affected the bison population. For example, when Indians acquired a campsite in a timbered point, they might have forced the bison to march cross-country to seek shelter elsewhere. When Indian warriors scared the animals off a road, the bison expended more energy traveling over the highlands or within a poorer road or river valley. Burning the grass, especially in the fall, to frighten the animals away from a Euro-American expedition may have saved the lives of countless animals in the short term by keeping them away from Euro-American guns. Yet, in the long term the burned plains may not have regenerated in time to provide winter pasturage. From a purely bison-centric standpoint, any diversion of the herds, which required the expenditure of energy to flee, adversely affected the animals. Indian horses also affected bison ecology and movements. The big horse herds fed on the same grass sought by bison. Some historians argue that the horse herds of the Upper Missouri seriously impinged upon the amount of available grass for the bison, thereby having an adverse impact on bison numbers.[100]

Even with those variations in migration patterns caused by Indian fire, warfare, hunting, camping, and competition from feeding horses, bison continued to follow the established roads to and from the big rivers. Variation undoubtedly existed in migration patterns, which led Euro-American observers to conclude that bison movements adhered to no discernible pattern. In other words, the animals moved in a chaotic, incomprehensible manner. This conclusion gained merit after the 1850s, but especially in the 1870s, when so many Indians and Euro-Americans pressed in on the last herds. An increased Euro-American presence in the Upper Missouri pushed the herds all over the plains. Bison did deviate from their established paths, but only when interrupted from their well-worn routes. So regardless of perturbations, bison still adhered to their primordial migration pattern into and out of the big river valleys.

Indians influenced bison migration patterns. Yet bison, their movements, and their road network also had a profound affect on Indian peoples, especially the Teton Sioux. Bison shaped Teton thought in ways that twenty-first-century Euro-Americans can only imagine. The animal influenced their art, language, rituals, ceremonies, spirituality, diet, dress, warfare, and geography. From the perspective of the indigenous buffalo hunters, the bison stood in the middle of the circle, at the center of the universe.

3

Buffalo People

The Influence of Bison on Indigenous Culture, History, and Geography

The buffalo is the most common animal of the Upper

Missouri and it is of the greatest usefulness to the large number

of wandering nations that dwell there.

—Pierre-Antoine Tabeau, French fur trader

The Teton Sioux (Teton) have long been portrayed as the pre-eminent equestrian nomads of the Upper Missouri. In the early and middle nineteenth century, they earned a reputation for best expressing the bison culture. The Teton found many uses for bison. The creature dramatically influenced Teton material culture—their technologies, tepees, diet, and dress—and (before its near extinction) dominated every aspect of Teton thought and action. Fluctuations in bison ecology also generated war between the Teton and the other Upper Missouri tribes.

A visitor to a Teton encampment at the height of the summer hunt entered a world where the line between bison and human blurred. Smells and tastes of bison flooded the senses from every direction. Soot-blackened kettles bubbled with boiling bison meat. Scaffolds, burdened arms outstretched to the sun god, held hundreds of pounds of fatty, cherry red meat, slowly browning, shrinking, and hardening below a withering sky. Packs of ravenous dogs, near cousins to wild wolves, trotted through camp, howling, barking, yipping, and begging for the tiny morsels occasionally flipped nonchalantly onto the ground by a bison-engorged Indian. Women, working hard at preparing meat for immediate consumption or winter use, scurried from scaffolds, to fire, to tepee, wearing halved bison robes loosely attached to their midsections. Men sat in circles, smoking, sucking on marrowbones, or nibbling on the last bits of a delicious tongue. Parfleches, made of rock-hard bison leather, lay at their feet, contents unknown. Then there were the tepees stripped of all bison hair, oiled with smeared bison brain, and bleached white by the grassland and its elemental tools of wind, rain, and sun (fig. 3.1). On the outside walls of their circular enclosures, the Teton painted the war exploits of the occupants. A picture depicted an Indian on horseback, high, proud, galloping, ready to slay an enemy with a battle-ax. Another etching displayed a warrior engaged in hand-to-hand combat with a member of the Crow nation, the avowed enemy of the Teton. Still another

Figure 3.1. An encampment of Assiniboine in the Upper Missouri. The equestrian nomads of the Upper Missouri relied on bison for nearly all the necessities of life, including food, fiber, fuel, and shelter. Bison pervaded all aspects of plains Indian culture. The tepee represented the most common form of shelter in the Upper Missouri territory prior to Euro-American occupancy of the region. Indigenes utilized an average of fourteen shorn bison robes to assemble a single tepee. (Courtesy of the W. H. Over Museum, Vermillion, South Dakota)

drawing showed an individual on a hunt. The hunter first strikes the bison with an arrow, it charges at its pursuer, it falls to its knees, and then it lies dead. The Indian male rides forward in triumph. Such illustrations represented family crests—emblems of stature and accomplishment. Clark wrote of Dakota (close relatives of the more western Sioux) tepees near Calumet Bluff on August 28, 1804, "The Camp which was handsum made of Buffalow Skins Painted different Colour, their Camps formed of a Conic form Containing about 12 or 15 persons each."[1]

Conversation in a Teton village revolved around bison, their behavior, where they might be found tomorrow or the next day, how to conduct an upcoming hunt, who would ride which pony during the hunt, who would have the distinction of leading the hunt, which individuals would actually participate in the hunt and carry out the surround. Teton males theorized about how best to approach the herds without frightening them away, how to police the village to maintain noise discipline once the hunters went forth, and what punishment would befall those who sought to hunt before the proper time. Teton men and boys talked about what part of the animal they would eat just after a kill and which tasty pieces they would eat later. They discussed how delicious those grilled marrowbones would taste tomorrow night and what a celebration they would have after the hunt came to an end, feasting, reliving the day's excitement, and dancing. Bison talk occupied much of a male's day during the summer months.

Teton men also discussed the land at their feet and the rivers flowing through it. For nomadic peoples, environmental and geographic knowledge was a prerequisite to survival. While traveling or in camp, Teton males constantly read their surroundings to learn their composition. The Teton and all the other tribes of the Upper Missouri needed to know the environment to decipher where the bison might be located during the hunt, where they might find water on the next day's route of travel, or where they would encounter their enemies. Indians could not afford to ignore their locale. They knew place out of necessity.

The names of the conversationalists indicated their link to the bison world. The Teton possessed descriptive names that tied them closely to the natural world and its inhabitants. The most commonplace names united Teton males with bison bulls and their observed characteristics. Popular names included One Bull, Standing Bull, Running Bull, Slow Bull, Lame Bull, Black Bull, Jumping Bull, White Bull, Mad Bull, Bad Bull, and the revered Sitting Bull (fig. 3.2). Naming individuals after bison bulls indicated

Figure 3.2. One Bull, Teton Sioux. The Teton Sioux, like all the tribes of the
Upper Missouri, identified strongly with their environment and its most notable
mammal, the bison. Personal names symbolized the connection between
humans and the bison world. Teton Sioux males often received names that
attached their personal identity to the bison bull. One Bull is an example of the
linkage between nomad and mammal. (Courtesy of the W. H. Over Museum,
Vermillion, South Dakota)

the import of this animal to Teton society. Naming an individual after an
animal also points to a high level of intimacy and identification with the natural world. For a person to associate himself with a "sitting bull" is to take on
the traits of that creature, to immerse oneself in another being's world, and
in the case of Sitting Bull, to become resolute in the face of danger.

Names linked the Teton Sioux to the environment. In contemporary
American society, significant numbers of females continue to take the last
name of their spouse. This is a form of enmeshment, seeking oneness with
another entity through naming. Additionally, many Americans today receive
a Christian first name; this is a sign that Christianity continues to play an
important role in society. Modern Euro-American names do not have the

environmental connotations once affiliated with Teton names. In many ways, contemporary American society, through its personal naming, displays its mass, anonymous character. That a person's Social Security number is increasingly as important as his or her name points to the state of society. Americans live in an ever more abstract world, a world of numbers and computers, often cut off from any perceived environment or animals. On the other hand, in the nineteenth century, the Teton so personalized their ties to bison that they readily named themselves after the creature.

The Teton did not just hunt bison. Referring to them as merely bison hunters is to either ignore or devalue all the other connections between nomad and mammal. In the early and middle nineteenth century, bison pervaded Teton culture and the Teton paradigm. The Teton not only hunted bison; they lived bison 365 days a year. A Teton Sioux recognized the world as ordered and sensible because he or she understood bison. Until at least the 1850s, the majority of the Teton could not comprehend or imagine living in a world without bison. War, peace, wealth, poverty, travel, technologies, tools, clothing, diet, village sites, and religion all reflected this one animal. Removing bison from the lives of the Teton meant social, political, and economic disintegration—it meant the end of the world. To a Teton, a reality without bison made no sense, appeared bleak, hopeless, and nightmarish. A Teton without bison was no longer a Teton. Strip bison from their lives and they would lose their identity, their sense of self, their sense of connection to their surroundings. Every Teton understood this fact. Without bison, their names would change, their identities would be radically altered, they would find themselves living in another place.

Bison ruled Teton geography. Teton migratory patterns mirrored those of the bison. *Homo sapiens* and bison moved in sync. Trader Tabeau observed, "The cow [buffalo] leaving the banks of the Missouri at the first good weather, the wandering tribes leave also in order to follow her by wandering as she does. From then on up to August, only the people who till the soil are seen there [in the Missouri Valley]; for the others are not able to subsist as the cow is their only resource."[2]

From the late eighteenth century up to the middle of the nineteenth century, the migrations of Teton bands occupying what is today central South Dakota imitated the grand pulsation of the Upper Missouri system. The Teton along the middle Missouri Valley located their winter camps in the bottoms at the mouths of the White, Bad, and Cheyenne Rivers. These bands remained at the Missouri Valley camps from November until March, frequently moving north or south within the bottoms to avoid complete depletion of timber and grass in any one area.[3] Maximilian's observations add weight to the argument that Teton Sioux wintered in the Missouri River trench: "They, the Yanktonans, generally come to the Missouri in the winter, but at this season it was mere chance that we met with them."[4]

In April or as late as May, depending on the severity of the winter, the middle Missouri Teton followed the tail ends of the herds into the Missouri's tributaries and out onto the high plains. By June or early July, the Teton reached their outermost range, at the foot of the Black Hills, at the headwaters of the Powder or Tongue, or within the Coteau des Prairies and Upper Minnesota River Valley. They then turned back toward the Missouri, reaching it in time for the rutting season. They arrived at the Missouri with the herds. At the close of the rutting season in mid-September and the commencement of the fall rains, the bison, lured by a new cover of grass, left the Missouri once again. The Teton, ever the stalkers, followed them, trotting west or east for their annual fall hunt. Only in late October or early November, as the herds embraced the Missouri Valley in anticipation of winter, did the Teton come back to the mouths of the White, Bad, and Cheyenne Rivers or Okoboji, Medicine, and Crow Creeks.[5]

Some variation existed in this pattern. To cite an instance, some bands, which left the Missouri River trench in April, did not come back to the Missouri for the late summer bison rut, instead remaining far up on the headwaters of the Missouri's tributaries until the fall rains made it practical for their horses to cross a greening Upper Missouri territory. These bands might stay in the higher elevations all summer, gathering berries and tubers in the foothills of the Bighorns or the Black Hills. They might go back to the Missouri only after cold forced them down from on high.

Other variations in Teton migration patterns became apparent during drought years, when the Indians decided to hold close to the Missouri River trench or one of its principal tributaries for an entire year or longer, fearing to venture out to the highlands. During just the opposite scenario, in an exceedingly wet year, or series of moist years, the Teton bands might stay up along the tributaries year-round, feeding on the bison that remained there with them. Another notable exception to the standard migratory pattern became visible after the 1850s and through the 1870s. An increased U.S. military presence in the Upper Missouri prevented many Teton from returning to either the Upper Missouri main stem or the Yellowstone main stem during the winter months. Rather than hazard a confrontation with the heavily armed Euro-Americans down in the Missouri or Yellowstone River Valley, the Teton remained encamped up the tributaries of these two streams for the entire year. The drainage system of the Upper Missouri territory determined Teton movements. If bison saturated the Teton paradigm, the Indians viewed those bison through the contours of drainage basins. The Teton determined summer and winter campsites by drainage, following the routes of flowing water and bison hooves. The world of the Teton was a world of bison and erosion lines.

Migration and seasonal use of the bottoms may have actually aided biological diversity. Human occupancy of the bottoms for short, intense periods possibly acted as an ecological disturbance. *Homo sapiens* compacted soils, inadvertently planted seeds, cleared old timber for new growth, denuded some grasses to entice others, preyed on mammalian species, netted birds, and harvested a variety of plants. All these actions could have potentially enhanced the habitat mosaic and biological diversity in the bottoms. The incredible degree of biological diversity within the Missouri Valley prior to Euro-American settlement lends legitimacy to the argument that nomadism and biological diversity maintained one another in a symbiotic relationship. Even the semisedentary tribes such as the Mandan, Hidatsa, and Arikara did not permanently reside in villages on the Missouri. Rather, they had winter camps, summer camps, and hunting camps. They, like the Teton, moved with the seasons. These movements did not necessarily overtax the bottoms. The evident sustainability of this nomadic pattern is illustrated in the Mandan presence along the Missouri. The Mandan had resided in camps along the Missouri since at least A.D. 900. Undoubtedly, they had successfully worked out a social, economic, and geographic order that enabled them to remain on the Missouri for close to one thousand years. They found a balance in relation to the bottoms. It appears that human movement represented the key to that balance. A permanent human presence in the bottoms had the reverse effect on ecology. Sedentary human occupancy led to the elimination of multiple habitat types, the eventual establishment of a single dominant habitat, and decreases in biological diversity.[6]

Bison influenced Teton geography in other important ways. Teton Indians lived within a fast-paced and amazingly mobile geography. Consider tepees. Up to fourteen sheared bison robes, sewn together and draped over leaning lodge poles, formed the primary mode of shelter for the Teton and the other plains tribes. The tepee represented an ideal domicile for equestrian nomads. Lightweight, of simple design, and quickly raised or dissembled (Edwin Denig claimed that Crow women could take down tepees and have all camp equipage packed and ready to go in less than twenty minutes), the tepee symbolized the exceptionally high degree of mobility within the bison world of the Upper Missouri.[7] To add to the mobility and speed of Indian peoples, the lodge poles, when not stacked for tent supports, served as the beams for the travois. The Teton hoisted the poles of the travois upon the shoulders of their dogs or horses, placed a taut bison robe atop the two poles, and then placed their luggage on top of that. The burdened dog or horse dragged the travois and its accumulated paraphernalia across the countryside.

Bullboats also played a significant role in Teton geography (fig. 3.3). The Teton relied on the readily available supply of bison to construct the highly maneuverable watercraft. A bison robe, soaked in water and heavy with absorbed moisture, would be placed around a woven, widemouthed basket of saplings. After a day or two in the scorching summer sun, the robe shrank around the perimeter of the bowed branches. Once dry and rock hard, the

Figure 3.3. Bullboat. The Indians of the Upper Missouri quickly constructed the simply designed bullboat for river navigation. The bullboat enhanced Indian mobility in the fast-paced world of the Upper Missouri. (Courtesy of the W. H. Over Museum, Vermillion, South Dakota)

bison robe, wrapped around its wooden frame, formed a boat of simple design and construction. The Teton, and all the tribes of the Upper Missouri,
used bullboats to ferry themselves across streams too deep to ford. Bullboats
represented a vital component of Indian transportation, aiding rapid cross-
country movement, especially in the spring and early summer when so many
of the Upper Missouri's rivers flowed at bank full or flood stage, keeping humans and horses from wading across their deep currents. Indians throughout the Upper Missouri built these boats to gain a river crossing; once across,
they left the boats at the ford for the next traveler or for their return trip.
Brackenridge, at the mouth of the Cheyenne River, recounted "forty or fifty
skin canoes, which had been left by some war party which had crossed
here."[8] If the Indians decided to hold on to the boat, its light weight did not
slow them down in the least. The boat, and its quick and easy construction,
fit nicely into Teton nomadism. The boat could be completed in a few hours,
used for a crossing, and then discarded on the far bank—abandoned to rot.
It required so little work that it did not slow the Teton in their occasionally
harried movements. Additionally, if the Teton needed to ditch the boat, they
forfeited very few labor hours. From any perspective, the bullboat represented an ideal blend of Indian ingenuity, bison ecology, and rapid movement.

Bison abetted Indian geography and mobility in so many ways—tepees
and bullboats being the most prominent. Yet bison also aided Teton travel by
providing what today's blitzkrieg U.S. Army calls "meal, ready to eat." Jerked
or sun-dried bison meat served as travel food—pure protein and energy.
Dried bison, occasionally mixed with pounded fruit to form pemmican, sustained human health. Jerked meat served the nomad perfectly: the food
packed tight, it did not spoil easily, and it concentrated protein into small
bundles. The Indians required lots of protein to keep their muscles on the
move. Another travel ration consisted of jerked bison preserved in bison lard.
Teton culinary experts placed dried bison meat inside a leather bag or a
cleansed bison stomach, then poured the grease from fried bison fat into the
bag. After the concoction cooled, the grease solidified around the jerked
meat, preserving it from spoilage. Apparently, this fatty lump kept for years.
A person could eat the mixture raw or toss the whole thing into a pot, let it
boil, and then gobble up the greasy mess. Several Euro-American fur traders
partook of this food while working in the Upper Missouri. None of them
wrote of it with relish. As a matter of fact, one writer remembered finding
gobs of bison hair packed in with the lard and jerked beef. Unable to separate

the hair from the lard, he ate the whole thing, swallowing hard on each blubbery fur ball.

Bison facilitated Indian and Euro-American movements by their overwhelming presence along the main routes of travel. Indians, and later Euro-Americans, readily killed bison while on the move and then feasted on everything from entrails to tongue. Maximilian in 1833 recollected that during his voyage from Fort Union to Fort McKenzie, "We had happily accomplished the voyage from Fort Union in thirty-four days, had lost none of our people, and subsisted during the whole time by the produce of the chase."[9] While floating up the wide Missouri, Brackenridge remembered well a banquet he partook of that consisted exclusively of bison meat: "Of all the animals given to satiate our carnivorous appetites, none can afford such a feast as the buffaloe. The hump is a delicious morsel; the tongue, the marrow, the tender loin, and the ribs are all excellent."[10]

Since bison numbers stood so high in the early nineteenth century all across the Upper Missouri, Indians never wandered far from the herds. They found meat on the hoof, which became meat "next to the fire." Indians, walking or riding along the main bison roads, could often secure meat at their convenience. In this way bison contributed to Indian geography and the dazzling mobility of the equestrian nomads of the Upper Missouri. Bison bestowed on Indian geography and mobility the material (leather and sinew) for the construction of light and tough storage containers (parfleches), saddles, dogsleds, snowshoes, and backpacks (fig. 3.4). Additionally, bison dung (not the soft, warm, straight-out-of-the-body kind but the old, brittle, been-on-the-ground-a-few-weeks kind) warmed food and bodies when wood could not be found. Bradbury recognized the efficacy of dung as a fuel while traversing the plains. He observed north of the Heart River, "At about half the distance across the plain we reached a small pond, where we halted, and having collected a sufficient quantity of dry buffaloe's dung, we made a fire."[11]

Bison, because of their supreme import to all facets of Indian life, played a major role in indigenous religious rites and spiritual beliefs (figs. 3.5 and 3.6). The Teton made few distinctions between themselves, bison, and the spirit realm—all moved as one. Other tribes, such as the Assiniboine, Mandan, Crow, Hidatsa, and Arikara, did the same. Bison robes, skulls, or symbols found their way into nearly every Upper Missouri tribe's religious ceremonies. The Teton's greatest religious rite, equivalent to Christianity's Easter, occurred each year in mid-June at the peak of the Upper Missouri's

Figure 3.4. Dogsled. Indians and Euro-Americans alike used bison robes to construct lightweight, durable dogsleds. In the early nineteenth century, dogsleds found widespread use on the smooth, frozen surface of the Upper Missouri main stem from December through February. Dogsled transportation abetted Indian and Euro-American mobility during the otherwise sluggish winter months. The contraption also furthered the harried character of the region's geography. (Courtesy of the W. H. Over Museum, Vermillion, South Dakota)

outward burst of energy. When life reached its zenith with the summer solstice, the Teton celebrated the Sun Dance, incidentally a ceremony of renewal and rebirth. During the Sun Dance, participants prayed and fasted for days. Oglala Teton engaged in sacred forms of self-flagellation. Prayers of thanksgiving and hope went out from large encampments, thanking spirits for bison abundance or pleading for an end to bison scarcity. Young men danced in circles around the sacred tree, seeking visions to guide their uncertain lives in a doubtful world. Oglala dancers pierced flesh with claws or notched bones, which were joined by thin leather strips to a bison skull lying on the bare earth. Dancers then jumped and plodded around and around the tree of life, dragging the skull or skulls behind their sweating bodies, suffering until the weight and tow of the skull yanked a slice of flesh from their backs, arms, or lower torsos. The fortunate gained a vision of their future;

Figure 3.5. Teton Sioux burial scaffold. Bison served a central role in Teton Sioux religion and spirituality. Here two bison skulls lie on top of the body of a deceased Teton Sioux. (Courtesy of the W. H. Over Museum, Vermillion, South Dakota)

the unfortunate or pious pierced their bodies over and over until they, too, gained a vision or met their self-imposed threshold for pain.

Bison skulls and robes appeared in other ceremonies, including the well-known sweat lodge ceremony, known to the Teton as Inipi. The sweat lodge ceremony is the oldest and most widely practiced of all religious ceremonies in the world, engaged in by indigenous peoples on every continent for thousands of years for both hygienic and spiritual reasons. The Teton participated in Inipi to cleanse themselves both physically and spiritually. They also entered the sweat lodge to pray, strengthen their personal values, and more clearly see the role of intent in their lives. The wonder of Inipi is its personal character. Each participant decides for him- or herself the significance of the ceremony and what he or she hopes to contribute to the act of sweating and praying. Inipi also involves personal and community hope and gain.

The Teton built the lodge itself, or the house of prayer, by burying one

Figure 3.6. Cheyenne medicine lodge. The most sacred
of tepees in a camp circle, the medicine lodge, is shown
here with a bison skull painted on its side. The image is
another example of the import of bison to Indian
spirituality. (Courtesy of the W. H. Over Museum,
Vermillion, South Dakota)

end of a sapling in the earth and then bending the sapling over and placing
its other end in the ground. Dozens of branches bowed one over another
formed a round frame upon which the Teton heaped bison robes, which
blocked out light and held in heat and moist air. In the center of the lodge
the participants dug a hole for the placement of hot stones. Outside the
lodge, flag poles, placed at the four directions, each held a small flag of either
white, black, red, or yellow. A bison skull lay just beyond the entrance to the
lodge. After the Teton heated stones (collected from the beneficent stone
people), they placed them inside the lodge, entered the structure, shut the
entrance, and engaged in the ceremony. After repeatedly dousing the stones
with water and praying and smoking, the participants left the womb of the

lodge and reentered their former physical reality. The first item seen upon exiting the lodge would be the bison skull to their front. That skull grounded the Teton to place, reminding them of where they were and who they were as individuals and as a people. That skull proclaimed their presence in the bison world; it quickly pulled them back to the grassland.

All Upper Missouri tribes conducted ceremonies to bring bison closer to their encampments to alleviate hunger and hardship. Maximilian recalled at Fort Clark, "It being reported that herds of buffaloes were at no great distance, a party of Indians resolved to give them chase on the following day, and to implore the blessing of heaven upon their undertaking by a great medicine feast."[12] Chardon, also at Fort Clark, either became a convert to the power of Mandan religious ceremonies or his dour journal actually contains a bit of sarcasm. He postulated on March 8, 1837, "Yesterday and to day are the two Coldest days, that we have had since last January, I expect that it is the Medicine that they are Making at the Village to Make Buffaloe approach."[13] The Mandan carried out a unique dance labeled by Euro-Americans the Buffalo Dance, which involved a fertility rite to bring the bison close to their village.[14] The Mandan also possessed a society of warriors known as the Bison Bull Society. Membership in this group was reserved for only the bravest of men (fig. 3.7).

The tribes of the Upper Missouri country built shrines to the bison, placing them at strategic locales along bison roads, near river crossings, inside bottomlands, at the mouths of rivers, or where two roads crossed paths. The shrines displayed indigenous respect for bison. Additionally, they indicated an Indian desire to appease or placate bison to entice them toward their encampments. Maximilian and Karl Bodmer, walking in the hills to the north of Fort Union, found a whole series of shrines erected for the bison, as recorded by Maximilian: "We observed on the highest points, and at certain intervals of this mountain chain, singular stone signals, set up by the Assiniboins, of blocks of granite, or other large stones, on the top of which is placed a buffalo skull, which we were told the Indians place there to attract the herds of buffaloes, and thereby to ensure a successful hunt."[15] Bodmer, so impressed with the sight, painted a depiction of one of these religious shrines (fig. 3.8). Henry Boller described a bison shrine he saw near Fort Berthold in the 1850s: "On the very summit were placed a couple of buffalo skulls, with pieces of scarlet cloth fastened around each horn. Two medicine poles were also set up with pieces of calico flying from them, gifts to propitiate the Great Spirit that he would send them plenty of buffaloes."[16] Bradbury

Figure 3.7. Bison Bull Society, Mandan. Only the
strongest, most courageous warriors joined the
Mandan Bison Bull Society. The society revered the
bison bull's vigor and steadfastness. Karl Bodmer
sketched this member of the society in full regalia in
1833. (Courtesy of the Joslyn Art Museum, Omaha,
Nebraska)

viewed one of the shrines near the Arikara villages and wrote: "Went early to
the bluffs to the south-westward of the [Arikara] town, on one of which I
observed fourteen buffalo skulls placed in a row. The cavities of the eyes and
the nostrils were filled with a species of artemisia [sage] common on the
prairies, which appears to be a nondescript. On my return, I told our interpreter to inquire into the reason of this, and learned that it was an honour
conferred by the Indians on the buffaloes which they had killed, in order to
appease their spirits, and prevent them from apprising the living buffaloes of
the danger they run in approaching the neighbourhood."[17]

Figure 3.8. Assiniboine bison altar near Fort Union, 1833. The Assiniboine and other tribes built altars to the bison at important choke points across the Upper Missouri. The shrines paid homage to the animal, appeased the bison spirits, and displayed Indian humility toward a world dominated by such a grand mammal. The Indians believed the tabernacles showed their deference to the bison, which in turn would attract the animals to the site and ease the rigors of the hunt. The shrines exhibited the presence of a spiritual geography in the Upper Missouri. (Courtesy of the Joslyn Art Museum, Omaha, Nebraska)

Brackenridge, in the summer of 1811, came on an old Teton encampment situated in a bottom on the Missouri's east bank, across from the mouth of the Cheyenne River. He remembered, "Our curiosity was attracted, by a space, about twenty feet in diameter, enclosed with poles, with a post in the middle, painted red, and at some distance, a buffaloe head raised upon a little mound of earth. We are told, this is a place where an incantation for rendering the buffaloe plenty, had been performed. Amongst other ceremonies, the pipe is presented to the head."[18] Maximilian described a similar piece of holy ground he saw at Fort Pierre in 1833: "Round an isolated tree in the prairie I observed a circle of holes in the ground, in which thick poles had stood. A number of buffalo skulls were piled up there; and we were told that this was a medicine, or charm, contrived by the Indians in order to entice the herds of buffaloes."[19] Hundreds of such shrines lay scattered across the Upper Missouri territory, temples to the bison gods and symbols of a spiritual geography.

One of the most remarkable memorials to Upper Missouri ecology lay near the mouth of the Poplar River. It embraced hundreds of elk, mule deer, and bison horns. Maximilian described this formation in 1833:

> The hunting or war parties of the Blackfoot Indians have gradually piled up a quantity of elk's horns till they have formed a pyramid sixteen to eighteen feet high, and twelve or fifteen feet in diameter. . . . All of these horns, of which there are certainly more than 1,000, are piled up, confusedly mixed together, and so wedged in, that we found some trouble in extricating, from the pyramid, a large one, with fourteen antlers, which we brought away with us. The horns are partly separated from the head of the animal with the skull, and partly single horns. Some buffaloes' horns were mixed with them. The purpose of this practice is said to be a medicine, or charm, by which they expect to be successful in hunting.[20]

Later, Euro-American visitors to the religious site disentangled the pile of horns, loaded them on keels, and sent them to St. Louis to be sold for knife handles and other ornaments (fig. 3.9).

From the time of Lewis and Clark until at least the 1960s, and even up to the twenty-first century, many Euro-Americans viewed the Sioux, especially the Teton, as warlike, savage, and the worst curs on the plains. Very early in the Sioux–Euro-American relationship, the Teton gained notoriety among Euro-Americans as being a fighting people, a tribe that reveled in war and killing. The modern historical consensus supports the conclusion that war played a pivotal role in Teton culture. Specifically, male advancement within the Teton sociopolitical order depended on achieving success on the battlefield. Along with this belief is a more subtle corollary idea, that the Teton possessed an innate predisposition toward war. In other words, these people liked to fight. They loved to go out onto the plains and beat others silly. Teton

Figure 3.9. Elk, deer, and bison antler altar, far Upper Missouri. Karl Bodmer and Prince Maximilian of Wied saw a large mound of antlers near the Missouri main stem in 1833. The stack of antlers represented another shrine to three of the region's prominent mammalian species. (Courtesy of the Joslyn Art Museum, Omaha, Nebraska)

males fought and killed as instinctively as bison rutted. No one understood exactly why; it just happened. Maybe they carried a combat gene, or their feistiness stemmed from their eating too much red meat. Whatever the cause, nature somehow preprogrammed the Teton to be the bad boys, and girls, on the plains. What is more, according to this theory, the Teton supposedly fought more frequently than other tribes. Granted, other tribes fought, but the Teton surpassed all tribes in the frequency and intensity of their wars.[21]

Euro-American literature is rife with accounts of the savagery of the Teton. The illustrious Thomas Jefferson feared Teton military strength. Meriwether Lewis, although educated to avoid gross generalizations or stereotypes, held a poor impression of the Teton before he even encountered his first Teton near the Bad River in September 1804. Jefferson and Lewis received their preexpedition impressions from French and Spanish traders who had met the Upper Missouri's most powerful tribe. Jefferson, Lewis, and even Clark placed the Teton into a steel trap of stereotypes. None of these men ever let the Teton out of that pigeonhole.

Lewis and Clark's nearly disastrous encounter with the Teton in September 1804 may have done more than any other event in early American history to firmly plant the impression of the Teton as savage and warlike within the Euro-American mind. After the confrontation at the mouth of the Bad, both Lewis and Clark wrote the Teton off as unredeemable thugs, forever on the dark side. When the expedition returned to the states in 1806 and approached the Bad River once more, Lewis, Clark, and all the men feared an encounter with the Teton. Clark wrote on August 26, 1806, "As we were now in the Country where we were informed the Sceoux were assembled we were much on our guard deturmined to put up with no insults from those bands of Seioux."[22] Below the White River, only four days later, Clark wrote again, "Imediately after 80 or 90 Indian men all armed with fusees & Bows & arrows Came out of a wood on the opposite bank about ¼ of a mile below us. they fired of their guns as a Salute we returned the Salute with 2 rounds. we were at a loss to deturmin of what nation those indians were. from their *hostile* appearance we were apprehensive they were Tetons."[23] Two years in the West, amid scenes of visionary enchantment, had not softened Lewis's or Clark's heart toward the Teton. The Teton would not receive forgiveness. Instead, the two explorers and their subordinates continued to loathe and fear them.

After the end of the expedition, Lewis and Clark, in their official capacities as governor of Louisiana Territory and Louisiana Territory's superintendent of Indian affairs, respectively, did much to promote the image of the Teton as warlike savages. These two men, whom the American people held in the highest esteem, utilized their institutional stature and public regard to promote the image of the Teton as brutes. In the years following the expedition, Meriwether Lewis and William Clark informed trappers, traders, military officers, government officials, common citizens, and foreign dignitaries of the decadent Teton and their wicked ways. In a period that lacked sophisticated communications, and when news literally traveled at a horse's pace, it is incredible how far afield went the word that the Teton loved war, hated Euro-Americans, and deserved a thorough thumping at the hands of white America. In a world as sparsely populated and personal as Louisiana Territory in 1807, a few prominent individuals, in this instance Lewis and Clark, could turn the public against an Indian people and lay the foundation of a stereotype that has not yet been debunked.

Consider what the Indian agent for the Upper Missouri Agency wrote in 1846 about the Teton: "The Teton alone are believed to have upwards of

5,000 lodges, averaging over ten souls to each lodge. A glance at the map will disclose the extent of the country. Their ceaseless wars, and fierce and treacherous character, have already been averted to."[24] Rudolph Friederich Kurz chipped in his two cents worth on the topic: "Without war an Indian is no longer an Indian. War is his means of educating himself. Success in war is his supreme aim in life. By nature imperious and full of energy, he finds in martial exploits his only chance to win distinction. In renouncing war he gives up his chief life purpose; he is forced to rearrange the plan of his whole existence."[25] He further elaborated, "The highest aim of an Indian brave is glory in war; accordingly there is perpetual hostility among the different tribes. His method of warfare is nothing more than a well-planned hunt; any sort of stratagem is permissible."[26] Army officer Gouverneur Warren commented, "Of all the aborigines in the Territory under consideration, the Dakotas [Teton] are probably the ones that have undergone the least material diminution of their numbers since their discovery by the whites. They are still numerous, independent, warlike, and powerful, and contain within themselves means of prolonged and able resistance to further encroachments of the western settlers."[27] Prince Wilhelm held one of the only contrary views of the Teton visible in the literature of the period. He asserted, "I had heard so many exaggerated reports regarding the Sioux. In St. Louis they were described as the wildest savages, who were the treacherous enemies of all whites and of all neighboring tribes. They were called the terror and the plague of the Upper Missouri. I was therefore very much surprised that this was not consistent with fact."[28]

Each time Euro-Americans engaged in combat with Teton warriors, the image of the Teton as belligerent barbarians received further reinforcement. In the 1850s and 1860s, the Teton fought a series of wars against the U.S. Army to protect their diminishing lands and vanishing herds. By the latter decade, the view of the Teton as lovers of war became a stalwart Euro-American perception. Custer's demise on the Little Bighorn sealed the stereotype and locked it firmly in the vault of American historical truths. Portraying the Teton as a mean-spirited martial people elevated the hero Custer. Not just any run-of-the-mill Indian people killed the beloved George Armstrong Custer; only the most overbearing Indians could kill such a man. White historians placed Custer on top of a pedestal of racial pride. From a military standpoint the Teton had to be placed alongside Custer to explain his horrendous defeat. In a sense, this interpretation of the Teton fostered the notion that America's indigenes outfought all other indigenous peoples in the world. America encompassed a great land- and waterscape and thus held the most magnificent savages the globe had ever seen. All this congealed under the umbrella of American exceptionalism, that favorite historical delusion and the bane of those who live outside the borders of the United States.

Questions about the Teton and war need answers. Did the Teton possess an innate propensity toward war? What drove them to war; or what variables propelled the Teton war machine into action? Did the Teton wage war more frequently and intensely than other tribes? Most important, for the purposes of this examination, how did Teton warfare relate to the Upper Missouri's bison ecology and geography?

The Teton did not possess an innate predisposition toward war. Yet many young Teton males actively sought combat. Military forays and horse-stealing raids bestowed laurels, respect, gratitude, and prestige upon the shoulders of a successful warrior. Young Teton males pursued the path of war for many of the same reasons young Euro-Americans did at that time. They craved the admiration of loved ones, the recognition of society, and the possibility that military prowess led to socioeconomic advancement. Boredom led to war, too. Nomadic life, with its routine of tearing down, packing up, and unpacking gear, became stupefying for vibrant, imaginative youth. The monotony of travel did not help the cause of peace either. Day after day on the trail, staring at the elusive horizon, eating the dust of those to their front, and thinking about another night inside the tepee pushed men to the edge of their wits. War offered an outlet, a gambler's obsession, a compulsion if you will, something to fill the dark spaces of the imploding mind, and a level of unmatched excitement.

War also lay deep in the roots of the grassland. The high plains environment did not always contribute to inquisitiveness, creativity, or compassion; it could foster just the opposite. Ignorance, parochialism, and an overcompensated arrogance often spewed from its depths. The Upper Missouri, with its eternal sun, rolling plains, sameness on all sides, and overbearing wind, frequently beat the Teton down, rather than raised them up. Distances induced a sense of smallness, insignificance, loneliness, and depression. War offered a quick reprieve from obscurity, a chance at greatness, an opportunity to fly above the plains on horseback, and an occasion to take back an identity subsumed by grass.

Not all Teton savored war. And not all Teton males needed war to overcome their perceived helplessness vis-à-vis the environment. Many Teton males discovered bison hunting as an adequate means of confronting and overcoming the grassland. Taking down a bison symbolized the Teton male's ability to force the plains to its knees. That bison lying on the ground, blood pouring from its mouth and nostrils and pooling around the edges of its slumped body, that body was grass—pure and simple. A certain satisfaction came over Teton males and females when they stood over the slain carcass of a bison. Butchering bison generated feelings of superiority, if only temporarily. When a Teton stuck his razor-sharp knife blade just below the animal's neck and ran it down to the bung hole before splitting the body wide open, he momentarily dominated the grassland, put it in its place, set it down beneath him. Hunting meant more than killing bison; it prevented the Teton from losing themselves on the plains.

Teton society placed the individual pursuit and killing of bison on a par with the display of bravery in battle. Everyone considered the bison hunt gravely serious (a matter of life and death). The hunt's import became apparent whenever a tribal member violated hunting protocol. A Teton who chased a herd prematurely or who scared it away suffered a severe chastisement at the hands of his cohorts. Repeat offenders faced the death penalty. The Teton beat or killed their own for poaching because this practice threatened everyone's life. Kurz remarked, "Woe be unto the man who, in overhaste, attacks inopportunely and upsets the plan; his horse will be shot dead from under him or his weapons will be broken in splinters."[29] While near the Knife River, Maximilian learned of the Mandan holding a white man for fear he would disrupt the bison hunt. The prince stated, "On the 2nd of February, one of the sledges sent to Picotte came back, having been broken on the way. The man who came with it fell in with the Mandans, who were going to hunt buffaloes, and detained him, lest he should frighten the animals away."[30]

If the Teton beat or even killed their own for spoiling a hunt, it takes no stretch of the imagination to understand why they would fight and kill members of another tribe who challenged their dominion over a bottomland and its herds. Edwin Denig remarked, "Not much blame can be attached to Indians who war against persons transgressing on their hunting ground."[31] Gouverneur Warren, after encountering a band of Teton near Harney Peak, on the edge of the Black Hills in 1857, displayed a high degree of awareness when he stated, "For us to have continued on then would have been an act for which certain death would have been inflicted on a like number of their own tribe had they done it; for we might have deflected the whole range of the buffalo fifty or one hundred miles to the west, and prevented the Indians from laying in their winter stock of provisions and skins, on which their comfort if not even their lives depended."[32]

The Indians did not always fight for revenge or honors. The Upper Missouri tribes, like their Euro-American counterparts, fought for strategic objectives. Kurz noted that the nomads possessed council tepees at each village site where men discussed geopolitics and strategy: "This [the assembly lodge] is the largest hut in the settlement and serves as meeting place for their deliberative assembly or council as well as for the soldiers' guardroom. There all important news is discussed and decisions arrived at concerning the chase, war, and wanderings."[33] Politics, and the odds of success or failure, affected all military decisions. Denig commented, "They [the Indians] seldom risk much to gain little. They do not fight grand battles merely from a thirst for blood."[34] Individual combat exploits served to advance geopolitical ends. Individuals did not fight randomly or without economic, political, or military considerations in mind. Young warriors going off on a horse-stealing raid, besides seeking to promote themselves in the eyes of their comrades, also promoted the general welfare of the tribe or band. Acquiring horses from an enemy weakened that enemy, while increasing the mobility, hunting efficiency, and military-strike capabilities of their own people.

Teton bands met to discuss long-term strategy in relation to their enemies. Each spring, often during the Sun Dance, political and military discussions among village elders centered around whom to fight in the coming summer months, when to launch attacks, and what objectives they hoped to achieve as a result. Author George E. Hyde mentions a council of all the Teton bands at Bear Butte in 1857. At this meeting, the affiliated Teton chiefs decided to resist any further Euro-American advance into the Powder River Country.[35] Brackenridge made a strong comparison between the Arikara strategic and political situation and that of any other nation-state: "We here see an independent nation, with all the interests and anxieties of the largest; how little would its history differ from that of one of the Grecian states. A war, a treaty, deputations sent and received, warlike excursions, national mourning or rejoicing, and a thousand other particulars, which constitute the chronicle of the most celebrated people."[36] Thus, the Teton and other Indian peoples of the Upper Missouri met regularly to discuss and decide on long-term geopolitical policy. They, like their Euro-American counterparts, weighed the pros and cons of peace and war.

Why did Euro-Americans view the Teton as so savage? For a whole host of reasons, all legitimate in their eyes. The poor reception received by Lewis and Clark, the occasional alignment of some Teton bands with the British out of Canada, and the fact that certain bands owned prime real estate wanted by the Euro-Americans engendered or reinforced negative stereotypes.

Still other factors contributed to this poor image. Throughout the nineteenth century, the Teton, rather than fleeing from American arms, resisted and often defeated American forces. Their battlefield victories did a great deal to stick the Teton with the savage label. Had the Euro-Americans quickly shoved them aside, the Teton may not have received the foremost savage cognomen. But since the Teton fought valiantly and effectively against the Euro-Americans, the Euro-Americans, wanting to inflate their tarnished self-image, elevated the Teton to the premier warriors on the continent. Labeling the Teton a warlike people, inducted into a military society from birth, allowed the U.S. Army to save face when its officers found themselves repeatedly having to explain their failures to superiors and the American public.

The Missouri River village tribes profoundly influenced Euro-American perceptions of the Teton. The village tribes, including the Hidatsa, Mandan, Arikara, Ponca, and Omaha, warred against the Teton at one time or another during the 1700s and 1800s. The combatants waged genocidal war. Eventually the village tribes, out of necessity, aligned themselves with the Euro-Americans to ward off the Teton and save themselves from extermination. Predictably, these peoples passed their strong anti-Teton biases on to their Euro-American allies. As early as the winter of 1804–1805, Lewis and Clark listened to the worst invective delivered by the Mandan against the Teton. Listening to those diatribes, Lewis and Clark, and the Euro-Americans who followed them up the Missouri to the Mandan villages, had little difficulty painting the Teton in the worst possible shades.

The Teton's nomadism did not win them friends among the Euro-Americans either. Euro-Americans liked horticulturists and despised nomads. Euro-Americans considered all Indian peoples as savages, but there existed degrees of savagery. Euro-Americans viewed Indians engaged in agriculture as noble savages, savages trying to emulate themselves and therefore worthy of some patronizing admiration. To the white race, Indian agriculturalists were potentially redeemable. Indian farmers might someday attain the benefits of civilization, since agriculture lay at the foundation of the great American nation. With agriculture and its sedentary requirements, the village tribes could more easily be assimilated into the larger Euro-American society. In other words, the Euro-Americans found it easier to relate to the semi-sedentary tribes because they both shared agriculture and village life. On the opposite end of the spectrum stood the nomads. Nomads were real savages. According to prevalent nineteenth-century thought, they remained hopelessly stuck in barbarism with their supposedly unpredictable hunter-gatherer life. Euro-Americans had difficulty relating to nomads. Nomadism presumably did not foster high culture, letters, science, the arts, or capitalism. Bradbury confirmed, "The belief in a future state seems to be general, as it extends even to the Nodowessies or Teton, who are the furthest removed from civilization, and who do not even cultivate the soil."[37]

Nomadism engendered harsh feelings from Euro-Americans for another crucial reason. The nomads, because of the requirements of their lifeways, interacted far less with the Euro-Americans than the tribes permanently settled on the Missouri River. Village tribes quickly learned the language and manners, as well as the likes and dislikes, of the Euro-Americans in their midst. Familiarity led to stronger trade ties and military alliances. Teton bands, out on the high plains for month after month, did not maintain long-term contacts with the Euro-Americans. Thus, Teton bands often did not know Euro-American customs and thereby had difficulty relating to them. Since the Euro-Americans interacted more with the river tribes, knew them better than the nomads, and felt comfortable in their camp circles, it is not surprising that they developed more amicable relations with those who were physically closer to them while remaining suspicious or openly hostile toward those at a distance.

Since the first English attempts to establish colonies in North America in the 1580s until the modern era, Euro-Americans expected Indian peoples to show deference. Euro-Americans believed their perceived superiority demanded respect from those they considered culturally, intellectually, and spiritually inferior. Indian reverence in turn reinforced the Euro-American sense of supremacy. Frequently, whites required Indians to show them esteem as a precursor to trade, negotiations, or peace. From the Euro-American viewpoint, good Indians showed them deference, while bad Indians did not. One U.S. Army officer recounted, "I was very favorably impressed by the dignified, *quiet manner* of this [Crow] chief. His whole deportment was so in contrast with the bluster of the Teton orators we met at Fort Pierre that it was remarked by all. The Teton were loud and rapid talkers, gesticulating most vehemently."[38] Ironically, the Teton believed they, too, deserved respect from other peoples. The masters of a domain that reached from the Minnesota River to the Missouri and on to the Black Hills, the Teton (like their Euro-American counterparts) demanded and received obsequiousness from the Indian peoples and European traders of the Upper Missouri. The Teton recognized their own power. For this reason, they did not flatter Euro-Americans. Instead, they wanted the Euro-Americans to bow to their perceived strength. And why shouldn't they? In the first decades of the nineteenth century, the Teton met only a handful of Euro-American explorers, traders, or trappers at a time. Not until the mid-1850s did they face the military power of the United States. Thus, for decades, the Teton conceivably could not believe that Euro-Americans possessed great might. In the Teton mind, a few Euro-Americans, standing on Teton territory, in the middle of hundreds (if not thousands) of warriors, should pay respect to the Teton. Why should it be the other way around? For the Teton to show obedience or great humility toward a small, weak, and vulnerable group such as the Lewis and Clark expedition would have been considered ludicrous. A lack of respect from the Teton toward Euro-Americans only strengthened the stereotype of the Teton as militant.

The fact that Indian peoples, including the Teton, fought in close proximity to Euro-American trading establishments did a great deal to foster the image among Euro-Americans that Indians, especially the Teton, reveled in war. Euro-Americans saw Indians fighting literally at their doorstep. That bloodshed contributed mightily to the idea of Indians as murdering savages. Additionally, since the Teton fought frequently at or near the Missouri River and Yellowstone River posts, Euro-Americans convinced themselves that the Teton represented the most warlike of all Upper Missouri tribes. In another great irony, Euro-Americans did not always recognize how their posts and trade items contributed to war on the Upper Missouri.

Euro-American traders established their posts in key ecological zones, the rich bottoms along the Missouri or Yellowstone main stems. The mere existence of these posts disrupted mammalian migration patterns. Perturbations of the bison migration pattern meant hardship for Indian peoples. When the bison did not show up on schedule at their allotted places of residence, Indians responded by changing their own migratory patterns. Any change in Indian movements increased the likelihood of war, since each new route of travel might throw one tribe or band into another.

Indian peoples wanted exclusive trading connections with Euro-Americans. All tribes wanted that privilege. Bradbury encountered a Teton chief near the Big Bend who "commenced by stating that they were at war with the Ricaras, Mandans, and Gros Ventres or Minaterees, and that it would be an injury to them if these nations were furnished with arms and ammunition."[39] Most often, Indian tribes sought a trading post deep within their own territory, far removed from the reach of their enemies. For Indians, gaining a post inside their own boundaries guaranteed against conflict with other peoples. They could travel to and from the posts without fear of attack. Yet the Euro-Americans did not want to establish posts within the domain of a single tribe because one tribe, with singular access to the post, could charge more for their peltries, and thereby squeeze the wealth out of the Euro-Americans. For the Euro-Americans, a post located in a contested or neutral zone served to generate competition among the tribes, which meant that they received a higher price for their products. In other words, no one tribe dominated the trade. Thus, in these contested slices of territory, a Euro-American post meant each tribe possessed less bargaining power, since any other tribe might undercut their bargaining offer in subsequent negotiations. A divide-and-conquer strategy served Euro-Americans well on the Upper Missouri.

Euro-Americans resisted the desire to establish tribal posts and instead sought intertribal posts, such as Fort Union at the Missouri-Yellowstone confluence. Advantageous to the Euro-Americans, intertribal posts spelled disaster for Indians. Forced to trade on Euro-American terms, Indian peoples gravitated to these forts, where they frequently found their foes. For instance, when Crow traders arrived at Fort Union, they often found Blackfeet Indians there at the same time. Mortal enemies, the Crow and the Blackfeet actually fought beneath the gates of Fort Union. Maximilian, who provides insight into how Euro-American trading posts fostered Indian warfare, wrote the following lines at the post at Bellevue: "It was near this place that a marauding party of twelve Ioways lately crossed the river, and pursued a defenceless company of Omahas, who had just left Belle Vue; and, having overtaken them three miles off, killed and plundered all of them, except some who were desperately wounded, and whom they believed to be dead."[40]

On the Missouri, the Teton traded at Fort Union, Fort Berthold, Fort Clark, and Fort Pierre, forts also utilized by their enemies the Mandan, Hidatsa, and Arikara. When Teton warriors approached Fort Clark, near the Mandan villages, combat often ensued between the two peoples. Francis Chardon witnessed numerous instances of war between the Teton and Mandan. Predictably, Chardon considered both peoples tepee trash, unaware of or unconcerned how his very presence contributed to their fighting. Euro-American trading posts spurred Indian conflict by concentrating Indian people. The resulting combat bolstered the Euro-American perception that Indians practiced incessant warfare. Denig summarized how forts contributed to Indian warfare: "For the fort built in their country has been the theater of more war and bloodshed both of Whites and Indians than any other spot occupied by the fur traders." Denig again: "The Sioux on the one hand, and the Blackfeet on the other, constantly in search of Crow Indians who are supposed to be near the fort [Fort Sarpy], make this place the center of their operations."[41] Kurz remembered the danger present just outside the walls of Fort Union. He remarked while approaching the fort, "The region we were traveling through was very dangerous ground; Blackfeet were said to be often roaming stealthily about, lying in wait for Assiniboin who passed this way constantly, one by one, as they went back and forth between the forts and their various settlements. We had to make haste."[42]

Trading posts affected Indian warfare in another important respect. The most intense periods of trade occurred in the spring (during March and April) and again in the fall (during September and October). Trade virtually ceased during the winter months because of the dangers inherent in traveling over the plains at that time. Trade also slowed down in the summer because animal peltries remained thin and the tribes departed the big rivers for the interior and the summer hunt. Since all tribes adhered to a spring and fall trading schedule, everyone showed up at the posts at the same time. Tribes knew when and where to find their enemies. As a result, Indian peoples hovered around the posts in March, April, September, and October, waiting for their enemies to appear. The Teton lurked outside of Fort Union, hoping to hit the Crow. The Blackfeet, also hoping to kill some Crow, hovered around Fort Cass or Fort Van Buren on the Yellowstone. And so it went all over the Upper Missouri.[43] Bloodshed begat further bloodshed.

Trading posts made Indian warfare more predictable, easing the previously troublesome task of locating an enemy over thousands of square miles of turf. Edwin Denig, with an air of disgust, mentioned the Arikara practice of stalking an enemy just outside the gates of Fort Union. With exasperation he wrote, "The height of their [the Arikara] ambition at war is to visit the mouth of the Yellowstone once a year or so and kill some stray inoffensive woman."[44] Furthermore, Indians patrolled outside of the posts to prevent their enemy from trading there at all. Teton warriors fought to turn back enemy tribes from Fort Union, Fort Clark, and Fort Pierre or the smaller, satellite posts across the Upper Missouri. Preventing an enemy from acquiring muskets, balls, and powder diminished their military strength, while enhancing one's own security. Once more, the Euro-Americans viewed these patrols as indications of Indian militarism, rather than a necessity. Euro-Americans also despised these practices (which curtailed the trade) because they impinged upon their profit margins. The fewer tribes reaching the post, the less competition among the Indians, and the higher the prices the Euro-Americans would be forced to pay. Euro-Americans wanted to trade with all tribes, while the Indians sought to limit that trade. Indian and Euro-American trading interests rarely coincided on the Upper Missouri.[45]

Finally, Euro-American traders downplayed, ignored, or remained utterly oblivious to the emotions Indians attached to the trade. Indians required muskets, balls, and powder above all else. Bradbury wrote, "The species of goods most in demand were carbines, powder, ball, tomahawks, knives &c."[46] They needed those materials to survive: to fight and hunt. Trade meant life or death. Bradbury, who understood the connection between trade and Indian survival, stated, "Expecting that on our arrival at the Aricara Town they should obtain a supply of fire arms and ammunition, which would give them a superiority over their enemies."[47] Maximilian described much the same scene at Fort McKenzie: "On our return to the fort, the trade had been resumed, and was going on very briskly; it gave occasion to many droll scenes; pleasure and discontent were expressed in many different ways. Many Indians were quite affectionate, and embraced the Whites; others were noisy and angry."[48] The stakes involved in trading were incredibly high for Indian peoples. What made matters worse for the Indians, and only fueled the flames of emotion, was that they understood that the Euro-Americans had only a limited amount of muskets, balls, and powder to trade each year. Even more frightening, Euro-Americans would trade those items to the highest bidder. Once the supply had been sold, that was it; the trade ended. Some Indians invariably went without. If you failed in the trade, you might die at the hands of your enemy who received those items. Needless to say, Indians became highly emotional during trade negotiations. Their lives were on the line. Indians commonly expressed a frantic exasperation, anger, and downright hostility toward Euro-American traders who lacked tact, compassion, or understanding of their difficult circumstances. Euro-Americans might push for outrageously high prices, insensible to the feelings and needs of the Indians. The disparity in how Indians and Euro-

Americans viewed the trade, with one seeing it as a money issue and the other as a life-and-death issue, combined with their different sociopolitical conditions, contributed to a great deal of misunderstanding. Henry Boller at Fort Berthold in 1858 witnessed the hysteria that might overcome Indians during the trade. He commented, "For the next three hours we had a lively time. Powder, balls, knives, looking glasses, hawk-bells, brass tacks, vermilion, awls, and other trifles were in demand, and when we stopped trading, having obtained as much meat as the wagon could transport, the pressure became very great, the squaws fearing that our stock of goods would become exhausted before all were supplied. Many of the women were exceedingly angry."[49]

Although firmly planted in the Upper Missouri, Euro-American traders occupied a different place perceptually. Euro-Americans interpreted Indian emotionalism during trade talks as proof of their uncouth character, their aggressiveness, and their unfamiliarity with civilized decorum. An Indian obsession with guns convinced Euro-Americans of Indian militarism. At the conclusion of trading, if the Indians got the goods, they held a dance. Successful indigenous traders had good reason to celebrate; they now possessed the necessary items to survive in the Upper Missouri. These celebrations marked an emotional release. Pent-up feelings of fear, anxiety, confusion, and doubt, which welled up during the trade talks, could finally be jettisoned. To Euro-Americans, the festivities, which occasionally turned into drunken melees, served as an additional reminder of the decadent Indian character. Simply put, everything associated with the trade (the discourse, the actual exchange, and the subsequent celebration) generated in the minds of Euro-Americans an image of the Indian as immoral, savage, and bellicose.

The trade influenced Indian gender relations, the militarization of Indian societies, and the Indian social order. Trade increased divisions within Indian societies by fostering disparities in individual wealth. Those Indian males with robes, as well as the women to work them, possessed more weaponry, blankets, horses, and other symbols of status than their colleagues. These wealthy males rose to become civil or military leaders. Additionally, females became increasingly relegated to the monotonous task of preparing bison robes for the trade. Consequently, their social status diminished to that of common laborers, with little influence in economic or military policy. The intensification of warfare stemming from the trade resulted in the militarization of many Indian societies. Militarization engendered hierarchy, which limited personal freedoms and democratic decision making. The trade increased the variety of material goods held by Indian peoples. Yet the acquisition of those goods came at very high social, economic, ecological, political, and military costs.[50] Capitalism did not come cheap to the tribes of the Upper Missouri.

The frequency and supposed meaningless character of Teton warfare engendered suspicions and animosities in the minds of Euro-Americans. It appears that very few Euro-Americans understood the ecological under-pinnings behind nomadic warfare. Indians in the Upper Missouri territory, and all across the plains, fought often and hard because they followed bison. Bison hunting, nomadism, and incessant warfare went hand in hand. The reason for this is astonishingly simple: bison did not stay put. Across the Upper Missouri, bison did not respect human territorial boundaries. The lumbering mammals trod from one drainage basin to the next, or from an overgrazed pasture to a virgin meadow. The Teton, or any tribe for that mat-ter, could not entirely control the movements of the animals, even though at times they tried to do just that. Indians did use fire to drive the animals in this or that direction. But attempts to direct bison had only a limited effect. Flames drove the animals off but did not guarantee their return in a day or two. Indian fire might frighten a herd from a valley bottom, but those ani-mals could conceivably reappear in that bottom the very next day. The plains tribes did not herd bison. Indigenes followed the herds rather than led them.

Since bison cut across the Upper Missouri unrestrained, every tribe in the region had to follow the herds. If any tribe put a limit on how far they would follow the herds, or if they honored a neighboring tribe's perceived border or territory, they might go without food as soon as the herds crossed over into the other tribe's domain. The Teton considered any impingement on their ability to move to be incomprehensible, unrealistic, or outlandish. To halt at an adjacent tribe's border meant the herds could potentially elude their grasp. Such an outcome could conceivably doom the Teton to want, hunger, and death. It is clear that all Indians experienced hunger when the bison did not show up. Maximilian made this assertion: "The Indians them-selves frequently suffer hunger, and their dogs, of course suffer still more." Tabeau noted, "If the hunt is a resource so general for the wandering na-tions, it is no less precarious and there are frequent instances of families and of entire tribes, which, notwithstanding their precaution of drying their meat against a shortage, have experienced horrible famine and sometimes died of hunger."[51] This ecological and geographic reality explains why many Teton, including Sitting Bull and Crazy Horse, adamantly opposed the establishment of fixed reservation boundaries in the 1850s, 1860s, and 1870s. Animals and ecology did not adhere to arbitrary Euro-American political boundaries. Within the Teton paradigm, reservation life (sedentary and restricted to sacrosanct borders) equaled poverty and starvation. Hard boundary lines meant an end to nomadism, the chase, and a way of life.

Following the herds, wherever they led, the Teton habitually clashed with warriors from neighboring tribes. Sadly, they could not avoid all of these encounters. The Upper Missouri was not so large and so full of bison that the various inhabitants did not come into regular, bitter contact. Bison followed established roads to and from the big rivers. The animals whiled away months in the well-known bottomland areas. Indian peoples, restricted to those same roads and camping in those same bottoms, inevitably bumped into each other, either along the roadways or down inside the valleys; combat ensued over control of bison trails and bottomland oases.[52] Some historians believe that buffer zones existed between various warring tribes. Bison supposedly found refuge in these buffers from the ravages of human conflict. Yet there is little evidence to support the existence of buffer zones within the Upper Missouri. Of the journals relied upon for this study, only Denig's account referred to the existence of such a buffer in the Yellowstone Valley, and that supposed safe zone disappeared as soon as the Teton Sioux took possession of the Lower Yellowstone Valley. From the mass of journalistic evidence, the Crow held no qualms about going into Blackfeet territory to wage war, the Sioux felt no compunction striking the Crow in their homeland, and the Mandan took every opportunity to pass into Sioux territory to kill or steal horses.[53]

Operating within an unstable ecological system, in which the bison supply never remained secure or guaranteed, the Teton and other nomadic tribes fought and died for access to bison roads and fecund ecological zones. Their future depended on that entrée. Luttig noted how conflicts erupted over bison: "Wednesday the 16th [December] at 1 in the Morning Garrow returned with the News that the Rees [Arikara] were willing to come if their critical situation with the Teton would allow it they had quarreled together and expected to fight a Battle to Day, the Teton wanted to force and go past the Rees, and camp higher and nearer to us, which the Rees opposed on Account of the Buffaloes."[54]

The ceaseless quest for access to the bison caused the Teton multiple dilemmas. For instance, if two enemy tribes sought the same sanctuary, only one tribe could acquire it. Tribes could not share the resource with anyone else or abandon it without a fight. To abandon a game-rich bottom to another tribe might be catastrophic. The evacuating tribe might not find bison anywhere else. Uncertainty stalked the Upper Missouri's ecology. Leaving game to someone else entailed greater risks than fighting for that game. Tribes that went without bison experienced a shortage of food. Denig wrote, "It also sometimes happens that from an entire disappearance of these animals they [the Assiniboines] are distressed by actual famine."[55] Chardon wrote on January 3, 1836, "The Sioux all moveing up from below—complain of being in a Starving condition."[56] Hunger among Indians could become so intense that they had to resort to eating rawhide. According to Prince Wilhelm, "The lack of food is at times so great among the Indians that they consume things that would seem very unwholesome for human beings. They often eat tanned or dried skins, grasshoppers, the bark of trees and all sorts of roots."[57] The Teton could not share their bottomlands, since they never knew how many bison or other game animals they would kill. If they shared the resource, there might not be enough meat to go around. Teton, and all other tribes in the region, preferred warfare and the ejection of the enemy from rich hunting grounds instead of compromise. Compromise with another tribe carried with it too much uncertainty.

Additionally, the Teton could not negotiate a permanent peace with any other tribe or with the Euro-Americans without abandoning their lifeway—an unthinkable prospect for most Teton until the 1850s and 1860s. Edwin Denig attempted to explain why the Teton fought so frequently. Denig did not grasp the ecological foundations of warfare across the Upper Missouri, although he did allude to the impossibility of establishing an enduring peace in the region. He alleged, "It is hardly possible for the Sioux nation to preserve peaceful relations for any length of time with any of the neighboring tribes. They are too numerous, warlike, treacherous, widely separated, differently ruled and advised, and only accede to peace proposals when the advantage is all on their side and felt by every individual."[58] With a bison population that fluctuated from year to year and moved at will, there could not be lasting peace because there could be no permanent boundaries. In an ironic twist of fate, Teton believed firm boundaries led to economic and cultural insecurity. Any curtailment of their movements harmed their future; and yet, unrestrained nomadism led to constant war, which also dimmed their future. On the stage of bison ecology, Indian actors danced an epic tragedy.[59]

Intertribal warfare increased markedly during drought years, years in which predation or disease decimated bison numbers, and, after the 1830s, when bison numbers went into an irreversible decline. A dry climate forced the Upper Missouri's ecology to shrink, leading to the congregation of bison in a few tight spaces. Indians went to those havens, and there they found their enemies, seeking sustenance from the same oases. Desperate to survive, and knowing the risk the other tribe posed to that survival, Indians fought for these pockets of fertility in an arid land. Denig noticed that war broke out during periods of scarcity: "When the Sioux have failed in their hunt, are not well provided with skins, and are suffering for provisions—and at the same time the Rees have a good crop of corn, the latter are obliged to give considerable quantities to preserve peaceful relations. It is at such times that disturbances happen. The Sioux are numerous, starving and consequently in bad humor."[60] Denig postulated that the historic decline of the herds led to warfare: "In proportion as buffalo recede from the Sioux country, that people are forced to follow them and being numerous must displace weaker tribes to provide for their own subsistence. Every year the battles between the Sioux and the Assiniboines become more frequent."[61] He continued, "But of later years the Sioux have become more formidable than they formerly were. It is believed that the great diminution of buffalo in the Sioux country will compel that nation to seek subsistence farther west. The district watered by the last 100 miles of the Yellowstone River offers great inducement for a hunter population."[62] Denig's prediction of a Teton migration into the Lower Yellowstone Valley would come true with dire repercussions for the Crow Indians and Custer's Seventh Cavalry.

The capitalist market also propelled the Teton Sioux west against the Crow, Kiowa, Shoshone, and other Upper Missouri tribes. The Sioux killed their enemies, and bison, for the markets of Europe and the eastern United States. As Dan Flores and Andrew Isenberg attest, Indian hunting contributed to the destruction of the bison herds. The Teton Sioux sold bison to Europeans and Euro-Americans for guns, powder, balls, and dry goods to further their expansion west and to satiate their desires. But Indian hunting was only one variable among many that contributed to the decline of the herds. Geographic constructs and a growing human presence in the Missouri and Yellowstone Valleys contributed mightily to the extirpation of the bison.

Within the Sioux paradigm, expansion and survival were one and the same. Without expansion west, Sioux culture declined and the individual suffered physically and psychologically. Lacking expansion, the Teton Sioux lost bison, horses, weapons, identity, and hope. For the Teton Sioux to stop driving west and attempt to hold a line ensured cultural collapse. The Sioux pushed west because their enemies lay at their backs, namely, the Ojibway in Minnesota and later the Euro-Americans along the Missouri River. Not to expand west would lead to Sioux subjugation, if not actual slavery. The reality of the Indian slave trade and the fate of the eastern Indians under Euro-American authority affected Teton Sioux military actions in the trans-Mississippi West. In the early and middle nineteenth century, the Sioux drove on to the Bighorns and Absarokas, believing such aggression to be their only recourse. The Teton Sioux practiced imperialism in the name of self-defense. Euro-Americans expanded west for many of the same reasons. The need for survival, the attraction of resources, the fear of subjugation back east, and the desire to preserve identities launched Euro-Americans into the Upper Missouri. For Euro-Americans to stop and hold a firm boundary also meant a loss of independence, opportunity, hope, and identity. It was as frightening for a Teton Sioux to consider returning to Minnesota to face the oppression of the Ojibway as it was for an Irish-American in the trans-Mississippi West to think of returning to the eastern seaboard or Ireland to confront Anglo-American, entrepreneurial, feudal lords. The Teton Sioux and Euro-Americans had at least this much in common—the perceived necessity of expanding west to acquire freedom.

Bison migration patterns, Indian nomadism, fluctuations in the Upper Missouri ecosystem, and the market economy operated in concert to spawn intense and frequent wars between Indian peoples. The Teton were not inherently predisposed toward warfare, yet their choice of lifeway (nomadic bison hunting) led to perpetual war. Following bison led to the warpath. Rather than see Indian warfare as largely a response to ecology, Euro-Americans saw it as a human character flaw. It was hard for Euro-Americans not to believe that the Teton controlled their destiny. Yet, within the parameters of the Upper Missouri ecosystem, the Teton and other tribes often had no other choice but war. If they chose boundaries and peace, they would die of starvation or be enslaved by their nomadic or sedentary neighbors. Thus, the seemingly warlike propensities of the Upper Missouri's Indian inhabitants, particularly the Teton, convinced successive generations of Euro-Americans that the region and its peoples should be incorporated into the American empire. To nineteenth-century Euro-Americans, the apparently aggressive, uncivilized, and immoral disposition of the Upper Missouri's Indians provided an ideal justification for the Euro-American conquest of the territory. Supposedly peace-loving, moral Euro-Americans belonged on the land, not unrefined equestrian nomads or semicivilized sedentary tribes. Henry Brackenridge believed the Upper Missouri deserved to be under Euro-American control when he wrote, "Mr. Bradbury had been an enthusiast, as most philanthropic Europeans are, on the subject of Indian manners, and I was myself not a little inclined to the same way of thinking, but now both agreed that the world would lose but little, if these people should disappear before civilized communities. In these vast plains, throughout which are scattered so many lovely spots, capable of supporting thousands such nations as the Arikara, or wandering Teton, a few wretches are constantly roaming abroad, seeking to destroy each other."[63] To Brackenridge, and the bulk of the Euro-American race at the time, the Upper Missouri should be a Euro-American territory of farms, fields, and towns, not bison and Indians. This assumption remains the foundation of the Euro-American position across the Upper Missouri.

At the commencement of the nineteenth century, Euro-Americans began to undermine the bison world and its Indian residents. In the first decade of that century, three prominent men worked diligently to subvert the ancient world of the Upper Missouri. Those three men are now worshiped as American heroes. Thomas Jefferson, Meriwether Lewis, and William Clark sought to overturn the Upper Missouri's ecological, geographic, and cultural order and supplant it with their own vision.

Explorers beyond the Platte

Lewis and Clark and

Early Euro-American History

In a true dialogue, both sides are willing to change. We have to appreciate that truth can be received from outside of—not only within—our own group. If we do not believe that, entering into dialogue would be a waste of time. If we think we monopolize the truth and we still organize a dialogue, it is not authentic. We have to believe that by engaging in dialogue with the other person, we have the possibility of making a change within ourselves, that we can become deeper. Dialogue is not a means for assimilation in the sense that one side expands and incorporates the other into its "self." Dialogue must be practiced on the basis of "non-self." We have to allow what is good, beautiful, and meaningful in the other's tradition to transform us."

—Thich Nhat Hanh, Vietnamese philosopher.

Knowing that he appeared tall, well-read, and frequently charming, Thomas Jefferson, that egalitarian, often slipped into haughtiness. In the 1780s and 1790s, many of Jefferson's colleagues in the American government suffered the same inclination. Washington, Madison, Hamilton, and Adams were all sure of themselves and frequently full of themselves. Their self-confidence became apparent in politics. Late eighteenth-century American leaders remained resolute in their policies and vehement in their opposition. Closely linked to personal assertiveness came an intense fidelity to the political system they framed following the War for Independence. They did not see a distinction between themselves and their government. Jefferson, like the others, maintained a deep conviction in the morality and promise of the American experiment. His nationalism matched his personal certitude.

Jefferson believed the newborn United States of America possessed tremendous potential as an economic and political unit. The Virginian considered America's destiny to be the protection and advancement of human freedom, equality, justice, and agrarian capitalism. He believed that the most effective means of advancing the cause of liberty would be for the young republic to engage in expansionism. If the United States did not expand, it risked encirclement by enemies of freedom: despotic and dictatorial European powers bent on its destruction. A fear of, and prevention of, encirclement propelled Euro-Americans into wars with Indians and other European peoples since the 1630s. To Jefferson, encirclement meant decline. A planter, Jefferson understood, like others of his profession, that the acquisition of agricultural land assured prosperity for the nation. Without westward expansion, farmers faced decreasing soil fertility, lower production, and reduced incomes. If farmers suffered, the entire economy and nation suffered with them.

At the time of his inauguration in March 1801, Jefferson took control of a militarily weak, geographically limited, and politically divided nation-state. In contrast, Great Britain stood at the top of the Atlantic world's hierarchy of nations. The preponderance of British power rankled American nationalists. But Jefferson knew the United States could never match British strength in the Atlantic. To even attempt to do so would drain wealth from the people through taxation and thus jeopardize individual liberty. Early in his administration, Jefferson faced a quandary. He envisioned an imperial America, but he held few tools to hammer his dream into reality. In 1801, and in the years that followed, the president could only accommodate British power, a real embarrassment for such a self-righteous man.

During his first term, Jefferson had to deal with all sorts of international difficulties. The on-again, off-again conflict between Great Britain and

France, the two world powerhouses, over European hegemony and oceanic empire detrimentally affected American commercial shippers. Impressment of American sailors and seizure of American vessels and their cargoes violated the United States' professed policy of neutrality in this latest European quarrel. Even more frustrating for Jefferson, the two military giants repeatedly disregarded the president's pleas to end their depredations against American ships. Jefferson understood that the French and British held the United States in contempt. Leaders in the two respective European capitals considered the United States comical, doubted whether it would survive, and did not believe it worthy of respect.

To compound matters, the new Republican administration had problems closer to home. Jefferson faced stiff opposition from Federalists, who despised him for his ongoing affair with Sally Hemings, his Francophile manners, and his loathsome republican comportment. Yankees in Boston and the rest of the Northeast feared that Jefferson's antiurban, antientrepreneurial, states' rights policies threatened to tear the new republic apart. Jefferson faced an ugly reality that first year in office. Like anyone with a mounting set of problems, he went fishing for a way out. Jefferson wanted to quiet his enemies, make an impression on Britain, France, and Spain, and thereby enhance the stature of the United States in diplomatic circles, garner faith among the American people in an overtly weak and ineffective government, and restore his waning political legitimacy.

By early 1802, American settlers had pushed into the Old Northwest—the region north and west of the Ohio River. By then, American trappers and traders had depleted the fur resources of western Illinois and Michigan Territory. Soon, large numbers of Americans would be flush up against the Father of All Waters, the Mississippi. The president believed the United States needed more land. Jefferson and Secretary of the Treasury Albert Gallatin gazed covetously at Spanish Louisiana—that massive tuft of earth that clothed the drainage basins of the Mississippi's western tributaries. Jefferson and Gallatin wanted that space.

Other possibilities for expansion undoubtedly presented themselves to the president, particularly in Spanish Florida and Texas, but Louisiana looked more enticing than the rest. Gallatin wrote in a letter to President Jefferson on April 13, 1803, "The future destinies of the Missouri country are of vast importance to the United States, it being perhaps the only large tract of country, and certainly the first which lying out of the boundaries of the Union will be settled by the people of the U. States."[1] Louisiana sat directly astride the path of an expanding United States. Jefferson and Gallatin considered the Ohio River the avenue of the American advance west, and that river flowed straight toward Spanish Louisiana. The inevitable, natural migration of the American people would be over the Appalachians to Pittsburgh, down the Ohio to its mouth, and then across the Mississippi and into Louisiana. Americans pouring out of the Ohio would accumulate in Louisiana and overwhelm it. Jefferson thought of the Missouri River in relation to the Ohio.

By 1803, Jefferson held a fairly accurate image of the Missouri River as far as the Mandan villages at river mile 1,600 (or 1,600 miles above the Missouri's mouth).[2] On the other hand, he did not know for certain the river's total length or its navigability beyond the Mandan. He knew the river entered the Mississippi approximately 165 miles above the mouth of the Ohio and that it coursed in a westerly direction for nearly 350 miles before turning to the north, northwest. That information convinced Jefferson that the Missouri could be linked to the Ohio as a route of empire. In Jefferson's mind, the Ohio opened the door to Louisiana, while the Missouri would one day allow the United States to penetrate deep into its interior parts.

Jefferson thought of the Missouri in other ways. That big muddy river might lead to the fabled Northwest Passage. Since the Columbian voyages, European peoples had sought an all-water route to Asia and the markets of China and India. The hope of a water route from the Atlantic west to Cathay had not yet died. Three hundred years after its inception, the apparition remained alive and strong within Thomas Jefferson. The geographic consensus at the time convinced Jefferson that the Missouri could be navigated with deep-draft boats (keels or river galleys and pirogues) to the Stony Mountains (today's Rockies). Once American traders reached the Missouri's highest point, a short portage would carry them over to the mythical River of the West (known to Jefferson as the River Oregon or Columbia River). In Jefferson's mind, the River Oregon, like the Missouri, could be navigated all the way to its head. Thus, after sliding their boats into the River Oregon, American shippers would quickly sail on to the Pacific and Cathay. This wishful vision of the West's hydrology held great appeal for Jefferson and others in his cabinet.[3]

Whoever found the Northwest Passage would be considered one of the great men in world history.[4] Discovering the passage would make Thomas Jefferson immortal. He knew it, and so did everyone else. Jefferson wanted that trophy. The Northwest Passage would provide a feast for his hungry ego.

If the United States found the passage, Jefferson would be guaranteed a place of honor in his own nation, and in the capitals of the great powers. Additionally, such a discovery would prop up his administration, bestowing honors upon it for its daring, vision, and boldness.[5] Perhaps even more important, the United States would finally gain respect and a place beside the old imperial rivals. Finding the Northwest Passage would announce to the world that the United States intended on participating in the imperial contest. European nations held a monopoly on voyages of discovery and conquest. Jefferson wanted to end that monopoly. From a commercial perspective, he understood that the existence of the Northwest Passage would make possible the creation of a transcontinental water route.

Jefferson was the first president to visualize a continental waterways system, one that would be the precursor to a later system promoted by the U.S. Army Corps of Engineers and various administrations in the late nineteenth and twentieth centuries. Jefferson imagined a North American water route that included the following components: the Ohio (from its forks at Pittsburgh), the Mississippi, the Missouri, possibly the Yellowstone (known in 1803 as the Missouri's great southern branch or by its French name, the Roche Jaune), the portage over the Stony Mountains, and the Columbia main stem. To Jefferson, these rivers would someday provide Americans with routes of expansion, sites for settlements, and arteries for trade and development.[6]

The president did not believe these rivers needed improvement for navigation, at least not initially. Rather, with the hydrologic data available to him, he thought these rivers ideally suited to the modes of transportation then in existence. Every river within the system could conceivably carry canoes, flatboats, rafts, pirogues, and keels. The only improvement necessary in this natural waterways system would be the portage over the low mountains separating the Columbia basin from the Missouri basin. If the portage did not traverse mountainous terrain for any great distance, the United States government would be able to build a canal from the head of the Missouri system to the head of the Columbia system and thereby tie East to West, Europe to North America, and North America to Asia. This waterways system would be the grandest commercial highway anywhere on the globe.

Decades before the advent of the railroad, the Ohio, Mississippi, Missouri, Yellowstone, and Columbia waterways system appeared the only feasible route to traverse the continent, integrate the west to east, settle the interior, and extract the West's wealth. As a result, the first Euro-American designs for the Upper Missouri envisioned utilizing the Missouri main stem as a route to preeminence. Jefferson considered the Missouri first and foremost as a navigation route, as one part of a much larger, more complex transportation system. He did consider the Missouri Valley as a site for agricultural settlement, but that role would be of secondary importance. Jefferson recognized that agricultural settlers might move slowly up the Missouri Valley, taking decades before being firmly established where feasible.

To make his transcontinental waterways system a reality, Jefferson needed more information on the Missouri, Yellowstone, and River Oregon. He needed to know whether keels could actually navigate to the Missouri's headwaters, whether the Yellowstone headed near the River Oregon, and where exactly lay the upper course of the River Oregon. He also had to pinpoint the location of the short, gentle portage between the Missouri drainage and the Columbia drainage.

Albert Gallatin understood the significance of finding the Northwest Passage and physically confirming the existence of the transcontinental waterways system. Gallatin wrote Jefferson, "The precise extent, therefore, of the country drained by all the waters emptying into that [Missouri] river, and consequently the length & directions of all the principal branches ought to be, as far as practicable, ascertained as well as that particular branch which may be followed for the purpose of examining the communications with the Pacific Ocean."[7] If under U.S. dominion, the Northwest Passage would grant the United States an unrivaled position of commercial importance. The United States would be in a position to dominate the commerce of North America and possibly capture a substantial portion of trade flowing between Europe, North America, and Asia. The Northwest Passage, if it existed, in conjunction with a transcontinental navigable waterways system, would ensure American greatness. Jefferson, Gallatin, and the American people needed that kind of assurance in the dismal year of 1802, when Barbary sailors, British pirates, and French seaman all took a bite out of American commercial shipping. The public needed to know that the American experiment would not only succeed but flourish. Discovering the Northwest Passage would boost public confidence in the struggling republic.

When brainstorming in his garden at Monticello or milling about the halls of the White House, Thomas Jefferson also thought about the Columbia River and its future. Jefferson wanted the United States' flag to fly on the sandy, log-strewn banks at the mouth of the River Oregon. He believed the Columbia's powerful currents would be the primary means of moving the furs and future crops of the far northwest to the Pacific Ocean. Whichever nation controlled the mouth of that deep river would garner the loyalties of the peoples of the West. Jefferson came to this conclusion because of the problems his administration faced with Spain over access to the port of New Orleans near the mouth of the Mississippi. In 1803, the president wanted American access to New Orleans, which Spain barred to American shippers. Jefferson feared that American citizens west of the Appalachian Mountains might gravitate toward Spain unless the United States acquired the port. In other words, Americans in the trans-Appalachian West might secede from the United States and join Spain in order to gain oceanic access for their commodities. When Jefferson considered a western exploration, he had the crisis surrounding New Orleans fresh in his memory. The president wanted the mouth of the Columbia claimed by the United States in order to avert any future possibility that the peoples of the Far West would align themselves to another nation-state, such as Great Britain, that might control the mouth of the river.

Jefferson also considered the Yellowstone, or southern, branch of the Missouri as a vital element in his western future. In Jefferson's study at Monticello, maps on his desk traced a southern branch of the Missouri that led toward the headwaters of the River Oregon. If the Yellowstone (William Clark often spelled it Rochejhone) led to the short portage and the River Oregon, it would be the link between the Missouri and the Columbia.

In addition, Jefferson wanted the Yellowstone examined because of its possible connection with the Rio Norte, known today as the Rio Grande. If the Yellowstone headed in close proximity to the Rio Norte, and both rivers could be navigated to their headwaters, then the Yellowstone–Rio Norte connection would enable American entrepreneurs to penetrate the Sante Fe market. Thus, the Yellowstone would serve to move American commerce east and west as well as north and south. The Yellowstone would be the vital river of the West—the chain linking the Missouri to the Columbia and to the Rio Norte.

In the ever-searching mind of Thomas Jefferson, the Yellowstone–Rio Norte route would allow Euro-Americans to draw the Spanish in New Mexico into the American orbit—it would be another river of empire. The Virginian did think of the Yellowstone and far Upper Missouri Valleys as the home of Euro-American agriculturalists, but he also understood that settlement of those western zones might take a long time. Additionally, those river valleys might someday be under the rule of another Euro-American republic, possibly modeled on the U.S. example. Products grown inside these two river trenches would feed western Euro-American multitudes. Any surplus production would be sold to the Spanish possessions to the south, fostering a trade that would enrich both peoples and someday consign New Mexico to the United States or its republican progeny.

By early 1803, Jefferson believed an exploring expedition up the Missouri and on to the Pacific might accomplish and support several administration goals and national purposes. Successful exploration of the Missouri and Columbia River systems might quiet administration critics, foster nationalism, achieve stature for the United States, inform European powers that the United States was a serious contender for dominance in North America, provide Jefferson himself with fame and an enduring legacy, open Louisiana to American penetration, claim the mouth of the Columbia for the United States, facilitate the use of a continental waterways system, and someday provide an outlet for western commodities.

Jefferson chose his personal secretary, Meriwether Lewis, to lead an expedition to the Pacific Ocean. The Lewis expedition (Jefferson did not consider William Clark Lewis's equal) fit Jefferson's conception of the military's role in a republic. Jefferson feared a large military establishment, with its hierarchical, undemocratic organization. He believed a strong military might one day overthrow a civilian, freely elected government, or at least undermine democratic, egalitarian values by its very presence. Military culture, and the threat of military force, might subsume other cultural values and beliefs. Jefferson also feared the taxation necessary to maintain a strong military. Three decades earlier he revolted against the British government over the issue of taxation. He took taxes seriously. Taxes stripped away individual freedom, initiative, and reward. Burdensome taxation stifled innovation, creativity, and ultimately democracy.

A small military party, originally planned to consist of between eight and ten men, later augmented to include at most twelve to fourteen soldiers and an undetermined number of civilians, with a peaceful mission, serving the purposes of geographic exploration, science, and empire, fit into the president's overall conception of the place of the military in society.[8] The expedition would require no new taxes because its budget would be small, it would not engage in warfare, it would rely on Indians for survival, and it would promote commerce. The Lewis expedition embodied Jefferson's minimalist approach toward the military, government, and empire. Whether he knew it or not, Jefferson placed an incredible onus of responsibility on the shoulders of a single man, Meriwether Lewis. Lewis needed to succeed, or the president's philosophical approach to government and empire would suffer a blow.

Jefferson liked the idea of a small Lewis expedition because a tiny group of supposedly apolitical, scientifically inclined explorers would not provoke the other imperial powers. Jefferson exhibited timidity vis-à-vis foreign powers because he wanted to avoid war. War would defeat his small-government, small-army, read-my-lips-no-new-taxes approach to rule. A fourteen-man expedition to the west would not incite suspicions, or opposition, from the big powers—or so Jefferson thought.

Jefferson told representatives from France, Spain, and Great Britain that the expedition would pursue knowledge, not empire. The passport issued to Lewis by the British government stated as much: "Captain Merriwether [*sic*] Lewis, citizen of the United States of America, is sent (under the authority of the said United States) to explore the headwaters and shores of the Missoury and the western parts of the North American continent, and that he carries with him no merchandise other than that which is necessary to assure a favorable reception among the native tribes, and to advance the scientific and literary objects of his voyage." The document went on to state that Lewis would undertake the exploration of the Missouri for scientific motives only.[9] Undoubtedly, in requesting this passport, Thomas Jefferson did not tell the British the other, less altruistic, purposes of the Corps of Northwestern Discovery.

Early on in the planning stages for the expedition, the president added scientific research as one of its primary purposes. He did this to cover the imperialistic motives of the endeavor. Over and over again throughout 1803, Jefferson publicly stated that Lewis and company would gather an array of information to advance Western science. Jefferson wanted to use science to ensure that the expedition remained fail-proof. Among early nineteenth-century Euro-American elites, science held a cultural position on a par with Christianity. For many, science represented an unassailable ideology. Yet Jefferson viewed it as a political tool. Science would add legitimacy to the expedition and deflect criticism from foreign and domestic opponents suspicious of the enterprise and its sponsor. Moreover, with science as a crutch, Lewis could not fail in his mission. If the explorers did not find the Northwest Passage or were forced to retreat in the face of British, Spanish, or Indian military force before reaching the Pacific, the exploring party would still return to the United States with scientific data of some value to the public.

The explorers could not help but make new discoveries. The West abounded in the unknown, the mysterious, the fanciful, and the scenic. So long as Lewis observed his surroundings and recorded his impressions in journals, he would acquire scientific information. It would be hard for the expedition to fail, unless catastrophe struck the party and its journals.[10]

Jefferson concealed the expedition's political and military objectives from the British, French, and Spanish ambassadors while elevating science's import. Jefferson lied about the expedition's true intentions. Science was not the primary purpose of the expedition, but Jefferson could not tell the British, French, or Spanish the expedition's ultimate purpose—to lay the groundwork for an American empire. If they learned of his true intentions and sought to stop the expedition, he would have been powerless to push the expedition through that resistance. From today's perspective it is surprising the British, French, and to a lesser extent the Spanish believed the president. Yet, with hindsight, it is not surprising. The thought of the puny, inexperienced, and hopelessly divided United States attempting to incorporate the trans-Mississippi West into its domain was considered preposterous by European diplomats and many Americans.[11]

That Jefferson believed an expedition to the western sea feasible and necessary places him on a pedestal high above the herd of mediocre American presidents. He displayed audacity, confidence, imagination, and arrogance in his conception of the expedition and how it served his larger vision for the West. Jefferson was audacious because he believed an expedition of between eight and fourteen military men and a motley crew of civilians could travel through the interior of North America, with all its physical and psychological dangers and its threats of British, Spanish, or Indian interference, and return home alive. The president evinced confidence because he believed that the land area of the Louisiana Territory, and the Columbia River drainage, might one day be incorporated into the United States or another Euro-American republic. In a transportation age dominated by foot travel, horse and wagon, pirogue, canoe, and keelboat (when horse travel averaged fifteen miles a day, and upstream keelboat travel only ten miles per day), Jefferson still considered the Upper Missouri and Far West a region that would likely be within the domain of the United States or one of its republican offspring. This was an absolutely astounding conclusion, especially for a man who had never been west of the Appalachian Mountains, had never seen the Mississippi, wide Missouri, Rocky Mountains, or Columbia Plain. The topographic and technological obstacles to integration of the trans-Mississippi West were absolutely daunting. Yet, Jefferson believed the area, which stretched close to seventeen hundred miles from St. Louis to the Columbia River's mouth, might one day be brought into the American Republic.

Jefferson imagined new worlds. He visualized the transformation of the lands of Louisiana, the Upper Missouri, and the Columbia drainage from wilderness to pastoralism. He pictured the rivers of the West as peaceful avenues of commerce, bearing manufactured goods between Indians and Euro-Americans and agricultural commodities from western farms to eastern cities. Jefferson wanted to establish his idea of the good life in the West: trade, agriculture, and small towns dotting a manicured landscape, with the rivers carrying keels. Jefferson envisaged a new order in Louisiana, the Upper Missouri, and the Columbia drainage, not a world of bison and nomadism. Jefferson's role would be transformative; he would be the great creator, a midwife to the birth of a vibrant, fresh reality in the West. At the President's House and at Monticello, Jefferson pored over his extensive collection of maps, thrilling at the thought of playing such a godly role in the formative process.

Jefferson's plans for the Louisiana Territory and the Upper Missouri displayed some of the contradictions streaming through the man's psyche. A professed lover of democracy and egalitarianism, Jefferson believed it might one day be necessary to force the indigenous peoples of the Upper Missouri to forfeit their lands and souls to Euro-America. Jefferson wanted to use the Lewis expedition to initiate the incorporation of Indian peoples into the United States. Shifting Indian trading patterns away from the British in Canada to the Americans at St. Louis would be the first step toward that end. Once the Indians became dependent on American commercial largesse, missionaries and educators would mingle among the tribes, baptizing them with river water and teaching them the rudiments of agriculture. He did not consider Indian lifeways a viable alternative for the region, either for the Indians themselves or for the Euro-Americans who would one day settle upon Indian land.[12]

Empires require complacency, indivisible thought, shared illusions, and organization. Fear, the widespread perception of a preponderance of governmental power, and the threat of coercion are necessary to force compliance to imperial ideals among a recalcitrant population. Jefferson hoped indigenes could be made peacefully complacent to Euro-American penetration and possession of their country through a dependence on American trade items. Failing that, the threat or actual deployment of military force would subdue uncooperative tribes. The requirements of empire go far toward explaining Jefferson's wish to convert Indian peoples to the American way. Jefferson thought he knew what was best for the Indians. He gave a passing nod to the legitimacy of nomadism, hunting and gathering, and Indian spirituality. On the other hand, he believed Indians lived in a hopelessly childlike state. They sought nothing more than comfort and allowed their desires or passions to govern their actions. Believing Indians approximated children, Jefferson justified the dismemberment of tribes, the undermining of indigenous cultures, and the integration of any remnant populations into the United States.[13]

Historians of many persuasions have long thought of Thomas Jefferson as brilliant, bold, and visionary for anticipating a Euro-American empire in the trans-Mississippi West. From another point of view, Jefferson might be considered somewhat delusional for his western dream. Taking into account all the environmental, economic, political, and military obstacles to American integration of Louisiana Territory, the Upper Missouri basin, and the Columbia drainage (including a semiarid environment, large, hostile Indian nations, British commercial competition, the possible absence of a Northwest Passage, and foreign threats to the long-term security of the United States), Jefferson's vision for the West is almost absurd. It is easy to believe that Jefferson wanted the impossible. But to his credit, the president knew it would take other men in other times to attempt the actual integration of the Upper Missouri and Columbia drainage basins. Jefferson also knew it might require a century or longer to achieve Euro-American settlement and development in the region. But like any intellectual worth an insignificant salary, Jefferson hedged his bets. The president understood that in the future the West could conceivably be under the rule of another Euro-American republic—one only loosely affiliated with the United States.

By April 1803, the larger political objectives of the expedition had been solidified in the mind of Jefferson. But before Lewis's departure for the West and history, the president and his key advisers added other, more specific objectives to the enterprise. Cabinet members Levi Lincoln, Albert Gallatin, and James Madison added their suggestions to Jefferson's policy repertoire. Lincoln worried that the expedition might not succeed if its members fell into Spanish or Indian hands or were forced back to St. Louis by one of America's many enemies in the region. Lincoln also wondered whether the Northwest Passage even existed at all. Lincoln did not want the Jefferson administration to chance a failure of the Lewis expedition. A failure out west for Jefferson, added to the growing list of administration setbacks, could conceivably hurt the president's reelection prospects or at least reflect badly on his leadership. Any loss of public confidence and legitimacy made ruling the nation and confronting foreign adversaries all the more difficult.

Lincoln inserted a significant goal for the expedition to bank against total failure and to quiet administration critics. He recommended that Lewis gather information on Indian peoples, for the sake of future exploitation and subversion. Lincoln wanted Lewis to learn Indian vocabularies, spiritual beliefs, rituals, material culture, trade practices, and military strength. This information would purportedly aid missionaries sent to Christianize and assimilate the Indians. If congressional and New England opponents to the administration heard that the expedition would assist in the eventual Christianizing of the savages, they would be more apt to support the president. Lincoln and Jefferson incorporated two sacred American ideologies, Christianity and science, to further the larger, imperial, aims of the expedition. Jefferson agreed with Lincoln's suggestions and added the proposals into his final orders to Meriwether Lewis.[14]

The secret letter from President Jefferson to Lewis, dated June 20, 1803, represents the clearest explanation of the purposes of the expedition. Jefferson wanted Lewis to first and foremost find the all-water route to the Pacific. The president wrote, "The object of your mission is to explore the Missouri river, & such principal stream of it, as, by it's course and communication with the waters of the Pacific ocean, whether the Columbia, Oregon, Colorado or any other river may offer the most direct and practicable water communication across this continent for the purposes of commerce."[15] Locate the water route to Cathay, the Northwest Passage, and the future prosperity of the United States will be closer at hand.

The second main objective of the expedition would be ethnological. Following the advice of Lincoln, Jefferson ordered Lewis and his cocommander to scrutinize and record all aspects of Indian culture. Jefferson's motives for acquiring ethnological information went beyond Lincoln's singular goal of Christianizing the natives. He sought religious, economic, linguistic, political, social, and military information on the tribes. Jefferson believed such information would make relations between Euro-Americans and Indians peaceful, since Euro-Americans would have a reference point to relate to the tribes. Knowledge of Indian languages, trade demands, and customs would reduce friction and misunderstandings between the two peoples as they engaged in business intercourse. Trade had long been the touch point, and at times the flash point, between Euro-Americans and indigenes. Knowledge of indigenous culture would ease the transfer of goods and services between the two peoples and avert the confusion that so often led to war.[16]

From a more practical point of view, Jefferson wanted ethnological facts to assist the expansion of the American fur trade into the Upper Missouri, Stony Mountains, and Far West. Once Americans learned which trade items the Indians preferred to purchase, they could begin to supply that demand, thereby gaining a foothold in the region. Euro-American entrepreneurs, priests, and friars required linguistic data to effectively communicate their wishes and demands to the tribes. Jefferson wanted to know the number of warriors residing within each nation. In modern parlance, Jefferson ordered Lewis to conduct a threat assessment. If trade did not bind the tribes to the United States, then he would use the strong arm of the U.S. Army to do the same. Finally, Jefferson, closely adhering to Lincoln's advice, hoped that Christian evangelicals would use the ethnological information to more effectively convert indigenes. Knowing Indian spiritual practices, American evangelicals would be in a position to modify their proselytizing techniques in ways that would undermine the Indian paradigm.

Jefferson ordered Lewis to perform a comprehensive resource inventory of the territory traversed by the exploring party. Inclusion of this goal demonstrated once again Lincoln's influence on Jefferson's thinking. The resource inventory served as the scientific element of the expedition. Lewis needed to observe and chronicle the West's soil types, flora, fauna, minerals, volcanic activity, and climatic variations. Jefferson wanted to know when plants flowered, leafed, and shed their leaves and when frost first bit the land. Such information would indicate the length of the region's growing season, a detail crucial to assessing the area's potential for agricultural development. A flourishing agricultural society would be the pot of golden wheat lying at the foot of the imperial rainbow. Jefferson did not intend for Lewis's scientific discoveries to only advance human understanding of the natural world. Science without result meant nothing. Instead, he believed science should determine the region's agricultural potentialities. Jefferson's science served agriculture and ultimately empire. It did not stand above politics; it reeked of subjectivity and utilitarianism.

Two final directives of the president to Lewis in his June 20, 1803, correspondence related expressly to the Upper Missouri territory. First, Jefferson told Lewis to learn the contours of the territory to the south and west of the Mandan villages. Perhaps the Missouri's great southern branch (the Roche Jaune) or the Missouri itself led to the Spanish possessions in New Mexico. Jefferson wrote, "Altho' your route will be along the channel of the Missouri, yet you will endeavor to inform yourself, by enquiry, of the character & extent of the country watered by it's branches, & especially on it's Southern side." Jefferson continued, "What are their [Colorado and Rio Grande Rivers'] distance from the Missouri, the character of the intermediate country, & the people inhabiting it, are worthy of particular enquiry."[17] Finally, Jefferson commanded Lewis, "Should you find it safe to return by the way you go, after sending two of your party round by sea, or with your whole party, if no conveyance by sea can be found, do so; making such observations on your return, as may serve to supply, correct or confirm those made on your outward journey."[18] Lewis followed this series of directives. In July 1806, Lewis sent Clark on an exploration of the Yellowstone River, while he examined the watershed of the Marias.

Before the expedition set forth westward, the United States acquired New Orleans and Louisiana Territory, which inflated the significance of the expedition. For a trifling sum of cash, an ambitious, messianic nation purchased from Napoleon Bonaparte the lands that enclosed the Upper Missouri. American diplomats bought an extensive piece of grass, wind, sky, and water not from its rightful owners but from French usurpers. After the Louisiana Purchase had been sealed with handshakes and smiles, the United States asserted control over a region still inhabited by powerful tribes. Historians long considered the Louisiana Purchase the Jefferson administration's greatest accomplishment. On its flip side, the purchase epitomized the hubris and cultural arrogance of the United States and its leaders. Indian peoples and their wishes did not factor into the negotiations that took place between French and American diplomats. President Thomas Jefferson and his cohorts utterly discounted the Indians; in one fell swoop they arbitrarily assumed authority over a territory occupied by indigenous peoples for at least eleven thousand years.

In the negotiations and subsequent purchase of Louisiana, the young American republic laid bare its imperial intentions. The purchase carried along with it many Euro-American assumptions, including the technological, social, economic, political, and military superiority of Euro-America. Additionally, Euro-Americans took it for granted that the land and Indians of the Upper Missouri would be integrated into an expanding American emplte. The only real question was when. What occurred in Paris in 1803 served as a precursor for what would follow. Euro-Americans did not consider Indians worthy of inclusion in their grand schemes for the Upper Missouri.

So much has been written about Lewis and Clark, and yet so much remains to be written. These men demand attention and analysis. William Clark and Meriwether Lewis successfully carried out the first American exploration of the trans-Mississippi West, and their trip and the printed record of it heavily influenced the subsequent history of the Upper Missouri. The two young men led the Euro-American drive into the Upper Missouri, both physically and perceptually. Perceptually they had the greatest influence on consequent history, geography, and ecology. The journals still affect how contemporary Americans perceive the Missouri River, Upper Missouri, and Far West. The perceptual legacy of Lewis and Clark is alive and well and will only intensify with the bicentennial of the expedition.

In the winter of 1803–1804, Lewis and Clark recruited expedition members, hutted at Camp Dubois in Illinois (located on the east bank of the Mississippi River across from the mouth of the Missouri River), and trained their troops and French rivermen for the hardships ahead. From the parade ground at Camp Dubois, the men gazed across the broad Mississippi to the Missouri coming in from the west. What came out of the Missouri's mouth induced fear in the inexperienced boatmen. The Missouri discharged greasy bile into the Mississippi. The shattered remnants of forests, farms, and animals passed before the men of the post. The Missouri's pageant of power troubled the men; nevertheless, expedition members were determined to stem the river of anxiety streaming through their psyches and the physical river over the horizon.

The Corps of Northwestern Discovery set out from Camp Dubois on the afternoon of May 14, 1804. The explorers cautiously ascended the Missouri's strong, dirty waters, swollen from spring rains and chock-full of floating debris and sunken trees. In those first weeks of May, when the rare moment of rest fell upon the crews, the men wondered what awaited them on the Missouri—death at the hands of Indian warriors, a violent drowning in the Missouri, maiming from accident, liaisons with virginal Indian women, undreamed-of sights and sounds, delicious foods, frolicking music, and jostling moments of dance? Imaginations ran with the river, blunted only by fatiguing work.

Traveling up the Missouri, the expedition encountered habitual delays and distractions. Crews pushed, pulled, or sailed upstream aboard two pi-rogues and a keelboat. Although possessing the best watercraft available on the market, the explorers moved slowly up the Missouri. Facing a current bulldozing downstream at up to six miles per hour, the corps averaged only nine miles per day. The greatest danger to keel and crew came when the corps crossed midchannel to reach the inside of the next upstream bend. In these crossings, the thalweg threw its full weight against the side of the keel and threatened to tip it over. Not until October 27, 1804, over five months after leaving Camp Dubois, did the Corps of Northwestern Discovery reach the Mandan villages near present-day Washburn, North Dakota, sixteen hundred miles above the Missouri's filthy mouth. The Mandan villages rep-resented the end point of existing Euro-American geographic knowledge. West of the Mandan the map drew a blank page.

Between October 1804 and April 1805, Meriwether Lewis and William Clark and their men questioned French and British traders, as well as Indi-ans, about the land and rivers to the west of Fort Mandan. Tightly packed in their quarters, next to blazing fires, Lewis and Clark learned about the far Upper Missouri and the Yellowstone. On April 7, 1805, only days after the Missouri River's ice burst and marched downstream, Lewis and Clark, twenty-nine men, one woman, and one child set out for the Pacific. The crew reached the Yellowstone River's mouth on April 25, 1805. The men and Sacagawea discovered the Great Falls of the Missouri and the plentiful supply of grizzlies in its vicinity on June 13, 1805. Fighting the Missouri's current and gingerly walking across its boulder-festooned shores, the corps reached the Three Forks on July 27, 1805. From there the party struggled up the Jefferson and Beaverhead Rivers. In September and October, it crossed the Rockies, passed down through the Snake River Valley, and even-tually canoed down the fishy waters of the Columbia. By fall 1805, Lewis and Clark knew that there was no easy portage across the Stony Mountains. A Northwest Passage did not exist. A transcontinental water route would never become a reality. The West's geographic realities destroyed Euro-American political and economic dreams.

The American expedition spent a soaking wet winter on the coast of present-day Oregon, huddled inside Fort Clatsop, impatiently waiting for spring and the chance to return to the United States. The party's presence at the mouth of the Columbia River did achieve one of Jefferson's goals: it upheld the American claim on the Oregon country and lent credence to future Euro-American use of the mouth of the Columbia as an outlet for American commodities and products. Anxious to leave the confines of Fort Clatsop, the explorers turned their faces to the east on March 23, 1806, still months before the snows melted in the high Rockies. After a layover among the Nez Percé that dragged on for weeks, the Americans attempted one, and later a second, crossing of the Stony Mountain barrier. After the second attempt, the men reached Traveler's Rest, near present-day Missoula, Montana. Here, on July 3, 1806, the expedition divided in two. Lewis and nine men hiked toward the Great Falls and Marias River; Clark and twenty-two others passed to the Three Forks, where he divided the contingent once more, sending Sergeant Ordway and nine men down the Missouri to join Lewis near the mouth of the Marias. Clark took Sacagawea, her son, Pomp, her anxiety-prone husband, Charbonneau, and nine men and pursued the Gallatin River to the east, southeast, seeking to locate the Yellowstone Valley and pursue its course to the Missouri. The separate branches of the expedition rejoined on the Missouri on August 12, 1806. Through the remainder of August and into September, the expedition hurried south and east down the Missouri, running sixty miles on some days, finally reaching St. Louis on September 23, 1806.

During their two-year, four-month voyage to the western sea, Lewis and Clark and company spent more time in the Upper Missouri than anywhere else in the West. Members of the Corps of Northwestern Discovery lived a total of fifteen months in the region between the Platte's mouth and the Three Forks. Over the course of those months, the Euro-American explorers became very familiar with the country, its rivers, its peoples, and its bison. Lewis and Clark first entered the Upper Missouri on July 21, 1804. Once through the portal on the Platte, these men of science and reason found themselves melding into the Upper Missouri's bison culture. By September 9, 1806, and their departure from the Upper Missouri, captains and crew had adopted much of the cultural baggage and some of the habits of the indigenes.

While in the Upper Missouri territory, the Euro-American explorers adhered to the contours of bison geography, following river drainages or bison roads in their movements. The men lived, worked, and hunted in the bottoms along the big Missouri, drank straight out of the river, camped and slept on those comfortable sandflats, wore elk and bison leather, slid their feet into Indian moccasins, cloaked themselves in Indian blankets, mounted Indian ponies, navigated in bullboats down and across rivers, slept on bison robes, and perfected a taste for roasted bison marrowbones. By the second year, the Upper Missouri felt as comfortable to the men of the expedition as the bison robes hanging over their shoulders and the elk skin moccasins cradling their feet. By September 1806, the Corps of Northwestern Discovery became acculturated to the Upper Missouri in ways that few Euro-Americans would ever match.

Yet, for all their comfort and ease with the bison world and its order, the explorers did not abandon their identities. Lewis and Clark and their men did not join with the Upper Missouri. They never once let the Upper Missouri, its ecology, climate, geography, hydrology, bison, or Indians, subvert their sense of superiority and distinctiveness. That the explorers upheld this attitude goes far toward explaining the expedition's success in crossing the trans-Mississippi West and returning home.

By the spring and summer of 1806, the men became increasingly anxious not only to return to the Missouri plains but also to return home. Arriving on the Missouri plains meant getting closer to St. Louis, the East, and their civilization. On July 8, 1806, Lewis commented that the men in his detachment are "much rejoiced at finding ourselves in the plains of the Missouri which abound with game."[19] Simple homesickness played a big role in the men's feelings of urgency. The explorers sorely missed their families, friends, and home-cooked meals. A desire to finally complete the long-drawn-out journey also impelled them eastward. But on a deeper psychological level, Meriwether Lewis, William Clark, and the others desired to get back to "civilization" so as not to lose themselves. By July 1806, if not earlier, the men perceived that their old selves, what previously constituted their identity, had begun slipping away. Powerful rivers, cyclonic storms, dusty winds, high mountains, monotone vistas of grass, ferocious grizzlies, and uncertain Indian friends and foes eroded the ramparts of their personalities, weakened their psychological defenses, and daily battered their sense of superiority.

Changes in physical appearance provided visual confirmation of the fear of losing their identity. On the Upper Missouri in summer 1806, the men began to resemble the dreaded Indians. Clark wrote on July 24, 1806, "[I] observed he [Hugh Hall] was necked, I gave him one of my two remaining Shirts a par of Leather Legins and 3 pr. Of mockersons which equipt him

Completely and Sent him on."²⁰ The bison world had shorn Hugh Hall of his garments. Hall's appearance worried Clark. What worried the brevet captain even more was that he had not noticed Hall's pitiful condition earlier. Clark realized he had normalized nakedness. In other words, he had come to accept nakedness as ordinary within the context of the Upper Missouri's bison geography and Indian culture. The contrast between the discipline and order usually evident in a military unit and the unprofessional appearance of Hugh Hall drove home in Clark's mind just how far Clark and his men had traveled both physically and perceptually from their pasts.

The similarity between the physical appearance of the explorers and that of the Indians—all of whom were charred dark from the sun, thin, haggard, wearing rags, or nothing at all—meant the Corps of Northwestern Discovery was falling into savagery. In the Euro-American mind, only Indians roamed the plains naked. White men wore clothes. Clothing symbolized the frontier between civilized man and his primitive and barbaric surroundings. Nakedness implied the absence of protection, vulnerability, the victory of environment and savagery over civilized, comprehensible self. The shoddy appearances of the men increased everyone's anxiety to leave the Upper Missouri. They had to return to the east before they lost even the last shreds of their clothing and whiteness.

Preservation of the Corps of Northwestern Discovery's identity goes far in explaining the successful return of the expedition to St. Louis. Maintenance of individual and collective identities depended on several interrelated factors. Unit size mattered most. The size of the expedition fostered unit cohesion and an esprit de corps, a shared identity of uniqueness. Unit size blunted acculturation. One man on a trip of two years and four months across the Upper Missouri and West would have had to acculturate more fully with one tribe or another in order to survive. Existing environmental, social, political, and military circumstances across the Upper Missouri prevented single Euro-Americans from surviving separate from Indian allies. Granted, John Colter trekked alone through the country in 1807, but Colter was lucky. His experience was exceptional. To go it alone in the Upper Missouri meant certain isolation and a very high probability of death by accident or war wound. Thirty-one men (the number in the permanent party) required Indian assistance but did not have to acculturate. They did not have to fully join with the Indians through marital contracts or binding military or political alliances. They could maintain strict lines of demarcation between themselves and the Indians around them. Their numbers and accumulated firepower offered the corps a measure of protection against total submission to the land and its dominant cultures.

The officers maintained unit and individual identity through ritualistic practice, for example, by marking holidays with parades or festivities such as an impromptu celebration at the Great Falls to mark Independence Day in 1805. Lewis remembered, "We gave the men a drink of sperits, it being the last of our stock, and some of them appeared a little sensible of it's effects the fiddle was plyed and they danced very merrily untill 9 in the evening when a heavy shower of rain put an end to that part of the amusement tho' they continued their mirth with songs and festive jokes and were extreemly merry untill late at night. We had a very comfortable dinner, of bacon, beans, suit dumplings & buffaloe beaf &c. in short we had no just cause to covet the sumptuous feasts of our countrymen on this day."[21] Rituals bonded the men with their cohorts and their country.

The captains occasionally initiated talks with Indian peoples by ordering the enlisted men to march in formation past the assembled dignitaries. Clark or Lewis periodically carried out inspections to maintain a semblance of military discipline. A call to arms recapitulated the military purposes of the enterprise. A military formation or random inspection of arms quickly threw the men back into another reality. Parades and inspections reminded the explorers of their affiliation with the U.S. Army and the United States, and of their identity as Americans.

A perception of unknown enemies on all sides strengthened unit cohesion and reinforced individual identities. To the men of the expedition Indians could not be trusted. In an Indian world, Euro-Americans had no friends, only potential enemies. Under such dangerous circumstances, with Indians moving all around, members of the exploring party could only trust one another. Unswerving trust among expedition members was of paramount importance, so much so that the captains court-martialed and then flogged those who broke that trust. Indians, no matter how friendly, always remained suspect. The choice of nightly campsites reflected this distrust and fear of Indians. Expedition leaders located campsites in relation to water, timber, and defense. While moving through today's central South Dakota, past the core geographic region of the Teton Sioux, the explorers camped on sandbars in the middle of the Missouri River channel to place distance and water between themselves and their tentative enemies onshore. By fostering an "us versus them" mentality in the men, Lewis and Clark maintained unit and individual identities.

The Upper Missouri's environment acted on Euro-American identity in contradictory ways. As mentioned earlier, rivers, grassland, and Indians might tear down Euro-American characteristics, particularly the newcomers' blind confidence in their technological prowess and political astuteness; but at the same time those forces might strengthen old identities. On the outbound journey the land oppressed the men, kept them confined, tore at them, and consequently pushed them close together. To leave the safety of their Euro-American community meant being thrust into an alien world. But on the return trip in 1806, their familiarity with the land offered opportunities and new avenues of discovery. By July 1806, the party felt so at ease with the Upper Missouri that its members broke into three small parties, each detachment going its own way—its members chancing defeat by Indians or disaster from a natural phenomenon in exchange for greater independence. Comprehension of the Upper Missouri's geographic system allowed the explorers that increased flexibility and freedom in travel. The splintering of the expedition on the return leg of the journey is also indicative of the acculturation process. A group with less familiarity with the Upper Missouri would not have risked a division of unit strength.

Commanders with less self-righteousness and patriotism would not have been able to keep a unit together for so long under such trying circumstances. A sense of Euro-American cultural superiority not only justified the expedition itself but also buttressed the planned Euro-American occupancy of the Upper Missouri. Lewis and Clark never questioned the rightness of their enterprise, and neither did their men. Even though the expedition spent years beyond the Euro-American settlements and their characters and cultural assumptions suffered numerous challenges, Lewis and Clark and their men did not abandon their dichotomous, sanctimonious ideals. They stayed true to cause and country. For Lewis and Clark or anyone else in the corps to have done otherwise would have raised grave doubts about the whole enterprise. Questioning the purpose of the expedition while in the Upper Missouri might have led to unit disintegration. The stakes were too high for the men to doubt any aspect of the expedition. Again, this explains the crucial importance of administering court-martials and lashings early in the journey. Those punishments strengthened unit cohesion.

Lewis and Clark and crew also had too much on the line personally to question or doubt the expedition and its goals. Each member had his own reasons for undertaking the journey. The men had career goals, hopes for government land grants, or lucrative government positions at the end of the endeavor. If the members of the exploring party considered the repercussions of their actions as being anything but positive, if they expressed misgivings about the expedition's justifications, it is possible they would have failed to reach the Pacific and return home as a singular unit. Failure as an expedition equated personal failure and the impossibility of reaping personal rewards after the return home.

The explorers admired Indian know-how and grudgingly admitted Indian superiority in their own realm. But the Euro-American adventurers never considered the Indians as equals; to have done so would have thrown their enterprise into question. To have viewed Indian cultures as deserving of respect, Indian land rights as viable and authentic, and the bison world as ordered, understandable, and worthy of preservation would have seriously challenged the underlying justifications for the expedition. The expedition was about overturning an established order, not upholding it. The expedition had meaning so long as it facilitated the destruction of the bison world. The Euro-Americans were revolutionaries, men bent on destroying one system and replacing it with another. The Lewis and Clark expedition was all about change, about replacing an old order with a new one, one dominated by Euro-Americans and serving Euro-American commercial interests. This was an expedition to spur Euro-American subversion of the Upper Missouri's ecology, geography, and indigenous cultures. Its ultimate objective was the integration of the region into the larger Euro-American body politic. Consistent with their mission, the explorers relegated Indians to the positions of savages, knowledgeable, yes, but savages nonetheless. Such a belief delegitimized the Indian hold on the Upper Missouri. Savages deserved to lose their lands to the superior white race. Whether or not Jefferson, Lewis, and Clark ever verbalized it, they unconsciously understood that absolutists make good imperialists and relativists do not.

Between May 1804 and September 1806, Lewis and Clark and several of the sergeants recorded their observations. Lewis and Clark regarded the journals, those incredible literary and artistic records, as blueprints for American expansion. Their science served an expansive nation-state and little else. The men believed knowledge for merely enlightenment or cultural understanding to be worthless. The information in the journals was never objective. Those journals supported, and continue to support, very subjective ends.

In an obvious understatement, Lewis and Clark continue to hold extreme symbolic importance. Their expedition to the western sea represents the dichotomous, all-or-none, them-versus-us, good-versus-bad thinking prevalent among Euro-Americans in the nineteenth century. Of course, that sort of thinking remains strong even today. Lewis and Clark passed through the Upper Missouri between 1804 and 1806; that passage weakened their links to the United States and its belief system in many ways but did not destroy the connections. The great tragedy of the Lewis and Clark expedition is that these explorers, these incredibly bright, articulate, and learned men, went to the Upper Missouri, lived with its Indian peoples, adopted many of its cultural artifacts, interacted closely with its bison geography and ecology, and returned to the United States still intent on destroying that world.

During their time in the Upper Missouri and West, Lewis and Clark and their men viewed an exotic realm—one stupendously different from their own. These explorers, through their journals, served as windows into a mysterious, ordered, rich, and ecologically sound bison world. But rather than seek a true dialogue with that world and a blending of the Euro-American reality of towns and farms with the Indian reality of bison and wild rivers, the Euro-American race worked (and continues to labor to this day) to replace the bison world with its own exclusive vision of the future. Euro-Americans also failed to recognize and uphold Indian cultural integrity, thereby missing opportunities to learn ecology and sustainable economy. What the Euro-American race did do is learn of the region and its cultures for assimilative purposes. Both Lewis and Clark returned to St. Louis intent on deconstructing the Upper Missouri. After September 1806, they worked from their offices in St. Louis to seek American expansion up the Missouri. They also diligently applied their energies toward gaining the control and submission of the Indian peoples living there.[22]

After 1806, the key goal of the United States government in regard to the Upper Missouri territory was to keep the Missouri River route open. Government officials understood that the Missouri River represented the single greatest resource in the Upper Missouri. The Upper Missouri main stem would factor heavily in all federal military, strategic, and economic decisions regarding the region between 1804 and 1877. The Missouri would allow the United States to penetrate the Upper Missouri, project military power into the region, commercially compete against the British traders who entered the region from Canada, push the British out, monitor the tribes in the area, and subdue or chastise recalcitrant indigenes. The river and the boats it supported would put farmers on the bottomlands, haul commodities downstream, and bring the materials upriver to build a new society out of wilderness. The Upper Missouri main stem would be the key element in the fur trade, the military conquest of the indigenes, the era of agricultural settlement, and the early town-building period. Across the Upper Missouri region in the nineteenth century, the Upper Missouri main stem took front and center stage.

Lewis and Clark, like most Americans in the nineteenth century, understood the frontier process: the steps that occurred as the Euro-American frontier advanced and new lands were integrated into the American political and economic sphere. The advance of the frontier was a national obsession. The public followed its advance and reveled in the ingenuity and might of the American nation as it pushed west. It was a decades-long American soap opera, with an ever-changing cast of characters and plots but with a predictable outcome. The advance of the frontier was an event resembling a community celebration—it bonded Americans together. What is more, by acquiring new lands, Americans further tied their loyalty to the American government. The frontier's advance was both participatory and observatory: those who participated in it became more patriotic, and those who watched marveled at its forward momentum. The process had been under way for hundreds of years on the North American continent, and it followed a discernible pattern. The first step in the process, as it had been most recently on the Illinois frontier, would be the fur trade. Following the inevitable depletion of the fur resource, the Indian inhabitants would be removed from their lands, either forcibly or through treaties, and then the agricultural settlers would advance onto the scene. Thus, in 1806, the national heroes Meriwether Lewis and William Clark sought to promote the fur trade across the Upper Missouri.

Lewis and Clark worked to repeat the frontier process on the Upper Missouri—the same frontier they watched advance across the Old Northwest in their youth. Upon their return, they made contact with St. Louis fur interests. In the fall of 1806 and the spring of 1807, the two young heroes divulged the Upper Missouri's geographic secrets to a handful of fur traders. In the spring of 1807, the fur traders set forth aboard keels for the Upper Missouri. The geographic and ecological transformation of the Upper Missouri began in earnest.

5

In Search of Place

The Sioux and Euro-America

Although for many years buffalo have been tolerably numerous
through the country of the Crees and Assinaboines [*sic*], yet they
are rapidly diminishing, and other nations have but few; besides,
their range is gradually becoming more limited; and the extensive
plains between the Coteau de Prairie and Saschawaine [*sic*],
formerly covered with these animals, are now entirely deserted
by both Indians and game.

—Alfred Vaughn, Indian agent, 1854

Riches and dreams led the Teton Sioux and Euro-Americans to
the Upper Missouri. Both peoples wanted to turn the resources of the region
into the good life. But the Sioux and Euro-Americans differed in their visions of what constituted an ideal society. The Sioux believed in nomadism
and the bison hunt. Euro-Americans believed in commerce, agriculture, and
sedentary living. A nomadic people required a very different approach to the
Missouri Valley than did an agricultural, commercial, and sedentary race.
The Sioux wanted the Missouri Valley as a haven, for themselves and bison.
Euro-Americans wanted the river as a commercial route and the valley as a
site for trading posts, farms, military forts, and towns.

The Sioux beat the Euro-Americans to the Upper Missouri by only a few
decades and used European guns and horses to build an empire out of the
grassland. They also tapped the bottoms, and the bison flowing through the

Upper Missouri system, to ride their ponies to greatness. Euro-Americans did the same. Guns, horses, bison, and rivers erected an American domain in the Upper Missouri. Soon after the return of the Lewis and Clark expedition to the United States, Euro-Americans began to redirect the Upper Missouri's energy flows. The Teton Sioux and Euro-American visions for the Upper Missouri joined in the beaver and bison robe trades, yet that trading gradually undermined the Sioux lifeway while supplanting it with a Euro-American economic and social system. Euro-American trading posts, hunting practices, and river travel adversely affected bison numbers. The decrease in the bison population and the increasing presence of whites in the Missouri Valley contributed to the outbreak of war between the Teton Sioux and Euro-Americans. By the 1850s, friction between two fantasies of the Upper Missouri sparked into violence.

It is not known when the Sioux first set foot in the Upper Missouri basin. What is known is that they found their way to the Missouri from Minnesota, drawn there by trade and the riches in the Missouri bottoms. By the middle 1700s, the western Sioux migrated back and forth between the meadows and forests of the Upper Mississippi River drainage and the tallgrass prairies east of the Missouri River trench. These seasonal movements followed recognizable routes and patterns. Sioux bands trod a path up the Minnesota Valley before diverging along two possible trails to the west. One avenue left the banks of the Minnesota, passed up the Redwood River, traveled on to Lake Benton, and from there skirted Medary Creek. Medary Creek led the Sioux to the Big Sioux River, which they crossed and then went on to Lake Campbell. To the west of Lake Campbell, the Sioux hopped from pothole to pothole until arriving along the southern tip of Lake Thompson. Water and bison drew them westward to Redstone Creek, across Firesteel Creek, and through Sand Creek. Eventually, the Indians arrived at either Wolf Creek or Crow Creek, both of which aimed the Sioux toward the shores of the Missouri.

A second thoroughfare from Minnesota to the Missouri traced farther to the north. This trail began in the Minnesota Valley near Marsh Lake, then scampered up the South Fork Yellow Bank River all the way to its uppermost heights, where it passed by Round Lake on its way to Willow Creek and the Big Sioux River. At today's Watertown, South Dakota, the trail cut a fairly straight path from Lake Kampeska westward. The road crossed over Timber Creek, Dry Run, and the James River before entering the South Fork Snake Creek at the point where it joins Snake Creek proper. Pursuing the South

Fork Snake Creek west, the Sioux came to a fork in the road near today's Faulkton, South Dakota. Here they either continued up the South Fork Snake Creek until reaching the head of Okoboji Creek or swerved to the southwest and found the head of Medicine Creek. Either one of those two routes pointed them to the Missouri River. Okoboji Creek dropped the Sioux into the Missouri Valley not far from the Little Bend, whereas Medicine Creek placed them solidly on the east bank between the Big Bend and the Bad River confluence.

In the middle eighteenth century, Sioux bands left the boreal forest during the spring and early summer to hunt bison as far as the Missouri's eastern flank. Much of the hunting occurred in the Coteau des Prairies. Loaded down with meat and heavy bison robes, the bands returned to the trees by late summer. They remained in the forest and along its periphery until the following year, when they repeated the cycle. On these annual hunting excursions, the Sioux encountered the Missouri River tribes. From the earliest years of the Sioux migration westward, the Sioux warred against these semi-sedentary Indians (including the Arikara, Hidatsa, Mandan, Omaha, and later Ponca).[1] The animosity between the Sioux and the river tribes preceded the arrival of Euro-Americans in the Upper Missouri. As a matter of fact, the river tribes, including the longest established tribes, the Mandan and Hidatsa, viewed the Sioux as unwelcome interlopers from the east. Mandan and Hidatsa leaders did not want more competitors vying for the bison herds and bottoms of the Upper Missouri.

Initially, the Sioux went to the Missouri to hunt on a seasonal basis, returning from whence they came before the onset of deep summer. But gradually the seasonal hunting camps extending along the Missouri's eastern bank from the mouth of Okoboji Creek to Medicine Creek became semipermanent village sites where Sioux bands spent the blustery winter months shielded by cottonwoods from gray clouds of snow and cold winds. These first Sioux colonizers in the Missouri River trench faced enemies on three sides: to the north, the Mandan and Hidatsa; due west, the Arikara and Cheyenne; to the south, the Omaha and the predecessors of the Ponca. All these tribes wanted to drive the Sioux back. Although facing resistance from the river tribes, the Sioux planted outlying colonies on the Upper Missouri main stem by 1750. A large population of young men, British guns, and a ferocious tenacity made it possible for the Sioux to hold to the Missouri. From the archaeological evidence, it appears as though the Sioux crossed the Missouri sometime in the early 1760s and established a beachhead on the Missouri's western shore near the Bad-Missouri confluence. The Teton Sioux winter count for 1764–1765 depicted men swimming, and its translation read, "They swim towards buffalo." This could mean that the Sioux swam the Missouri River in search of bison on the west bank.[2]

In the late 1760s, massed infantry attacks by gun-toting Sioux removed the Arikara from their heavily fortified village at the mouth of Crow Creek. The destruction of this village secured the Sioux's southern flank, which allowed the Sioux to move down the Missouri, James, and Big Sioux Rivers into today's southeast South Dakota. The Sioux victory at Crow Creek also enabled them to advance en force across the Missouri without fear of encirclement by the Arikara. Straight out from the mouth of Crow Creek sat an ideal ford across the Missouri main stem. Destroying the Arikara position at Crow Creek and capturing the ford gave the Sioux the ability to project their power to the west and southwest toward the Oacoma bottom and White River; it also made the Arikara position on the Missouri's west bank less tenable.

During subsequent decades, the Sioux solidified their hold on the Missouri's east bank, spreading south to the James-Missouri confluence and north to the Great Bend in today's North Dakota. But the Sioux did not stop there. In the late eighteenth century, Sioux bands on the Missouri's west bank wrestled six prominent sanctuaries out of the hands of the Arikara and Ponca. The warfare in the Missouri Valley centered on the bottomland sanctuaries, where the Teton Sioux waged genocidal wars to capture biologically diverse ecological zones. The Sioux seized the bottoms at the mouths of the Cheyenne River, Bad River, Medicine Creek (on the south bank of the Missouri, not to be confused with the other Medicine Creek flowing into the Missouri from the north), American Creek, and the White River, as well as the mesa inside Big Bend.

Of these six bottomland sanctuaries and tributary mouths, the bottom bestride the mouth of the Cheyenne was the most strategically important. As mentioned earlier, the Cheyenne River road coupled the Missouri Valley with the Black Hills. The road was the most heavily utilized route between the Black Hills and Missouri; it was also part of a larger trade route across the plains, serving as a link in the chain that joined the Missouri Valley, Black Hills, Platte Valley, central plains, Rocky Mountain frontal range in today's Colorado, and Sante Fe market. Additionally, the Cheyenne River road cut through the epicenter of the Upper Missouri bison range. Superb hunting existed in and around the Cheyenne Valley. Moreover, the bottom at the mouth of the Cheyenne River served as the linchpin between the western plains and the eastern prairie-plains and between Spanish horses and British guns.

The import of the Cheyenne bottom became apparent in 1795, when Sioux infantry launched an all-out attack against the Arikara village at the mouth of the Cheyenne. In a war that foreshadowed the total wars of the twentieth century, the Sioux killed at least 125 men, women, and children before taking the stronghold. Once inside the earthen breastworks that encircled the fortified village, the Sioux proceeded to erase all vestiges of Arikara occupancy. Warriors leveled the village's earth lodges and incinerated whatever remained standing. With that victory, the Sioux established a defensible anchor on their north and west flanks. They also positioned themselves for an empire across the Upper Missouri. They could now move west, to the Black Hills and beyond, without anxiety that their rear would be compromised by the Arikara. With the capture of the Cheyenne bottom, the Teton Sioux had muscled and murdered their way into a prominent role in the Upper Missouri (fig. 5.1).

By 1804, the Sioux's Missouri Valley properties laid the groundwork for their imperial expansion to the south and west. By the time of the Lewis and Clark expedition, the Teton Sioux held firm control over a 150-mile reach of the Missouri River trench. Dominion over one of the richest ecological areas in the Upper Missouri bioregion bestowed on the Sioux a preeminent role in the geography and economy of the Upper Missouri. Their Missouri Valley holdings would put them on a collision course with another imperial power moving up from the southeast.

The Lewis and Clark expedition inaugurated the Euro-American presence in the Upper Missouri. When Lewis and Clark returned to St. Louis in the fall of 1806, the public greeted the exploring party as national heroes. The resounding welcome received by Lewis and Clark and the other men, along with the extreme public interest in the physical details of the continental crossing, fulfilled another of Jefferson's goals for the expedition, which was to rally the populace behind the administration and the nation-state. Patriotism and optimism rose up the flag pole of nationalism. French and Spanish fur traders, who only recently swore allegiance to the United States, expressed gratitude for the return of the explorers to St. Louis. They heartily welcomed home Lewis and Clark not out of a sense of patriotism but for more self-interested and entrepreneurial reasons. These fur traders wanted to tap the fertile beaver streams of the far Upper Missouri basin.

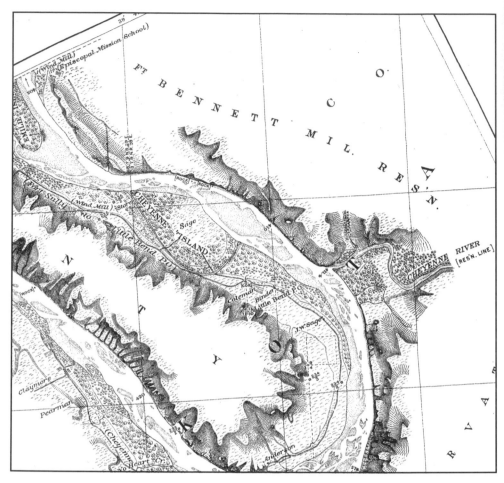

Figure 5.1. The Cheyenne bottom (view toward south). This 1894 Missouri River Commission map of the Cheyenne bottom shows the Cheyenne–Missouri River confluence in the lower right corner. Just downstream from the Cheyenne River's mouth, on the Missouri's right bank, lay the well-known and heavily used bottomland. In the 1790s the Teton Sioux fought a vicious war against the Arikara for dominance of this crucial choke point in the Upper Missouri territory. Once the Teton captured the Cheyenne bottom, the tribe positioned itself for hegemony over the plains to the west, southwest. (Missouri River Commission Map, 1894)

Lewis and Clark would serve their selfish desires. Manuel Lisa and Pierre Choteau Sr. sought out Lewis and Clark for the geographic and ethnographic information they gathered in the Upper Missouri. They wanted to know where they could and should establish fur trading posts, where they could find the highest concentrations of beaver, which Indians would be willing to trade furs for guns, powder, balls, and trinkets, and which tribes would kill their men.

Lewis and Clark understood that the legacy of the expedition would be as important as the actual act of traversing the continent. The only way the expedition would continue to hold meaning and significance in the American consciousness (besides the impressive physical obstacles it had overcome in its two-year, four-month journey) would be if the knowledge gathered on the trip reached the widest possible audience. Without the dissemination of information through the publication of the journals, correspondence, and conversation, the explorers would fail in the most important mission of all: to make the expedition historically relevant as a tool for imperial America's drive to the Pacific. Their discoveries needed to aid American expansion into the Upper Missouri. If the American people had failed to follow the explorers up the Missouri, it is unlikely the United States would be celebrating the bicentennial of their journey. It is the legacy of imperialism that made the men great. Distilled from the westward movement, the Lewis and Clark expedition loses its impact, becoming just a footnote in American history.

Lewis and Clark did not want to become historically irrelevant. Patriots to the core, and seeking recognition and institutional advancement within the American sociopolitical structure, the two men freely shared the wealth of their experience and knowledge of the Upper Missouri with the fur men of St. Louis. Lisa and Choteau, in the fall of 1806 and winter of 1806–1807, mined the two captains for details on the Upper Missouri's geography, hydrology, ecology, and ethnography. In candlelit rooms, over brandy and cigars, Lewis and Clark told the eager traders what they wanted to hear. They provided them with details that kindled their imaginations. Lisa and Choteau heard of the incalculable numbers of beaver at the Missouri's Three Forks and along the banks of the gravelly Yellowstone. The captains also offered their opinions on the best locations for fur trading posts, which would be collection centers for the furs and distribution points for trade items. According to both captains, the premier location for a fur trading post would be on the south side of the Missouri main stem just above the mouth of the

Yellowstone. Lewis wrote of this site on April 27, 1805, "On the Missouri about 2½ miles from the entrance of the yellowstone river, and between this high and low plain, a small lake is situated about 200 yards wide extending along the edge of the high plain parallel with the Missouri about one mile. On the point of the high plain at the lower extremity of this lake I think would be the most eligible site for an establishment."[3] Clark thought a site closer to the confluence would serve traders better than Lewis's location. Nonetheless, with their knowledge of hydrology, Lewis and Clark correctly gauged that the width and water volume of both the Missouri and the Yellowstone indicated one thing—the far Upper Missouri basin (the land area to the west, southwest, and northwest of the mouth of the Yellowstone) drained a huge area. Those two big rivers would carry Indians and furs to this juncture. Their assessment of the geographic importance of the Yellowstone-Missouri confluence would be confirmed on the return trip in 1806. By August 1806, the captains knew that the Upper Missouri and Yellowstone, in addition to their tributaries, resembled a funnel that could pour forth the wealth of the far Upper Missouri into the hands of any Euro-American willing to reach for it (fig. 5.2).

Another superb site for a post existed where the Gallatin, Madison, and Jefferson came together to create the Missouri. Beaver waddled all over the bowl-shaped valley enclosing the Three Forks. Erect a post where the Missouri gave birth, and the traders could net beaver and Indians. The explorers recommended a third site for a post at the mouth of the Bighorn. In July 1806, Clark noticed that beaver dens and dams blotted the land and waterscape in the vicinity of the Bighorn-Yellowstone confluence. The beaver were there; they just needed to be trapped out. In addition, the largest tributary of the Yellowstone would quickly put trappers into the beaver fields along the Bighorn itself and the foothills of the Bighorn Mountains, while carrying their beaver peltries downstream in bullboats or dugouts.

Lewis and Clark recommended constructing a geography of extraction across the Upper Missouri. Choteau and Lisa concurred in that recommendation. While the captains represented the architects of a Euro-American geography in the Upper Missouri, Choteau and Lisa supervised the first construction crews who erected it. Consequently, the rivers of the Upper Missouri, especially the Bighorn, Yellowstone, and far Upper Missouri, would be great siphons, pulling resources out of the land and pushing them downstream to the great port at St. Louis. Lewis and Clark saw the Missouri main stem as the central element in their geographic system. It would be the pri-

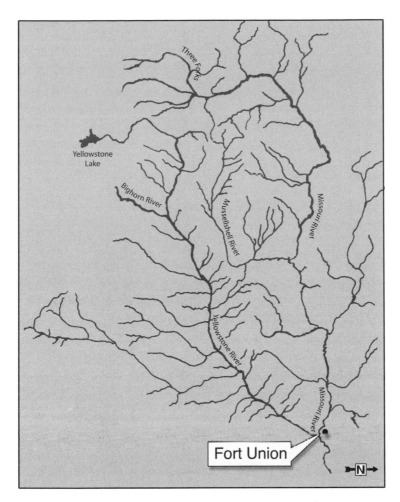

Figure 5.2. Fort Union and the funnel-shaped drainage basin of the far Upper Missouri to its west. The hydrology of the far Upper Missouri basin made the Yellowstone-Missouri confluence an ideal location for a Euro-American collection and distribution center within the region's fur trading system. (Paul Davidson, South Plains College, Levelland, Texas)

mary route into and out of the Upper Missouri territory until the advent of the railroad.

Lewis and Clark told the fur men about the tribes of the Upper Missouri. In simplified terms, the captains warned them about the Sioux and the Blackfeet, while espousing the amiable qualities of the Mandan and the questionable character of the Crow. After having his head filled with advice,

Lisa went northwest to the Upper Missouri in spring 1807 to establish a post at the mouth of the Bighorn named in honor of his son, Ramon. Thus began the construction of a Euro-American geography. Lisa would have been better served had he chosen the Yellowstone-Missouri confluence for the site of his post. As it turned out, Fort Ramon, perched at a choke point on the Little Bighorn, Bighorn, Alkali Creek, and Musselshell River road, maintained only a fleeting presence in the Upper Missouri. To its detriment, it lay too far from downstream centers of support. Positioned approximately two thousand river miles from St. Louis, the post could not be easily or cheaply resupplied by Lisa's fledging company. Lacking U.S. military backing, the enterprise on the Bighorn became untenable from a defensive standpoint. Hence, the post operated for less than a year before its owner abandoned it to the sage and buffalo grass. Its distance from the East and pressure from the Blackfeet forced its closure. Fort Ramon's brief history illustrates the nature of the Upper Missouri beaver and bison robe trade. In the decades that followed, posts rose and fell across the Upper Missouri with a frequency hard to track and a history impossible to chronicle; but all the posts, from the big to the small, played similar roles, occupied analogous locations, and set in motion comparable ecological transformations.

Traders often went up the Missouri in the spring, set up a ramshackle post by fall, collected furs in the winter and early spring through barter, and then returned to St. Louis with their peltries atop either the spring fresh or the June rise. Consequently, small trading houses appeared and disappeared on an annual basis. This modus operandi continued on the Upper Missouri from 1807 until the end of Indian independence in the late 1870s. A few examples will illustrate the fluidity of the Upper Missouri fur trade and its geography. At the Yellowstone-Missouri confluence numerous fur trading posts came and went in the nineteenth century; most lasted only a few years. Traders built Fort Henry in 1822 and abandoned it in 1823. Fort William survived but a year between 1833 and 1834, while Fort Mortimer lasted from 1842 to 1845. Only Fort Union lasted more than a decade; it thrived from 1828 to 1867. The Bighorn-Yellowstone confluence witnessed the same instability. Fort Ramon set the example for all the posts that followed in its stead. Fort Benton on the Yellowstone was built by the Missouri Fur Company in 1821 and deserted by its traders in 1823. The American Fur Company built Fort Cass at the Bighorn-Yellowstone confluence in 1832 only to leave it to rot in 1835. In 1875, Bozeman entrepreneurs established Fort Pease. The U.S. Army rescued Fort Pease's war-weary residents from certain death at the hands of the Sioux in March 1876. The geography of the Upper Missouri fur trade displayed a temporal quality that matched the region's fluctuating ecology and mobile geography.

The Euro-American fur trading system developed a semblance of permanence when the American Fur Company established the bigger facilities of Fort Union (1829), Fort Clark (1831), and Fort Pierre (1832).[4] Each post served as a center in its own right while offering support to the other two units in the network. Although all these forts remained along the Missouri main stem for over two decades, the transitory nature of the system continued in the form of satellite posts. Satellite posts, at the time referred to as trading houses, often consisted of nothing more than a log cabin or tiny stockade manned by a handful of brave or desperate souls. The American Fur Company and its competitors established trading houses on a yearly or seasonal basis. The houses sat on the periphery of the geography of trade—tenuously situated on the edge of the areal reach of the big forts. To cite an example, in 1832, Fort Union supported two satellite posts, one at Fort McKenzie near the mouth of the Marias River and one at Fort Cass at the Bighorn-Yellowstone confluence. Fort Cass lay nearly 300 miles from Fort Union, while Fort McKenzie sat about 350 river miles away. At those distances, Fort Union's occupants could do little to assist the satellite posts if they came under assault from hostile bands of Blackfeet. Furs collected at the peripheral facilities went downriver to Fort Union in April or as late as May, where the peltries would be placed on the June steamboat for transshipment to St. Louis (fig. 5.3).

After the fall in beaver numbers in the 1820s and early 1830s, the bison robe became the key item in the fur trade. The positioning of Euro-American trading posts throughout the Upper Missouri territory dramatically influenced bison ecology. For the most part, the fur traders built their trading posts along the Missouri and Yellowstone River main stems. They did this to access the deep waters of the region's two most navigable rivers. Even more significantly, the road network of the Upper Missouri conveniently touched both of these two large streams, allowing posts to attract Indian traders to their gates. Euro-Americans constructed their trade houses and larger forts within the rich bottoms situated at the mouths of the tributaries flowing into either the Yellowstone or the Missouri. The timber, game, and grass flourishing in the bottoms made the oases ideal for the placement of trading posts. Post occupants needed timber for palisades, storage facilities, housing, and fuel, grass for stock, and game to satiate their gnawing appetites.

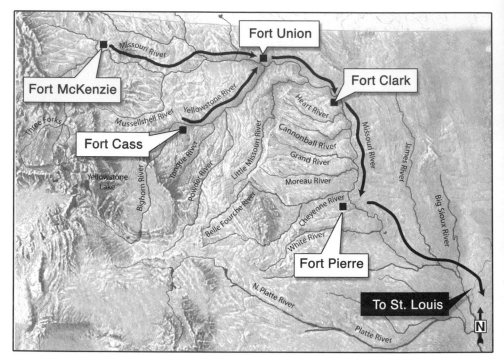

Figure 5.3. The beginnings of Euro-American geography in the Upper Missouri. Euro-American fur traders redirected a portion of the Upper Missouri's energy flows down the Missouri main stem. (Paul Davidson, South Plains College, Levelland, Texas)

The posts also sat high above the floodplain, most often atop a second or third terrace, immune from annual freshets. One individual said the following about Fort Pierre's location: "The site selected was a level plateau some three hundred feet back from the river, about three miles from the mouth of the Wapka Shicka [the Bad River]."[5] Frequently, trading houses and forts arose where a gravel bank to their front offered long-term protection against the wanderings of the Missouri or Yellowstone. Gravel banks held the river's erosive currents in check. The posts and their human and animal occupants also resided where a deep, stable channel of the Missouri or the Yellowstone could bring keels, mackinaws, and later steamboats to their front. The Fort Union site is a case in point. At the place where the American Fur Company erected Fort Union, a firm, high gravel bank line sloped down to a deep river channel only feet from the fort's main gate. To the east down the Missouri's north bank, timber grew in healthy, tall stands, offering carpenters a perfect source for hewing palisades and storage facilities. To the rear of the fort, a wide, open plain grew grass for stock. Game ran amok in the confluence area, with its wide array of species habitats. Post site selection also involved considerations of defense. Euro-Americans wanted clear fields of fire around the margins of any post—to ward off Indians showing a belligerent face to the fort. Fort Union possessed excellent fields of fire, especially to its rear, where a plateau presented a view of the countryside that militated against any surprise attack.

Yet the most important geographic consideration when establishing a trading post in the Upper Missouri region related to the ancient bison and Indian road network. Euro-Americans set up their fur trading posts along the Missouri and Yellowstone main stems at locations that intersected the great roads and straddled the largest, most fruitful bottoms. During the height of the fur trade era, between 1807 and the 1840s, trading houses or forts arose at the toe of the Sixty-Mile Bottom at old Council Bluffs (the one that lay on the Missouri's western shore opposite the Boyer River confluence). The Boyer and Little Sioux Rivers, which mouth at the Missouri within miles of one another, delivered Indians, traders, and furs from today's northwestern Iowa to the trading forts inside the Sixty-Mile Bottom. Through the years, a variety of trading houses arose at the head of the Sixty-Mile Bottom, in the vicinity of the Omaha village. As late as the mid-1850s, a trading house operated by a Mr. Thompson nestled under the loess hills near today's Sergeant's Bluff. Thompson traded with the Omaha and possibly with the Sioux moving up and down the Floyd and Big Sioux Rivers.

Another trading house existed at the mouth of the Big Sioux, where today's South Dakota jabs its lowest extremity into Iowa. A French Canadian named Bruguier traded at that spot. Bruguier's post tapped the Big Sioux Valley to the north and the Missouri Valley to the northwest, catering largely to the Sioux coming down from those two directions. The cottonwood bottom on the south side of the Vermillion River, close to its confluence with the Missouri, served for decades as a trading center. Its coverage area included that bountiful tallgrass prairie land lying to the northeast. Farther up the Missouri, where the soiled James entered the Big Muddy, temporary trading houses came and went in the tall cottonwood forest on the James's southeast bank. Small-time operators placed trading houses at the Niobrara bottom, on the Missouri's eastern shore opposite the mouth of Ponca Creek, and within the bottom situated at the mouth of the White River. The bottom on the Missouri's western shore opposite Crow Creek and the Sioux Three

Rivers Pass held Fort Kiowa in the 1820s. Traders built a house on a high, protected island near the mouth of Medicine Creek. The bottom to the north of the Bad River–Missouri confluence contained Fort Tecumseh and then Fort Pierre, both of which intercepted Indians and bison coming down three well-traveled roads—Okoboji Creek from the east and the Bad and Cheyenne Rivers from the west. A post also once sat at the bottom situated on the Missouri's west bank facing toward today's Pollock, South Dakota. The Heart, Knife, and Apple Creek embouchements saw their share of short-lived trading posts. Fort Berthold later dominated the Missouri's northern shore close to where the Little Missouri road crossed the Missouri trench. The traders at Fort Berthold and their Indian allies in the neighborhood thus oversaw the mammalian traffic passing from the Missouri trench to the Little Missouri badlands to the southwest. Fort Berthold presented its owner-operators with a superb location for trading, especially after midcentury, when the only remaining bison roamed in the lands to the west and south of the fort.

The American Fur Company assembled Fort Union at the greatest intersection of roads in the Upper Missouri. Roads from the southwest, west, northwest, northeast, and east came to a single foci at the confluence. Those roads made Fort Union into a grand spectacle, where extravagant and colorfully dressed characters from the far corners of the Upper Missouri joined to barter for their needs and wants. Fort Peck made its apperance in 1866–1867 near the mouths of Big Dry Creek and the Milk River. Through the years, forts found their way into the flowery Musselshell bottom, the wooded Judith bottom, and the wet Marias-Teton bottom. The Three Forks also contained a post in the first years after Lewis and Clark came home. Traders abandoned that fort after the Blackfeet made it obvious they did not appreciate a Euro-American presence in the middle of their favorite hunting and trapping grounds. In the Yellowstone Valley, Euro-Americans built additional wooden fortresses. The Bighorn confluence witnessed the placement and cession of five posts during the fur trade era. One post found its way into the bottom in the vicinity of modern-day Hysham, Montana; another one lay down in the vegetated bottom near the mouth of the Big Porcupine; and two more sat close to the mouth of the Rosebud. This list is by no means definitive, since many trading houses lasted only a few months before vanishing into historical obscurity. The main conclusion to be drawn from the history of post site selection is the relationship between Euro-American trading facilities and the existing Indian-bison road network. Euro-Americans utilized the Missouri and Yellowstone River trenches to connect their constructs to Indian and bison movements. The posts represented a Euro-American adaptation to an ancient geographical system.

Interestingly, Indians often informed Euro-Americans where to erect the fur trading posts. John Luttig remembered the Sioux telling the Euro-Americans where to built their fort: "3 Chiefs and 2 young Men remained to fix on a spot for a trading house they went with us across the River to the North Side 1 Mile below where we had camped, laid out the house for Mr. Bijou who was to remain to trade with the Yentonas, Sioux and Shaunee."[6] Culbertson asserted in 1850, "The trading houses are built of rough logs and are intended but for one winter; they are built wherever a party of Indians happens to locate for the hunting season, and traders are sent out with an equipment according to the prospect for robes."[7] Indian tribes wanted posts along their routes of travel, within the bottoms where they camped in late summer and winter, inside their core geographic region, and at a safe distance from the campsites of their enemies. If the Indians did not choose the location for a trading post, they permitted, or grudging accepted, its existence so long as they benefited from its presence. But when a post quit serving their needs or largely assisted their enemies, tribes might lay siege to it until its occupants withdrew or died.

The fur trade, trading houses, and forts in the Upper Missouri had some unforeseen repercussions on bison ecology, ones that accumulated over time. For starters, the fur trade disrupted the ecology of the bison hunt. Previous to the trade, Indians took the bulk of their animals during the summer, when bison ran fat and grew less hair. More fat meant more food, while less hair meant less work in turning robe to tepee, container, or tool. But the traders demanded a heavy bison coat, which meant the Indians shifted their hunting pattern to take more animals in the winter months. Often the Indians might remain all winter near a post, killing any bison that came near and then immediately processing the robes for trade. Hunting close to the forts lessened Indian labor, since it was not necessary to transport the robes over long distances. Such practices put tremendous stress on a bison population already pushed to its limits by the weather. The shift to winter hunting resulted in the wholesale killing of animals down in their valley sanctuaries, which in turn forced them out of the valleys in the winter, where they suffered greater predation on the uplands or succumbed to cold, snow, and hunger. The fur trade altered the seasonal character of the hunt and increased bison mortality.

An ever-increasing Euro-American presence kept bison away from the Missouri and Yellowstone Valleys at crucial times during the year. If hard weather (drought, cold, or snow) gave bison no choice but to move into the bottoms next to the Euro-American forts, the creatures risked being destroyed. Luttig, at a post located on a peninsula of land on the Missouri's west bank near present-day Kenel, South Dakota, recalled that on a blustery December day in 1812, the bison flooded down Spring Creek into the Missouri Valley. The presence of the bison so close to the Euro-American fort made the killing of the animals quite easy. Luttig remarked, "Cloudy, opposite the fort the Prairie is covered with Buffaloe, Bapt and Men arrived this morning had Killed 4 Cows and 2 Bulls."[8] Chardon spoke of a band of bulls that approached within range of Fort Clark during the rut in late August 1834: "News of a band of Buffaloe, below—Mandans went to run them—Accompanied them to the chaise and Killed one—on our way home we were overtaken by a shower of rain, and thunder, the Indians say that we Killed all the band amounting to 27 Bulls."[9] James Chambers at Fort Sarpy, in the Yellowstone Valley, wrote on January 5, 1855, "A very cold day large bands of Bufflo on the opposite side of the river. Valle Lamarche & all hands out on a hunt Valle approached & kill'd one cow Faillant at the report of the gun took after the Band on foot fired in the band some five or six shots without effecting wound of all the fools I have ever seeen Faillant bangs all."[10] What these accounts indicate is that Euro-American occupancy of an increasing number of bottomland sanctuaries in conjunction with their hunting practices severely impacted bison.

Indians killed bison to dominate or temporarily overpower the intrusive grassland. They also killed the animals to survive and prosper. Euro-Americans hunted bison for more complex and elusive reasons. For a white male in the Upper Missouri during the waning days of the bison world, killing bison had less to do with putting meat on the table (although that did factor into the equation) and more with proving himself manly. Euro-Americans have long exhibited an obsession with trophies. Since the dawn of the Euro-American presence in the Upper Missouri, and before that along the eastern seaboard, whites hunted and fished to snatch trophies. They clung to the belief that bigger is better. In taking down a mammoth bison bull, a white male proclaimed to the world, but especially to those in his immediate community, that he was as virile as the bull he just blasted into oblivion. A white male did not become a true man of the wilderness, or, as they called them in the nineteenth century, a mountaineer, until he killed a bison on horseback. Hunting to kill a trophy bison reeked of machismo and contributed much to the slaughter and demise of the herds, since hunters always wanted a bigger bull, or more cows, or a more difficult or exciting kill. For some, shooting bison became addictive; the adrenaline rush and the inflation of the ego made it an aphrodisiac. Men just had to go back to the hunt again and again to satiate their bloodlust. Whites wanted to make the hunt better next time by displaying a more adept handling of their horse during the chase or to show their comrades just how well they could pull out their big rifle and slam a bison into the earth. It had so much to do with showing others, and proving to oneself, just how much of a man one could be in the wilds. To kill bison with more skill than a plains Indian, or at least with equal adeptness, meant a lot. Euro-Americans could then claim special status: they resembled the rough-and-tumble mountaineers, men who took down bison as easily as they bedded Indian women or swallowed dram after dram of cheap whiskey (fig. 5.4).

The trophy complex emerged from the longitudinal landscape of the Euro-American agricultural world. Sport hunting distinguished a "civilized" man from a savage. Civilized men hunted for sport, whereas Indians hunted out of necessity. Euro-Americans killed for entertainment, camaraderie, and personal distinction; indigenes killed for food. In an added twist, Euro-American males considered their own form of hunting far superior to that of the Indian. Killing for sport bestowed stature and elevated its perpetrator beyond the confines of the wilderness. Only Indians and uncouth mountaineers killed for a livelihood. This Euro-American mentality came up the Missouri with fur traders, eastern elites, and European tourists. Celebrated travelers who visited the region in the early and middle nineteenth century, such as Maximilian, Nicollet, Culbertson, Audubon, and Harris, recognized when they entered the Upper Missouri frontier because bison became the standard fare at the dinner table. Yet these men participated in repeated bison hunts from a perceptual place of sport rather than from a perceived necessity. Hunting for sport kept the wilderness at a distance. Sport separated upper-class whites both socially and economically from the Indians and mountaineers. It proclaimed that the wilderness had not subsumed their identities as the upper echelon within American society. They may have killed to put meat in their mouths, but they still saw this killing as distinct from the Indian practice, since they infused it with notions of sport. Sport drew one more boundary between themselves and the Indians or the trashy whites who had gone native.

Figure 5.4. The mountaineer. Mountaineers occupied a perceptual space between civilization and savagery. They found various kinds of work while in the Upper Missouri, including hunter, trapper, trader, and scout. Nineteenth-century elites who visited the Upper Missouri both idealized and despised the mountaineers for their daring, skill, and occasional reckless abandon. (Courtesy of the Thomas Gilcrease Institute of American History, Tulsa, Oklahoma)

Edward Harris, a clumsy, bespectacled intellectual who visited the Upper Missouri in 1843, wrote profusely about hunting bison. Harris composed the following lines after a day of shooting bison with his male colleagues in a region southwest of Fort Union: "We now regretted having destroyed these noble beasts for no earthly reason but to gratify a sanguinary disposition which appears to be inherent in our natures. We had no means of carrying home the meat and after cutting out the tongues we wended our way back to camp, completely disgusted with ourselves and with the conduct of all white men who come to this country. In this way year after year thousands of these animals are slaughtered for mere sport and the carcasses left for the wolves."[11] Oddly, Harris's guilt over this incident would not stop him from doing the same thing less than three weeks later.[12]

Notions of sport helped maintain perceived civilization in the face of wilderness. Sport bolstered Euro-American ideas of cultural, intellectual, and physical superiority by proving that whites had not entirely lost their more earthy or primitive natures. In other words, it proved that civilization produced strong men. Paradoxically, sport gave Euro-Americans the opportunity to claim they controlled wild nature in themselves. Whites could go out in the morning, defeat the wilderness, and still go home in the evening to the wife, kids, cabin, and corn. Sport offered whites one-upmanship, a means of outperforming Indians at their own game, while still enabling Euro-Americans to serve as upstanding members of civilized society. Additionally, by engaging in hunting as sport, or infusing it with an element of entertainment and frivolity, Euro-Americans separated themselves from the land at their feet and the ecology moving all around them. Since they hunted for sport, they did not need the land or its ecology for survival. Sport gave Euro-Americans the illusion of independence from ecological limitations. Whites had supposedly freed themselves from the ecological processes that kept Indians bound to the earth and its wild creatures. Whites, with the wonder of agriculture and the capitalist economy propping it up, did not have to obey nature's dictates as Indians did. Whites convinced themselves that if sport hunting failed them, they could still look to markets for food and fiber. Euro-Americans believed civilization offered them protection from ecological disturbances, ecological collapse, and dramatic fluctuations in mammalian populations. This idea (that Euro-Americans did not face the same ecological limits as Indians) served to elevate the Euro-American superiority complex even higher.

Interestingly, Lewis and Clark, who spent over two years beyond the fringe of civilization and who hunted daily for food and fiber, did not fully abandon sport hunting. It is easy to understand why. Sport perpetuated old identities under stress and strain. Along the Yellowstone River in July 1806, when identities began to buckle under the weight of the bison world, Clark and company engaged in day after day of sport hunting. Clark's journals made it obvious that he and the other men engaged in an ongoing quest to kill still more game and/or bigger bison bulls, bears, elk, and deer. On July 19, 1806, he wrote, "killed Seven Elk, four Deer, and I wounded a Buffalow very badly near the Camp imediately after I arived. in the forepart of the day the hunters killed two deer an Antelope & shot two Bear."[13] This widespread killing had little to do with feeding or outfitting the thirteen people in his detachment. Days later Clark noted that he killed the biggest deer of his life:

"Saw emence number of Deer Elk and buffalow on the banks. Some beaver. I landed on the Lard Side walked out into the bottom and Killd the fatest Buck I every Saw."[14] One day after killing his "fatest" buck, Clark wrote of wanting to kill a trophy bighorn sheep. He commented, "I wished very much to kill a large [bighorn] buck, had there been one with the gang I Should have killd. him."[15] Trophy fever had seized the young explorer. Clark, through ritualistic slaughter, exorcised his own doubts and savage demons. In the act of shooting trophies, he reminded himself of his civilized demeanor and background.

There was really nothing civilized at all about sport hunting. Killing is a dirty business; it is bloody, violent, and noisy. A bison in the throes of death can make quite a scene. After several slugs pierce its body, the animal might shudder, drop down on its front knees, mourn its own death with deep, guttural wails, open its mouth and dangle its tongue over its chin, bleed copiously from its nose, and even cry out a death song before leaning over on its side and kicking its legs straight out in rigor mortis. Killing bison, or any creature, for the thrill of it, to remind oneself of who one is, or to impress colleagues is without question a shallower justification for killing than killing for survival.

Sport hunting had serious consequences for the bison herds of the Upper Missouri, contributing to a separation of Euro-Americans from the Upper Missouri's bison world. Hunting for sport placed Euro-Americans outside the perceptual and ecological boundaries of the region. In the Upper Missouri, Euro-Americans proved their otherworldliness, or outsider status, by wantonly slaughtering bison, elk, and other large fauna. Euro-Americans did not need hunting to maintain their culture, but whites well knew that bison supported Indian culture. Euro-Americans showed their disdain, snobbishness, and disrespect for Indians and their world by killing bison.

Sport hunting severed Euro-Americans from the bison world's land, rivers, ecology, and cultures. This is what Euro-Americans wanted anyway. Sport hunting, and all the English cultural baggage attached to it, removed any brake (either moral or economic) on killing. Since Euro-Americans did not believe they needed bison (or any other native species) to uphold their culture, perpetuate their economy, or maintain their religious systems, and since the act of killing actually strengthened waning identities, Euro-Americans saw no reason not to participate in an orgy of slaughter across the Upper Missouri. An added incentive to kill was the knowledge that it cleared away the old order in preparation for the new. Once the bison left the Upper

Missouri, the region would be primed for the dawn of a new age of agriculture. There existed no higher power, and no human authority, able to stop the killing. Indians attempted to slow the slaughter of bison by whites, but to no avail.

Navigators on the Missouri inflicted major damage on the herds. To cite an instance, if steamboat passengers eyed a herd swimming in the river in front of the bow of the boat, and the animals swam within shooting range, men ran for their guns, and in minutes shots rang out across the valley. When Euro-Americans spied animals onshore within range, they took the animals down. The journal records indicate that Euro-Americans rarely passed up the chance to shoot bison. On the steamers, most men and boys killed as many of the animals as they possibly could, while only refined and proper ladies did not engage in the practice. The journals are replete with tales of wanton slaughter by steamboat passengers. Mary E. Cook, on the steamer *Henry Atkins,* stated, "Great excitement on board caused by seeing an antelope in the river; every man rushed for his gun and over sixty shots were fired at the poor creature without killing him, and he was finally captured by going out with the Yawl and catching him by the horns."[16] Daniel Weston, on board the *Colorado* west of the Missouri-Yellowstone confluence, remembered, "This afternoon we had an exciting time with buffalo of which we have seen large herds today. Right under a steep bank which they could not climb and just at the water's edge we came upon seven, and as the boat approached they took to the river—I fired twice and have the credit given me of bringing down one with the shot that killed him."[17]

John Napton, on the *Imperial* below Fort Benton, wrote of bison hunting from the steamer: "Just as we were about to tie up for the night, an immense herd of buffalo were seen crossing the river a short distance below. This broke the monotony of our every day life on board and everybody was eager for the chase. Both yawls were soon full of men and on their way down the river. Several who could find no place in the yawls concluded to go by land. . . . All was confusion for a while until the hunters returned safe and with abundance of buffalo meat."[18] Near the Cannonball River, John James Audubon recounted the excitement of coming upon bison in mid stream:

At one place where the bluffs were high, we saw five Buffaloes landing a few hundred yards above us on the western side; one of them cantered off immediately, and by some means did reach the top of the hills, and went out of sight; the four others ran, waded and swam at different places, always above us, trying to make their escape. . . . Unfortunately for them, we had been gaining upon them; we had all been anxiously watching them, and the moment they began to swim we were all about the boat with guns and rifles, awaiting the instant when they would be close under our bows. The moment came; I was on the lower deck among several of the people with guns, and the firing was soon heavy; but not one of the Buffaloes was stopped, although every one must have been severely wounded. . . . Mr. Charles Primcau, who is a good shot, and who killed the young Buffalo bull the other day, assured me that it was his opinion the whole of these would die before sundown.[19]

Military expeditions that established posts in the region, or passed through, also wreaked havoc on the herds and other mammals. During the Yellowstone Expedition of 1818–1819, sponsored by the federal government to build a military post at the Yellowstone-Missouri confluence, a detachment left the main party to hunt in the valley and its environs. Hunters killed three hundred deer and twenty bears during the brief excursion.[20] Prince Maximilian, on the Missouri fourteen years after the Yellowstone Expedition, still heard of the destruction it wrought on the region's mammalian life. He wrote, "At that time there was so much game that they [the soldiers] entirely subsisted on it. We were told that in one year they killed 1,600, and the other 1,800 head of game [white-tailed deer], besides elks and bears; and wounded, perhaps, as many more of those animals, which they were unable to take."[21]

Knowing the danger posed by forts and their occupants, bison began to stay completely clear of them. In 1823, Paul Wilhelm recollected, "These animals have not been seen here for years, having been frightened away by the military station at the Council Bluffs."[22] In 1873, when the U.S. Army escorted the crews of the Northern Pacific Railroad survey into the Yellowstone Valley, Custer's men freely partook of sport. James Calhoun recalled near Pompey's Pillar, "We found the supposed horses were elk. There were about fifty in the herd, and after watching us for some time, they broke for the hills. With fifteen or twenty men General Custer pursued them and succeeded in getting fifteen. Other officers got about ten more, so that one half of the herd was killed."[23]

It seems as though travelers to the Upper Missouri did not fulfill their itinerary until they had gone on a hunt. Visitors to the fur posts participated in an obligatory bison hunt. Many men recalled their first hunt in detail, as a rite of passage in their lives, akin to losing some sort of virginal innocence to a woolly bison. The German Rudolph Friederich Kurz reminisced about his first bison hunt: "This has been a splendid day in my experience; I have been on the chase for the first time and shot my first buffalo. Sketched my first buffalo from life."[24] The killing of bison reached a fever pitch in the 1830s, with an increase in steamboat traffic, an intensification of the robe trade, and a general rise in Euro-American numbers in the Missouri River trench.

In 1831, the first steamboat made its appearance on the Upper Missouri. By that date, steamers had already displaced keels on the Lower Missouri as the primary mode of carrying cargo and passengers. The debut of steamers north of the Platte both resulted from and spurred the intensification of the bison robe trade, which was marked by the establishment of the first large, permanent trading posts. Deemed faster, more efficient, more reliable, and thus more profitable than keels, steamboats quickly supplanted keels as the heavy cargo–carrying vessels in the Upper Missouri trade.

Throughout the 1830s, smoke-spewing steamboats increasingly threw their soot into the air along the Mighty Mo. Prince Maximilian, on board the steamer *Yellow Stone* in 1833 (two years after its maiden voyage to the Upper Missouri), remembered how the boat, with the thump, thump of its engine, the shattering splash of its side wheel, and the rattle of its metal parts, caused a commotion while it pushed itself against the Missouri. Animals and Indians, who had never before heard or seen the loud, shrill sound of the industrial era, ran before the steam-spitting dragon. All fauna retreated before the odd-looking contraption. Maximilian recounted: "The noise and smoke of our steamer frightened all living creatures; geese and ducks flew off in all directions";[25] "Opposite to the mouth of Otter Creek, in the woods and thickets of the west bank, behind which rose the green hills of the prairie, there were many elks, which were frightened by the noise of the steamer";[26] and "Continuing our voyage, we saw the buffalo hasten away, and moored our vessel at twilight to some trees on the north bank."[27] Audubon saw firsthand how the *Omega* alarmed bison: "We have seen this day about fifty Buffaloes; two which we saw had taken to the river, with intent to swim across it, but on the approach of our thundering, noisy vessel, turned about and after struggling for a few minutes, did make out to reach the top of the bank, after which they traveled at a moderate gait for some hundreds of yards; then, perhaps smelling or seeing the steamboat, they went off a good though not very fast gallop, on the prairie by our side, and were soon somewhat ahead of us; they stopped once or twice, again resumed their gallop, and after a few diversions in their course, made to the hill-tops and disappeared altogether."[28] Steamers and their heavily armed passengers terrified bison.

Steamboats disrupted bison ecology in a number of ways. The brown-water cruisers forced bison out of the Missouri Valley. The sound of the boat itself, along with its trigger-happy passengers, made the Upper Missouri main stem unsafe from March through October. Granted, one or two boats on the river per year did not have too great of an effect on bison movements or population numbers. But by the 1860s, dozens of boats made multiple trips each year along the Upper Missouri. In 1864 alone, at least thirty steamboats ran up and down the Upper Missouri main stem between March and November.[29] Combine all that steamer traffic with that of hundreds of mackinaws, canoes, and bullboats, and you have a recipe for ecological disruption. Bison, rightfully wary of heavily armed Euro-Americans and their strange sounds and smells, steered clear of the Missouri River trench. Euro-American steamboats, and the accompanying activity, caused bison to avoid an essential biological corridor.

What hurt the herds the most was the timing of the boats. Steamboats came up from distant St. Louis atop the spring rise, reaching the Upper Missouri by early April or sometimes as late as May. The calving season lasted from mid-March to May. The big boats frightened mother and calf from the valley into the uplands. Atop the grassland, the yearlings and still-weak mothers faced an increased likelihood of predation by wolves. The effect that steamers had on calving is hard to gauge, but the boats likely increased stress on the animals and magnified the effects of predation. Correspondingly, the animals that concentrated in the Missouri River trench through May offered plenty of sport to bored steamer passengers. Debilitated cows and inexperienced yearlings made easy targets.

Steamboat pilots working the Upper Missouri turned the bows of their boats downstream in July, August, and sometimes as late as September or October. No pilot or crew wanted to spend the winter months locked in the ice along some remote reach of river where cold and Indians might make life unbearable. That downriver journey, which by the middle 1860s might be accompanied by hundreds of drunken miners in bullboats and mackinaws, occurred simultaneously with the bison rut. Miners, freed from the back-breaking labor involved in placer mining and glad to be going home, showed little restraint when descending the Missouri. Miners and other river travelers complicated the bison mating ritual. Bison found it more difficult, if not impossible, to mate while Euro-Americans, using fifty-caliber rifles, shot slug after slug through the air. The traffic descending the river during the rut disrupted bison propagation and thus affected herd numbers. The cumulative effects of decades of such human activity caused large-scale reductions in the bison population. Additionally, when those boats came down from the heights of the Missouri, their passengers and crews killed thousands upon thousands of animals, which immediately reduced bison numbers (fig. 5.5). Bradbury, somewhere south of the Calumet Bluffs, saw the valley filled with bison in rut. The members of his boat crew fired at the animals for no apparent reason: "We saw some buffaloes swimming, at which the men fired, contrary to our wishes, as we did not intend to stop for them."[30]

Steamboats contributed to deforestation within the Missouri River trench, especially in the bottoms and on the wooded islands. Steamboats consumed an average of 25 cords of wood per day. A trip on the Upper Missouri might last three months. It took two to two and a half months to get upstream to Fort Union, and then about two to three weeks to get back down to Omaha. That number of days amounted to a maximum of 2,250 cords of wood burned in their furnaces in one round trip between Omaha and Fort

Figure 5.5. A steamboat on the Upper Missouri. Steamboats adversely affected bison ecology. In this illustration, a boat plows straight through a herd of swimming bison while an Indian on horseback shakes his arm in outrage at the scene. When steamers pulled up to a herd in midchannel, the male passengers on board habitually shot as many animals as possible in the name of sport before the boat moved upstream. (Courtesy of the Thomas Gilcrease Institute of American History, Tulsa, Oklahoma)

Benton. All that kindling came from the valley, most of it offered up by the timbered bottoms near the Missouri's major tributaries, the same bottoms periodically occupied by Indians and bison. The continuous harvest of timber led to deforestation within the Missouri River trench by the 1850s and 1860s (fig. 5.6).

As early as 1833, Maximilian noted the deforestation present around Fort Pierre, not so much as a result of steamboat traffic but from overuse by Indians and Euro-Americans: "The timber for this fort was felled from forty to sixty miles up the river, and floated down, because none fit for the purpose was to be had in the neighborhood."[31] Steamboat operations only exacerbated the problem of deforestation in the Missouri Valley in today's central South Dakota. By 1850, Culbertson noted the insufficiency of timber in this area. He remarked, "There is nothing that would be called a forest, except at some places along the Missouri. To-day we have seen very little timber; most of the banks are destitute of it entirely, except the willow; occasionally a point is seen well timbered with young cotton wood. I have been told that

Figure 5.6. African-American roustabouts gather wood on the banks of the Missouri. Steamboats burned an average of twenty-five cords of wood per day in their furnaces. Consequently, the boats contributed to deforestation in the Missouri Valley by the 1850s and 1860s. (Courtesy of the Sioux City Public Museum, Sioux City, Iowa)

they go from Fort Pierre, one hundred miles above, to get timber for their boats and other purposes."[32] The trees in that heavily used bottom at the Bad had been stripped bare. As a result, the inhabitants there traveled far upstream to cut timber and float it down to Fort Pierre. Those trees burned up in steamboat furnaces had once kept the stinging Upper Missouri winds off the backs of bison or provided Indians with fuel. Deforestation denied both bison and the Indians the resource they needed to survive the winter months. What happened at the Bad River bottom also occurred throughout the bottoms of the Upper Missouri after the dawn of the steamboat era.

To make matters worse, steamboats did not just stop anywhere during the day or night. Pilots nudged their boats up against the high banks adjacent to the bottoms so that African-American roustabouts could harvest wood just before nightfall or hunt game in the early morning hours before sunup. Culbertson again: "We stopped before breakfast for fuel, the procuring of which here is not like that in the States; there are here no wood-yards, with the wood all cut and in proper order, but whenever a lot of dry timber appears, it the boat needs it, she puts ashore, and all hands fall to work cutting and carrying on board; with the number of hands on board, it takes very little time."[33] Overnight stays put still further pressure on the bottomland resource base. Boats quickly injected large numbers of people into the bottoms. Hundreds of people might disembark from a boat in the evening hours, many of them armed to the teeth. Gawking Euro-Americans hurriedly overwhelmed the flora and fauna they encountered in the bottoms. If all those humans running through the lowlands and up on the river's terraces did not actually exterminate creatures; at a minimum they drove the life from the lowlands. Steamboat, keelboat, mackinaw, and bullboat traffic on the Missouri main stem quickly dropped large numbers of Euro-Americans in the midst of the bison world, displacing bison with *Homo sapiens*. The bottoms and the bison could not take the pressure.

Why didn't the Teton Sioux stop the steamboats traveling through their territory? Occasionally they tried to do just that. But the Indians confronted insurmountable problems when attempting to halt steamboats. First, the Teton Sioux had to remain on the move in order not to overexploit a river bottom. Thus, they could not establish permanent, fixed posts on the Missouri to wait for the steamers and then stop them as they attempted to pass their positions. To wait in one area resulted in the very ecological disruption they wanted to avoid, namely, the overexploitation and eventual depletion of resources. To wait too long in one place meant no food, the loss of fodder for their horses, and less timber for themselves in the long run. Their quality of life, in both the present and the future, deteriorated the longer they remained in one locale. Because of their need to remain on the move, it was often only a chance occurrence when the migratory Teton Sioux intercepted a passing steamboat. To effectively halt steamboat traffic on the Missouri, or at least impede it, the Sioux would have been required to surrender the very nomadism they wanted to preserve. Such a permanent attempt to stop the boats also would have risked the wrath of the U.S. Army, something the Teton Sioux wanted to avoid up to the 1850s.

Second, at the very time the Sioux hunted bison out on the uplands in May and June, steamer traffic on the Missouri reached its yearly peak. Accordingly, the Sioux lingered far from the Missouri Valley while steamers rode the spring and summer rises upstream. The Sioux needed to be on the uplands at this time to fatten their horses, acquire bison meat, and lay in a supply of robes for clothing, shelter, and equipage. To wait in the bottoms for a chance encounter with a steamer made no sense economically. Moreover, waiting in the valley meant consuming resources in the spring that they would desperately need in the winter.

The strategic results derived from stopping steamers were also very dubious. Namely, most Teton Sioux bands up to the 1850s wanted the goods that were being brought upriver by the steamers. The Sioux needed weapons and ammunition to wage war on their enemies and continue to defend or expand their domain. The Teton Sioux faced a dilemma in this respect: they needed arms to fight and expand, but the acquisition of those arms meant inviting the steamers into the Upper Missouri, which in turn led to the shrinkage of resources and the implosion of their domain. The Teton Sioux could not cut their ties to the boats, or they risked eventual decline. Yet to keep the ties with the boats also meant eventual decline. The Sioux found themselves in a double bind. In their time in the Upper Missouri, they never discovered a long-term solution to the dilemma of trade.

Any Sioux who wanted to strike at the boats confronted the steamers' irregular appearance on the river. Steamboats did not come upriver on a regular, announced schedule. Not keeping to a predetermined schedule prevented interception by the Sioux. The Indians did not know when a boat would come around the bend below or above them. And even if the Indians located a steamer, the cultural, economic, and military inducements to attack it were minimal. Assaulting a steamboat was not considered glamorous in the Sioux way of war. Sioux warriors fought on horseback against other equestrian warriors. To shoot at a steamboat offered little opportunity for a Teton to display courage, prowess, or strength, all important individual reasons to fight. Undoubtedly, stopping the boats would achieve strategic objectives, yet the individual's objectives had to tie into strategic goals for a Sioux warrior to want to risk life or limb. There had to exist individual rewards for combat, or it would not make sense. A Sioux could not count coup on a passing steamboat. A Sioux counted coup by touching his enemy. A boat, or its Euro-American passengers, floating in midchannel could not be touched by a warrior, so a couple of angry potshots was all a steamer might be worth to a Sioux. In economic terms, the boats represented a considerable prize with their store of goods, but to take one might result in long-term negative repercussions, the curtailment or cessation of trade, or an army expedition against the band or entire tribe.

From a tactical standpoint, the boats were hard, if not impossible, to take. Floating in midstream, maybe hundreds of yards away from the banks, the boats were out of range of most musket balls, and a tough target for even the best marksmen. To actually engage a steamboat crew in a firefight would have invited intense return fire from crew members with rifles and possibly cannon loaded with grapeshot. If sixty white men on board a boat could deliver a fusillade against a single bison, they certainly could do the same against an Indian. The price of attacking and taking a Euro-American steamboat was just too high, while the rewards were dubious at best and meaningless at worst. So the steamboats continued to run up and down the Missouri, depleting the timber and bison as the Sioux watched, powerless to halt the traffic.

The Teton Sioux did attack the woodcutters strung out along the Missouri. Tiny woodcutter encampments sprouted along the far Upper Missouri in the late 1860s and early 1870s. Tough mountaineers felled timber to sell to the boats. Since the Sioux could not strike the boats, they decided to strike those who actually cut down their timber and shot their bison. As an incentive to assail the woodcutters, Teton warriors could count coup on them. In 1866, on the far Upper Missouri, what became known as the Woodcutters War erupted between the Teton and Euro-American loggers. This war would be an on-again, off-again affair until 1870. In 1868, Mary Cook experienced the effects of the war. Near the Musselshell she noted, "Stopped at a deserted wood-yard and took on wood; one man killed here. . . . stopped at Grand Island to get wood, also the two men who owned it got aboard, as it was dangerous for them to remain ther [sic]."[34] Of course Cook labeled the perpetrators of these attacks as "ferocious savages," utterly failing to make the connection between the military strikes against woodcutters and Indian perceptions of self-defense.[35]

The majority of Euro-Americans at the time interpreted such attacks as did Cook, as proof of Sioux savagery. Yet J. A. Wells understood the causes of the Woodcutters War when he inscribed, "Therefore, when they [the Sioux] saw white men in great numbers enter the river bottoms, there build their houses and commence the destruction of the timber, they waged a bloody and relentless warfare, to keep them away from, or to drive them out of this great game preserve."[36] Chief Standing Elk, at a meeting with government officials at Fort Pierre in the early 1860s, made it plain why the Sioux attacked the Euro-Americans in the bottoms: "The whites had for a long time been killing off their cattle (buffaloes) and cutting down their timber and the time had come to stop all intercourse with them and drive them out of the country."[37] The Sioux killed woodcutters because they took the Indians' trees without permission or compensation.

By the 1850s, the bottoms began to feel the strain of Euro-American geographic constructs, hunting practices, and river traffic. The grasslands and forests in the vicinity of Forts Pierre, Clark, and Union became more and more impoverished, unfit for bison or humans. In 1855, Lieutenant Gouverneur Warren glimpsed the debilitated state of the Bad River bottom: "At the site of the fort [Fort Pierre] the grass has been killed by the Indian lodges, and all the cottonwood destroyed in giving the barks to their horses in winter; there is also a great deal of wild sage growing on this plain. It, in fact, seems to be the most barren of the low prairies I have visited [on the Missouri]."[38] By the 1850s, visitors to Fort Union noted that bison no longer came close to the post because of all the human activity in its immediate environs and the poor state of the vegetation in the area. Bison only began to reappear on the land thirty to forty miles southwest up the Yellowstone Valley.[39]

As the bison disappeared, the remnant herds retreated farther and farther up the Missouri, retreating from the southeast toward the northwest. The withdrawal of bison mirrored the advance of Euro-Americans. Wilhelm observed as early as 1823 near the Elkhorn River, "Here were many skulls and skeletons of the bison, which at that time still frequented these regions during the winter. Since then these giant creatures of the prairie have withdrawn farther and farther. It is possible that the Ponca [Creek] or even the White River is now the geographic boundary of these animals along the Missouri. This boundary is constantly being pushed over farther to the north and west. The demand of the valuable hides of these animals together with the wanton destruction at the hands of hunters who roam over these regions is bound to reduce their number greatly."[40]

In 1804, bison rambled all across the Upper Missouri from the Platte to the Marias and from the Boyer to the Three Forks. By the 1850s, Euro-Americans remarked that their range included only the lands to the west and southwest of the Little Missouri–Missouri confluence. Warren, who traveled widely across the Upper Missouri in the 1850s and who knew the bison's range, stated in 1855:

Of the various kinds of animals and their distribution I might here say a few words. Many of them are fast passing away, and in a few years those upon which the Indian is now dependent will become extinct. The buffalo, which have been so important an agent in the preservation of the Indian, are now gradually gathering into a smaller area, and although in the valley of the Yellowstone, and along the upper Missouri, thousands may yet be seen, they are annually decreasing at a very rapid rate. In 1850, buffalo were seen as low down on the Missouri as Vermillion river, and in 1854, a few were killed near Fort Pierre, but at the present time none, unless, it be a stray bull, are seen below Fort Clark [at the Knife River]. Even at the base of the Black Hills it would be difficult for a party of white men to support themselves by hunting.[41]

Edwin Denig, who probably understood bison demographics and distribution better than anyone else in the Upper Missouri, wrote that by 1856 bison had all but been exterminated east and northeast of the Missouri in today's North and South Dakota. Even west of the Missouri main stem, the animals did not appear in notable numbers until the Little Missouri–Missouri confluence.[42] Still others confirmed this conclusion, including Kurz, who did not see bison in 1851 until near Fort Clark and who said that by that date a person rarely saw bison near Fort Pierre, except maybe a random bull (fig. 5.7).[43]

In the early and middle nineteenth century, bison numbers decreased across the Upper Missouri. A variety of factors combined to decimate the herds. Indian hunting played a role in the decline of the herds. The competitive nature of the fur trade did not encourage conservation. Across the Upper Missouri, no single tribe controlled the herds or determined the num-

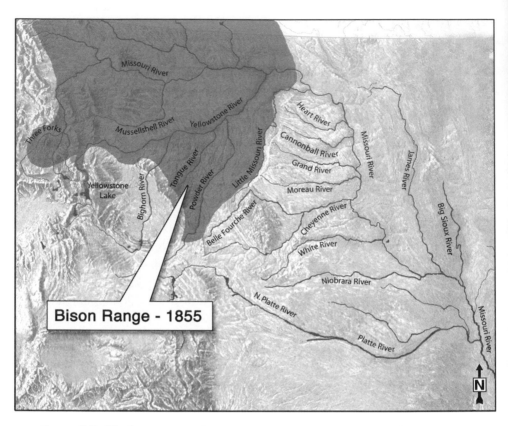

Figure 5.7. The bison range, Upper Missouri, circa 1855. By 1855, the concentrated range of the bison shrank to include a region encompassing the Little Missouri, far Upper Missouri, and Yellowstone River basins. (Paul Davidson, South Plains College, Levelland, Texas)

ber of bison sold at the trading posts. Consequently, in the early nineteenth century the Upper Missouri experienced the tragedy of the commons. The incentives to waste bison occasionally outstripped the reasons to conserve the herds. One tribe might attempt to conserve bison, while its neighbors killed those same animals for trade or domestic needs. Once the Teton Sioux gained a near monopoly over the herds in the Powder River Country and Lower Yellowstone Valley, they stabilized the bison range and worked to maintain the bison population. Between 1855 and 1877, the Teton Sioux in these areas controlled the herds and the number of robes sold for trade, and they prevented Euro-Americans and other tribes from hunting in the region. As a result, a substantial number of bison remained in the territory up to

1877. Teton Sioux policy since their arrival in the Upper Missouri may have been to gain a monopoly over the herds. Unfortunately for themselves, they did not achieve that goal until too late. The Teton Sioux in the far western Upper Missouri practiced conservation after 1855. Competition to dominate the herds led to war. Competition to own and sell the herds contributed to waste. In contrast, centralized control over the herds and control over output conserved the animals.

Drought, disease, blizzards, and predation also diminished the herds. Yet one of the greatest causes of the decline in bison numbers stemmed from the construction of Euro-American trading posts in the crucial bottomland sanctuaries from the Platte to the Three Forks and from the Yellowstone confluence to the Bighorn. The trading posts and their human occupants preempted bison from those preserves, which adversely affected the bison population. Euro-American sport hunting and river traffic (especially the steamboat traffic after the 1830s) frightened bison from the Missouri Valley, contributed to an increased slaughter of the animals, and facilitated deforestation and the overexploitation of the bottoms, all of which hurt bison numbers. The bottoms and their bison could not handle the pressure of a permanent Euro-American presence. As a result, the bison population went into a tailspin. The collapse of bison ecology was readily apparent to observers by the 1850s, who noted the absence of bison from much of the Upper Missouri. With bison numbers decreasing, and Euro-Americans continuing to push up the Missouri, the Teton Sioux faced a momentous decision: whether to become sedentary wards of the federal government or wage war against the Euro-Americans to conserve the bison and preserve their lifeway.

6

To the Horizon

The Teton Sioux Move West

When we came to the tall soldier lying on his back naked, Bad
Soup pointed him out and said, "Long Hair [Custer] thought he
was the greatest man in the world. Now he is there." "Well," I
said, "if that is Long Hair, I am the man who killed him."

—Pte-san-hunka, White Bull, Teton Sioux

By the middle of the nineteenth century, Teton Sioux territories
extended from the Missouri River trench to the Black Hills and the eastern
limits of the Yellowstone basin. Bands of Hunkpapas occupied lands along
the Lower Yellowstone and Little Missouri Rivers. Oglala and Brule hunted
and lived near the head of the Tongue and Powder. Still more Oglala resided
along the Platte Valley. A number of influences gave rise to this Teton Sioux
empire. The bison robe trade represented a major factor in encouraging
Sioux expansion. Trade supplied the Sioux with the guns, balls, and powder
necessary to wage imperial war. Also, the inducements of the trade drove the
Teton onto the lands of neighbors in pursuit of bison. Since the trade benefited the Teton, a tense but workable peace existed between the expansionist
Euro-Americans and the equally aggressive Sioux. But in this limited and
chaotic world, two imperial peoples eventually bump into one another.
When they collide, they either work out a compromise through negotiation
or go to war for dominance of the other. In the 1840s and 1850s, the Sioux
came head-to-head against the Euro-Americans who flooded both the Platte
and the Missouri Valley. By the late 1840s, Euro-Americans covered the

Platte Valley with wagon ruts and way stations as they pushed on to Oregon. Along the Lower Missouri, Euro-Americans had cut and planted the low-lands into farms. In 1856, white settlers landed on the banks of the Big Sioux River, where they founded a colony. Ironically, they named the settlement Sioux City, even though the town's very existence stood in opposition to the Sioux way of life. As Euro-Americans and the Teton Sioux increasingly con-fronted one another along the Platte and Missouri Rivers, strains appeared in the relationship (fig. 6.1).

While Euro-Americans shouldered their way into the Upper Missouri, the bioregion witnessed a series of overlapping ecological disturbances. The

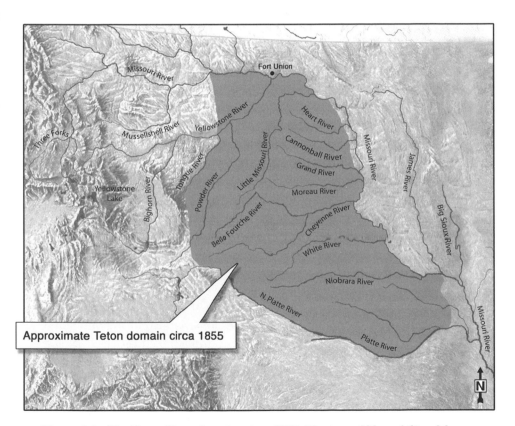

Figure 6.1. The Teton Sioux domain, circa 1855. The incredible mobility of the Teton Sioux in conjunction with the fluidity of the Upper Missouri's ecology prevented the establishment of fixed boundaries between nomadic tribes. Nonetheless, the historical record indicates that the Teton ruled over a large piece of the Upper Missouri by the middle of the nineteenth century. (Paul Davidson, South Plains College, Levelland, Texas)

cumulative ecological effects of Sioux expansion, warfare, and hunting, Euro-American movements and hunting, the presence of a large Euro-American population in the Missouri and Platte River trenches, drought, introduced European and Asian diseases, and Euro-American geographic constructs caused extreme gyrations in the ecosystem. As the Upper Missouri system trembled, its human inhabitants responded to the fluctuations with corresponding intensity. Yet concerted human action only provoked a furious ecological reaction. In the 1850s, the entire ecosystem, humans included, operated in a horrific feedback loop that spiraled toward ecological collapse. Yet circumstances required humanity to act quickly and dramatically toward the Upper Missouri. The Teton Sioux responded to these wild oscillations in ecology by migrating still farther and fighting even more. When the Teton struck the Euro-Americans on the Platte to conserve the bison and preserve themselves, the Euro-Americans responded by sending the U.S. Army en masse to the Upper Missouri. More U.S. troops in the region put a greater strain on the ecosystem, which in turn forced the Teton Sioux to greater efforts at self-preservation.[1]

The Grattan affair set off the first war between the United States and the Sioux. The incident came on the heels of eight consecutive years of drought, a drought that by 1854 had swept the plains clean of grass and bison and was about to sweep the Teton Sioux along with it. Besides the drought, diseases (such as smallpox and cholera) introduced to the Upper Missouri by the travelers on the Great Platte River road added one more deadly element to the Teton Sioux's dire circumstances.

The Grattan affair holds great symbolic importance. On August 19, 1854, Sioux warriors camped six miles southeast of Fort Laramie found a lame cow that had wandered away from a Mormon traveler trudging along the Platte River road. The Indians took the cow into their camp and butchered it, hoping to relieve the jolting hunger tearing through their rib cages. By late summer 1854, the Sioux faced starvation, since the bison did not show up when and where they expected them. A tough, gnarly old cow looked fairly delectable after weeks or months without bison or dog. The Mormon who lost the animal reported to the soldiers at Fort Laramie that the animal had been stolen by the Indians at the camp below.

A young, ignorant, recent West Point graduate, Lieutenant John Grattan, stationed at Fort Laramie, wanted action. He requested from the post commander permission to bring in the perpetrators of this supposed crime. The commander consented to his wishes. Immediately, Grattan took twenty-nine

soldiers and an interpreter and rushed down to the Indian village. Once
there he met with the head chief, Conquering Bear, and demanded that he
turn over the mastermind behind this heinous crime to the U.S. Army for
appropriate sentencing and punishment. When Conquering Bear refused to
turn over the culprit, Grattan decided to make larceny into a crisis. He ordered his men to open fire on the camp, mortally wounding Conquering
Bear in the ensuing melee. The Sioux responded to Grattan's stupidity and
lack of diplomatic tact by surrounding his command and summarily execut-
ing the lieutenant and all his men.

The Grattan affair set off a chain of events that metamorphosed the
Teton Sioux's geographic position in the Upper Missouri. The brief battle
also contributed to over twenty years of intermittent warfare between the
U.S. Army and the Sioux that culminated in the death of George Armstrong
Custer in eastern Montana Territory, in 1876, and the killing of Crazy Horse
at Fort Robinson, Nebraska, in 1877.

The beginning of the military era along the Upper Missouri occurred as a
consequence of the Grattan affair. Incidentally, the military era coincided
with the demise of the robe trade. In 1853, the agent for the Upper Missouri
estimated that one hundred thousand bison robes had found their way from
the Upper Missouri posts to St. Louis. Informed mountaineers and observers
of the scene such as Alfred Vaughn, Indian agent for the Upper Missouri
Agency, calculated that for every robe shipped downstream, an additional
three bison perished in the Upper Missouri. Thus, in 1853, a total of four
hundred thousand animals died across the Upper Missouri. Vaughn concluded, "I have taken no little pains to ascertain the supposed number of
buffalo annually destroyed in the agency [Upper Missouri], and, from the
best information the number does not fall very far short of 400,000. Not less
than 100,000 robes have been shipped by the two companies who are li-
censed to trade amongst the Indians under my charge. 150,000 are destroyed, of which a small portion of their flesh is consumed; they are killed
for their hides, to make lodges, which they are compelled to make very secure to protect them from the extreme severity of the weather during the
winter."[2]

Such a heavy harvest of bison meant the end of the trade was near at
hand. By the middle 1850s, fur traders, including Edwin Denig, predicted
the ultimate demise of the herds and the end of the fur trade era in just a
matter of years. The robe trade diminished quickly after 1855. In 1855, Fort
Pierre closed up shop. In 1860, Fort Clark, in operation since 1831, shut its

doors to business. And then in 1865, the run-down, overused, and collapsing Fort Union also ceased its operations. The dates of the closing of these fur trading posts corresponded to the disappearance of bison in and around their walled enclosures. One can trace the shrinking bison range to the north and west by the date each post closed its gates. By 1855, bison no longer inhabited the Missouri Valley or plains to the east or west of Fort Pierre. Thus, the fort's usefulness to the trade vanished with the bison. By 1860, the bison had retreated from around Fort Clark, so it, too, went out of business; and by 1865, the animals occupied a smaller piece of territory to the west and south of Fort Union. Changing bison ecology remade Euro-American geography.[3]

Rather than entirely retreat from the Upper Missouri as the fur trade ended, the Euro-American race established military posts alongside the river to hold the territory for the United States. The U.S. Army built the forts to keep the Missouri Valley out of the hands of the Teton Sioux. Officials wanted the forts to maintain a tight rein over the Missouri main stem, keep the navigation route open, protect settlements in the lower valley, guard settlers streaming up the Missouri, and contain the Teton Sioux to the west.

Although the army requisitioned the American Fur Company's Fort Pierre in 1855, Fort Randall was the first and most important post actually constructed by army personnel on the banks of the Missouri. The fort, which stood over the Missouri by 1856, gave the army the ability, at least perceptually and to a lesser extent physically, to watch the Teton Sioux who lived beyond the ridgelines. The fort also denied, or impeded, any Sioux attempts to disrupt Missouri River navigation. It accomplished this task by lying so close to the southern end of the former Sioux geographic core, which consisted of the Missouri Valley from the Cheyenne River to the White River. The army wanted the fort and its armed occupants to pose enough risk to the hostile Teton Sioux that they would not dare approach their former homeland. The post sat close enough to that core area to make its occupancy or even temporary use by the traditionalist Sioux difficult, risky, or impossible. Military leaders concluded that unfriendly Sioux bands could not get too close to the fort without chancing a strike by the army. The army also took control of Fort Pierre to gain a tighter grip within the former Teton Sioux center. Pierre, like Randall, prevented any recalcitrant Teton Sioux from using the bottomlands at the mouths of the Cheyenne and Bad as well as the Big Bend. Fort Pierre nudged the Sioux west, farther away from the Euro-Americans passing up and down the Missouri River.

In the middle 1850s, the Sioux faced a dilemma. They could either remain on the Missouri and subject themselves to federal oversight or abandon
the Missouri altogether and go west, somewhere far west, beyond the sight of
the U.S. Army, the guns of tourists, the sounds of steamers, and the stench
emanating from forts. They could go where bison still roamed in generous
numbers. The question of whether to stay on the Missouri or leave it split
Sioux society between traditionalists who wanted to continue to hunt bison
and live nomadic lives without any interference from the federal government and accommodationists who desired to stay on the Missouri, fully or
partially abandon their previous lifestyle, and tether themselves to the Euro-
Americans.

Sioux leaders debated the merits of abandoning the Missouri or staying
close to it. The issue of leaving the Missouri struck at another more divisive
problem facing the tribe: whether to resist the Euro-Americans or reconcile
with them. To hug the Missouri Valley meant surrender. The only way to
remain there was to rely on the Euro-Americans and the annuities they
brought upriver on steamers. To stay meant to settle down, abandon the old
nomadic ways, take up farming, and depend on the largesse of the United
States government. There just was not enough game in the valley to do otherwise. The Teton Sioux who chose to remain on the Missouri could not survive in the denuded valley without Euro-American assistance. General W. S.
Harney in 1856 recognized this fact when he said that the bands staying on
the Missouri would be peaceably inclined toward the United States, and that
those who moved to the interior would be considered hostile. To leave the
Missouri River meant resistance to the Americans and an attempt to continue the old ways.

During the talks surrounding the Harney Treaty of 1856, the Teton Sioux
who came to Fort Pierre expressed their concerns about remaining along the
Missouri. They informed Harney that his demands that they stay next to the
big river caused the tribe to divide on the issue. Chief Smutty Bear told Harney why he and his people had grave doubts about becoming sedentary agriculturalists: "I have tried to do this [raise corn], and have worn all the nails
off my fingers trying to do it. Ever since I have tried to work that corn, and I
am still at it, but can't raise it. I have listened and want to do it, but could
not."[4] To Smutty Bear and others, the uncertainty of agriculture in the
Upper Missouri entailed more danger for the Sioux than the uncertainties
associated with nomadism and the hunt. Bear Rib of the Hunkpapas made it
clear that Harney's insistence that the Sioux remain on the Missouri would

splinter the tribe. He remarked to the crusty general, "I heard you; for women and old men that have no wings, this is good." What Bear Rib meant is that the treaty and its promised annuities would be good for women, the elderly, the infirm, and the very young, but it would stultify the warriors who wanted to continue to roam and live in the old manner. Bear Rib continued, "My brother [Harney] wants me to throw away a part of my nation and make me cry [by leaving some of his people on the banks of the Missouri while others left it for interior lands]."[5]

Denig rightly predicted where the traditionalist Teton Sioux would go: "It is believed that the great diminution of buffalo in the Sioux country will compel that nation to seek subsistence farther west. The district watered by the last 100 miles of the Yellowstone River offers great inducement for a hunter population. At this time, the entire south side of the Missouri as high up as the Musselshell and as low down as the confluence of the Little Missouri of the Big Bend, extending for 100 miles into the interior, is unoccupied by any Indians. This is one of the best game districts in the world."[6] There was also little question in the minds of the Teton Sioux leadership regarding which direction to follow. There existed only one option: they needed to reach the region with the greatest concentration of ungulates in North America, the Bighorn, Powder, Tongue, and Yellowstone River drainages. That region was still, as Denig made clear, filled with bison.

The trails the Teton Sioux took to the west followed the Upper Missouri's ley lines (fig. 6.2). The indigenes literally let the bison guide them to their new promised land. Treading along the bison roads, the Sioux passed up the Cheyenne, Bad, or White and found their way into the Belle Fourche, then up it to its Great Bend. From there they walked or rode over the gentle rises between the Belle Fourche and the Little Missouri. At that point they branched off to either the north or the west, going down the Little Missouri or pursuing a westerly course to the Little Powder, Powder proper, or Tongue, where they dragged their travois down to the Yellowstone River or up to the foothills of the Bighorns. This migration took years, lasting from the 1840s into the late 1850s. By 1860, the Sioux integrated the Lower Yellowstone Valley, from the mouth of the Tongue River to the mouth of the Roche Jaune, into their empire. Once more, in geographic terms, mastery over the mouths of such streams as O'Fallon Creek, Powder River, Tongue River, and the Yellowstone River itself meant dominion over the lands to the south of those confluence zones. The Teton Sioux converted the Lower Yellowstone into their new core, replacing the Missouri (fig. 6.3).

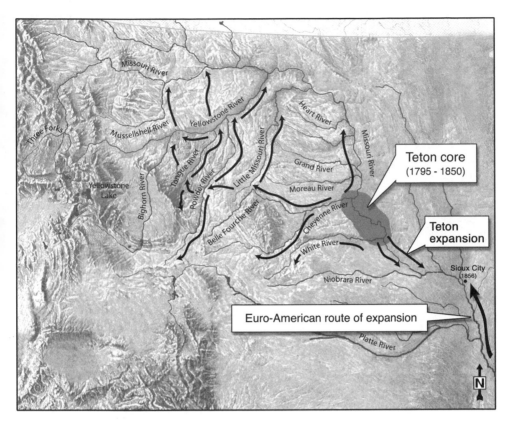

Figure 6.2. The routes of Teton Sioux expansion from their core area in the Missouri River trench. (Paul Davidson, South Plains College, Levelland, Texas)

Yet the traditionalists in the Powder River Country and Lower Yellowstone Valley could not cut themselves off completely from the accommodationists or the Euro-Americans at their backs. The accommodationists became the conduit through which arms and ammunition moved to the interior bands. Those Sioux in the Yellowstone basin needed powder, balls, and rifles to keep the Crow at bay. The supposed traditionalists had to rely on the accommodationists and ultimately the Euro-Americans to pursue their traditional way of life and defend it from Crow and white hunters.

Once they moved into the Yellowstone Valley, the Sioux pushed aside both the Crow and the Euro-Americans there. They also shut down the region to the robe trade in an attempt to preserve the herds that gave them life and culture. Thus, Teton Sioux hostility closed the last bison refuge to the robe traders and ensured the preservation of the herds until the late 1870s.

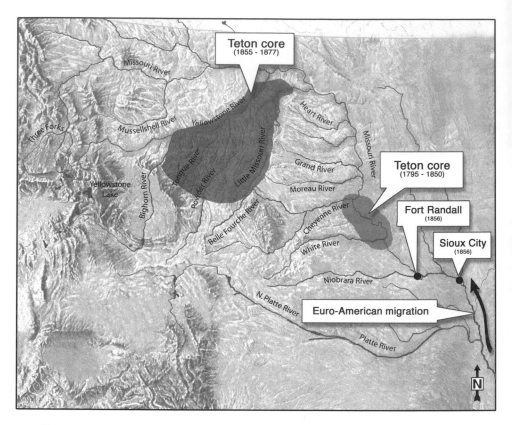

Figure 6.3. The Teton Sioux abandon the Missouri Valley, circa 1855. In the late 1840s and early 1850s, traditionalist Teton Sioux bands departed from the Missouri River trench and migrated west, northwest, to establish a new geographic core in the Yellowstone basin. The increasing Euro-American presence along both the Platte and the Missouri River set off this migration to the northwest. (Paul Davidson, South Plains College, Levelland, Texas)

Denig admitted as much in 1856: "Neither the Crow Indians nor traders could be brought to station themselves there for any length of time and the Yellowstone has been abandoned by both."[7] The Crow expressed anger at the Sioux move west onto to their former lands. Chief Mato-Luta of the Crow told First Lieutenant John Mullan in 1860, "Our hearts are bad. The white man is no longer friend to the Crow Indian. . . . The white man has set our enemies [the Sioux] upon us; some of our warriors have been killed, and we have lost many horses. They have taken our trading post [Fort Sarpy, on the Yellowstone River] away from us. We could go there and trade with the whites without being killed by our enemies, the Sioux; but now we have no presents; we cannot trade our robes for blankets anywhere. The Sioux will not let us trade at Fort Union." By the late 1850s, the traditionalist Teton Sioux held the Lower Yellowstone basin in a firm clasp.

The inaccessibility of the Yellowstone Valley worked to the advantage of the Teton Sioux by restraining the white advance. At midcentury, no major Euro-American road bisected the Yellowstone basin. The Yellowstone River was barely navigable for any watercraft, including the mackinaw and keel, but especially the steamboat, whose pilots stayed away from the Yellowstone's notoriously rocky channel. The inability of Euro-Americans to get into the Yellowstone basin meant relative safety for the Sioux and the bison herds there. The Yellowstone and its southern tributaries and the far reaches of the Upper Missouri main stem were the last sanctuaries available to bison. This region represented the last line of defense for equestrian nomadism.

The Sioux did not restrict their movements to the Lower Yellowstone basin. Ever the nomads, they continued to move north and west. In the late 1850s and early 1860s, Sioux bands reached the far Upper Missouri River trench, sliding along its south bank until eventually touching the banks of the Musselshell. Those Sioux at the Musselshell punted the Blackfeet to the north side of the Missouri. Farther south, Teton bands trod down to the shores of the Little Bighorn and Bighorn, all the while driving the Crow before them like so many startled bison.

The Sioux position in the Yellowstone basin and far Upper Missouri came under assault not long after the indigenes moved there. In 1862, Euro-Americans in southwestern Montana found the metal that drove men to madness. Gold, and all the dreams attached to it, convinced otherwise committed men to abandon wives, children, friends, and family for the western wilds and a chance at quick riches. The gold strikes at Alder Gulch set off a rush to the Montana diggings. By 1864, the rush reached full steam. Thousands of men left the war-torn East for the calmer alpine meadows of Montana. Miners took four primary routes to the mines. One path to Virginia City began at St. Joseph, Missouri, on board a steamboat. From that port on the Missouri, the boat passed to Fort Benton, Montana Territory, the head of navigation on the Missouri main stem situated thirty miles east of the Great Falls of the Missouri. At Fort Benton miners gladly disembarked from the overcrowded steamboats and traveled via wagon train to the gold fields.

A second route traced the Platte to Fort Laramie, where it turned northwest, gripping the foothills of the Bighorn Mountains until reaching the Bighorn River just a few hundred yards from where it saws its way through Bighorn Canyon. From thence the trail wound over the tablelands toward the Yellowstone. Once on the Yellowstone, it followed the river's south bank until attaining the ferry crossing at Benson's Landing. The trail climbed the pass that separates the Missouri and Yellowstone watersheds and then slipped down to the Three Forks, went up the Madison, and into Virginia City. In 1864 John Bozeman surveyed this route, which would be named after his courageous or insane personage. He was courageous because he charted a road through Sioux territory; he was possibly insane because the Sioux would have killed him, beat him, or stripped him naked and taken all his possessions (or maybe carried out all three perverse acts in reverse order) had they caught him on their land. The third road to the golden apparition went up the Platte River Road, over South Pass to Utah, then north through the Bitterroot Range to Virginia City. A fourth route darted up the Columbia Valley to Walla Walla and from there to the gold fields.

The steamboat route up the Missouri to Fort Benton, although full of twists and turns, presented the miners with the quickest and safest mode of travel to Montana. Not until the completion of the transcontinental railroad in 1869 did the Platte, North Platte, Utah, and Bitterroot Mountains route become quicker, cheaper, and safer than the Missouri River passage. But in the mid-1860s, miners preferred the Missouri or the hazardous Bozeman Trail. Many miners went to Montana on a seasonal itinerary, reaching Virginia City in the early summer, digging until the fall, and then returning home before the onset of those killer cold Montana winters. On the return to the states, miners overwhelmingly chose to drift down either the Missouri or the Yellowstone Rivers, which carried miners home for free and at a fairly decent clip. Miners went to Fort Benton on the Missouri or Benson's Landing on the Yellowstone to begin their downriver trips. At Fort Benton, they either boarded steamboats for home or teamed up and built a mackinaw. Mackinaw navigation on the Missouri could be slower and more challenging than a steamboat ride, but in the 1860s and 1870s, thousands of miners took mackinaws from the Upper Missouri or Yellowstone to the Lower Missouri because the cost of transporting body and soul to the states in this manner amounted to almost nothing. If a miner chose to take the Yellowstone from Benson's Landing, he floated downstream aboard either a mackinaw, a bull-boat, or a dugout canoe. The Yellowstone River offered a faster route home because Benson's Landing sat closer to Virginia City than Fort Benton. The Yellowstone also possessed an added bonus—its current moved quicker than the Missouri's. Yet the Yellowstone River route held out the possibility of mortal danger to any prairie sailor. The river broke up mackinaws on its rocks with horrifying regularity, especially during the low-water months when most miners headed for home. To add to the terror of the miners, the Lower Yellowstone Valley contained the Sioux who wanted to count coup on whites (fig. 6.4).

The Sioux did not take all the Euro-American activity along the Missouri, Yellowstone, and Bozeman Trail lying down. Instead, they struck back in vengeance, killing white trespassers and soldiers whenever the opportunity presented itself. Warriors carried out the attacks for strategic purposes—to protect Sioux territorial integrity, preserve bison from indiscriminate Euro-American hunting, conserve the bottomland timber and grass, prevent or halt the general depletion of game that accompanied the presence of Euro-Americans, and loosen the Euro-American noose around the Sioux home-

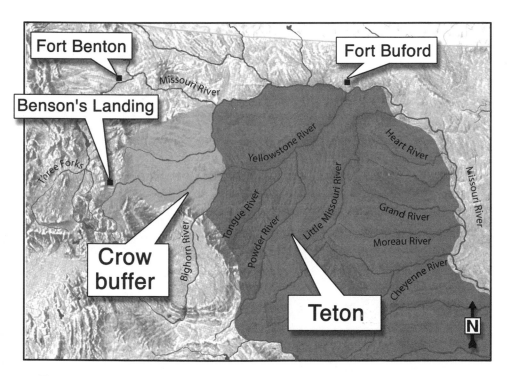

Figure 6.4. Fort Buford and the head of steamboat navigation on the Upper Missouri and the head of mackinaw navigation on the Yellowstone. Fort Buford, with its boot-bound infantry units, offered only limited protection to those who dared navigate the far Upper Missouri and Yellowstone Rivers in the 1860s and 1870s. (Paul Davidson, South Plains College, Levelland, Texas)

land. A Teton Sioux fear of encirclement encouraged the killing. The Montana gold rush resulted in an informal siege of Sioux territory, one that, if continued, would result in the loss of the Sioux core along the Yellowstone River, as well as the depletion of the rich bison range skirting the edge of the Bighorn Mountains.

The Sioux felt hemmed in on the north along the far Upper Missouri by steamers, traders, and woodcutters. In 1865, four boats docked at Benton. A year later, when the Missouri route gained in popularity, thirty boats put to shore at Fort Benton. Steamboat arrivals increased slightly in 1866, when thirty-one boats reached that port. A year later, thirty-seven boats stopped there.[8] The traffic going to and from Fort Benton after 1862 ran off the bison from the Missouri Valley. A repeat of what had occurred along the Missouri east and south of Fort Union in the 1840s and 1850s now played out along the far Upper Missouri.

The Sioux also felt confined on the west by the Bozeman Trail and its miners, held in check to the south on the Platte by cattle, wagons, and those bound for Oregon, and barred from the east by the forts and steamboats along the Missouri River. Encirclement meant a limitation on movement and access to the herds, the possibility of which the Sioux could not accept. If the Sioux could not follow the herds to their sanctuaries in the far Upper Missouri and Lower Yellowstone Valleys or pursue the animals up to the head of the Tongue, then they faced cultural disintegration. Although referring to reservation boundaries, the following passage accurately describes how borders of any kind led to death and disease among equestrian nomads: "To isolate them in small strips of territory, where they cannot subsist under surrounding circumstances upon the large lands they now occupy, would be only to deliver them over to the ravages of disease, in addition to the miseries of famine. If penned up in small secluded colonies they become hospital wards of cholera and smallpox, and must be supported at an immense annual cost to the government."[9]

To Sioux thinking, the valleys and other oases in the Yellowstone basin had to be kept safe for bison and Indians or it was all over. Reservation life would kill them, from either starvation or disease. So the Sioux struck out, hitting whites and soldiers on the Bozeman Trail, firing on steamboats on the Missouri, plugging away at miners dumb enough to descend the Yellowstone in an open mackinaw, and scalping woodcutters for stealing their cottonwood trees and scaring off their game. The U.S. Army responded to these attacks with force.

Following the Civil War, the army implemented an intensified policy to contain the Teton Sioux. Containment, as an American policy, existed long before the cold war between the United States and the Soviet Union; it did not originate in the mind of U.S. diplomat George Kennan. Euro-Americans had practiced the encirclement of enemies since the colonial era. The United States sought to contain the Sioux through the construction of a series of posts along the Missouri main stem and to the west below the Bighorn and Gallatin ranges. Along the Bozeman Trail, the army raised the pickets of Forts Reno, Phil Kearney, and C. F. Smith in 1865–1866. Fort Buford went up in 1866 at the confluence of the Yellowstone and Missouri, only a few miles east of the much older Fort Union. As early as 1818, the U.S. Army had sought to build a post at the mouth of the Yellowstone to intercept the various Indian trails that converged there and to stem British influence in the Upper Missouri (fig. 6.5). Fort Stevenson, close to the Knife River–Missouri River juncture, served as another link in the chain of posts on the Missouri. In 1872, the army erected Fort Abraham Lincoln in the bottom just south of the Heart River. In 1864, the army built Fort Rice fifteen miles below where Apple Creek enters the Missouri. In 1866, it built the new Fort Sully, named after General Alfred Sully, in a bottom just north of the mouth

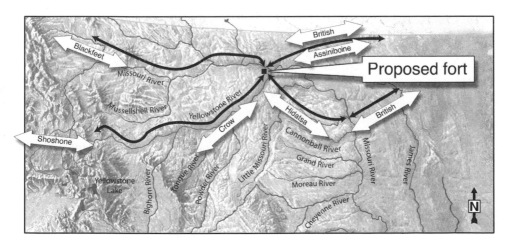

Figure 6.5. The proposed U.S. Army fort at the mouth of the Yellowstone, 1818. The U.S. Army believed that a post at the Yellowstone–Missouri River confluence would give the United States the ability to stem British influence in the Upper Missouri while providing American traders with the protection needed to tap the region's fur resources. (Paul Davidson, South Plains College, Levelland, Texas)

of Okoboji Creek. The first Fort Sully, built in 1864, replaced the debilitated Fort Pierre, while the second offered the army a better position to requisition timber and grass and oversee the Big Cheyenne road. The army maintained Fort Randall in southeast Dakota Territory. Also in 1867, army personnel erected Fort Ellis, just a few miles to the west of the heights of Bozeman Pass.[10] Fort Ellis rounded out the system of new posts across the Upper Missouri (fig. 6.6).

Army engineers chose the site for each post based on specific environmental characteristics. In addition to overseeing an extensive trail network, Fort Buford, although manned by infantry, gave the army a modicum of control over access to the Yellowstone Valley to the southwest. The fort also pro-

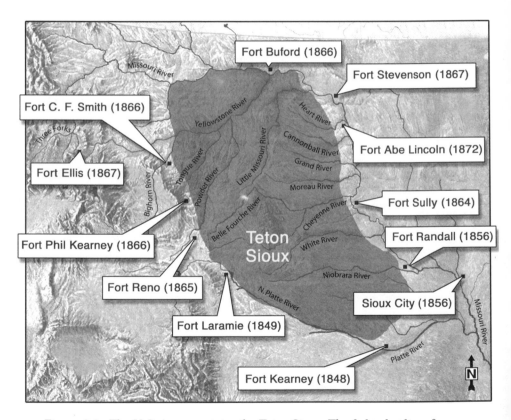

Figure 6.6. The U.S. Army contains the Teton Sioux. The federal policy of military containment did not originate in the middle twentieth century during the cold war. Rather, the U.S. Army established a series of posts around the Teton Sioux between the 1840s and 1870s to prevent the tribe's military and economic expansion. (Paul Davidson, South Plains College, Levelland, Texas)

vided the army with the ability to go into the Yellowstone River trench if and when the need arose. Fort Buford steered the Teton Sioux away from the all-important crossroads of the confluence while also protecting steamboat traffic on the Missouri. Fort Stevenson defended several U.S. allies from the Sioux, including the Mandan, Hidatsa, and Arikara. Stevenson, near the Great Bend on the east shore of the main-stem Missouri, secured the Missouri in its vicinity and oversaw the Knife River road all the way to its head near the Little Missouri badlands. Stevenson gave the army the ability to go after the Sioux who hunted in the Little Missouri drainage; the post could also project U.S. power farther west into the Yellowstone Valley. Fort Abraham Lincoln controlled access to the Heart River road. Fort Rice, which furthered American control over the all-important bottom that extended from the Cannonball north to the Great Bend, controlled southern access to today's Bismarck Bottom. Fort Sully kept a watch over the Missouri River route, commanded the Cheyenne–Okoboji Creek road, and blocked any Sioux bands from moving back east toward the settlements in Minnesota or southeast Dakota Territory. Fort Randall guarded the white communities developing in southeast Dakota Territory. Forts Reno, Phil Kearney, and C. F. Smith assisted the army with a number of tasks—checking the Teton Sioux's western advance against the Crow while contributing some protection to miners treading the Bozeman Trail. Fort Ellis provided protection to the agricultural settlers dashing down from Bozeman Pass to drain, plow, and seed the Three Forks area.

The army built every fort along and atop the existing Indian and bison geographic system, thereby granting the military dominion over vital crossroads and river-road junctures. Additionally, each post sat squarely on the back of the Upper Missouri's oases, ensuring the army food, forage, and timber. These forts taxed and strained the already hard-pressed ecology of the Upper Missouri. The military forts on the Missouri main stem, with their troops and the increased steamer traffic needed to support them, eliminated virtually all large mammals from the Missouri River trench from Fort Randall north to the Yellowstone confluence by the late 1860s. Emma Dickinson, on board the *Mollie Ebert* bound for Fort Benton in May 1869, recorded seeing only five elk between Sioux City and Pierre. She did not spot a single bison along that entire reach. Three days after passing the Yellowstone–Missouri confluence, the boat's passengers saw their first bison, a herd of two standing near shore.[11] By 1870, the once-humming Missouri River Valley became eerily quiet—a dead zone, devoid of most furbearers except maybe the still-prolific prairie dog.

Out of necessity, the army placed the posts along the Bozeman Trail inside three high-country oases. Fort Reno covered the meadowlands at the head of the Powder, Fort Phil Kearney did the same near the Tongue, and Fort C. F. Smith lay where the bountiful Lower Bighorn Valley began its sinuous course to the Yellowstone. Sioux leaders, including Crazy Horse, considered Fort Phil Kearney to be the most disruptive of the three forts because its palisades rose above fields filled with bison and elk. Additionally, from Phil Kearney, army personnel could potentially hit the Sioux on the Tongue, Little Bighorn, Rosebud, and Powder River roads.

The Sioux launched repeated military forays against the forts situated along the Bozeman Trail. They held a special contempt for Fort Phil Kearney. From the time Kearney went up in 1866 to its fiery end in 1868, the Teton Sioux constantly hovered outside its walls, waiting to kill, maim, or harass any soldier ignorant or brave enough (the two characteristics often go hand in hand) to venture outside the picketed enclosure. From the Teton Sioux point of view, the fort had to go. Crazy Horse and two thousand other Sioux sent that very message to the whites on December 21, 1866. Just to the north of Lodge Trail Ridge, and beyond the sight of those still inside Fort Phil Kearney, Crazy Horse and his companions destroyed a force of eighty men led by Captain William J. Fetterman.

The Fetterman Massacre (as Euro-Americans at the time labeled it) or the Fetterman Battle (as later chroniclers termed it) loudly proclaimed to the army to get out of the Powder River Country. General William T. Sherman (that hard-nosed proponent of total war) heard the message. In 1868, the United States and the Teton Sioux negotiated a treaty to end hostilities across the Upper Missouri region, particularly the fighting on the Bozeman Trail and the killing on the Missouri's banks west of Fort Buford. Oglala chief Red Cloud signed for the Teton Sioux, and Sherman penned his name on parchment as a representative of the United States. The die-hard conservatives among the Teton Sioux (including Crazy Horse and Sitting Bull) considered Red Cloud's acceptance of the treaty a sellout. The Fort Laramie Treaty of 1868 prompted a further splintering of Sioux society. The accommodationists of 1868 agreed to the treaty, but stalwart traditionalists refused to consider its provisions. After 1868, the most passionate anti-American Sioux permanently resided in the Yellowstone basin, cut off from contact with Euro-Americans and determined to defend their territory. These Sioux isolated themselves from the mollifying influence of their more liberal Sioux brothers and sisters to the east. The provisions of the Fort Laramie Treaty of 1868 set the stage for the Great Sioux War.

Both the United States and certain elements within Sioux society got what they wanted from the Fort Laramie Treaty. The United States abandoned the Bozeman Trail to the Sioux because of incessant Sioux attacks along the trail, the absence of traffic along the route, the existence in 1868 of a new route to western Montana's gold fields, and the transfer of the army's energies to the southern plains. General Sherman believed the costs of holding on to a little-used trail far outweighed the benefits. So Sherman agreed to pull the army out of the Powder River Country. Red Cloud made several concessions to the United States. Most important, he accepted the creation of a reservation, which included today's western South Dakota. The government placed the eastern boundary of the Great Sioux Reservation on the east bank of the Missouri River trench for several reasons. Federal officials wanted to utilize the Missouri navigation route to supply the Sioux with promised annuities. Additionally, the Missouri River route would be used to move troops quickly up the Missouri to punish or chastise any Indians that resisted federal policies. Finally, the Euro-American negotiators of the treaty recognized that very little land across the Sioux domain could be farmed profitably. The Missouri River bottoms on the main stem's western shore would be the lands that would be farmed. Federal negotiators saw the Missouri Valley as the key means of assimilating the tribe. It would carry missionaries and educators to the reservation, and the military if necessary, and would provide the fertile lands needed for agriculture. Agriculture in turn would create a new Sioux, a domesticated, benign, civilized people. The Missouri River took center stage in federal policy objectives for the Sioux, who, as stipulated by the treaty, could remain in the Powder River Country so long as the herds remained in sufficient numbers to justify the chase (fig. 6.7).

The treaty appeared ideal to Red Cloud. It essentially affirmed Teton Sioux domination over all the lands they now occupied and established boundaries, but not the firm boundaries that spelled an end to nomadism. The Sioux could still leave the reservation to pursue the herds to the west. The treaty also provided the Sioux assurances that the reservation boundaries would not be violated, nor would their position in the Powder River Country be challenged by Euro-Americans.

From Red Cloud's perspective, the 1868 treaty gave his people a lot. First, it guaranteed Sioux lands against further Euro-American encroach-

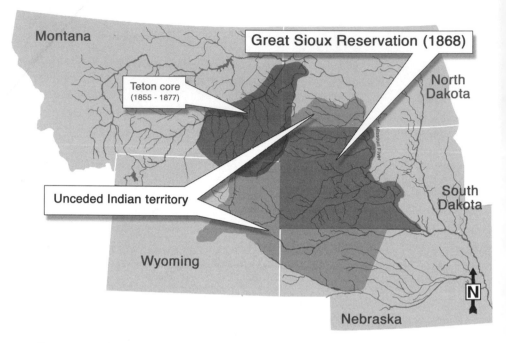

Figure 6.7. The Great Sioux Reservation and Teton Sioux core geographic area. The Fort Laramie Treaty of 1868 established the Great Sioux Reservation, which included all of present-day western South Dakota. The treaty engendered a split in the ranks of the Teton Sioux between traditionalists and accommodationists. The traditionalists did not abide by the treaty provisions and remained in the Powder River basin and Yellowstone Valley, where bison still flourished in large numbers. (Paul Davidson, South Plains College, Levelland, Texas)

ment. Second, it delineated boundaries, which thereby avoided future land disputes with Euro-Americans and possible conflict with Euro-Americans and Indian enemies. Within those boundaries lay all the best hunting grounds in the Upper Missouri. Third, the treaty granted the Sioux a position on the Missouri River and the dwindling resources there. This was considered incredible from Red Cloud's thinking; since the Oglala had long left the Missouri, they could now go back. Fourth, the treaty promised annuities, foodstuffs, clothing, and weapons that would improve the lives of Red Cloud's people and ensure against winter starvation. Starvation became more and more a possibility as the herds continued to dwindle. Fifth, the treaty legalized Sioux occupation of the Black Hills. Sixth, the treaty authorized the Sioux to remain in the Powder River Country and Yellowstone basin so long as there were animals in numbers suitable to the chase. This last point would not be an issue because the Sioux, if their lands were respected, would conserve the herds. The treaty meant the Sioux would still hunt, preserve their culture, and draw on the Euro-Americans for the requisite trade items. Red Cloud and the other Sioux signatories saw the treaty as a boon; it legitimized all that they currently possessed, offered them the Missouri River, and gave them annuities. The deal seemed even sweeter because it cost the Sioux nothing, or so Red Cloud thought. Red Cloud signed the treaty on November 6, 1868, and in so doing became an accommodationist. He split with his traditionalist allies, who did not want any treaties with the Euro-Americans. From 1868 onward, Red Cloud sought accommodation, and that accommodation was reflected in geography. Red Cloud's bands gravitated toward the Platte, White, and Missouri Rivers and the American annuities to be found in those locations.

Not all Sioux leaders agreed to the provisions of the treaty. As a matter of fact, three influential chiefs and their followers did not sign the treaty or recognize its provisions. Those three chiefs, Sitting Bull, Crazy Horse, and Gall, continued to live in the Yellowstone basin, disengaged from Euro-America and its supposed corruption. Sitting Bull, Crazy Horse, and Gall would not go to the Great Sioux Reservation; instead, they would reside "permanently" in the Yellowstone country, whether in violation of the treaty or not.

Although some Sioux agreed to reside "permanently" on the Great Sioux Reservation, the Fort Laramie Treaty stipulated that the tribe could hunt in the region west of the reservation, in the unceded Powder River Country. The treaty did not specify the status of the Yellowstone River trench to the north, which left open the possibility that the Sioux could remain there. However, the treaty stated that Sioux could not maintain a "permanent" presence in those unceded lands. The treaty stated explicitly, "The tribes who are parties to this agreement hereby stipulate that they will relinquish all right to occupy permanently the territory outside their reservation as herein defined, but yet reserve the right to hunt on any lands north of North Platte, and on the Republican Fork of the Smoky Hill River, so long as the buffalo may range thereon in such numbers as to justify the chase."[12] How the Indians and the Euro-Americans interpreted the word "permanent" would be of crucial import to later events, as would the interpretation of how many animals there needed to be on the range to "justify the chase."

Did permanent residence on the Great Sioux Reservation mean that the

Sioux must immediately (as of 1868) remain on that reservation year-round? Or did permanent residence imply that that reserve would be their permanent home after the demise of the bison herds in the unceded territories? By stating that the Sioux could not maintain a "permanent" residence in the unceded territories, did the treaty imply they could not live there permanently in the future or permanently year-round? In other words, did the Sioux in the unceded lands have to return to the reservation each fall? Additionally, how many animals needed to be in an area to "justify the chase"? A great deal of leeway existed as to how one interpreted the word "permanent" and when the number of bison either continued to justify or no longer justified the chase. In short, the Fort Laramie Treaty of 1868 left much room for misunderstanding. Misunderstanding between peoples often leads to war.

Some Sioux bands upheld the Fort Laramie Treaty, whereas others disregarded all its provisions. Those bands "permanently" residing in the Powder River Country and the Yellowstone River trench did not abide by it. There existed no peace in those regions, especially along the Yellowstone Valley and the far Upper Missouri Valley. The Sioux there continued to attack Euro-Americans at will. Sioux warriors under Sitting Bull continued to kill wood-cutters and soldiers along the the Missouri River trench and the Yellowstone River Valley after 1868.

In 1872 and 1873, the Teton Sioux warred against the surveying expeditions moving up the Yellowstone Valley under Stanley and Custer. These attacks enraged top military officials, including Generals Sheridan and Sherman, who interpreted them as Sioux perfidy. In other words, the Sioux could not be trusted to uphold the Fort Laramie Treaty. Yet, along the Yellowstone and the Missouri, the Sioux perceived their own actions as necessary; they must protect their last stronghold from all challengers. By 1873, any trust engendered by the Fort Laramie Treaty began to wane. The big battles between the Sioux and the U.S. Army in the Yellowstone Valley did much to generate animosity between the two sides. The seeds were being sown for the Great Sioux War.

In 1874, Sherman ordered George Armstrong Custer and his calvary to "explore" the Black Hills to see whether gold existed there. Custer's forces cut across the Great Sioux Reservation from Fort Abraham Lincoln (near Bismarck, North Dakota) to the hills. Custer proceeded to the hills and explored the region, enjoying the expedition tremendously, particularly the opportunities to hunt bears. Afterward, having returned to base, Custer announced to the eastern press that gold in abundance lay in the streams of the Black Hills. That news sent hundreds of miners to the hills with the result that relations suffered between the Teton Sioux and the U.S. government.

In 1874, Euro-American miners, in clear violation of the Fort Laramie Treaty, crossed the boundary of the Great Sioux Reservation and climbed into the Black Hills, where they panned for gold. Their diggings set off another gold rush. The army initially attempted to keep the miners out of the Black Hills, but a long reservation border combined with too many miners and too few soldiers enabled thousands of gold seekers to slip through the army's dragnet. In response, the Sioux started to scalp and mutilate miners, actions that also violated the Fort Laramie Treaty. Not suprisingly, the miners in the Black Hills, who by the summer of 1875 numbered eight hundred, called for protection. The army concluded that much of the bloodshed was being committed by traditionals who moved into the hills from the Powder River Country.

The federal government came up with a solution to the crisis besieging the Black Hills, a crisis growing with the swelling population of miners, who by the winter of 1875–1876 numbered fifteen thousand.[13] Rather than uphold the treaty provisions agreed to at Fort Laramie and clear the hills of Euro-Americans, President Ulysses S. Grant decided to try to purchase the Black Hills from the Sioux, the rationale being that if the United States owned the Black Hills, the pretext for the Sioux attacks would end. In 1875, emissaries for the federal government went to the Great Sioux Reservation to purchase the hills. But the reservation Sioux expressed outrage that the Great Father wanted to abrogate a key provision of the Fort Laramie Treaty. The Sioux refused to negotiate the sale of the hills. Feeling snubbed by presumably ignorant and inferior savages, U.S. emissaries returned to Washington, D.C., to urge the Grant administration to chastise the intransigent Teton.

Without any resolution to the problem of the Black Hills, Grant, Sherman, and Sheridan decided to crush the Sioux in the Yellowstone basin. The three men believed the Yellowstone basin held the Sioux who instigated violence against the miners in the Black Hills. A war would either kill the hostiles west of the Great Sioux Reservation or force them onto a reduced reservation in Dakota Territory. Either way, the United States would win.

Grant wanted the Black Hills. If the president and his generals needed to incite a war with the Sioux to take the land, then so be it. After a meeting with President Grant in November 1875, Sherman issued an order that all

Sioux in the Yellowstone basin return to the Great Sioux Reservation by January 31, 1876, or else be considered by the United States government to be in open rebellion. According to how one interpreted "permanent" in the Fort Laramie Treaty, the order may have violated treaty provisions that granted the Sioux permission to hunt and live in the Yellowstone basin. Sherman's order was unrealistic. The Sioux wintering in the Powder River Country, along the banks of the Tongue, Powder, Yellowstone, or Little Bighorn, either did not receive news of the order or ignored it. The Teton Sioux could not move to the reservation during the dead of winter. To do so risked being caught out in the open in a blizzard and perishing in the cold and snow. In addition, the winter of 1875–1876 was one of the worst in years on the plains. Hence, thousands of Sioux remained in the Powder River Country after the January 31, 1876, deadline. Sherman subsequently labeled them hostile. After that date, he geared up the American war machine for a campaign.

Sitting Bull, Crazy Horse, and Gall disregarded Sherman's deadline. They may have wanted war with the whites, or at least they did not intend on abiding by what they perceived as an arbitrary order with no means of immediate enforcement. Accordingly, in late spring and early summer 1876, Sherman and Sheridan sent their troops into the Powder River Country and along the Yellowstone River in search of the Sioux. The plan of attack involved three forces, each converging on the Sioux from a different direction. One prong, led by Colonel John Gibbon, would come down the Yellowstone from the west. A second column would be headed by General George Crook. Crook's command would leave Fort Fetterman, Wyoming Territory, and proceed to the north and the headwaters of the Rosebud. The third column would be led by General Alfred Terry. Under Terry's overall leadership would be the tactical commander of the Seventh Cavalry, George Armstrong Custer.

Custer possessed an awesome fighting record from his Civil War days and from his time spent on the southern plains. The American public knew him as a commander who took the battle to the enemy—he was not afraid to fight. By the 1870s, Custer held a reputation for being the best Indian fighter in the U.S. Army. Custer, unlike so many other commanders across the plains, found, ran down, and killed Indians. Custer displayed a flair for the dramatic and a love for pomp and circumstance. That he was eccentric cannot be doubted. Supposedly, Indian and white females found themselves attracted to this daring cavalier, although photographs of him show a rather homely individual. He wore his blond hair long, over his shoulders (but for the campaign of 1876 he cut it short). He dressed flamboyantly, even outrageously, creating his own uniforms. One uniform designed by the boy wonder consisted of a yellow leather jacket and pants, a large-brimmed, floppy campaign hat, and a flashy red scarf bouncing around his neck. That he made a tempting target for his own men, and the enemy, is obvious. Like most narcissists, Custer held a reputation for insubordination. He could be headstrong, self-righteous, and unwilling to take orders when he considered those orders absurd or just plain wrong.

Sherman and Sheridan wanted the three prongs under Gibbon, Crook, and Terry/Custer to close in upon the Powder River Country. Sherman and Sheridan hoped that one column would contact the Sioux and either engage them in battle or drive them into the arms of one or both of the other two prongs. Eventually, the three units would grind the Sioux down between them.

Opposing this U.S. Army force was one of the largest Indian contingents ever assembled in United States history. An estimated fifteen thousand Sioux, Cheyenne, and Arapaho camped along the Little Bighorn River in the third week of June 1876 to participate in their annual ceremony of renewal and thanksgiving. In plains Indian culture, the Sun Dance was, and is, the biggest religious ceremony of the year, occurring in June with the solstice, when the earth is at its greenest and life in the Upper Missouri at its fullest. Of the fifteen thousand Indians camped along the Greasy Grass, between three and four thousand warriors paraded through the camp that stretched for three miles from north to south and a half a mile from east to west.[14]

Three men led the Sioux: Sitting Bull (a medicine man who earlier received a vision that soldiers would fall into camp upside down, meaning the Indians would kill many bluecoats); Crazy Horse (an Ogalala commander of repute, deeply spiritual, a persuasive speaker, and a man committed to resisting the white advance); and Gall (a Hunkpapa with a chiseled chin, impressive height, and barrel chest). Gall looked the part of a chief.

Custer's force was supposed to move south toward the headwaters of Rosebud Creek, all the while searching for the Sioux or signs of their movements. Once at the head of the Rosebud, Custer and his troops were to turn west, northwest, into the Little Bighorn Valley. Terry's orders to Custer gave the brevet general leeway regarding when to engage the enemy. If Custer found the Indians, he had the authority to pursue them. Terry and Custer both feared that any delays might give the Indians time to flee beyond the reach of the cavalry.

On June 22, 1876, Custer and his men departed the Yellowstone and moved up a good bison road along the Rosebud. All the while, Custer's Indian scouts scoured the countryside for signs of the Teton Sioux. At the same time, scouts from the Sioux camp on the Little Bighorn watched Custer's movements. The Indians at the Greasy Grass knew of Custer's approach, but rather than run away, they decided to stay put and risk a battle, knowing that the tactical advantages rested on their side. The Teton Sioux recognized their own strength. They allowed Custer to come to them. This was a tactical decision on the part of the Sioux leadership. It was not just happenstance that Custer found the big encampment; the Sioux allowed him to do it, knowing that they had the numbers to overwhelm any single prong of the three moving against them. Crazy Horse had done just that on June 17, along the upper Rosebud, when his warriors turned back the troops commanded by General George Crook. With Crook out of the picture, the Sioux felt confident they could take on Custer's cavalry.

Late on June 24, 1876, Custer's Indian scouts discovered a massive, fresh trail heading due west over the Wolf Mountains toward the Little Bighorn Valley. The raw nature of the trail meant one thing; the Indians were close, within only one day's march. Custer decided late in the evening on June 24 to move immediately on the Indians to his west rather than continue south. He had found the Sioux and wanted to engage them before they scattered to the far corners of the Upper Missouri. He feared that the Indians would disperse and not be destroyed or captured as so often happened in Indian warfare on the plains. With no misgivings, he ordered his troops to follow the Indian trail.

At dawn the next morning atop the Crow's Nest, Custer's scouts spotted an Indian encampment next to the banks of the Little Bighorn fifteen miles away. The scouts concluded that the camp contained a large number of Indians. The camp was big, but they did not know how big. Nonetheless, Custer decided to hit the village. He ordered his troops to the Little Bighorn without knowing how many Indians occupied the valley to his front. It is likely that he did not really care how many Indians were down there. Custer, imbued with strong notions of the superiority of the Euro-American race, believed his force of cavalry, if properly deployed and led, could take on any Indian force and defeat it, no matter how large. Custer's arrogance was born of experience. The man had not been defeated by Indians in all his years on the plains, so why would this battle be any different? Furthermore, during his southern plains campaign, whenever a cavalry unit struck an Indian village by surprise, the Indians panicked and retreated rather than stand and fight in an organized, disciplined manner. If Custer could strike fast and hard, he would roll the village up, or so he thought as he prepared to launch his attack.

Custer divided his troops into three separate arms. One arm under Captain Frederick W. Benteen was ordered to the south, to prevent the Indians from escaping up the Little Bighorn. A second arm, under the command of Major Marcus A. Reno, would hit the Indian village along its southern end. The third arm would be under Custer's direct command and would strike the village at its upper end. Custer hoped that the two assault forces hitting the village nearly simultaneously would cause maximum consternation among the Indians, leading to a pell-mell exodus from the village and the abandonment of all its baggage, bison meat, and horses.

Custer must have cursed under his breath when he first saw the size of the Indian village from the rugged hills overlooking the Little Bighorn Valley. An estimated fifteen hundred tepees nuzzled the valley floor below his now seemingly tiny detachment of 215 cavalrymen. But by the time he saw the village with his own wide eyes, it was too late. He had already committed himself and his men to battle. Custer's column descended a ravine toward the center of the village, only to be quickly repulsed by an onrushing wave of screaming, excited warriors. Custer may have died at the mouth of the ravine, at the point where it opens into the Little Bighorn Valley. Custer led his troops into battle. He was not a commander who sat on a horse on a high hill at a distance from the battle and directed the course of combat through runners or signal flags. Rather, he liked to be in on the action. When he came down that ravine toward the village, it is likely he was at the front of his column, and he would have been the first to witness and feel the solid thump delivered by the roughly one thousand warriors who hit the cavalry as they descended from the ridgeline above. The brevet general may have been shot dead only minutes into the fighting. Rather than leave his corpse in the ravine to be disfigured by the Indians, his troops may have thrown the limp body on a horse and carried it toward Custer's Hill. Whatever the case may be, this initial strike by the cavalry failed miserably, and the column retreated back up the ravine and then northward in a haphazard, every-man-for-himself manner. If Custer survived the initial Sioux blow in the ravine, he, too, raced to the northwest, fighting a rearguard action to keep the Indians off his horse's tail.

By the time the young brevet general reached the top of the hill named in honor of him, the end of his life closed in around him. No sooner had he reached the summit than a thousand warriors under Crazy Horse swooped down on him and his few remaining troops with the force of a sledgehammer. In the final minutes of the battle, an estimated two thousand warriors circled the remnants of Custer's cavalry detachment, firing arrows and rifle balls into the rapidly shrinking ring of soldiers. Custer and his command died without much of a fight. Less than an hour after the first shots went off in the ravine, Custer and all his men lay dead, completely overwhelmed by a far superior and better-led force.[15]

Decades after the battle, another explanation for Custer's death emerged from a Sioux warrior named White Bull, who received his name from the sacred white buffalo, the most important religious entity in the Sioux spiritual world besides Wakan Tanka, the Great Spirit. According to White Bull and numerous corroborative eyewitnesses, White Bull, who did not recognize Custer through the haze of battle, rode up to the mounted general from the rear and pulled him off his horse. The dismounted Custer then turned and fired his carbine nearly point-blank at the still-mounted White Bull. The shot missed the Sioux warrior, who then dismounted and ran through the dust toward the bewildered general. The two men struggled for several moments in hand-to-hand combat, with Custer hitting White Bull several times with his fists and even grabbing his long braids. White Bull in turn delivered several hard raps against Custer's head. White Bull then took Custer's carbine out of the general's hands, turned it on him, and shot him dead. White Bull, the bison world in human form, killed George Armstrong Custer on June 25, 1876.[16]

Custer's defeat was the direct result of the U.S. government's policy of removal, concentration, and assimilation. The Battle of the Little Bighorn, or the Battle at the Greasy Grass, as the Indians refer to it, occurred because the U.S. government violated previous treaties with the Teton Sioux and tried to force them onto a smaller reservation. The Indians defended their land, their bison, their families, and their rights. The Battle at the Greasy Grass was a battle, not a massacre. In 1876, and for decades thereafter, the eastern media portrayed the combat as a massacre, as if Custer and his men went out on a lark and just happened to be struck down by Indians. That could not have been further from the facts on the ground. Custer went to kill and destroy, and he died in battle as a result of his intentions. At the Greasy Grass the Indians outfought, outmaneuvered, and conducted a far better strategic campaign than their Euro-American opponents.

The news of Custer's defeat arrived on the eastern seaboard with the sound of a thunderclap. The public felt outrage and wanted revenge. Revenge is what they got. Congress appropriated funds later that summer to irrevocably crush the Teton Sioux in the Yellowstone country. During the campaigns of late summer 1876, the army, with the aid of a small fleet of steamboats, established depots, forts, and stockades at the major choke points in the Yellowstone Valley. These army compounds monitored traffic moving on the region's significant north-south roadways. Facilities arose at the mouth of the Little Bighorn, Bighorn, Rosebud, Tongue, and Powder, and across from the mouth of Glendive Creek, opposite of where today's Glendive stands. These posts, or depots, gave the army the ability to sweep the region to the south of the Yellowstone. The army used the posts and patrolling steamers to keep the larger bands of Teton Sioux from crossing the Yellowstone and pursuing a northerly course into Canada and safety (fig. 6.8).

The defeat of the Sioux came in the winter of 1876–1877, when units

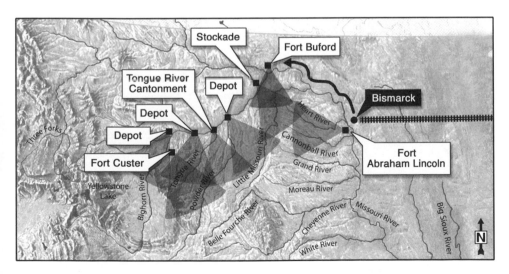

Figure 6.8. U.S. Army depots, posts, and supply lines utilized to overcome Teton Sioux resource advantages in their core area in 1876–1877. The depots, the military forts, and the Missouri–Yellowstone River navigation route enabled the U.S. Army to project power into the Teton Sioux core following Custer's defeat. (Paul Davidson, South Plains College, Levelland, Texas)

under the charge of Colonel Nelson Miles, nicknamed Bear's Coat, pursued the remaining Sioux and Cheyenne trapped to the south of the Yellowstone. In May 1877, the last Teton Sioux military commander, Crazy Horse, surrendered himself and his warriors at Fort Robinson, Nebraska. Sitting Bull, to the astonishment of American military commanders, evaded the net laid down along the Yellowstone. He and his people went to the east of the forts and stockades and fled into Canada. He would reluctantly return to the United States and imprisonment at Fort Randall in 1881.

Following the Battle at the Greasy Grass, a number of lithographs emerged that supposedly depicted the final moments of Custer's command. The most famous painting, which found its way into thousands of drinking establishments across the country, was sponsored by Anheuser Busch and executed by artist Otto Becker. In Becker's depiction, Custer is shown as one of the last white men standing atop Custer's Hill. Dead or dying soldiers at his feet, Custer stands alone, holding a sword in one hand and a reversed pistol in the other. The general stares resolutely forward, sword over his head ready to strike and kill the Indians. The Sioux circle around the great general, about to consume him.[17]

The Becker lithograph possesses symbolic importance. On one level, it displays the courage of Custer, the individual, in the face of staggering odds. Custer is portrayed as a brave soldier who will die with his boots on, standing firm against his enemy. On a deeper level, the painting displays the Euro-American race and its battle against the forces of savagery and disorder. Custer the man is the Euro-American race, and that race will not flinch when it confronts a brutal world. The Indians are symbols of anarchy; Custer's pose is that of a man sure of himself and his cause. Take that image even further, and you have a snapshot of the Euro-American interpretation of its confrontation not only with the Teton Sioux but also with the Upper Missouri bison world. The Sioux represented the bison world. The white race must stand firm against the Sioux and their world, must civilize the Upper Missouri, the very grassland that supported such savagery and disorder. Custer was only one man who died on the grassland, but what he ultimately represented was Euro-America's ongoing battle to subvert the Upper Missouri and transform its cultures, ecology, and geography to mirror American values and ambitions. Custer was a soldier in that decades-long effort, and that is why so many visitors still travel to the site of the Battle at the Greasy Grass. "Custer's last stand" symbolized the last stand of the bison world as much as the general's. The battle signaled the end of one geographic and ecological reality and the beginning of something markedly different.

Custer got beat at the Greasy Grass because he made the mistake of going into the Sioux's geographic core with a force operating on the periphery of U.S. influence and eastern centers of supply and support. Custer died because he attacked the Sioux at a time when their physical, and corresponding military, strength reached its annual peak. He set out for the Little Bighorn when the Upper Missouri's energy flows attained their greatest areal extent. By June of each year, the Sioux ran strong on bison meat and the protein derived from it, while their ponies became vigorous off the grasses sprouting across the region. The energy pulsing through the system contributed to Sioux military power. If the army had hit the Teton Sioux in the late winter or early spring, when the original campaign plans called for it, the energy flows moving through the Upper Missouri system would have been at their lowest. Subsequently, the Sioux would have been considerably weaker and less able to fend off and defeat U.S. Army forces. The army would do just that in the winter of 1876–1877. The military leadership, learning from its deadly mistakes in the summer of 1876, conducted a winter campaign under the leadership of Colonel Nelson Miles. Miles, with base camps and supply depots along the Yellowstone River trench, including the all-important Tongue River cantonment at the mouth of the Tongue, put better-supplied troops into the tributary valleys south of the Yellowstone to defeat or drive out the Sioux residing there. Winter served the Euro-Americans (who could draw on outside sources of supply in those months), whereas summer served the Sioux by providing grass and bison.

The defeat of the Sioux in 1876–1877 meant the bison lost their protectors. As the Sioux went to the reservation in Dakota Territory, the curtain opened on the bison world's grand finale. The coup de grace for the Upper Missouri's bison came swiftly (fig. 6.9). As soon as Euro-Americans shoved the Indians off the stage, ranchers, farmers, traders, and market hunters moved into the Yellowstone Valley. Once there, they established ranches, farms, and hunting cabins inside the bottoms situated at the mouths of the Yellowstone's perennial tributaries. Euro-Americans also took their cattle into the sanctuaries located along such tributaries as the Tongue, Rosebud, and Powder.

In the first years after Crazy Horse's surrender, market hunters concentrated around the military posts, especially Fort Keogh, which granted access to the Tongue–Sunday Creek road and provided protection to the hunters

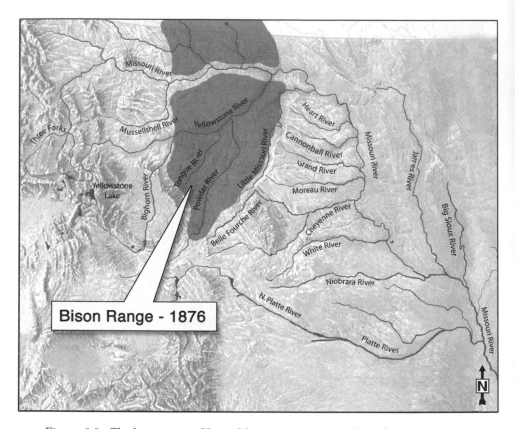

Figure 6.9. The bison range, Upper Missouri, circa 1876. Steamboat operations, agricultural settlement, disease, drought, trading posts, military forts, Indian hunting, Euro-American hunting, and U.S. Army operations caused a dramatic reduction in the bison range by 1876. (Paul Davidson, South Plains College, Levelland, Texas)

against tiny bands of unredeemed Indians unwilling to accept the new socio-economic order. Fort Keogh and Miles City also offered bison hunters a market for their meat and robes. Hunters moved up Sunday Creek and the Tongue, tapping the bison passing over that north-south thoroughfare. In only a few short years, Euro-Americans occupied the key junctures in the Yellowstone Valley, including the bottoms at the Bighorn, Alkali Creek, Big Porcupine, Little Porcupine, Rosebud, Tongue, Sunday Creek, Cedar Creek, Powder, and O'Fallon Creek.

The flood of humanity into the Yellowstone Valley after 1877 denied the trench to bison. When hard winters came in 1876–1877, 1877–1878, 1880–1881, and 1881–1882, the weather, in a repeat of the ancient ecological ritual, drove bison herds toward the Yellowstone Valley. But the animals did not find succor there; instead, they met a barrage of gunfire. The *Yellowstone Journal,* of Miles City, Montana, noted that "the killing was all done in winter,"[18] winter being the time when the animals concentrated in the bottoms. Oscar Brackett, who entered the Yellowstone Valley during the winter of 1876–1877, wrote how bison came to the Yellowstone during the coldest months: "We went in on an island just above mouth of Little pocupine [*sic*] & built us a cabain there was no Bufaloo up to that time on the Yellow Stone the Morning after we had got our Cabbain done it had turned very Cold. I went out so I could see up & down the bottoms & the Bottoms was covered with them & from that time untill Spring the Country was full of Buffaloo."[19] Stationed at the mouths of perennial tributaries to the Yellowstone, the hunters had an easy go of it as cold and wet placed bison in front of their barrels. To no one's surprise, bison numbers quickly fell. In the winter of 1879–1880, an estimated 35,000 hides found their way to the train depot at Miles City. The *Yellowstone Journal* reported, "The winter of 1880–81 was the record breaker in buffalo killing, owing no doubt, to the very deep snows of that winter, making it almost impossible for the herds to move. It was estimated that fully 250,000 were killed that winter in what was then Custer County."[20]

The animals found it more difficult to go into the Yellowstone Valley after the Northern Pacific laid track from Glendive to Livingston in 1882–1883. The noise of the locomotives and the passengers they carried further hastened the extermination of the herds. In that later year, at least 45,000 hides sold at Miles City. By 1884 it was all but over. Most informed, or barely informed, residents of the Yellowstone Valley knew it.[21] The last paradise of hunters, the Yellowstone Valley, had been cleared of large fauna in just a few short years.

One of the last hunting excursions for wild bison on the plains of the Upper Missouri occurred in 1886. On September 20, 1886, William Hornaday, with the Smithsonian Institution, boarded a train in Washington, D.C., bound for Montana, his purpose being to kill about thirty of the last three hundred free-range bison for the sake of posterity. Hornaday wanted a collection of bison shot, stuffed, and put on display in his prestigious museum. Along the Big Dry–Big Porcupine road, Hornaday and his colleagues discovered a remnant herd and proceeded to methodically kill its members one by one.

On October 16, 1886, one of the team members shot a large bull. But as dusk closed the window to the sun and the grass turned purple with the sky, the hunters reluctantly left the bull where it lay, hoping to return to it in the morning to dress it. As the hunters trotted back to base camp, they feared the night would bring wolves to the carcass, carnivorous scavengers that would devour the bison. But when Hornaday and his fellows came back to the bison kill site the next morning, they found something completely unexpected lying on the ground. The bison bull had been stripped of its meat and hide not by wolves but by the sharp knives of Indians who must have been following the team's movements and came to the kill site after Hornaday and his men abandoned the animal to the night. The nighttime visitors painted the animal's shorn head. Streaks of burnished yellow and red decorated the skull. A flag of red and yellow cloth hung from one horn. The other horn revealed eleven small notches, cut to express a cryptic numerology. To Hornaday and his colleagues, it was apparent that the Indians had held a ritual over the dead creature, one of the last of its kind to roam freely across the Upper Missouri. The death of that bull, and the Indian ceremony surrounding it, marked the passing of the bison world into forever.[23]

A Hydraulic Empire

The Corps of Engineers and

the Reclamation Service

Control of the water of the West is control of the West.

—Joseph C. O'Mahoney

The direction of water influences the path of society. Across the semiarid environment of the Upper Missouri, the course of empire followed rivers. At the end of the fur trade and military eras, Euro-Americans commenced the construction of an agricultural world in the Upper Missouri. They wanted to spread their image of peace and affluence across the land- and waterscape. But Euro-Americans disagreed on how to achieve a prosperous agricultural, sedentary society on top of the grassland. They understood water would be the key to well-being, but how should that liquid be used to achieve the ideal society? Differing views on the Upper Missouri's future revealed themselves through two institutions and their respective policies toward the Yellowstone and Missouri Rivers. The Corps of Engineers sought to build a society in the Upper Missouri by turning the waters of the Upper Missouri and Yellowstone Rivers into barge navigation channels that would carry agricultural commodities to markets in the South and East. Reclamation Service officials believed the two biggest rivers of the Upper Missouri should be directed toward irrigated fields. No one within the new dominant culture of the Upper Missouri thought of allowing the waters of the Missouri and Yellowstone to continue to flow through ancient, nomadic channels.

The Yellowstone River and the steamboat traffic it supported played a pivotal role in the eventual defeat of the Teton Sioux living south of the Yellowstone main stem. Steamers also enabled the U.S. Army to maintain a strong Euro-American presence in the Yellowstone Valley in the years prior to the arrival of the railroad. The initial Euro-American hold over the Yellowstone Valley depended on the reliability of the steamboat connection to the Missouri Valley and eastern centers of power. The Euro-American grip on the Yellowstone Upper Missouri region remained as strong or as weak as the transportation connections between the territory and eastern zones of supply. The Corps of Engineers' work in improving the Yellowstone between 1879 and 1883 must be considered in that light. River development advocates in the nineteenth century referred to engineering projects that dammed or channelized rivers as "improvements," perceiving public works as embellishments of the natural characteristics of the riparian and riverine environments. Improvement of the Yellowstone served as an adjunct to military operations and as a means of reinforcing the links between the Yellowstone Valley and the outside world (fig. 7.1).

Once the Northern Pacific Railroad laid tracks between Glendive and the Bighorn River, the status of the Corps of Engineers along the Yellowstone

Figure 7.1. The Lower Yellowstone Valley near Miles City, Montana. (Photograph by author, 1999)

changed in significant ways. The army engineers no longer needed to "improve" the Yellowstone River to ensure supplies reached Fort Keogh or Fort Custer. The railroad maintained the valley's ties to the east and west.

Consequently, in the years after 1883, the army engineers found their position in the Yellowstone Valley and Upper Missouri in general eroded by Northern Pacific Railroad tracks. Army officers in St. Louis, at the Western Division office, debated what to do with the Yellowstone. Should the army admit defeat at the hands of the railroad, abandon the river altogether, and send its work boats scampering down the Missouri? But nineteenth-century Euro-Americans, especially those of a military persuasion, had an aversion to retrograde motions. The word "retreat" rarely found its way into the Euro-American lexicon. As a result, the army engineers brainstormed other possibilities for the Yellowstone, projects that linked the Yellowstone to larger, more complex hydraulic schemes.

The central question posed by the railroad's arrival at the Bighorn River (which Yellowstone River navigators considered the ostensible head of navigation on the stream) was whether or not the Corps of Engineers should attempt to maintain a position on the Yellowstone River. In the minds of many army officers, if the corps surrendered the Yellowstone, the people residing in the valley would forever suffer at the hands of the supposedly exploitative railroad companies. The problem facing the corps and the residents of the Yellowstone River Valley after the arrival of the railroad had ramifications far afield, striking at the heart of the Euro-American political, economic, and social order of the era. The crux of the issue was whether the American people had the inherent right to a competitive transportation and economic system or whether they should be victimized by monopolies.

Between 1883 and 1911, the corps alternatively sought justifications for improving the Yellowstone. The two primary explanations for early improvement of the stream had been to assist the army against the Sioux and then help the Northern Pacific Railroad in the construction of its route to the Pacific. By 1883, both arguments no longer held water, and the army engineers went searching for new arguments so they could continue to tinker with the Yellowstone. Yet, by the end of the first decade of the twentieth century, engineering hurdles and hydrologic realities rendered any corps justification for manipulating the Yellowstone unconvincing.

The Corps of Engineers' relationship to the Yellowstone River cannot be viewed in isolation. The corps' actions along the Missouri and even the Mississippi influenced its policies toward the Yellowstone. Events in one river basin influenced circumstances in the other two; it is impossible to view the Yellowstone alone. To illustrate, channelization techniques developed for use along the Missouri and Mississippi would be deployed on the Yellowstone. Additionally, the establishment of the Mississippi River Commission in 1879 and the Missouri River Commission in 1884 generated enthusiasm and hope among corps officials that they would be able to channelize not only the Mississippi and Missouri but also the Yellowstone. The Missouri River Commission's disbandment in 1902 diminished hope among army engineers that the Yellowstone would ever be united to a larger corps-administered Mississippi-Missouri-Yellowstone navigation network.

The Corps of Engineers began work along the Yellowstone River in 1878. In that year, army engineers surveyed 145 miles of the river. Men standing aboard skiffs and armed with long poles took a total of 59,731 soundings of the river channel's depth along that entire reach. The U.S. Army Corps of Engineers conducted this survey, and another one in 1879, as a precursor to the "improvement" of the stream for steamboat navigation. On September 5, 1879, the engineers began to actually "improve" the Yellowstone.[1] Army personnel focused their efforts at Buffalo Rapids, the rocky shoal situated twelve miles east of Miles City and Fort Keogh. The corps concluded that Buffalo Rapids and its rocks represented the single greatest obstacle to steamboat navigation on the Yellowstone. Its presence made it difficult and sometimes impossible to send supplies upstream to Forts Keogh and Custer.

Between 1879 and 1880, teams of men, often wet and cold, drilled hundreds of cylindrical holes into rock, and into those holes dropped sticks of dynamite. In 1880 alone, the engineers detonated a total of 273 explosions at Buffalo Rapids, hoping to reduce the rapids to rubble and clear a pathway for steamboats. The army blasted two other rapids into smithereens in 1880: Baker's and Wolf's rapids got pounded by corps crews. This work helped steamboat companies haul a total of sixty-six hundred tons of material into or out of the Yellowstone Valley. Miles City saw twenty-four steamboat arrivals that year.[2]

The year 1881 signaled the height of the army's work along the Yellowstone. The Corps of Engineers intensified its efforts on the stream to aid steamers supplying the construction crews of the Northern Pacific Railroad. Much of the work that year and in 1882 centered around Glendive, where the railroad first touched the banks of the Yellowstone (fig. 7.2). Crews built wing dams at several locations at or below Glendive to concentrate the Yellowstone's flow and deepen the thalweg. This channelization work materi-

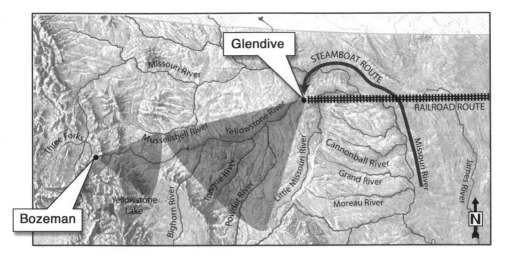

Figure 7.2. Glendive as the gateway to the Yellowstone Valley, 1877–1882. (Paul Davidson, South Plains College, Levelland, Texas)

ally assisted the steamers that ferried supplies between Bismarck, North Dakota, and the Northern Pacific Railroad construction crews inching their way up the Yellowstone Valley toward Bozeman Pass and the Three Forks. The chief of construction for the NPRR expressed his appreciation for the Corps' labors in a letter dated November 17, 1882: "The work done by you has been a great benefit to the navigation of the Yellowstone River."[3]

The influence of the railroad on steamboat traffic became readily apparent In 1882, when only two railroad company construction boats plied the river. No steamboat companies engaged in long-haul traffic could work the river in the face of the railroad's existence. In 1883, the Northern Pacific Railroad completed its transcontinental route. The corps' work on the river reflected the changing transportation scene. In that year, the engineers did almost no work on the Yellowstone. In the blink of an eye, the railroad rendered the army engineers insignificant players in the field of frontier development. The engineers admitted as much in the *Annual Report of the Chief of Engineers:* "It is doubtful if the Yellowstone above Glendive will ever again be of any importance as a line of transportation, unless the railroad company should exact too much."[4] If the army wanted to stay on the river, and thereby maintain an institutional presence and power base there, it needed to redefine its mission.

Just as the corps began its withdrawal from the Yellowstone Valley, events along the Missouri and Mississippi valleys forced a reevaluation of the corps' role in the entire Mississippi basin and nation at large. Prior to the 1880s, the corps accomplished piecemeal engineering work around the country as the need arose. For instance, along the Missouri, Congress assigned the corps the task of shoring up the collapsing banks at various riverside communities, including Kansas City, St. Joseph, Sioux City, and even the rather insignificant town of Vermillion, Dakota Territory. During this period, the engineers saw themselves as objective, apolitical scientist-engineers who carried out or fulfilled the public interest.

But beginning in the late 1870s and early 1880s, the Corps of Engineers began a consideration of its role within the federal system that stemmed from the organizational revolution sweeping the country at that time. Since the Civil War, government and private institutions had grown in size, complexity, and social and political reach. As institutions expanded, they began to stake claims on specific resources, regions, or policies. The federal government remained the single largest organization within the American sociopolitical-economic system throughout much of the nineteenth century. Through conquest and other forms of acquisition, the federal government gained control over the land area that today encompasses the contiguous forty-eight states and Alaska. That same government encouraged the American citizenry to settle upon those lands. Once geographic empire became a reality in the 1870s, various institutions maneuvered to establish institutional empires under the larger federal geopolitical umbrella.

Corporate empires existed prior to the 1880s, but during that decade and into the 1890s, institutions in both the private and the public sphere made a frantic effort to divvy up the nation's land, water, mineral, and forest resources. The institutional empires of the 1880s were continental in scale, controlling large tracts of land or copious resources. The railroad companies were the first post–Civil War institutions to establish a series of empires across the western United States. The railroads owned big chunks of the West, granted by the federal government. Those land grants endowed the railroad companies with imperial power, through control of the resources and the transportation grid to and from specific regions. Monopolization of a territory's transportation system gave the railroads unprecedented power to extract wealth from an area's resource base and its inhabitants. Because of that power, railroads became the largest nongovernmental organizations in the United States by the 1870s. In 1883, the Northern Pacific Railroad established itself solidly across the land area between Minneapolis–St. Paul and Puget Sound. As the railroad's hold over the land and its people intensitied, calls for railroad regulation and/or competitive water transportation arose among the populace.

In the late 1870s and early 1880s, cries of unfair railroad rates and the need for deep-draft barge traffic on the nation's three biggest midcontinental rivers reached a fervent pitch. Into this storm of protest and discontent stepped the Corps of Engineers. Corps officials, including Brigadier General Andrew A. Humphreys and Brigadier General Horatio G. Wright, recognized that the Corps of Engineers could conceivably create a national waterways system. A number of interconnected rivers, deepened by the corps and capable of carrying barges, intersecting the United States, would capture traffic from the railroads and lessen their influence over the nation's economy, while at the same time assuring the corps' institutional survival and even expansion during the railroad age. A national waterways system would lead to the growth and expansion of the corps' organizational size and territorial influence and supposedly increase the economic prosperity of the United States. The corps in the 1870s and early 1880s developed an imperial vision, one that opposed the railroads. This imperial image took shape at the same time that the corps' role on the Yellowstone River came into question.

The Corps of Engineers drew up a plan that was spectacular in scope. Corps officials hoped to create a deep, channelized river system from the Great Lakes south to the Gulf of Mexico and from the Appalachians all the way to the Rockies (fig. 7.3). The hydraulic system would include the Mississippi (the key artery of the waterways network), along with the two largest branches of the Father of Waters: the Mighty Missouri and the more placid Ohio. Extending out from these three big rivers, a series of tributary barge channels would penetrate even farther inland, touching the far corners of the continent. The army engineers saw the Yellowstone River as a potential barge route tied to the Missouri. A Yellowstone barge channel would tap the bountiful Yellowstone Valley and maybe go as far as the base of the Rocky Mountains, with its timber and mineral wealth. Engineers stated, "Aside from the picturesque and historic interest attached to the Yellowstone, it possesses an interest as a navigable stream of no mean order. Constituting as it does one of the main arteries of Montana, it will increase in importance as a line of transportation for the productions of what will ultimately, and at no late date, become one of the most important states of the Union."[5] The corps wanted to deepen all the rivers in the system through a program of channelization. Channelization and the resulting constriction of flows would

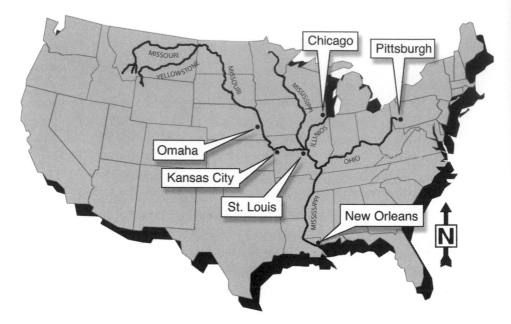

Figure 7.3. The Corps of Engineers envisions a hydraulic empire. This illustration depicts the corps' proposed Lakes-to-the-Gulf Waterways System. (Paul Davidson, South Plains College, Levelland, Texas)

increase depths so that rivers could float tows and barges hauling tons and tons of cargo. Deep-draft barge traffic would hurt the railroads, take their business, and free the American people from their tyrannical rates.

By conceptualizing such a hydraulic system, the Corps of Engineers became involved in economic and social planning. This occurred two decades before the ascendancy of the Progressive Conservationists and five decades before the social planning schemes of the New Deal. The corps' hydraulic blueprint, if carried to fruition, would make the army engineers major players in economic development, on a par with the railroads. It would develop the nation along rivers, not rails; it would build or dismantle cities according to their proximity to deepened rivers; it would make St. Louis and New Orleans ports of amazing wealth and stature; and it would redirect resources and political power away from the railroads, and especially Chicago and New York, to the corps and its handpicked municipalities.

The corps' river navigation system helped establish the idea that the government had not only a right but also an obligation to acquire natural resources (in this case rivers) and develop those resources for the benefit of the American people. The corps' plans for the nation's midcontinental rivers established the precedent for the later government acquisition of timberlands in the West and the government prohibition against private ownership of dam sites. Once its river plans had been drawn up, the corps received authorization from Congress to carry out those plans.

In 1879, Congress created the Mississippi River Commission to channelize the Mississippi from its mouth to St. Louis to create a channel deep enough to support barges and to supervise the construction of a system of riverside levees for flood control. In 1884, Congress formed the Missouri River Commission to deepen the Missouri from its mouth to Sioux City, Iowa. The Missouri River Commission's charter left open the possibility that the Missouri might, at a later date, be channelized from Sioux City, Iowa, through the Dakotas and into Montana. The establishment of these two commissions offered the Corps of Engineers the real chance to make its imperial vision a reality. The corps had no idea how much it would cost to channelize the Mississippi or the Missouri. In 1881, Major Charles Suter, a member of the Missouri River Commission based at the corps' St. Louis office, calculated the Missouri could be channelized for $10,000 per mile. In Suter's estimation it would cost $8 million to channelize the river to Sioux City and another $12 million to channelize it through the Dakotas and into eastern Montana to the confluence of the Yellowstone and Missouri. Twenty million dollars to channelize two thousand miles of river appeared reasonable to Suter and his colleagues in St. Louis. As a matter of fact, they considered the project to be a bargain. Suter believed the navigation channel from Sioux City south alone would result in $5 million in savings per annum for Missouri Valley farmers. Thus, the channel from Sioux City to the mouth would conceivably pay for itself in roughly a year and a half of operation. A channel all the way to Montana would pay for itself in less than five years.

With the possibility of building a channel from New Orleans to St. Louis and from St. Louis to the mouth of the Yellowstone River, the Corps of Engineers did not want to rule out the likelihood of extending the barge route up the Yellowstone as far as practical. By the middle 1880s, some corps officials, including Suter, became hopeful they would be able to tie a Yellowstone River barge channel to a Missouri River barge channel. A channelized Upper Missouri and Yellowstone held out the possibility that the corps would pull the northern plains and northern Rockies (the Upper Missouri territory) into its orbit and away from the railroads (fig. 7.4). This prospect was so tempting that the corps could not let the Yellowstone go. For this reason,

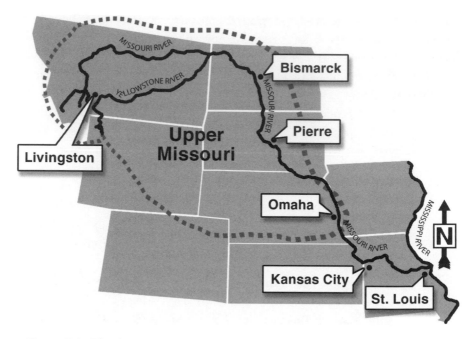

Figure 7.4. The Corps of Engineers along the Missouri and Yellowstone. In the 1880s and 1890s, corps officials hoped to join the Missouri and Yellowstone to the Mississippi to create a far-reaching inland waterways system. The corps also sought to seize an empire by building a barge channel from St. Louis into the Dakotas and Montana that would profitably compete with the monopolistic railroad companies. (Paul Davidson, South Plains College, Levelland, Texas)

the St. Louis office and later the Sioux City office continued to include the Yellowstone River in its *Annual Report to the Chief of Engineers* throughout the 1880s and 1890s. Inclusion of the river in the annual report was a means of stating the corps had vested interests in the Yellowstone. The continued mention in the annual report symbolized the corps' hope of coupling the Yellowstone to the Missouri and ultimately to the Mississippi.

The corps did not receive any appropriations for channelization work along the Yellowstone after 1887, yet even as late as 1895 the army continued to claim an interest in the stream. In that year the army went so far as to insist the Milwaukee Railroad company build its bridge at Fairview, Montana, with a span that ascended high enough to allow steamboats to go under it. This requirement, which substantially increased the cost of the bridge, not only made clear the corps' hostility toward the railroad companies but also served as a reminder that the engineers hoped that one day the Yellowstone River would be a viable steamboat or barge channel. While the corps kept its options open on the Yellowstone, trying not to foreclose the possibility of a future barge channel in the river, events were transpiring along the Missouri that would dash corps hopes for the Upper Missouri basin as a whole (fig. 7.5).

Congress charged Major Charles Suter, head of the Missouri River Commission, with building the Missouri barge channel from the mouth to Sioux City and possibly beyond. Suter and his engineers were struggling with the Missouri in the 1890s. The river displayed a propensity to outflank, undermine, or completely wash away the corps' channelization structures (which included permeable pile dikes, willow mattresses, stone revetments, and willow and stone weirs). The Missouri's shiftiness and vivacity caused unbelievable delays in the barge channel's construction. The river punished the engineers with cost overruns, which in turn undermined the corps' legitimacy with Congress. To cite an instance, Suter once believed, back in 1881, that the army could finish the channel to Sioux City in five years at the relatively low cost of $10,000 per mile. But as late as 1895 (fourteen years after the first Suter cost estimate), the engineers had completed only forty-five

Figure 7.5. Railroad bridge across the Lower Yellowstone River, Fairview, Montana. The Corps of Engineers insisted this bridge not obstruct potential steamboat and/or barge traffic along the Lower Yellowstone River. As a result, the bridge's builders included a weight and pulley system to lift the far-left span above any passing steamboats and/or barges. Today the Yellowstone's thalweg has shifted to the other bank, leaving the unique span over dry land. (Photograph by author, 1999)

miles of the barge channel at the whopping price of $58,000 per mile. By this later date, prospects for finishing the Missouri River barge channel quickly and cheaply had long been abandoned. A year later, in 1896, many corps officials seriously doubted whether the river could ever be channelized at all. The forty-five miles of channelized river did not provide the army with enough experience or data to accurately estimate how much it might cost to channelize the river to Sioux City or much less through the Dakotas. Channelization could conceivably cost far more along certain unstable reaches of the river, or it might cost far less; the engineers just had no clue. Their ignorance worried a budget-conscious Congress.

Delays in the work schedule (occasioned by the Missouri's ability to destroy structures and slow down the engineers), along with the wishes of river communities to take Suter's operating budget and spend the dollars on their own local bank stabilization projects, combined with the terrible cost overruns, the corps' uncertainty about ultimate project costs, and the total absence of steamboat or barge traffic on the river, convinced Congress to suspend channelization of the Missouri River in 1896. Suter, frustrated and angry with local intransigence and congressional interference, resigned from the Missouri River Commission soon after.

By 1896, the Corps of Engineers' scheme for the Missouri and Yellowstone collapsed in the face of the hydrologic realities. After 1896, Congress did not appropriate any money to channelize the Missouri. When the dream of Missouri River navigation died, the hope for the Yellowstone barge channel expired with it. In 1900, the engineers struck the Yellowstone River from the pages of the *Annual Report of the Chief of Engineers.* The report commented, "No appropriations for the general improvement of the Yellowstone River have been granted by Congress since 1886, and it is considered that the further improvement of this river has been abandoned. No further reports will be submitted."[6] The Yellowstone had been literally scratched from the corps' plans. As if the cut in appropriations had not sent a loud enough message to the advocates of Missouri River and Yellowstone River channelization, in 1902 Congress disbanded the Missouri River Commission.

The corps had been dealt a resounding defeat in the Missouri basin, and with that political chastisement, the Yellowstone River remained beyond the periphery of the corps' dreamed empire. But in 1903, a superflood ripped through the Lower Missouri Valley, swamping Kansas City, Missouri, and drowning the rich agricultural lands that bound the river through central Missouri. The flood of 1903, in addition to the floods of 1907 and 1908, revived interest in the Missouri Valley barge channel and consequently the Yellowstone River as a navigation route. By 1908, the corps' imperial plans for the Missouri and Yellowstone were dusted off and looked at once more.

Since the 1870s, the corps' primary concern had been reengineering the Mississippi, Missouri, and Ohio—the ostensible Big Three of American rivers. The Yellowstone never lay at the center of the corps' thinking or planning. Nonetheless, if the Missouri River could be channelized, there always existed the chance that the Yellowstone River would then be improved and coupled to the Missouri and Mississippi. That the Yellowstone did not factor too large in the corps' plans was evident by the fact that in 1904 the recently established Reclamation Service (RS) received congressional authorization to construct two low dams across the Yellowstone, one at Huntley, Montana (twelve miles east of Billings), and another at a site eighteen miles downstream from Glendive. The RS's construction blueprints for these two structures did not possess navigation locks capable of allowing steamers or barges to pass safely through the dams. Therefore, the completion of these dams, especially the one near Glendive (eventually named the Intake Dam), would preclude any possibility of steamboat and barge traffic on the Yellowstone. The two dams would enable the two-year-old RS to lay claim to the waters of the Yellowstone, establishing its jurisdiction over the river. The dams would end any navigation on the river and eject the Corps of Engineers from the Yellowstone Valley (figs. 7.6 and 7.7).

A Yellowstone River redesigned for irrigation would forestall a stream engineered for navigation. By a historical twist of fate, the legislation authorizing these two dams came before Congress in a year when the corps displayed no interest in the Yellowstone River. The army scuttled its navigation plans for the Missouri and Yellowstone in the first years of the twentieth century when the Missouri River Commission had been disbanded. Taking its cue from the corps and receiving strong support from the Northern Pacific Railroad, Great Northern, and Milwaukee Railroad, the RS proposed the two dams and received a congressional authorization.

It is not coincidental that the RS, early in its history, aligned itself with the railroad companies. The RS and the railroads both had vested interests in blocking the goals of the Corps of Engineers. The railroad companies had lands to sell in the Yellowstone Valley. If and when RS water dripped onto those semiarid properties, the price per acre would go sky-high, benefiting the railroad companies. Commodities produced on those irrigated farms would provide carrying trade for the railroads, which meant even more

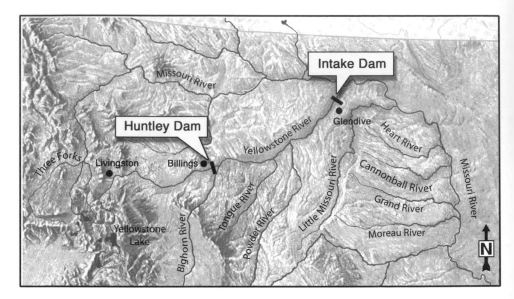

Figure 7.6. The Huntley and Intake Dam sites. (Paul Davidson, South Plains College, Levelland, Texas)

money. The RS needed the entrenched power of the railroads to support its own agenda and counter the schemes of its older, more experienced and politically savvy rival, the Corps of Engineers. What is more, irrigation projects meant institutional survival for the RS and personal career advancement for its engineers. Navigation and irrigation were inherently at odds. Western rivers, with their often low and erratic flow regimes, could be used for only one or the other purpose. The Yellowstone and the Upper Missouri did not hold enough water to support both purposes simultaneously. So the RS joined the railroads to get the two dams, while the corps kept quiet.

Reclamation Service engineers began construction of Huntley and Intake Dams in 1905. These two structures would be run-of-the-river dams, meaning they would not regulate the Yellowstone's flows; instead, they would allow the river to pour over their crowns. The idea behind such a dam is to create a high enough head of water, or reservoir, to effectively divert a portion of the river onto adjacent cropland. The raised reservoir would provide the elevation and gravity to hurl descending water atop fields. Most important, neither dam would possess navigation locks to allow for the passage of steamboats or barges through the structures. Consequently, construction of the two dams would spell the end of through navigation along the Yellowstone River.

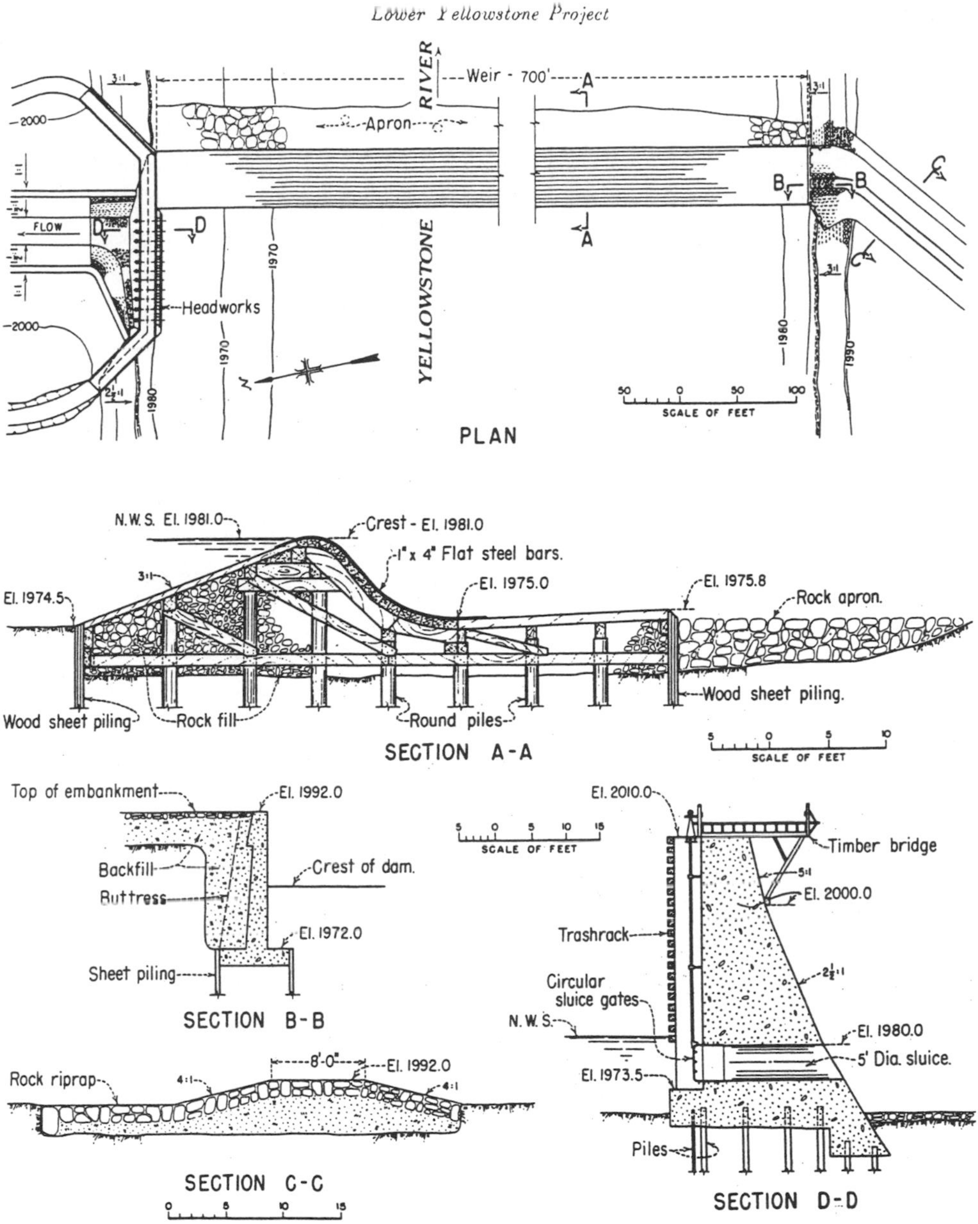

Figure 7.7. The design of the Intake Dam, Lower Yellowstone River. (Courtesy of the Bureau of Reclamation, Denver, Colorado)

Huntley and Intake Dams, two of the first to be built in the West by the newly founded RS, were going to be showpieces. Both critics and supporters of the RS watched closely to see how it would handle the two Yellowstone projects. The RS's chief engineer, Frederick H. Newell, felt the pressure to showcase the dams. The RS needed to prove its expertise and the necessity for its existence. It needed to succeed on the Yellowstone in order to receive moneys for future projects and ensure the future viability of the organization itself. It could not afford to bungle these projects.

By 1905, the Corps of Engineers had been awakened to the threat posed by the RS and its run-of-the river dams along the Yellowstone. In that year, the corps acknowledged it might lose the river to an upstart competitor. The army engineers had a new rival for control of the rivers of the West, one that openly sided with the railroads. The Corps of Engineers wanted to humiliate, challenge, oppose, and in any way obstruct the RS on the Yellowstone. So in 1905, just as the construction of Intake Dam got under way, corps officials sought to prevent the dam's completion. Besides trying to denigrate the RS, the corps in 1905 began opposing Intake Dam because interest in Missouri River navigation, and by fiat Yellowstone River navigation, began reemerging along the Lower Missouri, especially in Kansas City. The desire among the public and the Kansas City Commercial Club to build a barge channel to Sioux City, and even farther upstream, increased markedly at the same time that the RS began building the lockless Intake Dam. Once more, the corps viewed the Yellowstone as a potential link in a large, continental waterways system.

Intake Dam, without a navigation lock, would forever keep the Yellowstone River in the railroad companies' pocket and within the domain of the RS. The Corps of Engineers thus had three strong reasons to oppose the dam in 1905: to obstruct the fledgling RS, to weaken the RS, and to keep the Yellowstone dam-free so that the corps might someday extend its inland waterways system along its banks. To accomplish these goals, the corps began insisting in 1905 that the RS had violated federal law by not seeking corps approval for Intake Dam. The army focused its opposition on Intake Dam rather than Huntley Dam because Intake Dam sat lower down the Yellowstone and thus posed a greater threat to any future barge traffic on the stream. Since Intake Dam would block a federal waterway, and the corps held jurisdiction over all federal navigable waterways, the RS was required by law to seek corps approval for the project. The army argued that the dam was illegal and that work on it should stop immediately so that the corps could examine the structure and determine whether it would impede navigation.

By insisting that the dam was illegal and that the RS must seek corps approval for its project, the corps hoped to weaken the RS and make it subservient to the army. If the RS followed the corps' urgings, the corps would gain final authority over RS projects, something the army engineers craved and the RS feared. If the dam was ruled illegal by the courts and the RS required to seek corps approval, then the RS would be seriously weakened and nothing more than an adjunct to the Corps of Engineers. The corps could then block RS projects throughout the West and secure its hold on the region's water.

Therefore, between 1905 and 1909, the corps insisted that the dam at Intake not obstruct Yellowstone River navigation. Steamboats and future tows and barges had to be allowed through the dam. Thus, the RS must build a lock. A lock added to the dam would keep the Yellowstone within the domain of the Corps of Engineers. More important, corps officials knew that building an expensive navigation lock on the Intake Dam would result in construction delays and astronomical cost overruns that would humiliate the RS in the eyes of the public and in Congress. The lock would render the dam too costly, putting the structure into the red and hopefully sinking the whole enterprise. Requiring the RS to build the lock would lead to such huge increases in the cost of the project that the RS might have to abandon the dam altogether and concede defeat. The army engineers relished that prospect. The corps could then regain sole control over the Yellowstone. The institutional dogfight over Intake Dam had tremendous import for the future of the RS and the corps, not only in the Yellowstone River Valley but in the West as a whole.

The Corps of Engineers' attempts to block the construction of Intake Dam intensified in 1906, 1907, and 1908 as the public demand to channelize the Missouri rose to a fever pitch. By 1909, a congressional authorization for the channelization of the Missouri appeared inevitable. The army believed that the Missouri would be channelized at least as far as Kansas City and eventually all the way to Sioux City. One day the channel might conceivably reach into the Dakotas and even Montana. The corps did not want to lose a potential Yellowstone River route, so its top officials raised objections to Intake Dam.

Reclamation Service officials did not take the corps' abuse. Instead, the director of the United States Geological Survey, Charles D. Walcott, and the chief engineer of the Reclamation Service, Frederick H. Newell, insisted they acted within their legal rights by moving forward with the Intake and Huntley Dams without corps approval. More important, Walcott and Newell pushed their engineers to get the dam into the river as fast as possible to forestall any future attempts by the corps to halt its construction. Once the dam rose above the Yellowstone, the corps would be hard-pressed to have it removed or modified with a lock. The RS also pushed its congressional allies to study the Yellowstone River and determine whether in fact the dam would impede navigation. Walcott and later Newell wanted to know if anyone would ever use a corps-built navigation channel along the Yellowstone. Walcott and Newell had called the corps' bluff—both men confident that the Yellowstone would never be a part of a corps hydraulic empire.

In the Rivers and Harbors Act of March 1909, Congress, responding to RS requests, ordered the Corps of Engineers to study the Yellowstone River to determine its future as a navigation route. In the summer of 1909, corps personnel from the recently formed Kansas City District office journeyed to the Yellowstone Valley to conduct the most extensive survey of the Yellowstone River to date. The engineers had two questions to answer. First, could the Yellowstone be reengineered to facilitate either steamboat or barge traffic? More specifically, did the river's hydrology make it a candidate for channelization or some other improvement for the purposes of navigation? Second, if the engineers deemed the river worthy of improvement, what effect might Intake Dam have on the future of Yellowstone River navigation? After months of careful study, the Kansas City District reached its conclusions. In early 1911, the Board of Engineers for Rivers and Harbors, the committee responsible for reviewing projects before submission to Congress for authorization, received two reports from the Kansas City district engineer, E. H. Schulz, with regard to the Yellowstone.

In a display of bureaucratic honesty, the board ruled against a Yellowstone River navigation channel. Senior board member Colonel William T. Rossell stated, "The proposed channel improvement, [below Glendive] involving an initial expenditure of $35,000 and $20,000 a year thereafter, is not deemed advisable on account of its excessive cost when compared with the commerce to be benefited. It is also clear that the expenditure of $200,000 for the construction of a lock [at Intake Dam] was entirely unnecessary for navigation in the natural condition of the river and is not now justified by the mere amount of water-borne commerce, and the board must so report."[7] With that statement, the board signed navigation's death warrant along the river. The board also made it plain that the Corps of Engineers would no longer object to the construction of a dam at Intake that did not possess a lock.

A number of hydrologic factors persuaded the Board of Engineers for Rivers and Harbors to rule against a Yellowstone navigation channel. A major disincentive to channelize the Yellowstone related to cost. Board members believed that traditional permeable pile dikes, similar to the ones used on the Missouri and Mississippi, would not work on the Yellowstone River. The Yellowstone destroyed pile dikes too quickly, at a pace far faster than those shredded by the Mighty Missouri. Those hard Montana winters froze the Yellowstone to depths not seen along the Lower Missouri. Each spring, the frozen Yellowstone broke apart and glided downstream, shoving portly blocks of ice into pile dikes. In March and April, projectiles sheered inches off the piles. After years of grinding by ice, piles shattered and fell into the river, utterly useless. The rapid deterioration rate of "control" structures along the Yellowstone made the expense of maintaining a barge channel along the stream prohibitive.

Even if the river did not rip apart the Corps of Engineers' blessed work, the river still could not be channelized. Army engineers knew that the compression of the Yellowstone's channel width through the deployment of pile dikes and revetments, in combination with the river's naturally steep slope, would accelerate current velocities to levels that would prevent either steamboats or tows and barges from pushing their cargoes upstream. The federal engineers believed the anomalous hydrologic character of the Yellowstone River meant it could not be channelized.

Yet the board believed the Yellowstone could be made navigable if the government threw enough money at it. But then again, any river in the world could probably be made navigable if humanity willingly bore the expense. A slack-water channel could be constructed along the river. Fifty or more dams, with locks, could conceivably be built from the mouth to Billings (the largest commercial market on the river). These dams and locks, and the resultant reservoirs, would allow barges free movement up and down the river. However, according to the army, the cost of building this system would be so exorbitant that no amount of Yellowstone River commerce could ever justify the expense of construction. An eternity of barge traffic could not repay the costs of building a slack-water channel. In its report on the Yellowstone, the Corps of Engineers admitted that the railroad companies adequately serviced the Yellowstone River Valley far cheaper than a navigation channel ever could.

Another reason the corps dropped the Yellowstone from its "to do" list related to the abject lack of interest among Yellowstone Valley residents in channelization of the stream. Of course, the absence of a public endorsement for channelization influenced Congress's response to the corps as well. There existed almost no support for a corps barge channel in the Yellowstone River. Glendive interests, particularly the town's Commercial Club, sat solidly behind the corps' efforts. If the channelization of the stream ever became a reality, Glendive would likely be the head of navigation. Upstream from that former military stockade, boulder-strewn rapids and riffles made steamboat or barge navigation a perilous endeavor indeed. Citizens of Sidney, Montana, located about twenty miles upstream from the Yellowstone-Missouri confluence, also wanted the corps to manipulate the Yellowstone. Billings, the largest city in Montana, contained only a few disciples of the Corps of Engineers. Even fewer Billings residents believed a barge channel along the Yellowstone all the way from the mouth to Billings to be economically sane or feasible from an engineering standpoint. One Billings businessman did write a letter to the corps, urging it to pursue its navigation plans along the stream, but that single letter represented about the extent of the city's support for the army's pipe dream.

Backing for the corps' navigation channel fell far short of what was needed to gain a congressional authorization for a channel from the mouth to Glendive, a lock inside Intake Dam, or an open water channel from the mouth all the way to Billings. In contrast, the Reclamation Service possessed widespread support for its plans for the Yellowstone River. Of crucial import, powerful interests based in Billings wanted the Reclamation Service to build dams and irrigation works in the Yellowstone Valley. Bankers, real estate brokers, farm implement dealers, and the railroads all favored the Huntley Project and the Lower Yellowstone River Project (the name designated for Intake Dam and its collections of irrigation ditches and laterals).

Without an ounce of public or congressional enthusiasm for its strategy along the Yellowstone, the army took steps to extradite itself from the river. The endorsement of valley residents would have made anything possible. With public backing, the army may have been able to force the Reclamation Service to build a lock at Intake Dam, build the dubious barge channel, or at the least improve the lower eighty miles of river, if not for navigation then possibly for bank stabilization purposes. Bank stabilization represented a nearly unassailable justification for river improvement. If a river could not be channelized for any other reason, then it could be channelized to stabilize its banks, protect private property from washing away, and keep the engineers employed in the name of the public good. Bank stabilization made a lot of people happy.

Political approval of a corps project often outweighed all else. With residents and politicians in favor of a navigation channel, the engineers could conceivably go ahead with a project even though the hydrologic, engineering, and economic arguments against such an enterprise were strong. Politics mattered most in moving forward with river work. Public advocacy could make questionable projects acceptable. Proof of that fact was visible along the Missouri, which was being channelized at that very moment, even though a mounting pile of engineering, economic, and hydrologic evidence contravened rationales for channelization of that stream.

The Corps of Engineers confronted very different circumstances on the Yellowstone and Missouri. Residents of the Missouri Valley solidly backed the army engineers and aggressively lobbied Congress for funds to pay for channelization. Along the Missouri Valley, the public's belief in the need for channelization of the stream defied all logic. Missouri Valley residents wanted a barge channel regardless of whether it would ever be cost-effective. Along the Yellowstone, residents believed the river's best use would be for irrigation.

One significant reason the corps did not find partisans of navigation along the Yellowstone had to do with the fact that a culture of navigation never flourished there. Residents of the Yellowstone Valley did not look to the river as a viable navigation route. The Yellowstone, even during the steamboat era, had a reputation for being barely navigable. Yes, it carried steamboats, but only for two or three months out of the year. In June and July it was possible to float a boat on the thing, but by August the Yellowstone dropped so low that it hardly carried rafts or mackinaws. There exist numerous horror stories of mackinaws descending the river in August or even as late as September and being blown to splinters on the river's hairy rocks. Hardly anyone took seriously the corps' insistence that the Yellowstone could, and should, be improved. The river had sunk so many craft in the past that any talk of its carrying deep-draft barges sounded nothing short of ludicrous.

On the other hand, Euro-American navigation of the Missouri River had been going on for six decades prior to the arrival of the railroad adjacent to its muddy banks. From the advent of the Euro-American presence in the Lower Missouri Valley in 1804 to the middle 1880s, Euro-Americans relied on the Missouri River as a navigation route. The Big Muddy floated keels, mackinaws, dugouts, pirogues, and hundreds of steamboats to and from St. Louis and the upriver ports. The Missouri River route served as the key transportation artery for fur traders, missionaries, the military, miners, and agricultural settlers into the late nineteenth century. The Missouri had been crucial to Euro-American expansion into the trans-Missouri West. Settlement of the Lower Missouri Valley long preceded the arrival of the railroad. For example, the town of St. Joseph, founded in 1841, depended solely on the Missouri River route for eighteen years before the arrival of the railroad in 1859. In 1856, entrepreneurs from the Omaha–Council Bluffs area founded the town of Sioux City as the gateway to the soon-to-be opened lands northwest and west of the Big Sioux River. Sioux City residents depended on the Missouri River to meet their needs, wants, and aspirations until 1868 and the arrival of the railroad at the town's doorstep.

From the age of Lewis and Clark into the early 1870s, a whole string of towns, farms, and ranches sprung up along the Missouri's banks from the river's mouth into the Dakotas and Montana. These cultural enclaves owed their establishment and gestation to the keels and steamboats moving on the Missouri. Euro-Americans developed a heavy dependence on the Missouri River. Although the Missouri was not an ideal navigation route (one thousand boats went down in its waters in the nineteenth century), Missouri Valley settlers still used the river for long-haul transportation and communication. Statistics illustrate this fact. In 1867, seventy-one boats worked the Missouri River north and west of Sioux City, Iowa, while dozens of others rode the Missouri below that point.[8] The Missouri and the steamboats skimming its waters threw a lifeline between the supposedly civilized East and the Upper Missouri frontier.

A culture of navigation flourished along the Missouri. That culture was strongest on the Lower Missouri, between Kansas City and St. Louis, where the deeper channel and larger population meant more boats pushing up- and downstream each summer. When the railroad reached the Missouri, it adversely affected steamboat operations. The decline of steamboat navigation was apparent by the 1860s, obvious by the 1870s, and completed by the 1880s. Ironically, by the 1880s, residents of the Missouri Valley perceived the once-welcome railroads as exploitative and once again looked to the Missouri as a navigation route, not as a steamboat route, but as a potential deep-draft barge channel to compete against the railroads.

Knowing the Missouri had once been navigable, and firmly convinced it could be made so again, Missouri Valley residents, particularly the members of the Kansas City Commercial Club, worked from the 1880s onward to have the river channelized for barge traffic. A culture of navigation fostered an illogical faith that the Missouri could be successfully deepened into a barge channel. What is so amazing about this situation is that in subsequent years the Missouri would over and over again shatter the Corps of Engineers' goal of establishing a barge channel in the river. Yet despite repeated setbacks, the army and valley residents persisted in their attempt to tame the Mighty Mo. Army engineers, including Major Charles Suter, fed the public's faith in channelization and navigation with professions of their engineering expertise and technological mastery. As a result, Missouri Valley residents and the Corps of Engineers embarked on a one-hundred-year struggle to channelize the Missouri River.

No culture of navigation emerged in the Yellowstone Valley. In the years between 1804 and 1883, Euro-Americans navigated the river with bullboats, rafts, mackinaws, keels, and steamers. On the river, Euro-Americans deployed primitive, often hastily built, mackinaws more than any other craft. A majority of journal accounts attest to the fact that prairie sailors found the Yellowstone hardly navigable, except in June when big flows came down from the heights of the Yellowstone plateau. Steamboats did not begin regularly using the river until the middle 1870s. In 1875, the steamboat *Josephine* under the command of Grant Marsh, darted into the Yellowstone. Thus, in the seventy years after Lewis and Clark, the Yellowstone carried only intermittent Euro-American traffic. During those same years, a prolific amount of traffic frequented the Missouri River.

In 1876–1877, the military campaigns and the establishment of forts on the Yellowstone main stem heralded a new era on the river. Yet the Yellowstone's steamboat era lasted only five years. During the peak years, steamboat numbers never even came close to approaching the number of boats that previously operated on the Missouri. In 1880, the port of Miles City reported twenty-four steamboat arrivals. Many of these arrivals resulted from the same boats returning to the port after shuttling back and forth to Bismarck. In 1881, at the height of railroad construction in the valley, twenty-one boats steamed up and down the Yellowstone, making it the busiest year on the river. In 1882, only two boats, both employed by the Northern Pacific

Railroad, entered the channel of the Yellowstone. By 1883, the same year that the Northern Pacific Railroad completed its road between St. Paul and Puget Sound, the Corps of Engineers' *Annual Report of the Chief of Engineers* did not report any steamboats on the Yellowstone.[9]

Those who settled in the Yellowstone Valley after 1877 were well aware of the troubles faced by steamboat crews on the river. Residents only had to stand on the river's edge and gaze at its white waters and narrow chutes to know that the Yellowstone presented pilots with a tremendous challenge. When the railroad reached Glendive in 1881 and the Bighorn's mouth in 1882, it ended steamboat navigation, cementing the idea that the Yellowstone lay beyond the pale of navigation. A culture of navigation did not have time to flourish along the Yellowstone for two reasons. First, the steamboat era did not last long enough, and the boats confronted too many obstacles across their path, for people to see the river as a viable navigation channel. Second, most settlers into the valley arrived after the steamboat era. The vast bulk of settlers came to eastern Montana and the Yellowstone Valley aboard railcars. These settlers had never seen the river navigated and thus never even considered it for such a task. They looked exclusively to the railroad to meet their transportation requirements. As a result, the Corps of Engineers did not have a clientele within the Yellowstone Valley.

In 1911, the Corps of Engineers scuttled the Yellowstone River. At the same time, the corps gave up its navigation goals for the Missouri River through the Dakotas. The corps pulled back from the Upper Missouri. If the Missouri in the Dakotas could not be channelized, it made absolutely no sense to channelize the Yellowstone. A channelized Yellowstone flowing into an unaltered Missouri would be completely useless, since that former stream had to be coupled to a Missouri River barge channel to be a viable route of commerce. In a comprehensive report issued in that year, the engineers concluded that the Yellowstone would not, into the foreseeable future, carry enough cargo to justify even modest improvement of the stream for traffic. The army also concluded that the Missouri above Sioux City would never haul enough cargo to justify the costs of channelization north of that point. The engineers also concluded that the river north of Kansas City, Missouri, should not be channelized for barge traffic. For all these reasons, in 1912 the Corps of Engineers and real estate interests in the state of Missouri only sought congressional authorization to build a six-foot-deep barge channel from the mouth of the river to Kansas City. The river beyond that metropolis would be left alone, free to wander and flood. The authorization of 1912 confined the corps' empire to the Lower Missouri.

The Reclamation Service finished Intake Dam in 1911—without a navigation lock. The failure of the corps to stop Intake Dam or maintain a position on the Yellowstone goes far toward explaining why the river would not be channelized or dammed in the twentieth century for navigation purposes.

8

Try and Try Again

Schemes to Dam the Yellowstone

The Yellowstone is certainly, viewed alone as a river, without

taking in the rugged and poor country adjacent, one of the most

beautiful rivers in the world.

—A nineteenth-century Euro-American visitor to the

Yellowstone Valley

The Corps of Engineers' role on the Yellowstone and far Upper Missouri evaporated after 1911. Without any hope of a navigation channel on either the Upper Missouri main stem or the Yellowstone, the corps had no reason to be there. Along the Yellowstone, the engineers conducted no surveys and wrote no reports on the stream in its *Annual Report to the Chief of Engineers.* But then, in 1918 and 1919, two hydrologic events occurred that brought the army engineers back to the valley, the first being the flood of June 1918 and the second a severe drought that seared Montana in 1919.

The largest flood since 1881, the Great Flood of 1918 tore ugly wounds through the irrigated lands on both sides of the Lower Yellowstone. This flood, coming during a month of bloody combat for American doughboys in France, inflicted far more damage on Yellowstone Valley residents than the flood of 1881. In that earlier catastrophe, a scattering of Euro-American ranchers and farmers lived in the valley. By 1918, the valley brimmed with people and their cultural artifacts, including automobile roads, crops, railroads, bridges, houses, fences, and towns. When the flood's crest rolled down the Yellowstone and spilled over its banks, it sank or scattered the results of decades of human labor. The valley below the Bighorn confluence experienced the heaviest losses. Forsyth, Montana, took a swim in the Yellowstone on June 16, 1918, when river water pooled on Main Street. Miles City and Savage, Montana, also took a beating from the river. Although the Yellowstone rose and fell within a week, the short duration of the flood did not dampen the anger felt by valley farmers, hundreds of whom lost their crops during a year when wartime demand had pushed commodity prices to all-time highs. In a business beset with price fluctuations and with prices seemingly low more often than high, the flood of 1918 stung farmers anxious to make a killing from the war.

In July and August 1918, cries went forth from several still-damp Yellowstone Valley towns, including Billings, Forsyth, and Miles City, to the Kansas City District, Corps of Engineers. Montanans wanted the federal engineers to examine the Yellowstone and find a means of stopping its floods. The corps responded to the public clamor with a survey—its purpose, to determine whether flood control dams and reservoirs could be built across the stream at a cost-effective price. What the corps learned along the river disappointed the Montanans. Flood control dams and reservoirs could not be profitably built to hold back the Yellowstone. The urban and rural real estate to be protected by a dam possessed a market value far below the total cost of any single dam. Evidently, it would cost more to dam the stream than to just let it flood the cheap lands along its banks.

A year after the flood of 1918, eastern Montanans found themselves sweating through the region's worst drought. The Yellowstone dipped to record-low levels in July and August, appearing dark blue as far as the mouth of the Powder. To see the river so clear so far downstream struck old-timers as odd. Irrigationists from Paradise Valley to Sidney went thirsty. They needed water to grow alfalfa or they were going to be hurting come fall. Once more, pleas for help went forth from the Yellowstone Valley. Farmers told their local, state, and federal representatives they wanted the river dammed. The logic behind the request: a dam would fix unreliable nature. The irrigationists wanted water stored in a reservoir or reservoirs somewhere south of Paradise Valley. That stored water could then be released onto their fields during a drought year or even during the dry months of late summer. Farmers demanded water. They felt as though they deserved water. Nature and the government had no right to deny them. None of these agriculturalists believed they should adjust their agricultural operations to the fluctuating hydraulic regime of the river. Many farmers feared what would happen to their financial status if 1920 proved to be as dry as, or drier than, 1919. Above all else, valley farmers wanted the river dammed to make it more reliable and its water deliveries predictable. They wanted to flatten the Yellowstone's flows by holding back the June rise for release during the skimpy months of July, August, and September.

In the summer of 1919, the corps's Kansas City District office received several requests to study the possibility of building dams across the Yellowstone. In September, army engineers boarded trains and rode west to the dusty Yellowstone basin. Once there they focused their attentions on two sites—Yankee Jim Cañon (near Corwin Springs, Montana) and Lower Cañon (situated five miles south of Livingston, Montana). After a few weeks in the field, the engineers stepped back on to a railcar at Livingston and journeyed home to Kansas City. After careful consideration, the engineers ruled against dams at the two sites. The corps could not build a cost-effective dam at either canyon.

During the summer of 1919, when pastel skies made men and women panicky and irrational, the issue of damming Yankee Jim Cañon and/or Lower Cañon was overshadowed by a much more controversial proposal. The Montanans, driven delirious by dust and led by Livingston business interests, wanted to dam the Yellowstone River within the boundaries of Yellowstone National Park. Businessmen wanted a dam built five hundred feet north of where the Yellowstone River exits Yellowstone Lake, or one hundred feet downstream from the famous Fishing Bridge (fig. 8.1). Livingston residents wanted a dam at the lake outlet because they believed it would revive the flagging economy in and around their town. E. M. Niles, who headed the movement and its organization (the Yellowstone Irrigation Association, formed in January 1920), proposed that either the federal government, the state of Montana, or private interests finance and build what he named the Outlet Dam. Niles and his colleagues chose the vicinity of Fishing Bridge for this tentative dam for a number of reasons. The site, according to Niles and engineers M. M. Galbraith, Henry Gerharz, B. C. Lillis, Charles Tabor, and R. H. Fifield, was ideal for the placement of a low dam. The valley tapered to a width of roughly five hundred feet at the spot, so the dam would be narrow, which would lower its overall cost. Additionally, the river streamed through relatively steep valley walls on each side. Those walls would hold the dam firmly in place. Even better, the dam would not create a new reservoir. The reservoir would be Yellowstone Lake itself. Thus, Outlet Dam would not require the inundation of large tracts of valuable real estate

Figure 8.1. The Outlet Dam site, view to the east, northeast. (Photograph by author, 1999)

within Yellowstone National Park. According to its proponents, the Outlet Dam would not materially subtract from the park's land area. Niles argued that Yellowstone National Park would not be harmed by the structure. The park's areal extent and sacrosanct borders would apparently remain intact.

The men of the Yellowstone Irrigation Association wanted a low dam (between twenty and twenty-five feet high), one that would raise the level of Yellowstone Lake by eleven feet over its low-water mark. Those additional feet would not inundate aesthetically pleasing parklands, so argued the project's self-proclaimed engineering experts, who made this claim because much of the eastern shore of the lake stood beneath sheer cliffs, in certain locales close to one hundred feet in height. The lake would be deeper, but for the most part only cliff faces would be flooded under the higher water level. Any other land inundated would be largely worthless from an aesthetic perspective. The engineers went so far as to claim, "This [the stored water] would make no change in the appearance of the lake, except the possible advantage, that any mud flats which may now show along the shore as the lake recedes would remain covered with water during the greater part of the tourist season."[1] To wit, the lake's appearance would be improved by the dam. The dam advocates admitted that lands in the far Upper Yellowstone Valley would disappear under the higher lake. But, as far as they were concerned, the far Upper Yellowstone had little or no value, since it lay in the most remote region of the park. Hardly anyone saw the far Upper Yellowstone, and therefore few would miss its partial disappearance.

The members of the Yellowstone Irrigation Association believed their pet project would have a dramatic influence on the Yellowstone's spring and summer flood heights. In a brochure published in 1921, the group made the confident assertion that the Outlet Dam "will almost entirely prevent the periodical flood damage in the Yellowstone valley above the mouth of the Clarkes [sic] Fork river and very materially lessen it below the mouth of this river."[2] To gain Lower Yellowstone Valley support for its scheme, the association argued that the dam would reduce flood damages in the valley by 40 to 60 percent of previous losses. But the main justification for this project remained unchanged—to provide irrigation water to farmers in the Yellowstone Valley. The project's boosters emphatically pronounced that the dam would store the Yellowstone's June rise for release in the dry months of late summer. A regulated Yellowstone River would provide water to fields laid flat by drought.

Besides the dam itself, the Yellowstone Irrigation Association called for the construction of an open ditch from possibly Yankee Jim Cañon down the left, or west, bank of the Yellowstone Valley to Livingston, a distance of fifty miles. To no one's surprise, the bulk of the lands to receive water sat to the north and east of Livingston. Much of that land grew sagebrush, but with Yellowstone River water it would be converted to profitable greenery. The total amount of land put under the plow after project completion would equal over 250,000 acres. Indirectly, this was an admittance that the lake water would be used to irrigate new land and not to ensure that already plowed land would have adequate water during drought episodes. Dam boosters admitted that the Yellowstone River already supplied the Livingston region with enough water, but they wanted more water for the expansion of the Livingston agricultural economy and ultimately the enhancement of their own material wealth (fig. 8.2).

The Livingston proponents went so far as to seek Lower Yellowstone Valley support for their irrigation plans. The project included the possible extension of the canal from Livingston to the east, northeast as far as Billings; the rationale: the longer the canal, the more public support. The closer the canal reached toward Billings, the more likely the powerful Billings business establishment would swing behind the project.

From the perspective of its Livingston backers, the dam and canal hydraulic system possessed numerous advantages and very few negative reper-

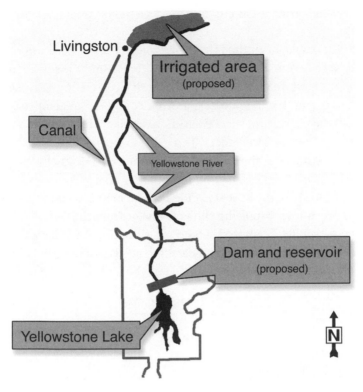

Figure 8.2. The Outlet Dam site, canal, and proposed irrigated area. (Paul Davidson, South Plains College, Levelland, Texas)

cussions. The dam and higher lake would not reduce the national park's aesthetic, recreational, or fish and wildlife values in the least. As for the park's aesthetic qualities, the elevated lake would appear the same as the present lake, only slightly higher and more expansive. Niles believed the dam itself, if built properly, would add to the beauty of the park. Its visual qualities would be such that park visitors would hardly notice it as a dam. The 1921 brochure proclaimed, "The combined dam and bridge can be so designed that the ordinary passer will never think of it as other than an artistic bridge."[3] Barring that, the dam might become a tourist attraction in its own right. A dam at the outlet would replace the old Fishing Bridge, since a road would be built across the dam's crown. Niles believed that the beautiful dam would represent an advance over the aging, gaudy bridge. All the design features of the dam and reservoir were for the purposes of making a minimal impact on the park and to convince the skeptical that a dam at the outlet would be a minor intrusion into this most sacred of American playgrounds (fig. 8.3).

What is notable about the Outlet Dam project is that its authors sought from the very beginning to deflect potential criticism of the scheme. They knew their project would cause a stir in certain circles. For that reason, they planned to extend the irrigation canal from Livingston to points east. They needed all the support they could garner to counter the possible tidal wave of opposition from park defenders. The canal extension east was also a ploy to convince farmers at the Clarks Fork Bottom, the Huntley Project, and Cartersville that Livingston had no intention of taking their water. Livingston wanted to share the benefits of the project, or at least give that impression. The brochure boosting the Outlet Dam emphatically declared that only excess flows would be captured behind the structure. All other water would be permitted to go downstream and meet the needs of those who relied on it. The water that once went unused would be used for beneficial purposes.

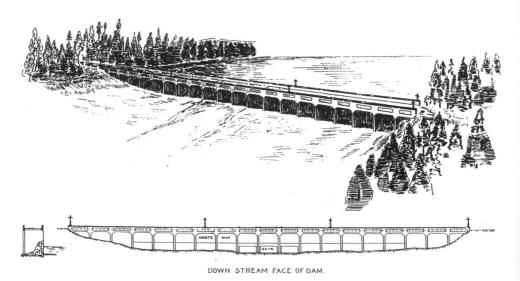

Figure 8.3. The dam at the Yellowstone Lake outlet. In the early twentieth century, Montana interests sought to build an aesthetically pleasing dam inside Yellowstone National Park where the Yellowstone River flows out of Yellowstone Lake. Park superintendent Horace Albright played an instrumental role in defeating the dam proposal. (Courtesy of the Yellowstone Irrigation Association, 1921)

The Yellowstone Irrigation Association increased its odds of success by soliciting the support of Montana's Democratic senator, Thomas Walsh. Walsh liked the idea of a dam across the Yellowstone, believing it would alleviate the affects of drought on his Montana constituency. That the dam would sit inside Yellowstone National Park did not outwardly trouble him. Walsh, who quickly became the project's most influential advocate, thought the Outlet Dam would be a win-win arrangement for everyone. Yellowstone National Park would not be harmed in any way, while Montana agriculture would receive sorely needed assistance. Walsh sincerely believed Montana would benefit from the project in significant ways. The state would get flood control and irrigation, two benefits that would increase land values and revive agricultural health.

Walsh boosted the project soon after its inception. His advocacy won him fame among Montana farm interests. Walsh's first task involved working through congressional channels to have either the Corps of Engineers or the Reclamation Service study the feasibility of a dam inside Yellowstone National Park. Any such study would be the precursor to congressional authorization of the dam. If Walsh achieved authorization, securing federal appropriations would be the next step. With money in hand, the engineers could begin the actual construction of the dam. But he and his federal engineers needed to get out to the dam site and look it over. Without a survey, nothing else would be possible.

As Walsh made preparations to have a study carried out by federal engineers, he ran into strong opposition from the young and very protective National Park Service (NPS), including Yellowstone National Park's superintendent, Horace Albright. Albright rightly perceived the Outlet Dam as a serious menace to the NPS, Yellowstone National Park, and the national park idea. If the dam went forward, two institutions and one grand concept might face imminent collapse.

Congress founded the NPS in 1916 to administer a growing system of national parks and national monuments sprouting up across the country. Only four years old when the Outlet Dam appeared in Congress, the NPS faced a significant challenge to its mission. If the Outlet Dam blocked the Yellowstone, the NPS's primary directive would be thrown into doubt. Failure to preserve the lake and the wonders of the park from developers could irrevocably weaken the NPS and contribute to its eventual demise.

Albright understood the danger the dam posed to the NPS's future. Rightly, he viewed the dam as a life-or-death issue for the NPS. The NPS needed to stand firm to uphold the sanctity of Yellowstone National Park. Failure to do so could have dire repercussions for other national parks. Albright also knew that if the NPS succeeded in stopping the dam, the institution's future would be more secure than at present. In addition, during this dam battle, the NPS could build a constituency of followers while distinguishing friend from foe within the federal bureaucracy.

National Park Service personnel believed that if Montana developers succeeded in building the dam, the former inviolate stature of the park, in place since its founding in 1872, would come to an end. The dam would open the door to all sorts of development schemes that had been previously proposed, were presently in hiatus, or had not yet even been dreamed up by some inventive mind. If the NPS and its parent institution, the Department of the Interior, did not keep out the dam, they would be unable to say no to other projects. Through the years there had been plans drawn up to tap the myriad geyser basins for geothermal energy, to open the park to hunting, to build a road network that would crisscross every section of the park, and to build more concession shops, hotels, and service facilities. A Pandora's box of construction might envelop the park if the Outlet Dam went forward.

Even more dramatically, while the Outlet Dam project fluttered into life, Idahoans to the west of the Grand Teton Mountains, who suffered from the same drought that hit Montana, thought about damming and diverting two other streams inside the park, the Falls and Bechler Rivers. The two rivers flowed through the remote southwest quadrant of the national park, where the dams and reservoirs would supposedly flood worthless, mosquito-infested, and visually unappealing swamplands.

All, or a portion of, these past and present projects might be set into motion if Senator Walsh's hopes for the Outlet Dam became a reality. Walsh's Outlet Dam traveled further through the legislative process than any previous proposal to tap the park's resources. That legislative fact frightened Albright to the core of his preservationist being. It also explains why the Outlet Dam demanded the most immediate and intense response. Albright faced a full frontal assault on the park. Yellowstone National Park could conceivably be dissected by one project after another. In the worst-case scenario, Congress would give permission to other development projects inside the park, and over time the park would resemble any other high mountain region developed in the West—gutted by mines, snared by tourist traps, sunk under hydroelectric dams, stripped of timber, and pierced with irrigation canals. At that point in time, Yellowstone would no longer be unique, its wonders exploited for private gain. If all this came to fruition, and there was no guarantee that it would not, Yellowstone would cease to be a park altogether.

The Outlet Dam tossed into question the national park idea, namely, that the national parks were to be preserved in perpetuity. Yellowstone National Park being the first, the largest, and the grandest of all the parks in the system, it represented the national park idea. If Yellowstone National Park, the jewel of the park system, could not be protected from covetous developers, then no other park in the system would be safe. Years later, Professor L. G. Rommell, a Swedish observer of the American scene, summarized the issue facing the NPS: "If commercial interests should be allowed to encroach upon Yellowstone Lake, this would mean far more than despoliation of a place where 'water never seemed so beautiful before' as N. P. Langford put it. It would be a terrific blow to the entire National Park idea which could not fail to have its repercussions throughout the world."[4]

The stakes in this controversy were huge. For this reason, Albright, upon learning of Walsh's plans for the park, immediately went to work to generate public and congressional opposition to Walsh's dam. He also took immediate personal steps, barring engineers from the Reclamation Service, Corps of Engineers, and the Yellowstone Irrigation Association from examining the dam site. Not a single engineer could get close to Fishing Bridge. Without a congressional order stating otherwise, Albright used his position as superintendent to keep the dam builders at bay.

Albright's apparent obstinacy angered Senator Walsh, but the senator remained powerless to order him to cooperate with the engineers until Congress okayed a survey. To accomplish that task and push the project toward the planning stage, Walsh introduced Senate Resolution 4529 on December 7, 1920. Albright, responding immediately to the threat of the Walsh bill, brought the controversy to the attention of the national media. *Collier's* and *Outlook* magazines ran articles opposing the dam. Albright also engaged well-known personalities to oppose the project, including author Lewis R. Freeman and landscape architect Frederick Law Olmsted. Albright lined up a host of institutional allies to stop the dam. The list of park supporters was impressive. The American Civic Association, American Automobile Association, American Forestry Association, American Society of Landscape Architects, National Association of Audubon Societies, National Geographic Society, National Parks Association, and Sierra Club all came out against Walsh and the Montanans.

The Senate Committee on Irrigation and Reclamation held hearings on the dam proposal from February 22 to March 1, 1921. Horace Albright, thin as a rail and hard as stone, came before the committee and effectively argued that the dam and higher lake level would seriously harm the national park. Damages to the park would include the inundation of hot springs near the lakeshore, the loss of Fishing Bridge to recreational fishing, the death of fish downstream from the structure during low flow periods, and the real possibility that the upper and lower falls might go without water during drought years.

The strongest oral arguments against the dam came from NPS engineer George E. Goodwin. Goodwin, relying on Yellowstone River hydrologic data collected by the United States Geological Survey, convincingly argued that the tentative dam would not provide either flood control or irrigation. The dam sat too far up the Yellowstone to substantially diminish flood flows east of Livingston. Additionally, the lake itself already dissipated floods descending from the mountains to the valley north of the site. The lake acted as a natural reservoir, so there was no need to improve on its natural regulatory traits. The additional feet of storage in a future reservoir would not appreciably add to the lake's storage capacity. Goodwin also stated that the dam would not provide any additional irrigation water. The river already delivered the water downstream in the dry months, so there was no reason to store more of it. During drought years, the Yellowstone still flowed out of the park with enough water to meet the needs of farmers downstream. To prove that point, the Senate committee was reminded that the dam and canal system were designed to deliver water to new lands, not those already under the plow. In an era when government representatives and businessmen prided themselves on their adherence to the principle of efficiency (this was the age when time studies, assembly-line production, and standardization spread through all industries), Goodwin's cries of waste and inefficiency captured a congressional audience. But more than any other factor it was the sanctity of the national park idea that swayed the Senate. Senators feared that development of the Outlet Dam would lead to a rush on the national parks. Walsh's bill died in committee in spring 1921. Albright, Goodwin, and the NPS scored a major victory. But Walsh did not accept this defeat. On April 12, 1921, a little over a month after his first bill, S.R. 4529, fell through, Walsh introduced two bills just like it, S.R. 274 and S.R. 275. The Committee on Irrigation and Reclamation held hearings on S.R. 274 on February 15, 1922, but once more, the eastern aristocracy and park allies dashed Walsh's hopes for a dam at the outlet.

The struggle between the NPS and Walsh was significant for a host of reasons. First, the NPS beat back a challenge to Yellowstone National Park and the unregulated Yellowstone River. The river remained undammed within the park. Second, and maybe most important, the Outlet Dam controversy represented an instance when Montana interests were stymied in their efforts to pursue a traditional development path by easterners and Californians who wanted the West, the park, and the Yellowstone River preserved for tourism. This dam battle was an example of elites turning a western river away from agriculture and toward tourism. Rather than serve irrigation, the Yellowstone would cater to the privileged few who wanted the river as scenery. Tourism, and the aesthetic needs of the industry, had everything to do with the NPS's success and Walsh's failure. Outlet Dam represented an example of Montana's colonial status as an emerging tourist destination for the wealthy and politically connected along the eastern seaboard and the California coast. Finally, Albright succeeded in preserving the park, the river, and the area's wildlife as nostalgic reminders of the ancient bison world. The two men did not want to save the old ecological order and its economy. Rather, they wanted the previous ecological order to support an emerging tourist economy. Inside Yellowstone National Park, ecology equaled scenery.

The Outlet Dam controversy was not the first time the Yellowstone River and the national park escaped large-scale industrial development. Over and over again in the twentieth century, the river and park would be spared development for hydropower, irrigation, flood control, and gaudy, convenience-driven tourism. Tourism represented a new form of eastern imperialism, designed to keep a subject region "pristine" or undeveloped. The domination of Montana's land- and waterscapes by outside tourists would accelerate after the 1920s. Tourism was old eastern imperialism disguised behind a kinder, gentler, preservationist mantra.

The agricultural depression of the 1920s, which was rooted in shrinking overseas markets, mechanization, low crop prices, and drought, explains why Montana interests sought to dam the lake outlet. Farmers north and east of Gardiner, Montana, convinced themselves that a dam, stored water, and more land under the plow would alleviate their pain. Montana agriculturalists were not the only ones looking upon the water of Yellowstone Lake with covetous eyes. Farmers in the plains of Idaho, west of the Teton Mountains, also wanted to divert water from Yellowstone Lake to irrigate their own, arid land. The Idaho-born proposals took many forms, but they shared the same origins as the Montana projects. All emerged as a means of lessening the uncertainty and suffering induced by agricultural depression and drought.

Even though none of Yellowstone Lake's waters originated in Idaho or flowed through that state, Idahoans believed they had as much of a right to Yellowstone Lake as anyone else. Farmers west of the Tetons had no qualms about making an interbasin transfer of water, from the Yellowstone basin to the Snake River basin. The first proposal of this kind, known as the Bruneau Plan and sponsored by the Fremont-Madison Reservoir Company of Idaho, emerged in 1919. The Bruneau Plan proposed that the lake outlet be dammed, the lake raised twenty to fifty feet over current levels, and the stored water, rather than irrigate Montana crops, should be siphoned off to the west, southwest. The company wanted canals dug from the lake's Flat Mountain Arm and South Arm through the Continental Divide and into the Snake basin. Once there, the water would flow down the Snake River into Idaho, where farmers would capture it and divert it onto their fields. Needless to say, the plan was complex, costly, and a political hot potato. This transfer of water from the Yellowstone basin to the Snake basin deeply concerned Montana and Wyoming interests, including the Livingston Irrigation Association.

The near-simultaneous submission of the Montana scheme and the Bruneau Plan to Congress, rather than convincing Congress of strong public support for the projects, had a very different effect. Congressional representatives recognized that the fears of the NPS had merit. It became apparent to everyone involved in the controversy surrounding a dam at the lake outlet that if either the Montana or the Idaho project received a congressional go-ahead, then one project after another would come before Congress, seeking to grab a part of Yellowstone National Park's natural wealth. If Congress signed off on one project, it would have to approve later requests. With this in mind, congressional representatives defeated the Bruneau Plan.

Drought in the 1930s forced the Idahoans to be persistent in their quest for water. In 1937, the State of Idaho, represented by the commissioner of reclamation of Idaho, R. W. Faris, decided once more to try to acquire water from Yellowstone Lake. The new plan, named the Faris Plan, hopefully would win the backing of Congress. It called for the damming of the lake outlet, the capture of the Yellowstone's summer rise, and the diversion of that supposed surplus water into a tunnel dug from the South Arm through the Continental Divide and on to Surprise Creek and the Snake River. Once in the Snake River, the lake's waters would flow into Idaho (fig. 8.4).

Oddly but understandably, Wyoming and Montana interests allied themselves with the NPS to kill the plan during its brief gestation. The State of Wyoming feared that the project would mar the scenic beauty of the national park and harm the tourist industry in the state. Montana believed the project posed a significant risk to its exclusive hold over the Yellowstone River. The project meant sharing the Yellowstone River with outsiders. An interbasin tranfer of Yellowstone water to Idaho might result in greater transfers in the future. Over time, the Idahoans, through legal action, could gain more and more of the Yellowstone, until flows into Montana diminished substantially. Montana could conceivably lose the Yellowstone to Idaho if this project went forward. No project at all was better than a project that allowed Idaho to tap the Yellowstone River. Without a project, Montana received all of the Yellowstone's flow, an occasionally diminished flow, but a flow nonetheless.

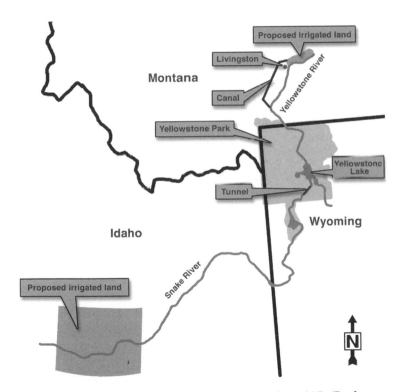

Figure 8.4 The Idaho project to dam the lake outlet, 1937. (Paul Davidson, South Plains College, Levelland, Texas)

With a project, Montana would have to share with someone else, which would complicate the whole issue of water rights. Just as important, Wyoming and Montana wanted to divvy up the Yellowstone River and its tributaries between themselves through a water compact. Idaho's project would muddle future negotiations and apportionment. Thus the Idaho project died only months after its birth. After the defeat of this project, the Outlet Dam never rose again. No one spoke of it in official circles. The sanctity of Yellowstone National Park remained intact, and the Yellowstone River continued to flow as an unregulated stream.[5]

In the 1920s, events in the Mississippi basin reverberated across the Yellowstone and Missouri basins. Most dramatically, the Great Mississippi River Flood of 1927 compelled the Corps of Engineers to reexamine the construction of dams across the Yellowstone River not for irrigation but for flood control. The engineers studied the feasibility of building dams athwart the Yellowstone to slow and diminish Mississippi River flooding. The army also examined the Missouri for the same purpose, to determine whether Missouri River dams would curtail Mississippi River floods. The two studies completed by the Corps of Engineers on the Yellowstone and Missouri Rivers had profound effects on the future of each of those rivers.

By volume the Mississippi is the largest river in the United States, with a daily average discharge past New Orleans of 470,000 cubic feet per second (cfs). In comparison, the Upper Missouri's daily average discharge past Omaha is close to 30,000 cfs. The Mississippi's daily flow volume is fifteen times greater than that of the Upper Missouri. Peak discharges over 1.2 million cfs have been recorded at the Crescent City of New Orleans. Every year, this riverine giant expels four hundred million tons of sediment, nitrates, and grime into the Gulf of Mexico, enough refuse to cover 3,240 square miles of land with a slick blanket an inch deep. The waters of the Mississippi come together at Lake Itasca, Minnesota, where it begins its 2,550-mile run to the Gulf of Mexico. The combined Mississippi-Missouri system is approximately 3,870 miles long, making it the third-longest river system in the world.

As the Mississippi throws its incredible weight past New Orleans, it appears steadfast, sure, and relentless. The Father (or Mother) of All Waters is, and always has been, a river worthy of fear and admiration. The Mississippi's dun waters originate atop a land area that extends from the Allegheny Mountains of Pennsylvania all the way to the Pioneer Mountains near Wisdom, Montana. From New Orleans and the plains of the Texas Panhandle, the river sucks in water north to the wheat fields of Alberta and Saskatchewan, Canada This riverine funnel incises a drainage basin equivalent to two-fifths of the contiguous United States, equal to 1,250,000 square miles. The Missouri basin makes up a little over 40 percent of the Mississippi drainage, and the Upper Missouri basin envelops over a quarter of the entire Mississippi drainage.

The Mississippi, in a manner similar to other rivers before the pell-mell engineering projects of the twentieth century, underwent a flood cycle each year. The worst floods in the Lower Mississippi (the river basin south of St. Louis) occurred when snowmelt from the Upper Midwest joined with heavy rainfall across Arkansas, Louisiana, Kentucky, and Mississippi to push the river over its banks and levees, usually in March and April. In 1926–1927, the lower valley endured an unusually wet fall and winter. In January 1927, at a time of the year when the Mississippi River should have been running low, the river approached flood stage in a number of locations between Cairo, Illinois, and the port of New Orleans. The Corps of Engineers, which had been tinkering with the river since the 1850s, warily watched it. In an era before the existence of large flood control dams on the Mississippi's tributaries, the corps banked its hopes for containing the flood, and possibly preventing it altogether, on a complex and extensive system of levees flanking both sides of the stream. Levees offered a sense of security against a swollen Mississippi.

The corps chose to build levees on the Mississippi for a number of reasons. For one, the army engineers believed levees, built close to the river's natural bank line, would concentrate the Mississippi's flows during flood episodes. Compressed water runs faster than dispersed water, a hydrologic fact that translates into a higher current velocity. An accelerated river supposedly increases its sediment transport capabilities. A big, rapid river can haul more silt downslope than a smaller, slower stream. Before the construction of levees, the Mississippi, when in flood, sprayed its waters out across its broad alluvial valley, which in turn lowered the height of its flood crests. The army engineers believed that confinement of the river's channel behind levee walls would force the river to compensate for its diminished width by digging out its bed and increasing its depth. It was hoped the Mississippi would scour away its bed material, causing a corresponding increase in its depth and carrying capacity. In the final analysis, the army concluded that a leveed Mississippi would be able to safely carry its flood flows into the Gulf of Mexico without inflicting damage on valley properties.

In the nineteenth and early twentieth centuries, the army engineers built levees that isolated the river from its side channels and flood outlets. Engineers felt confident that the Mississippi would respond to these changes in its hydraulic regime by excavating its bed to accommodate more water. The army had an additional incentive to adopt the "levees-only" policy. A narrower, concentrated, and hopefully deeper Mississippi River would serve barge navigation. As an added bonus, levees, by keeping the Mississippi away from its traditional haunts in the valley lowlands, would allow for land reclamation and agricultural production on their leeward sides. Mississippi Valley farmers could drain protected lowlands and convert marshland to cotton. Besides, levees allowed for community development on the valley floor. Towns could arise where malarial swamps once predominated. Levees, and a constricted river, made a sedentary civilization possible, while a nomadic river challenged the Euro-American socioeconomic order.

The Corps of Engineers, like any federal agency, also responded to the wishes of the people of the Lower Mississippi Valley, who understandably wanted levees for the same reasons the Corps of Engineers wanted them: levees meant a barge channel, flood control, reclamation, and urban and rural development in the floodplain. To the corps and its constituency, levees appeared to be a panacea, the answer to a whole host of hydraulic, economic, agricultural, and transportation problems. Levees offered stability where uncertainty once flowed. Anyone challenging the "levees-only" policy found themselves labeled a naysayer or worse.

And yet there existed skeptics of the program, civilian engineers who said the levees would lead not to bed scouring but to a rise in the riverbed. Some predicted more frequent floods at lower stages of water the moment the corps choked off the river's outlets and the Mississippi lost its connections to its floodplain. But the skeptics found themselves outgunned and outmaneuvered by the corps and its powerful backers. Too many influential interests wanted levees. By the 1880s, the "levees-only" policy sat firmly in place. When the Corps of Engineers closed the river's biggest outlet, the Atchafalaya, early in the twentieth century, more water than ever roared down the Mississippi's main channel. The murmurs of Corps opponents went largely unheard. Fortunately for the corps, the levees went up during a period of relative stability in the Mississippi's flow regime and morphology. From the 1880s to the 1920s, the Mississippi did not rise up and challenge the levees. When the river did threaten the levee system, the engineers, rather than heed the warning, just built the levees higher.

The unprecedented high flows descending the Mississippi in 1926 and 1927 worried some army engineers. Those floodwaters moving against their levees tested the decades-old levees-only policy like nothing else. If levees collapsed under the weight of water, both the levees-only policy and its primary sponsor, the Corps of Engineers, would lose credibility with the public, the engineering community, and Congress. Yet even as floodwaters flowed south in March 1927, the Corps' top echelon voiced confidence that the levees would hold against the river's growing crest.

But on Thursday, April 21, 1927, the army's confidence in its levee system dissolved in an instant of whipped water when the levee at Mounds Landing split wide open and the Mississippi immediately ran into the fissure. Within hours, the river stabbed a three-quarter-mile gash along the levee. The water did not let up. The river continued to eat the levee's sides while pushing twelve-foot-high waves through the hole. Engineers believed the Mississippi dug a channel through the levee aperture that measured at least a hundred feet deep. The levee break at Mounds Landing pummeled the Mississippi Delta region, the personal fiefdom of Leroy Percy and his fellow white patriarchs. The break and subsequent deluge affected a large land area. A piece of territory sixty miles wide by ninety miles long turned to river, and an estimated ten million acres of the richest land in Mississippi choked under ten feet of water. Along some reaches of the lower valley, floodwaters remained until July. Before the flood of 1927 finally came to a close, the Mississippi inundated twenty-seven thousand square miles, killed at least 246 people (mostly African-Americans), displaced 700,000 people, damaged or destroyed 137,000 buildings, and inflicted a $347 million financial loss. When it was all over, the Great Mississippi River Flood of 1927 represented the single most devastating flood in Euro-American history.

The Corps of Engineers and its levees-only program also fell victim to the Great Flood of 1927. Floodwaters punched big holes in numerous levees in the spring of 1927, and each breach struck a body blow against the corps' prestige and expertise. Rather than scour its bed during the flood, the Mississippi lifted itself out of its bed. A major portion of the silt moving downstream with the flood settled on the river's floor, driving the river ever higher. That rising bed, in conjunction with escalating flows, pressed the Mississippi River on top of its levees. By the end of the flood, a humbled chief of engineers, Major General Edgar Jadwin, admitted that levees alone could not contain the Mississippi River. In one fell swoop, the river had proved the fallacy of past corps predictions.

By the summer of 1927, the top brass in the Corps of Engineers, including General Jadwin, concluded that the next big Mississippi River flood could only be curtailed through the construction of flood control dams and reservoirs on tributary streams. Those structures would hold back high flows from the river, keeping the Mississippi within its banks. Additionally, long-closed outlets or side channels needed to be reopened to let the river spread its wings and lower its crest. Jadwin and his subordinates also proposed to repair, raise, and maintain most existing levees to provide additional protection to agricultural and urban real estate. Most levees had to remain in place. Decades of human labor, expended to convert wilderness to civilization, could not now be abandoned to a savage river. The engineers firmly believed dams, outlets, and higher levees would keep the Mississippi in check.

Amazingly, the Corps of Engineers, rather than admit defeat along the Mississippi, decided to up the ante and attempt to achieve greater control over the river's hydraulic regime. The engineers, although reeling from a major setback, did not retreat into a defensive posture. On the contrary, Jadwin, playing the part of an aggressive, take-no-prisoners general, opted to go on the offensive. The corps would not retreat from the Mississippi. Instead, the engineers would take their battle with the stream up its tributaries. In military parlance, the army planned on extending the field of operations.

In 1927, Jadwin pulled victory out of the jaws of defeat, using the flood and the fear it generated among policy makers and the public to push a new corps agenda. The army engineers would create a new empire, one based not solely on navigation but on a combination of navigation and flood control. The corps' institutional and areal influence stemmed from its legal authority over the nation's navigable waterways. Congress had traditionally charged it with improving streams for navigational purposes. This task gained it influence along the Mississippi, Missouri, and Ohio. Flood control offered the corps an entirely new arena within which to operate. If the corps received congressional authorization to engage in flood control efforts, it could expand its influence all over the Mississippi River basin and to the farthest corners of the United States. The Mississippi alone had roughly 250 tributaries, all potential pathways toward power.

Flood control offered the Corps of Engineers an empire far greater than anything possible through navigation. Flood control structures could conceivably be built on any stream in the country, whether navigable or not. Flood control could open wholly new avenues for corps expansion. The corps could leave the few large streams that carried commerce and move up even the most minuscule tributaries. The task of flood control presented the army engineers with all kinds of opportunities for growth and greatness. Jadwin and his cohorts wasted no time in pushing for congressional authorization of flood control legislation. In 1928, Congress passed a flood control act that granted the army engineers the ability to study and build flood control structures to contain future Mississippi River floods. The Great Mississippi River Flood of 1927, rather than driving the corps from the Mississippi basin, lifted the engineers to new heights.

Congress ordered the corps to conduct a series of river basin surveys as a first step toward controlling the Mississippi. The surveys would determine whether tributary flood control structures would lower flood heights on the Mississippi itself. Congress also ordered the corps to study the Mississippi's tributary river basins to ascertain how the streams could be engineered for hydroelectricity, irrigation, and navigation, or what was known as multiple-purpose development. Once again, the Mississippi's tributaries would serve as adjuncts in a large hydraulic system. The Mississippi would be the center of the system, and the tributaries would be on the periphery supporting the core. This is the same sort of rationale that existed when the corps pushed for a navigation channel along the Mississippi in the 1880s. Tributary routes along the Missouri and Ohio would support the main trunk line along the Mississippi.

Even before the onset of the Great Depression and New Deal, Congress and the corps drew up plans for social and economic development along the contours of river basins. Interestingly, officials within the Corps of Engineers began to view drainage basins from a bioregional perspective. Although not naming it as such, the army engineers laid the foundation for modern bioregionalism. They looked at river basins as distinct environmental and hydrologic entities requiring unique developmental approaches. The corps made some connections between rivers and basins, water and land.

In the early 1930s, the Corps of Engineers engaged in the most extensive examination of America's rivers in United States history. The Government Printing Office (GPO) published the studies carried out by the corps in a series of reports, collectively known as the "308" reports. The Kansas City District and the Omaha District offices examined the Missouri and Yellowstone Rivers. The 308 report for the Yellowstone, published in 1934, had far-reaching repercussions for the future of the stream. The main justification for a survey of the Yellowstone was to determine if flood control dams could cost-effectively be built across the stream and whether such dams would lower flood heights on the Mississippi River. The corps also looked at the

Yellowstone to see whether it could be developed for multiple purposes, including hydroelectric production, navigation, and irrigation. The 308 report, discreetly titled "The Yellowstone River, Wyo. and Montana," remains the most thorough hydrologic and engineering study ever conducted by any governmental agency of the Yellowstone River. The study included information gathered from all the previous Yellowstone River surveys, plus new data obtained by corps personnel who traveled into the valley in the early 1930s.

After a review of the Yellowstone River's navigation history or the lack thereof, and recognizing the monopoly that railroad companies held over the region's transportation grid, the army once more ruled against reengineering the Yellowstone to create a barge channel. The corps concluded that neither channelization to engineer an open-water barge channel nor a system of dams and locks to erect a slack-water barge channel could ever be economically justified for the Yellowstone. The railroads met the region's transportation needs more cheaply and efficiently than a barge channel ever could or would.

Besides studying the feasibility of remaking the Yellowstone into a navigation route, the Corps of Engineers investigated the river to determine whether its waters could in some way augment flows in the Missouri River. Since 1926, the corps had expended millions on a Missouri River barge channel between Kansas City and the river's mouth. The engineers designed and built a six-foot-deep, two-hundred-foot wide barge channel along the lower 380 miles of the Missouri. The army engineers, when building this channel, believed the Missouri would never dip below 20,000 cfs at Kansas City. As long as the Missouri carried 20,000 cfs, the barge channel would stay six feet deep. With these predictions and flow statistics, the corps built the barge channel. By the early 1930s, the army had expended tens of millions on the navigation channel. While the corps spent the money, the Missouri defied the army's earlier predictions. On September 19, 1931, the Missouri slipped to an all-time low of 10,700 cfs at Kansas City. This represented half of the water needed to keep barges afloat in the navigation channel. Such a low stage meant one thing: the corps based the dimensions of the six-foot channel on an inadequate data set. The engineers had to find water for their shallow, expensive, unusable barge channel. If they did not find that water, the channel would never carry barges. The investment of public moneys to date would have been wasted. Barge operators would avoid a navigation channel that frequently dropped to a three-foot depth or lower. The corps needed to find a reliable source of water to maintain a consistent six-foot depth in the channel even during drought years. Where to find the water plagued the engineers in Kansas City and St. Louis.

The situation along the Missouri below Kansas City gave the Corps of Engineers one more reason to examine the Yellowstone. The engineers wanted to know if they could dam that later river, store its waters in a sizable reservoir, and then release those waters downstream to the Missouri navigation channel to raise its water levels to the requisite six-foot depth. But along the Yellowstone there were very few tentative dam and reservoir sites capable of meeting this requirement. A good dam site is one with road and rail access, a narrow valley, a chalk or shale foundation, and a large potential reservoir area. East and north of Springdale, Montana, there existed no feasible dam sites on the Yellowstone River. The population density of the valley was relatively high, and the potential reservoirs were too small—too small to justify the placement of a dam across such a big river as the Yellowstone.

Thus, when considering dam and reservoir sites to augment the Missouri's flows, the engineers had no choice but to look at sites south of Livingston and north of Yellowstone National Park. Along the 671 miles of Yellowstone River flowing through Wyoming and Montana, the army engineers had only a 60-mile stretch of stream to work with, but within those 60 miles, they found two locations that held potential as dam sites. One site sat inside the Lower Cañon at a place called Allenspur, which army personnel examined back in 1919. Allenspur lay five miles south of Livingston, where the Absarokas slide down toward the Gallatin Range. The engineers considered Paradise Valley—which opens to the south of Allenspur—a decent reservoir site. Since high mountain faces flanked each side of the lowlands, Paradise Valley could conceivably hold a large body of water (fig. 8.5).

The other dam site fomented beneath the waves inside Yankee Jim Cañon. The Corps named this site "the second Cañon of the Yellowstone." Situated fifty miles south of Livingston and thirteen miles north of the national park boundary, Yankee Jim Cañon shakes the Yellowstone into lather. Both Allenspur and Yankee Jim possessed three of the four prerequisites for a feasible dam site. Each dam site sat squarely between tall, narrow canyon walls. Each canyon had superior rail access, provided by the Northern Pacific Railroad spur running between Livingston and Gardiner; that rail line would make it easy for the Corps of Engineers to get men and materials to either location. Furthermore, at both locales, solid bedrock lay in seams close to the surface, which meant that dams could easily and inexpensively be attached to the material (fig. 8.6).

Figure 8.5. The Allenspur or Lower Cañon Dam site, view toward the north. (Photograph by author, 1999)

Figure 8.6. The Yankee Jim Cañon Dam site, view toward the southwest. (Photograph by author, 1999)

The two sites looked very good in three out of four categories, but the lack of adequate reservoir storage capacity convinced the army to rule against both dams. The corps did not believe either Lower Cañon Dam or Yankee Jim Cañon Dam, singularly or in combination, could store enough water to sustain a 6-foot depth in the Missouri River below Kansas City during drought periods. The Lower Cañon Dam, which the corps envisioned at a height of 282 feet from toe to head, would back water far south into Paradise Valley. This reservoir would store 1,384,000 acre-feet of water, a sizable slab of liquid but not enough to keep the Missouri barge channel 6 feet deep. Yankee Jim Dam would stand 215 feet high and would flood the Yellowstone Valley as far south as the Yellowstone National Park boundary at Gardiner; the reservoir would hold a mere 279,900 acre-feet of water. Yankee Jim Dam could have conceivably been built higher, but the inviolable park limited dam and reservoir size. The corps could not violate the park's boundary, as the earlier Outlet Dam controversy made so clear. Neither Yankee Jim nor Lower Cañon would substantially augment flows in the Missouri River barge channel below Kansas City during drought episodes because neither dam could store enough water. The most water that would likely come down to Kansas City from the reservoir at Lower Cañon would be about 5,700 cfs, only a quarter of the total amount needed. Furthermore, the corps could not predict with certainty whether that water would be in the reservoir when it would be most needed at Kansas City. The corps even observed that both dams, operating in tandem, would not contribute significant flows to the Missouri River east of Kansas City in drought years.[6]

While the corps examined the Yellowstone, it also scrutinized the Missouri. By early 1933, the engineers found a dam site on the Missouri main stem to supply water to the cherished navigation channel. The Fort Peck Dam site (located just upstream from the fort that once straddled the Big Dry–Milk River road) not only would provide the necessary water storage to ensure a 6-foot channel depth below Kansas City but also would supposedly deliver enough water to maintain a 9-foot channel from Sioux City, Iowa, to the mouth if and when that deeper channel received congressional authorization. Fort Peck Dam, if built, would save the Missouri River barge channel from obsolescence. That same dam might lead to an extension of a still deeper channel all the way to Sioux City. Fort Peck could accomplish these tasks because it would rise 250 feet above the Missouri's bed, extend over 20,000 feet from valley wall to valley wall, and store close to 19 million acre-feet of water, enough to form a reservoir 134 miles long. The reservoir would hold back the equivalent of four years of the Missouri's average flow volume past the dam site. Predictably, the corps wanted Fort Peck Dam and not the smaller dams on the Yellowstone. Fort Peck would accomplish the immediate goal of providing water to the river south of Kansas City, while leaving open the possibility that the corps would be able to build a 9-foot channel at a later date from the mouth all the way to Sioux City. Fort Peck offered too much to the corps for it not to endorse it.

In October 1933, the army sought and received Public Works Administration approval for the construction of Fort Peck Dam. The decision to build the dam meant the Yellowstone would not be dammed to support the Missouri River barge channel. Hydraulic factors (the small reservoir sites available on the Yellowstone) and political realities (including the need to protect Yellowstone National Park) dissuaded the corps from seeking dams across the Yellowstone. The Yellowstone, once more, could not fit into a corps-dominated hydraulic system. Had the Missouri lacked a suitable site for a big dam, then there existed a higher probability that the Yellowstone would have been dammed to support Missouri River navigation. But as it turned out, the Missouri's development spared the Yellowstone.

Although the Kansas City District office and its politically astute commander, Theodore Wyman, decided against damming the Yellowstone as a means of propping up Missouri River navigation, Wyman and his engineers continued to examine the Yellowstone to determine whether dams and reservoirs at Yankee Jim and Lower Cañon might be suitable for reducing flood heights in the Lower Missouri Valley and the Lower Mississippi Valley. Dams on the Yellowstone might not be warranted for navigation, but they could be justified if they significantly reduced flood damage in either of the two populous valleys. But once again the engineers concluded that having two flood control dams on the Yellowstone would not be cost-effective. Most important, the Yellowstone River Valley itself did not need flood control. The Yellowstone River's flood regime differed from the Lower Missouri's and Mississippi's. Floods in the latter two valleys covered extensive portions of their respective lowlands for long periods, sometimes months on end, a circumstance that hindered agricultural production. The Yellowstone, on the other hand, flooded in March or April and again in June. When it topped its banks, it did so for only a few days and then fell back below its high banks. Thus, the Yellowstone Valley's flood damages were limited in both space and time. Short, localized floods caused far less damage than long, widespread floods.

The value of Yellowstone Valley real estate also affected how much damage the river inflicted on the agricultural sector. The land at risk of inundation in the Yellowstone Valley held a valuation far below that of lands in the Lower Missouri Valley. Most often, farmers utilized nonirrigated lowlands near the river as pasture for livestock. During the years of the Great Depression, that land might be worth only a few dollars an acre. In contrast, along the Lower Missouri Valley the price of an acre of lowland could reach over $100. In 1931, the average price for an acre of Iowa farm land stood at $109.[7] The corps estimated that flood damages in the entire Yellowstone basin in the previous fifty years equaled a mere $103,940 per year. A system of flood control structures, on the other hand, would cost at least $23,934,000. These statistics indicate that over the fifty-year life of the dam projects, the army would spend roughly $478,680 per year on flood control, an amount that did not include the accruing interest on the initial investment. Hence, flood control structures in the Yellowstone basin possessed unfavorable cost-to-benefit ratios; based on the statistics presented here, they would have cost about $5 for every dollar protected from flood damages.[8]

A further reason the Yellowstone did not need flood control structures had to do with the height of the river's banks. The river's stable gravel banks, in some locals as much as twenty feet from the low waterline to the apex, served as a natural levee against flood flows. Rarely did the Yellowstone overtop its steep banks. According to the Corps of Engineers, those natural banks provided valley ranchers, farmers, and town residents with adequate flood control. Finally, the dams at Yankee Jim and Lower Cañon would not hold back enough water to appreciably decrease flood flows. The dams would not do anything about the flooding of the Lower Yellowstone (below the Bighorn confluence) in March and April. That early-season flood occurred due to ice-out and the resultant ice jams. The river also flooded in the spring when snowmelt began streaming off the plains. The dams at Yankee Jim and Lower Cañon would be too high up the Yellowstone to stop ice jams and run-off in the lower valley. The Yellowstone's unique combination of hydraulic characteristics made flood control dams absolutely unjustifiable.

Unable to construct dams to achieve flood control on the Yellowstone proper, the army tried to determine if a regulated Yellowstone would measurably lower flood heights on either the Missouri River or the Mississippi River below St. Louis. The corps tried desperately to find a way to dam the Yellowstone. If the army could find a justification, it was going to plug that river. The corps discovered that dams at Yankee Jim and Lower Cañon would not affect flood flows on the Missouri River in the least. The Mighty Mo hopped over its banks in April and June. Just as the Missouri flooded in April, the corps would be forced to draw down the reservoirs behind Yankee Jim and Lower Cañon Dams in anticipation of the Yellowstone's upcoming June rise. The corps would have to let water out of the two reservoirs at the same time the Missouri left its banks in order to create storage space for the high flows that would soon descend the Yellowstone. As a result, the two dams would not halt the flow of Yellowstone water into the Missouri during its April rise. Rather, they would be required by the stream's hydraulic schedule to contribute water to an already burgeoning Missouri. Yankee Jim and Lower Cañon Dams would not at all diminish the size or duration of the April rise on the Missouri. In June, the Missouri flooded early in the month. Along the Yellowstone, the peak of the June rise came in the last weeks of that month or the first weeks of July. Hence, Yankee Jim and Lower Cañon Dams would hold the Yellowstone's June rise after the Missouri's June rise. The corps believed that flood control structures on the Yellowstone would only skim between an inch and a half and three inches off any Missouri River superflood at Kansas City. The expenses involved in erecting two gigantic dams could not be justified for such a minuscule reduction in flood heights in the Lower Missouri.[9]

The same issues arose concerning the tentative Yellowstone River dams and Mississippi River flood control, namely, the Lower Mississippi River flooded in March and April, months before snowmelt would enter the Upper Yellowstone River dams. So once again, the reservoir or reservoirs would be drawn down as the Mississippi's flows peaked in the spring. In addition, the two reservoirs would be so small, sit so high up in the Mississippi basin, and capture such a small portion of water draining into the Mississippi itself that the effect of the reservoirs on Mississippi floods would be barely perceptible at best and immeasurable at worst. The corps admitted that Yellowstone River dams would have almost no effect on Mississippi River flood flows. The corps estimated that Yankee Jim Dam would have lowered the 1927 flood at Cairo, Illinois, by only two inches and concluded, "Therefore, the construction of reservoirs in the Yellowstone Basin, to be operated primarily for Mississippi flood control, would be unsound and uneconomical, because of the unfavorable item of silting, relatively minor benefits to be derived, and the excessive costs for such minor benefits."[10] After its exhaustive analysis and number crunching, the corps rejected dams on the Yellowstone River to provlde either Yellowstone, Missouri, or Mississippi Valley flood protection. Besides not being justified for each river individually, the dams could not be justified as a means of providing flood control on all three big rivers simultaneously.

But the corps did not quit studying the river and the possibility of damming it. The army engineers tried to determine whether dams could be built for hydroelectric generation or irrigation agriculture. The corps quickly learned that no market existed that was large enough to absorb the hydropower generated by a future Yankee Jim or Lower Cañon Dam. Livingston did not have the consumers to take all the power coming out of the turbines of a Lower Cañon Dam, and the power from a Yankee Jim Dam would have nowhere to go. What made matters even worse, the cost of building transmission lines to another large market such as Billings or Butte would negate the dam's hydropower benefits. Power lines would cost more than the value of the electricity generated by the structure. So the river could not be dammed for hydroelectric production. The army engineers concluded that the two dams could not be justified for irrigation either. All the potential irrigation land in the valley had already been put under the plow and ditch. Even more interesting, there existed no need to build a dam to deliver water. The natural slope of the Yellowstone and its gravitation adequately delivered water to cropland along its banks. A high dam and reservoir would in no way deliver water more efficiently to downstream lands.

After ruling out damming the river for any single purpose, the army engineers threw around their statistical data to determine whether the river could be dammed for the combined purposes of irrigation, hydropower, Missouri River navigation, and flood control. Remarkably, the Yellowstone could not be dammed at Yankee Jim or Lower Cañon for any reason whatsoever, whether singularly or in combination. The astronomical costs of the projects still outweighed the associated benefits of the dams. The corps ended its comprehensive survey of the Yellowstone by recommending an even more intense development of the river for gravity irrigation. In one respect, that conclusion granted the Yellowstone River a reprieve. The dam-building plague that swept the West in the 1930s and 1940s passed over the Yellowstone Valley on its way to other rivers and other regions.

What is fascinating about the 1930s in general, and the 308 report in particular, is that if the corps could have found some way to dam the Yellowstone River, it would have done so. In a decade of drought and depression, when Montana suffered from unprecedented economic hardship, including poor crop production numbers and sky-high unemployment, the corps and the federal government needed few, if any, justifications to build dams across big rivers. Dams and channelization projects were seen as a means of employing men while infusing sorely needed capital into destitute regions. Projects of a questionable character still received federal money. A case in point: the Missouri River navigation project received millions of federal dollars during the Dirty Thirties, even though no one provided data to support the contention that that barge channel would ever actually carry barges. Fear and hope blinded the corps and Missouri Valley residents to the impracticality of the Missouri River navigation channel.

That the corps did not build a dam or a series of dams across the Yellowstone River had nothing to do with a lack of trying. Captain Theodore Wyman at the Kansas City District (the corps district with jurisdiction over the Upper Missouri basin until the formation of the Omaha District in 1934) advocated some rather shady projects during his tenure as district commander. If Wyman had found even a flimsy reason to dam the Yellowstone, he likely would have used it to gain project authorization and appropriations. But he and his companions could not find any way to fit the river into other, larger hydraulic systems. That Wyman and the army engineers could not uncover even a shred of economic evidence to support the damming of the Yellowstone River is utterly incredible and a testament to the exceptional character of that remarkable river.

9

Vanishing Act

Pick, Sloan, the Upper Missouri,
and Yellowstone

The promises of Pick-Sloan have proven to be largely a
disappointment to the people of South Dakota. Of the 972,000
acres of irrigation originally promised the state, only 24,100 acres,
or just over two percent, have been developed under the program.
Furthermore, it is a sad fact that the vast majority of the
hydroelectric resources in South Dakota—South Dakota produces
67% of the entire Pick-Sloan system power—is exported to other
states. . . . Enormous benefits have been received in other parts
of the basin, grossly out of proportion with the contributions of
these states to the cost of the Pick-Sloan program.
—South Dakota governor George S. Mickelson, 1989

By 1989, Governor George S. Mickelson and the people of
South Dakota felt outrage toward the Corps of Engineers and the Pick-Sloan
Plan for Missouri Basin Development. In 1944, the Pick-Sloan Plan author-
ized the construction of five earthen dams across the Missouri main stem in
North and South Dakota. South Dakota's share of the Missouri Valley would
be dammed and flooded by four of the five structures. In the 1930s and

1940s, South Dakotans went to Omaha, Kansas City, and Washington, D.C., to beg the Corps of Engineers for big dams across the Missouri. They wanted water to fill the dust bowl. South Dakota got the dams but not the water. Subsequently, the state's citizens believed they had been wronged by the Corps of Engineers and its hydraulic system. A river the South Dakotans believed rightfully belonged to them, and which they wanted to use for irrigation and recreation, was being drained away to the southeast to buoy the navigation channel below Sioux City. By the late 1980s and 1990s, South Dakotans no longer accepted the colonial status assigned to them and the Upper Missouri River by the residents of the Lower Missouri basin. They wanted the main-stem dams and reservoirs conceived by Lewis Pick and Glenn Sloan to serve their own economic ends rather than agriculture, urbanism, industrialism, and tourism in the Lower Missouri Valley. Yet it remains to be seen whether the Dakotans and Montanans will redirect the Missouri toward a new, more equitable society.

Lewis Pick represented his time. Like the majority of straitlaced men in the Corps of Engineers in the 1940s, he held an extreme faith in the efficacy and inherent goodness of technology. The man firmly believed American know-how and American gadgets could overcome any physical obstacle in the path of Western civilization. Rivers, mountains, seashores, and even powerful nation-states fell before the power of the United States' technological prowess and the expertise of its military engineers. Pick and his cohorts convinced themselves that they represented the spear point of American civilization at home and abroad. Nature's wildness and the savagery of foreign peoples met their masters in the field when confronted by Euro-American males wielding technological wands.

Pick had the luck to be in the right place at the right time. In 1927, to his good fortune and career aspirations, he served as district engineer at New Orleans during the Great Mississippi River Flood. He assisted with relief efforts in the Lower Mississippi Valley during that natural flood event and human catastrophe. His job performance during the flood and its aftermath quickly propelled him into the upper echelons of the Corps of Engineers. In 1942, Colonel Pick took the reins of the Missouri River Division, U.S. Army Corps of Engineers, headquartered in Omaha, Nebraska. Pick just happened to be at the helm of the Missouri River Division when the Missouri experienced its greatest flood. Two big floods, and Pick's response to both, helped launch the man to the highest position in the Corps of Engineers: chief of engineers. The Missouri River flood of 1943 began in the first week of April and lasted into June. During the intervening weeks, the Missouri inundated its valley lowlands three consecutive times. In May, it threw brown water into Omaha–Council Bluffs, covering the airport under several feet of grime.

Floods, which had occurred annually on the Missouri since its glacial formation between 30,000 and 9,500 B.P., represented in Pick's mind nature's wrath, its vengeful side, its unwillingness to abide by God's laws and man's dictates.[1] In Pick's reality, the floods of 1943 clearly illustrated that a rampaging Missouri lay beyond the pale of civilization. In other words, the Missouri opposed civilization and symbolized the antithesis of American society. An undammed, unchannelized, free-flowing, nomadic Missouri could never be a part of American civilization, in the same manner that "wild," equestrian, nomadic Indians could not.

In 1943, Pick and many Euro-American residents of the Missouri Valley placed the Missouri River on the other side of admissible reality. Once more, Euro-Americans dichotomized the world, depicting the Missouri as untamed and destructive, while perceiving their own society and themselves as civilized, peaceful, and well-intentioned. Once Euro-Americans viewed the river as a malignant force, thoughts of compromise with that natural entity vanished from their minds. The Missouri became the hated enemy, a force to be defeated and then subjugated to the will of the people. The Missouri, in an odd sort of way, became like the Japanese and the Germans—only the river's unconditional surrender would suffice. There could be no half measures in dealing with the Missouri, no semiwild, partially dammed, or unchannelized river, just as there could be no reasoning with a madman like Hitler. To Euro-Americans in the 1940s, the entire river had to come under total control. Pick and residents throughout the Missouri Valley determined to defeat the Missouri.

Colonel Pick believed the flooding along the Missouri to be utterly unnecessary. As a matter of fact, he thought it ridiculous, preposterous that the most technologically sophisticated, militarily powerful, and economically robust nation in the world should have to endure the hardships, inconvenience, and nuisance of a large river pouring over its banks. Americans should not have to put up with flooding rivers, which were a thing of the past—a bygone, unregulated, unplanned, irrational past. Pick found it unfathomable that the Missouri should be allowed to flood and to disrupt the smooth functioning of the United States' social, political, economic, and military systems. The Missouri in its unregulated condition did not factor into Pick's vision of an ordered, progressive, modern society. Wild rivers

were antiquated, outdated, and dirty. Pick wanted an efficient and clean
river.

Pick undertook to tame the Missouri and its tributaries, including the
Yellowstone. On May 13, 1943, the House Committee on Flood Control or-
dered the Corps of Engineers to devise a plan to stop the Missouri's April
and June rises and provide enough water to maintain a barge channel in the
Missouri main stem south of Sioux City, Iowa, for eight months each year.
This congressional assignment passed to the desk of Pick in Omaha. For
week after week in the summer of 1943, Pick scanned maps of the Upper
Missouri basin, read and reread various hydrologic studies, including
Schulz's reports of 1909 and 1910 and the voluminous and comprehensive
308 report of 1934. By August 1943, Pick finished his report to Congress.
The Pick Plan, although a mere twelve pages long, was the grandest river
engineering proposal ever considered for the northern plains and Upper
Missouri. Pick wanted big dams built at twenty locations throughout the Mis-
souri basin. If Pick got his way, dams would rise across the paths of the Yellowstone and Bighorn. Along the Missouri main stem, he wanted dams at
Garrison, Oak Creek, Oahe, Fort Randall, and Gavin's Point.

All these structures would serve two overlords, the Corps of Engineers
and its Lower Missouri basin constituency. Valleys would disappear under
lakes, and dams would rise above plains for the purpose of flood control and
navigation. If the corps bulldozed the dams into existence, South and North
Dakota and Montana would become the water colonies of the Lower Missouri Valley and the Corps of Engineers. Pick did not give a damn about the
Upper Missouri's past, its former order, it previous geography, its Indian
peoples, or its history. He saw only the future, a time when the northern
plains properly bowed before the more populous midcontinental region and
its protector, the Army Corps of Engineers.

Pick proposed the construction of a high earthen dam across the main
stem of the Yellowstone at the Lower Cañon site, five miles south of Livingston, Montana. Even though he was familiar with the conclusions of the 308
report concerning the site, Pick decided to reverse earlier recommendations
against Lower Cañon Dam. Pick made an unsound hydrologic conclusion
but a politically astute decision. He proposed a dam at Allenspur because he
needed Montana support for his plan, especially the state's backing for his
Missouri main-stem hydraulic system. Not one big dam on the Missouri
would be built in Montana under his scheme. Additionally, irrigation would
take a backseat to navigation. Montana would get water from the main-stem

system for irrigation only after the needs of the navigation channel had been met. Pick knew that that prospect, of being deprived of irrigation water, would raise the ire of Montana residents and their state and federal representatives. He made it clear that Fort Peck, built between 1933 and 1940, would continue to serve downstream navigation flows, not Montana agriculture. Lewis Pick's navigation and flood control vision for the Missouri River offered nothing to Montana. The Lower Cañon Dam would be a pork-barrel project, pure and simple, served up on a silver platter to entice Montana's people into agreeing to the entire Pick Plan. Paradise Valley and the world-class trout fishery there would be the sacrificial lambs, killed to preserve the larger objects of the plan—those massive dams planned for the Dakotas.

Pick, hoping to create a hydraulic system designed for navigation and flood control, believed that the Lower Cañon Dam would serve irrigation and hydropower purposes, two acute needs for Montana. The dam would not provide any flood control or navigation benefits, on either the Yellowstone main stem or the Missouri. Lower Cañon Dam would be of local benefit only. That the dam would have only local benefits pleased the Livingston business community tremendously; its members alone would profit from the dam's construction and from the water stored in its bottomless reservoir.

Pick's apparently irrational proposal to build Lower Cañon Dam makes sense when the dam's larger, systemwide contribution is taken into consideration. Pick wanted a dam at Lower Cañon because it would cost the Corps of Engineers nothing in lost influence in the Upper Missouri basin. More specifically, the corps could build Lower Cañon and still protect and sustain its gift horse, the navigation channel south of Sioux City. That channel's viability had been the corps' main concern on the Missouri since the 1880s. Lower Cañon Dam would sit so high up the Yellowstone main stem that its reservoir waters would not in any way take water away from the flows required to maintain the nine-foot-deep navigation channel proposed on the Missouri from Sioux City to the mouth. Pick understood this fact, and that is why he included the dam in his plan. Lower Cañon Dam would win Montana's support and require no sacrifice from the Corps of Engineers: a win-win proposition for all involved. Pick, a solid, red-blooded American, devised a perfect compromise, the very type of compromise that had made the United States a superpower and contributed to its social and political viability. That the compromise required the inundation of a river valley did not mean squat to Pick. A dam and reservoir represented an improvement on nature anyway. Even nature was going to benefit from the dam. Pick knew the dam would require the wasteful expenditure of public moneys because it would not be cost-effective by any stretch of an army engineer's accounting book, but that waste was justifiable if it led to Montana's support of the Pick Plan, a plan that would be so beneficial to society at large that Lower Cañon Dam's costs would easily be absorbed by the Pick Plan's overall benefits.

Pick did not see Lower Cañon Dam as a part of a larger hydraulic system controlled and operated by the Corps of Engineers; the dam was insignificant to his grander vision. Lower Cañon Dam represented an outlier, a monument to pork and the compromises necessary within the American political system. Pick admitted that the Bureau of Reclamation could build and operate the dam at Lower Cañon—an indication that he did not see the structure as a threat to the corps.[2]

Above all else, Pick and his superiors in Washington, D.C., wanted the corps to have control over the Missouri main stem. Chief of Engineers Eugene Reybold told Congress after submission of the Pick Plan to that legislative body, "It is essential, however, that the main-stem projects be built, operated, and maintained by the Corps of Engineers."[3] The Upper Missouri main stem represented the ultimate prize, an incomparable resource to achieve empire. Control of the Missouri main stem would give the Corps of Engineers a decisive role in the Upper Midwest, northern plains, and Rockies. If the damming of the Yellowstone, with a worthless dam, accomplished that end, so be it.

Lewis Pick did not propose any other dams on the Yellowstone River main stem because he did not want any more. A large dam lower down the Yellowstone might actually capture enough of the Yellowstone's flow volume to appreciably affect the flows needed to sustain the Missouri River barge channel below Sioux City. One dam, high up on the Yellowstone, would be acceptable; two dams would be one too many. The matter was moot anyway, since there were no feasible dam sites beyond the Mission Creek site, located sixteen miles east of Livingston.[4] No dam could be built on the Lower Yellowstone for the purpose of flood control. The 308 report of 1934 and a series of corps studies done later in the 1930s concluded that flood control dams across the lower Yellowstone would never justify the cost of their construction. The lands along the Yellowstone inundated by the river's spring or summer rises were of low value. Valley lands were mostly used for ranching or planted in inexpensive alfalfa. Dams to protect such lands could never be justified. Additionally, the Yellowstone River's high banks, ten feet in many locations east of the Bighorn confluence, kept the river from reaching over its bank line. High flows did not contribute to a flood problem in the Yellowstone Valley itself, which remained largely immune to devastating costly floods. Rather, the Yellowstone's high May and June flows caused problems in the more heavily populated urbanized, and agriculturally valuable, Missouri Valley.

Yet Pick believed he had to capture the waters of the Lower Yellowstone River somehow, since the Yellowstone dumped more water into the Upper Missouri than any other stream. It was the Yellowstone that contributed the most to the Missouri's frequent May and June floods. During the 1943 floods, the Yellowstone contributed high flows to the Missouri from the third week of March until the first week of August. In the last days of March 1943, the river dumped almost 90,000 cfs into the Missouri at the confluence. That huge volume of water caused much of the flooding in the Missouri Valley to the east and south. The flooding experienced three months later, in June 1943, had everything to do with the high flows coming into the Missouri from the Yellowstone. In that month, the Yellowstone discharged close to 90,000 cfs into the Big Muddy for days on end, while the Missouri itself contributed at most 10,000 cfs to flows east of the confluence.

The colonel needed to find a dam site to hold back the Yellowstone's June rise, the very rise that had shot down the Yellowstone, bullied its way into the Missouri, and then come down through the Dakotas to swamp the colonel's beloved Omaha. Controlling the Yellowstone would appreciably reduce flood heights on the Missouri. Pick proposed to control the Yellowstone by damming the Missouri River. Seventy-five miles northwest of Bismarck, North Dakota, the Missouri Valley narrows appreciably before turning sharply to the west. That turn in the river—nicknamed the Great Bend—was where Pick wanted a big dam. Garrison Dam's purpose would be twofold. First, it would dissipate the Yellowstone's spring and summer rises to prevent both from going downstream and wreaking havoc. Garrison would prevent a repeat of the flood of 1943 by holding the Yellowstone in check. Pick also wanted Garrison to capture the waters entering the Missouri River from the Little Missouri, Milk, and Little Muddy.[5]

Pick factored in siltation rates when deciding on the sites for his Upper Missouri dams. Garrison, which would be 210 feet high and create a reservoir 178 miles long, would hold enough water to prevent rapid siltation of its reservoir, a real concern across the Upper Missouri basin, with its thick rivers. Dams on the Lower Milk, Little Missouri, or Lower Yellowstone would have silted within decades; not so with a massive Missouri River reservoir.

Garrison reservoir, gigantic and enclosed by high valley walls, could absorb tens of millions of tons of earth each year and still maintain storage capacity for 920 years.[6]

Pick had to consider the character of the Upper Missouri basin's geology. That geology, especially the erosive soils lying on the surface of eastern Montana and the western Dakotas, played a significant role in his choice of dam sites. The existence of that gumbo goes a long way toward explaining why the Yellowstone and Little Missouri would be spared dams. Those rivers held too much silt and would kill a dam and reservoir too fast. Pick, although a big spender and a believer in the efficacy of pork, had to consider cost in choosing his dam sites. The pug-nosed colonel did not have a blank check from his congressional overseers, which explains why he favored big dams rather than small dams. A few big dams at strategic locations would cost the federal government far less than numerous small dams spread out across the entire Upper Missouri basin. Pick estimated Garrison's cost at $130 million. Additionally, big dams impounded more water in their larger reservoirs, which meant they lasted longer than smaller structures and reservoirs. A longer life expectancy in relation to siltation meant a better long-term return on the initial investment. Big dams on the Missouri main stem meant more bang for the buck.

Small, dispersed dams spread out across the northern plains region meant more political maneuvering, haggling, and power sharing. From a hydraulic, political, and jurisdictional point of view, big dams on the Missouri main stem kept things far simpler. A few colossal dams on the main stem guaranteed firm corps and federal control over the water resource. The corps' authority over the Missouri was clear and virtually beyond challenge because of the historical role of commerce on the river and the stipulations of the commerce clause of the Constitution granting the engineers jurisdiction over navigable waterways. Dams along barely navigable tributaries would have been more difficult for the corps to gain control over. As a result, the Corps of Engineers would have had to cut more political deals to acquire the water needed to float barges on the Lower Missouri.

Dozens of dams on the Missouri's tributaries and smaller structures on the Missouri main stem, all serving navigation and flood control, would have been more difficult for the corps to operate efficiently. The corps would have found it tough to coordinate the release sequences of so many dams sprinkled across great distances. Pick and his colleagues feared that a plethora of small dams might make it impossible to maintain a reservoir release se-quence that delivered reliable flows to the tentative nine-foot navigation channel below Sioux City. The reservoir control center in Omaha would be jostling reservoir levels up and down, trying to put that 30,000 cfs into the channel at Sioux City. That might be a difficult task if the corps had dams all over the map. Six big dams on the main stem would be hard enough to coordinate, but the size of the reservoirs, their location on the main stem, and their control by only one agency meant a higher degree of certainty that the army would deliver water to the navigation channel.

Pick did not need Garrison to control the far Upper Missouri main stem (the river reach west of the Yellowstone-Missouri confluence). Fort Peck Dam accomplished that in 1940. Most important, Fort Peck served the navigation channel south of Sioux City. Army engineers built it as a drought buster, a structure designed to deliver reliable flows to the six-foot barge channel during the Missouri basin's all-too-frequent drought episodes. Federal officials also wanted to employ men on public works projects during the Great Depression. Make-work on a dam like Fort Peck kept men off the streets, out of trouble, and away from leftist literature. Peck fulfilled all these goals.

Garrison appealed to Lewis Pick and the Army Corps of Engineers for one other important reason—the dam and its resultant reservoir would inundate Indian land rather than Euro-American homes, farms, and communities. The Fort Berthold Reservation and the lands of the Three Affiliated Tribes of the Mandan, Hidatsa, and Arikara would be inundated to create Garrison Reservoir. The flooding of those Indian lands did not represent a loss to Pick, the corps, the Bureau of Indians Affairs, the state government of North Dakota, or the off-reservation population of North Dakota. Rather, Euro-Americans believed that creating a reservoir out of the Indian bottomlands would be more economical and socially beneficial than using the Missouri Valley as Indian homelands. Additionally, once Indians lost the valley lowlands and the resources there, they would be easier to assimilate into the dominant culture. Indian assimilation had been a goal of the United States in the Upper Missouri since the time of Lewis and Clark. The geography of the Pick Plan was blatantly racist.

Pick submitted his rather hastily written dam-building program to the Chief of Engineers on August 10, 1943. After review of its contents, the chief of engineers passed the Pick Plan to Congress on December 31, 1943. Once revealed to the public in the spring of 1944, the plan drew immediate and concentrated fire from representatives of the Upper Missouri basin states of

North Dakota, Montana, and Wyoming. South Dakota remained quiet because its governor, Merrill Q. Sharpe, wanted the Pick Plan's dams at any cost.

Senator Joseph C. O'Mahoney of Wyoming did not believe the plan did enough for the Upper Missouri. The Pick Plan promoted lower basin interests at the expense of the upper basin's desire for irrigation. Water impounded by Pick's proposed main-stem dams would be either held back or released on schedule, depending on the needs of Lower Missouri Valley rural residents and urbanites. A substantial portion of any water in the Dakota reservoirs would find its way down the navigation channel south of Sioux City. It became obvious to O'Mahoney and others in the northern plains that irrigation water would be supplied to Upper Missouri basin farmers only after the navigation channel received its requisite flows. The deficiencies of the Pick Plan led Upper Missouri basin interests to oppose its congressional authorization. President of the Yellowstone Basin Association, H. W. Bunston of Hardin, Montana, urged his representatives to prevent the congressional passage of the Pick Plan, stating, "Protect us gentlemen, in our right to the first use of our water to the extent of our needs."[7]

The upper basin, led by O'Mahoney, requested that the Bureau of Reclamation (charged by Congress with the irrigation and hydropower development in the semiarid and arid West) submit its own plan for the systematic development of the Missouri River basin. Reclamation engineers had been working on a development plan for the river since 1939. Glenn Sloan, a mild-mannered, rather austere, and taciturn engineer located at the bureau's Billings Field Office, supervised the writing of the bureau's plan for the Missouri. Sloan was everything Lewis Pick was not. Quiet, thin, and meticulously dressed, Sloan was a technocrat par excellence. He saw himself as apolitical. He also sought to devise an efficient, cost-effective, socially acceptable hydraulic system for the Missouri basin that stood beyond politics, one based on objective science and mathematics, not subjective politics. Sloan believed fervently that the Missouri's best purpose would be to provide irrigation water to the rural, agricultural states of the northern plains. He did not believe these states should be made subservient to the lower basin. Rather, he wanted them to build their own agricultural paradise out of the grassland. He considered the navigation channel taking shape south of Sioux City the height of folly. To let the Missouri flow south and east to maintain a barge channel represented an utter waste of a vital resource, the squandering of dollars, and the loss of future economic potential. Not surprisingly, Sloan did not particularly care for the sometimes disheveled Pick, who could be overbearing and occasionally cocky. Pick played the part of a politician as much as an engineer, and these traits did not endear him to Sloan. Even more annoying to Sloan, Pick brazenly, and with blind faith, promoted his own development plan for the Missouri basin.

Sloan kept his political views largely to himself, but he questioned the feasibility of Pick's proposal based on its engineering principles. Sloan believed the Pick Plan to be bloated with unnecessary projects. He considered the proposed dam at the Lower Cañon site to be one of the wasteful projects included in the plan. Sloan read the 308 report on the Yellowstone and agreed with its conclusions with regard to the Lower Cañon site: a dam there would not be cost-effective under any future scenario—politically expedient but not cost-effective. Sloan argued that Montana did not need a dam at Allenspur, especially one of such limited value and effect.

When Sloan submitted his plan to Congress on May 5, 1944, it did not include a dam at Lower Cañon. In fact, Sloan's plan did not have any dams across the main stem of the Yellowstone River. Instead, Sloan believed that gravity irrigation represented the best and most cost-effective present and future use of the Yellowstone River. More specifically, the Yellowstone River in its natural state would adequately meet the agricultural needs of Yellowstone Valley farmers far into the foreseeable future. Sloan did seek the construction of a dam in Bighorn Canyon across the Bighorn River near Fort C. F. Smith. Water from this dam's reservoir would be dumped on fields in the Lower Bighorn Valley, from Fort C. F. Smith to the Hardin area. But the biggest difference between Sloan's plan and Pick's related to the proposed damming of the Missouri main stem in the Dakotas and Montana.

Sloan's main-stem system included three big dams in South Dakota at Fort Randall, Big Bend, and Oahe. These three dams would provide flood control to the Lower Missouri Valley while holding back high spring and summer flows for late summer irrigation. Sloan knew that flood control had to be part and parcel of his plan if he was going to gain lower basin support for his proposals. Flood control signaled Sloan's concession to the Lower Missouri Valley states. What he did not anticipate was the extreme commitment the Lower Valley states maintained in the navigation channel. His plan disregarded navigation's role in the Missouri basin (as evident in the absence in his plan of a reregulating dam for navigation releases southeast of Fort Randall). That omission eventually cost Sloan his dream.

The most important aspect of Sloan's plan related to irrigation. His dams would provide millions of acre-feet of water to irrigate land in North and South Dakota, especially in the James River Valley of eastern South Dakota. He also wanted to change the primary purpose of Fort Peck Dam and Reservoir from supporting navigation to providing irrigation water. Sloan believed flood control and irrigation compatible uses of the Missouri River. Sloan's dams would impound the Missouri's annual rises, preventing Lower Missouri Valley damages. In July, August, and September of each year, those same flood flows would be pulled out of the reservoirs to irrigate parched lands throughout Montana and North and South Dakota.

Sloan did not believe the federal government could develop the Missouri for both navigation and irrigation; each of those uses canceled out the other. Missouri basin residents could not have irrigation unless they abandoned the navigation channel. Drawing down the reservoirs to feed water into the nine-foot navigation channel would not leave any water in the reservoirs for irrigation. Thus, Sloan's plan did not propose reservoir storage space for downstream navigation. Sloan would abandon the navigation project, or supply it with water after irrigation needs had been met. Sloan's exclusion of navigation posed a real threat to the viability of the corps' lower river barge channel. Having invested nearly $250 million in a rarely navigated barge channel by 1943, Sloan's proposals meant that that quarter-billion-dollar investment would be thrown away and written off as a testament to bad engineering and hubris. The Corps of Engineers had faced many challenges to its Missouri River navigation channel in the past, and its officials, including Pick, were not about to let Sloan's plan derail their dream of building a barge channel from the mouth to Sioux City. Lower basin interests, such as the Kansas City Chamber of Commerce and Kansas City mayor John B. Gage, determined not to let Sloan succeed in killing the barge channel. Too much had been spent along the Lower Missouri to date on thousands of pile dikes and revetments and on the monstrous clay dam at Fort Peck to allow Sloan and the politically weak upper basin states to get their way. Lower basin interests worked hard to turn Sloan's challenge back on its heels.

Sloan's plan contained two aspects that related to the Yellowstone. First, Sloan's Oahe Dam (located six miles north of the South Dakota state capital at Pierre) would serve the same purpose as Pick's Garrison Dam, namely, it would capture and dissipate the Yellowstone River's June rise. The other important proposal made by Sloan related to the construction of a dam across the Missouri main stem at Canyon Ferry. Canyon Ferry lay inside a deep gorge along the Missouri seventeen miles northeast of the Montana state capital at Helena. Sloan saw his tentative Canyon Ferry Dam as a hydroelectric and irrigation bonanza, producing upwards of fifty thousand kilowatts and irrigating over 150,000 acres. A new Canyon Ferry Dam (an older, smaller structure already existed just upstream from the proposed Bureau of Reclamation dam site), besides being cost-effective, would be Sloan's means of gaining Montana support for his plan for Missouri basin development rather than have the state sidle up to Pick's plan (fig. 9.1).

The submission of the Sloan Plan to Congress set off a period of intense political haggling between the Upper Missouri basin states of Wyoming, Montana, and North Dakota and the Lower Missouri basin states of Nebraska, Iowa, Kansas, and Missouri. South Dakota representatives, including Governor Sharpe, decided to align the state's interests with the lower basin and the Corps of Engineers, a choice that still haunts South Dakota. Additionally, the two plans precipitated an intrastate political feud between interests in western and eastern Montana.

Predictably, Helena, Butte, and Missoula came down in favor of the Sloan Plan and the construction of Canyon Ferry Dam. The electricity and water produced by Canyon Ferry would benefit western Montana. Power lines from Canyon Ferry would first reach Helena (the closest city to the dam site) and then likely reach to Butte and Anaconda, with the extensive mining districts there. Any remaining power could conceivably be sold to the

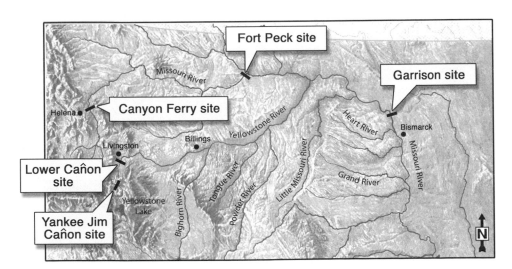

Figure 9.1. Dam sites across the Upper Missouri and Yellowstone main stems. (Paul Davidson, South Plains College, Levelland, Texas)

residents of western Montana, including the anticapitalist leftists, anar-
chists, and communists residing in Missoula. Opposing Helena and the pro–
Canyon Ferry state government were the residents of Livingston and
Billings, who favored the Pick Plan and its Lower Cañon Dam. Lower Cañon
Dam would provide thousands of jobs to the residents of the Yellowstone Valley from Livingston to Billings, spur business in Livingston and Billings, and
possibly open new lands to irrigation in the Livingston area.

In the fall of 1944, the Corps of Engineers and the Bureau of Reclamation joined to present a unified development plan to Congress. At the urging
of the Bureau of Reclamation and its Montana supporters, especially real
estate, banking, and governmental interests in western Montana, Canyon
Ferry Dam found its way into the discussions and negotiations surrounding
the merging of the two plans. The state of Montana and city of Helena
wanted Canyon Ferry rather than Lower Cañon because of its apparent cost-
effectiveness and its proximity to the capital city. In late 1944, when the
Pick-Sloan Plan came into being in the committee rooms of Congress, it included a proposal to build Canyon Ferry Dam. The politicians and engineers
erased Lower Cañon Dam from existence. The Yellowstone would not be
dammed at Allenspur.

Why did the Canyon Ferry Dam and not the Lower Cañon Dam find its
way into the pages of the Pick-Sloan Plan? First and foremost, Canyon Ferry
Dam gained a powerful following within Montana's political and economic
hierarchy. Helena's astute power brokers and the governor and senators of
the state favored Canyon Ferry over Lower Cañon. With that kind of backing, the tentative dam went ahead. Lower Cañon Dam never attracted such
a group of enthusiasts. Interestingly enough, Lower Cañon Dam found few
proponents outside of the Livingston area.

To build a big federal dam anywhere in the West, dam boosters needed
both demographic and geographic support for the project. In other words, a
significant segment of the population had to want the dam. Just as important, the dam had to possess popular appeal over a wide-ranging piece of
territory so that future benefits (either water, electricity, or flood control)
could be spread around the countryside. Canyon Ferry Dam met these two
criteria, whereas Lower Cañon Dam did not. As a matter of fact, even in
Livingston, where the dam would be built, residents split on the issue. Conservationists, concerned about the Yellowstone trout fishery, opposed the
dam, while farmers and business owners wanted the earthen barrier.

Canyon Ferry Dam would extend its benefits throughout western Montana and to a number of interest groups. Mining, rural, and urban interests would benefit from the dam. Meanwhile, the benefits of Lower Cañon would be limited to Livingston and its immediate environs and would consist of irrigation water and hydropower for a market already well supplied with both commodities. Federal engineers concluded that any power lines built from Lower Cañon Dam could not be erected cost-effectively more than a few miles from the dam. No market existed in that area of the state to consume the hydropower or justify the expense of the power lines. Livingston would be the only market for the dam's power, and it did not have enough industry or housing to burn all the energy running from Lower Cañon's turbines. On the other hand, a large, ready market existed in western Montana for Canyon Ferry hydroelectricity. Helena, Butte, and the lumber district of western Montana could consume cheap energy at a vociferous rate. In a nutshell, more people would prosper from Canyon Ferry than from Lower Cañon.

The death knell for Lower Cañon Dam came when the federal government accountants crunched the numbers and arrived at the end of the long, arduous, and subjective cost-to-benefit analysis. According to Bureau of Reclamation estimates, the dam at Canyon Ferry possessed a favorable cost-to-benefit ratio; that meant that for every dollar spent on the dam, more money would be returned in benefits to the public. The dam would be a money-maker. Lower Cañon did not have a favorable cost-to-benefit ratio. It was just not economically justifiable, and it became politically unjustifiable after October 1944.

By that late date, Montana's government elites swung behind Canyon Ferry Dam. They also let it be known that Canyon Ferry Dam would be the price the Lower basin and the Corps of Engineers would have to pay to get Montana's support for the comprehensive development of the Missouri basin. If the corps wanted to dam the Missouri at five places in the Dakotas and use the stored water to float one or two barges each year, fine, but Montana would support the harebrained scheme only if the federal government built Canyon Ferry Dam. Once Canyon Ferry Dam went on-line, the lower basin and the Corps of Engineers could do whatever they wanted with the remainder of the Missouri River. And so it happened that Canyon Ferry Dam wiggled its way into the pages of the Pick-Sloan Plan.

A war-weary and obviously declining Franklin D. Roosevelt signed into law the Pick-Sloan Plan for Missouri Basin Development on December 22, 1944. The plan authorized federal dams across the Missouri main stem at Canyon Ferry, Garrison, Oahe, Big Bend, Fort Randall, and Gavin's Point.

The legislation did not authorize any dams across the Yellowstone main stem. The Pick-Sloan Plan represented a victory for the Corps of Engineers and the Lower Missouri basin. The Missouri River main-stem dams in the Dakotas would be controlled by the corps and operated for downstream navigation and flood control—not irrigation. Canyon Ferry Dam, a minor structure in the much larger Missouri River hydraulic system, would be under Bureau of Reclamation control and managed for hydroelectricity and irrigation (fig. 9.2).

Amazingly, the Pick-Sloan Plan, which authorized 137 dams and reservoirs within the Upper Missouri basin, did not dramatically alter the Yellowstone's hydraulic regime, at least not until Yellowtail Dam went on-line across the Bighorn in 1966.[8] The Missouri, under the Pick-Sloan legislation,

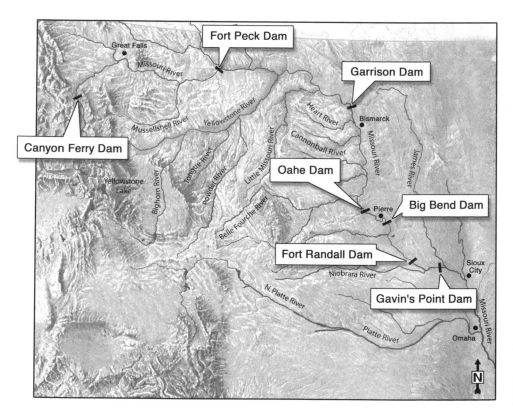

Figure 9.2. The Pick-Sloan dams built across the Missouri main stem. Although the Corps of Engineers completed Fort Peck Dam in 1940, Congress included its operation in the Pick-Sloan Plan. (Paul Davidson, South Plains College, Levelland, Texas)

would not be so lucky. The Missouri would be manipulated and dammed over and over again. Canyon Ferry Dam eventually rose over the Missouri, while Lower Cañon Dam lingered as a pipe dream of Livingston businessmen. Garrison Dam would block the Missouri at the Great Bend, while the Lower Yellowstone River would never see a flood control structure astride its path. Federal engineers sacrificed the wandering Missouri in the name of economic progress. Dam and reservoir construction represented one more step in erecting a Euro-American agricultural, urban, and industrial world across the Upper Missouri. Yet the federal engineers allowed the Yellowstone to escape their grasp. Actually, the Yellowstone simply glided past their lustful eyes.

It was not luck or fate that kept dams off the Yellowstone main stem in the 1940s and 1950s, during the peak years of America's obsession with big dams. Rather, the Yellowstone River in its natural state (with its unique hydrologic characteristics, especially its excessively steep slope and high banks) met the needs of irrigationists with gravity irrigation. Farmers in the Yellowstone Valley could not fathom any need for a gigantic dam across the Yellowstone. In addition, the Yellowstone River lacked good, cost-effective dam sites. Ultimately though, it was the Yellowstone's anomalous hydrologic regime that kept the earthen dams off its back. The river's high flows arrive in July, when farmers begin to demand copious amounts of water for their irrigated fields, its high banks limit the severity and areal extent of floods, and its steep slope delivers water through gravity irrigation systems, which means there is no need for high dams and high reservoirs across the Yellowstone to deliver water to dry land. That the Corps of Engineers and the Bureau of Reclamation did not plant a big, fat earthen dam atop the Yellowstone River as part of the Pick-Sloan Plan illustrates how politics, hydrology, and geography interacted to keep the Yellowstone dam-free—it remains the longest, largest unregulated river in the lower forty-eight contiguous states. In contrast, the Missouri River became one of the most heavily engineered rivers in the world.

A private company, Canyon Constructors, under hire by the Bureau of Reclamation, inaugurated construction of Canyon Ferry Dam on May 28, 1949. After five years of labor, a solid block of reinforced concrete, 225 feet high, 1,000 feet long, and containing 349,500 cubic yards of cement, crossed the Missouri River. Canyon Ferry Dam rolled the Missouri back on itself in successive layers until a dead-flat reservoir fell down behind the dam. Canyon Ferry reservoir obliterated twenty-five miles of the far Upper Missouri

Valley; it calmed splashing rapids, riffles, and fast water, turned valley walls to mud, and left a white film on rouge rocks. But Canyon Ferry Dam and the alpine lake to its rear did not compare in size or effect to the pyramidal dams thrown athwart the Missouri main stem in North and South Dakota. Those structures subsumed a primeval world.

The Corps of Engineers commenced construction of Fort Randall Dam on August 1, 1946, a year after the defeat of Japan, and at a time of certainty in the American way. The engineers did preparatory work on Garrison in 1946 and began actual construction in 1947. It took the world's largest engineering organization and national economic powerhouse six years to pen the Missouri behind Fort Randall Dam. In July 1952, only months after a superflood darted around the construction site, the army closed Fort Randall's ponderous steel gates. The rising reservoir obliterated the remnants of the old ecological order. Evidence of the change appeared on the surface of Fort Randall Reservoir (later named Lake Francis Case), where wreckage floated downstream and lodged against the dam's embankment. Logs, branches, and organic flotsam clogged the entrance to Fort Randall's outlet tunnels. The Missouri River surrendered and threw up wooden flags to signal defeat. Between the fall of 1952 and the summer of 1954, Lake Francis Case slid northward, its waters sluicing atop 140 miles of river valley. Everything withdrew before the advancing wetness; valley residents recalled seeing scores of ring-necked pheasants, mule deer, and coyotes dashing out of the bottoms, seeking relief on the stingy uplands. Much of the wildlife driven from the valley perished during successive winters. Lack of food and cover, along with exposure to winds, cold, and predation, took a huge toll on creatures. Hundreds of Sioux Indians on the Lower Brule and Crow Creek Reservation also left the Missouri Valley. By the fall of 1954, darkness hid American Island and the once-bountiful bottoms at the mouth of the White River and at Oacoma. In their place stood stark, lifeless, tree trunks.

After 1954, the inundation of the Upper Missouri continued unabated. What happened inside Fort Randall Dam's reservoir area occurred four more times in the next twelve years. The army shut the gates down on the Missouri at Garrison in 1953, Gavin's Point in 1955, Oahe in 1958, and Big Bend in 1963. By 1964, the Corps of Engineers had inundated 680 miles of the Upper Missouri Valley between Yankton, South Dakota, and the Yellowstone River's mouth. By the late twentieth century, the Upper Missouri contained only 10 percent of its former timbered bottomlands. The rest went to reservoirs, real estate developments, or channelization projects. The bison world lost its ecological center, and the Upper Missouri's Indian inhabitants (including many Teton Sioux) forfeited their geographic core.

From the 1850s until the 1880s, federal authorities created Indian reservations along the Missouri main stem. The Winnebago, Omaha, Ponca, Santee, Yankton, Rosebud, Crow Creek, Lower Brule, Cheyenne River Sioux, Standing Rock, and Fort Berthold Reservations sat adjacent to the Missouri (fig. 9.3). Several of these reservations enclosed those once-wealthy Missouri River bottoms. The displaced Winnebago, along with longtime valley

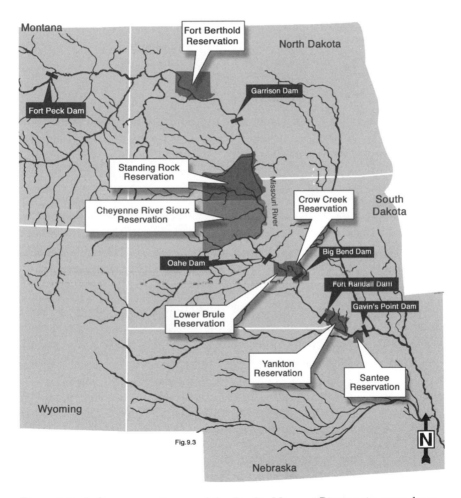

Figure 9.3. Indian reservations and the Big Six Missouri River main-stem dams. Indian peoples forfeited hundreds of thousands of acres of land to provide storage space for the Pick-Sloan Plan reservoirs. (Paul Davidson, South Plains College, Levelland, Texas)

residents the Omaha, held land at the head of the Sixty-Mile Bottom. Ponca Indians had a reservation at the Niobrara-Missouri confluence. At various times, reservation boundaries encircled the White River, Oacoma, Big Bend, and Cannonball River bottoms. At the end of the Indian wars, government troops forced Teton Sioux bands to the Rosebud, Lower Brule, Cheyenne River Sioux, and Standing Rock Reservations. In addition, many Oglalas settled on the Pine Ridge Reservation at the head of the White River. The Arikara, Mandan, and Hidatsa lost their bottomlands from the Cannonball to the Knife to Euro-Americans who erected Bismarck in the center of that zone. The Fort Berthold Reservation contained no large bottom, but its fertile valley lands still allowed for agricultural production. Although by the 1880s the Missouri River bottoms no longer held the bison or other large ungulates they once did, the government still planned on using the oases for other purposes.

The federal government wanted the tribes next to the Missouri River for a host of reasons. Along the Missouri, Bureau of Indian Affairs officials and the U.S. Army could keep a close eye on the tribes. General W. S. Harney admitted as much during a speech he gave to Sioux leaders in early March 1856 at Fort Pierre: "I would like to see all the bands of the Missouri have their villages on the river, with big fields of corn, where they can live and be happy; and those on the Platte can do the same there. We can then keep them." He continued, "If his people [Smutty Bear's band of Yankton Sioux] will make a settlement where we can get at them, I will have the ground ploughed, and do all that I can in that way for them. That's all I can do, as long as they behave themselves as they ought to do. . . . perhaps his [Smutty Bear's] children's children may be like the whites; and I want him to commence [with agriculture], that they may have our habits, &c." A German observer of the American scene in the early 1850s gave another reason why the Indians needed to settle down next to the Missouri: "Baptizing savages and roving hunters does not make them Christians; loyalty to the soil forms the foundation on which Christian communities rest, just as, generally speaking, the peasantry forms the core of organized states. . . . Hunters with no fixed abode are not for a moment bound by sentiments of loyalty to any land or by attachment to the soil or to human associations."[9] Such a policy, according to Harney, "will very much simplify our relations with these Indians, and at the same time render our control over them more effectual."[10] Harney and other government officials, besides wanting to restrain the Indians, wanted to make the nomads sedentary agriculturalists. The Missouri River navigation route and the fertile valley lands would contribute to those federal objectives.

Control over the Indians came upstream aboard steamboats. The Missouri River enabled the federal government to project its power into the Upper Missouri territory and thereby check the autonomy of the Indian peoples there. Additionally, the river route allowed the government to supply the tribes with annuities, which became increasingly important to the tribes after the 1850s and the precipitous decline of the bison herds. American policy makers also understood that the Missouri River had been, and would remain, crucial to Indian life in the region. The Indians needed the resources of the river valley, especially the valley's timber, water, and grass, to survive as cattle ranchers and farmers.

The Missouri Valley and the diminished mammalian life still attracted to it maintained a semblance of Indian culture in the Dakotas after the commencement of the reservation era. The Missouri River trench kept alive many traditional cultural attributes during the succeeding decades of federal assimilation programs. River valley lands placed perceptual and physical distance between Indian culture and Euro-American culture. The Missouri River enhanced Indian independence. The Bureau of Indian Affairs admitted that fact in the late 1940s and early 1950s; its officials recognized that the Missouri Valley bottoms allowed the Indians to pursue aspects of their old, traditional lifestyle and resist integration into the Euro-American cash economy and mass culture. Free produce from the valley enabled the Indians to hold on to a level of self-sufficiency. Self-sufficiency equaled influence, and that influence translated into resistance to federal dictates. The Missouri River Valley perpetuated an ancient reality into the atomic age. That the river valley was of key import to Indian culture cannot be denied. A Bureau of Indian Affairs report from 1954 proclaimed, "Certain desirable conditions in the [reservoir] taking areas which cannot be fully duplicated in the new areas [on the uplands] involve intangible losses. The pleasant living environment afforded by the wooded protected valleys, the good quality water from some springs and wells, the abundance of game and wild products, the recreational values of the streams and wooded areas, the association with old friends and neighbors, and the attachment which people have to their home locality, are things that cannot be fully replaced."[11]

An even more convincing indication of how important the river valley was to the reservation Indians of the Dakotas, and to their cultural integrity, became evident by the middle twentieth century in Indian landownership patterns. After decades of federal, state, and private efforts to divest them of their autonomy and land, and despite incredible environmental, social, political, and economic pressures, the Indians held firmly to the lands in the Missouri Valley. This not only is a testament to Indian cultural tenacity in the face of Euro-American subversion but also points to how they valued those lowlands and used that territory to sustain their culture.

A map of the Crow Creek and Lower Brule landownership in 1954 (prior to the inundations induced by Fort Randall and Big Bend Dams) illustrates that the Indians on these two reservations continued to hold most of the bottoms or valley lands on the reservations. In contrast, the members of those two reservations lost much of their less agriculturally viable or culturally valuable lands located at a distance from the river. The map is a checkered banner of Indian sovereignty and triumph, proclaiming both cultural continuity and cultural resistance. The Lower Brule and Crow Creek Indians did not remain on the uplands. In one sense, for the Indians to attempt to settle the uplands, as Euro-Americans had been trying since the 1860s, meant repudiating the Indian past. Indian peoples never lived on the uplands year-round. To settle up high would have gone against the grain of their history and their common sense. Ironically, the loss of those upland acres did not necessarily reflect Indian failure but Indian victory, or at least resilience. The fact that Indians abandoned those lands to the Euro-Americans could be viewed as an example of their unwillingness or inability to adopt an alien and ecologically impractical Euro-American land-use pattern. Ecology, history, economics, culture, and politics combined to move Indians down to the Missouri Valley by the middle twentieth century. What occurred on the Lower Brule and Crow Creek Reservations was repeated on the other Indian reservations of the Dakotas. The Lower Brule and Crow Creek example represented not an exception but the rule. On all the Missouri main-stem Indian reservations between the 1870s and the 1950s, Indian peoples lost their upland acres to Euro-Americans but continued to hold the lands down in the Missouri Valley.

The Indian peoples of the Upper Missouri did not go willingly onto the destitute uplands as their valley lands withered under the weight of army dams and reservoirs. Rather, they protested this most destructive of Euro-American intrusions on their world. The following comments by Jiggs Thompson, a member of the Lower Brule Tribe, testifies to the import of the valley lands to the Indian way of life and lends further credence to the argument that the Indians perceived the Missouri River as the center of their realm. Thompson made this statement after learning that the Corps of Engineers would go ahead with the construction of Big Bend Dam. That dam, he knew, would result in the inundation of all the remaining valley lands on the Lower Brule and Crow Creek Reservations. Thompson stated in February 1959, "We are opposed to the construction of Big Bend Dam. It is the wish of our people that no more land be taken from us. With us, the point is simple. When our land is gone, our way of life is gone, our tribes are destroyed. The bottom lands the Corps of Engineers want to take are the very best on the reservations. They are our heart lands. They can never be replaced. No similar lands are for sale. We depend on land for our livelihood, it furnishes us our income. To take our land is to take our homes and income, and a part of our history and heritage."[12] John Danks, a member of the Three Affiliated Tribes (Mandan, Hidatsa, and Arikara) on the Fort Berthold Reservation (which lost 152,000 lowland acres behind Garrison Dam), said something similar: "Before they flooded this area, the Fort Berthold people were pretty self-sufficient." He went on, "I find it truly unfortunate. . . . To me they just took the heartland of the reservation and one of the most fertile valleys of North Dakota and flooded it." By 1966, the Indians on the Yankton, Lower Brule, Crow Creek, Cheyenne River Sioux, Standing Rock, and Fort Berthold Reservations abandoned their valley lands to the Corps of Engineers. The Indians of the Upper Missouri River trench relinquished not just their valley lands but also a good portion of their geographic heritage and culture.

Glenn Sloan and Lewis Pick wanted empire for their respective institutions. Pick's empire would be based on navigation and flood control, and Sloan's would feed upon irrigation and hydroelectricity. Each man saw his form of empire as benevolent, efficient, and democratic for the Euro-American race and the Indians of the Upper Missouri. The Missouri main stem would be the workhorse of empire, harnessed by dams and roped to power lines and pipes. The river would pull the Corps of Engineers and/or the Bureau of Reclamation and the American nation toward greatness. Dams and reservoirs represented the culmination of the American dream. Hydropower, flood control, irrigation, and navigation would create an agricultural, industrial, and urban world of prosperity and happiness. But in order to make that world a reality, the army and reclamation engineers divorced water from life. They severed the Missouri River from the land at its edges and from the Indian cultures that relied on it. Federal engineers in the 1940s and 1950s did not see the Upper Missouri or Yellowstone basins as living systems, interconnected ecologies, or entities in their own right. They only considered rivers as multiple-purpose resources to be developed for abstractions such as irrigation, flood control, navigation, hydroelectricity, and/or recreation. Water would be dammed, channelized, and rerouted because it was seen only as water, not life. The perception of water as commodity made the water a commodity.

In the institutional struggle to dominate the Upper Missouri and establish a hydraulic empire there, the Corps of Engineers defeated the Bureau of Reclamation; army men succeeded in bending the Missouri to their imperial will, while the bureau was thrown the leftovers in the river's headwaters region. The bulk of the water passing through the Upper Missouri basin would be held, released, and directed to support a barge channel in the Lower Missouri Valley. The people of the Lower Missouri basin, as well as the Corps of Engineers, forced the Upper Missouri region to serve as a colonial appendage.

The World We Have Wrought

Current Ecological and Geographic Status of the Upper Missouri

The sun shines not on us, but in us. The rivers flow not past, but through us, thrilling, tingling, vibrating every fiber and cell of the substance of our bodies, making them glide and sing.

—John Muir

The ground cries out, I am Truth and Glory Is Here.

—Rumi

The geographic constructs lying atop the northern Great Plains and the region formerly known by its folk name, the Upper Missouri, are designed for extraction. The system of dams and reservoirs in the Dakotas and Montana is the clearest example of extractive geography. The Big Six main-stem reservoirs pour out their water into a navigation channel that does not serve upper basin interests. Meanwhile, the bulk of the water left in the reservoirs is there to serve a nonresident, tourist economy. Upper basin states have little influence over the management of the river. In the 1980s and 1990s, upper basin residents failed to hold water in the reservoirs or revise the *Missouri River Master Manual* (the document that stipulates the volume of reservoir releases and their schedule). Railroads, interstate highways, and the grid system of fences and fields interact with the Upper Missouri ecosystem in ways similar to dams and reservoirs. These constructs capture energy flowing through the system along ancient ley lines and redirect that energy outward. No doubt, a portion of the Upper Missouri's energy remains in place, cycled back into the system, but much of it is exported to eastern, western, or southeastern centers of power. The Upper Missouri bioregion is a plundered province.

Euro-Americans, since the Lewis and Clark expedition, strenuously labored to erect an extractive geographic system. They did so believing trade, agriculture, and urbanism would lead to prosperity and social stability. They wanted the American way. Hardworking farmers, laborers, miners, engineers, and ranchers continue to labor on, or within, extractive constructs, hoping to achieve those long-sought-after objectives. Yet at the beginning of the twenty-first century it is debatable whether the Euro-American geographic system will deliver prosperity or security. As a matter of fact, increasing instability is apparent throughout the Upper Missouri, especially since the onset of another severe drought at the end of the twentieth century. Rural flight (known as Dakotization), the near-complete depopulation of dozens of counties in the Dakotas and eastern Montana, the decline of the cattle industry, low crop prices, the rise of tourism, and the social disintegration associated with all these events plague the Upper Missouri country. A maladjustment to ecology explains the occurrence of these contemporary phenomena. That maladjustment is most conspicuous in the present geography, which is out of sync with the Upper Missouri's ecological and hydrologic rhythms (fig. 10.1). So long as Americans work, live, and play within the geography of extraction, that geography remains in place. On the other hand, cognizance of that geography enables humanity to reevaluate and question its role in perpetuating it. Why continue to maintain a geographic system of dams, reservoirs, fences, and roads that has led to such cultural, economic, and political poverty? Who do the colonists in the Upper Missouri serve by building walls?

The very first underpinnings of Euro-American geography across the Upper Missouri rested on the Missouri River as a navigation route and as a pathway to penetration, integration, and exploitation. In a major departure from previous Indian precedent, Euro-Americans created a Missouri River through-navigation route, running from St. Louis to the Yellowstone confluence and eventually to Fort Benton. There exists no evidence from the historic period that Indians utilized the Missouri River as a through-navigation route during their centuries-long occupancy of the Upper Missouri. Rather,

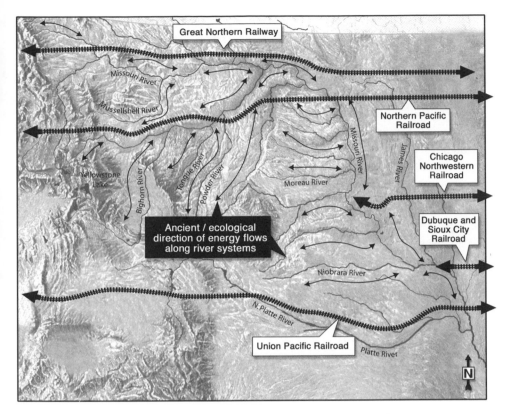

Figure 10.1. The Upper Missouri's energy flows are captured and sent over linear lines of transport to the east and west. (Paul Davidson, South Plains College, Levelland, Texas)

the Indians used the Missouri River trench as the core area of their nomadic or semisedentary lifeway. Bottoms held game, timber, and wintering sites. The Missouri Valley as a biological haven served Indian interests for a millennium and the Teton Sioux for a century. The differences in how Euro-Americans and Indians related to the Missouri Valley and the Upper Missouri became apparent in how the two people hunted for bison. Indians hunted for food, fiber, and trade, whereas Euro-Americans hunted bison largely for sport.

Euro-American and Indian geography joined in the Missouri River trench. The bison and Indian trail network touched the Missouri at particular junctures—at the mouths of the Upper Missouri's perennial tributaries. Euro-Americans established trading posts such as Fort Peck in the bottoms where the Indian trails crossed the Missouri. Traders built the fort on the north shore of the Missouri main stem opposite the mouth of the Big Dry and only a few miles west of the Milk River confluence. Fort Peck stood on the axis of the Big Dry–Milk River road. Trading posts tapped Indian geography and bison ecology and rerouted the energy flowing over those Indian and bison trails to the southeast, down the Missouri main stem. This redirection of bison and Indian energies in the form of beaver and later bison robes represented the first instance of Euro-Americans extracting the region's resources.

Euro-American culture in the Upper Missouri first arose along the Missouri River trench. Trading posts, military forts, Indian agencies, farmsteads, and towns rested in bountiful bottoms, intersecting Indian trails. Initially Euro-Americans modified Indian geography, bending it in their direction. But as whites increasingly occupied the land- and waterscape, they began to establish their own unique geography across the Upper Missouri.

Euro-Americans perceived the bison world to be wilderness, and the wilderness to be chaotic and destined for destruction. On the flip side, they saw their world as ordered, sensible, and representative of a new, rational, progressive age. Holding such views, whites, from the mountaineer to the missionary, worked to undermine one ordered system and replace it with one of their design. Yet in the process of deconstructing a world based on bison ecology, they contributed to chaos. Euro-American actions and cultural constructs, including the fur trade, its posts, steamboat traffic, and the market hunting of bison, precipitated a startling transformation of the Upper Missouri's ecology and geography.

The collapse of bison ecology in the Upper Missouri followed the path of the Euro-American advance rather than the route of Teton Sioux expansion. The bison range retreated to the north and northwest as a response to the increased white presence in the Missouri Valley and Upper Missouri country. Thus, the bison range shrank until by the 1870s it encompassed only the Lower Yellowstone basin and a portion of the far Upper Missouri basin. Then, in the 1880s, the bison world disappeared once market hunters and settlers took the bottoms along the Yellowstone River. Had the Teton Sioux been the primary culprits in the slaughter of the bison, the geography of that extermination would have been revealed differently across the land. The shrinkage of the bison range would have been from east to west, from Minnesota to Montana, rather than emanating outward from the Missouri Valley and the whites there. Indian hunting played a role in the decrease of the herds. Yet the historical geography of the Upper Missouri indicates that

Euro-Americans (through their activities and cultural constructs) in the Missouri and Yellowstone Valleys contributed more than any other factor to the destruction of the bison.

Oddly, the very ecological upheaval Euro-Americans set in motion reinforced white ideas of cultural and racial superiority in relation to Indian peoples. That sense of superiority further reinforced justifications for the integration of the Upper Missouri into the American sociopolitical order. For example, Indian warfare as a response to ecological change convinced many whites of the savagery of indigenous peoples. Consequently, such savages did not deserve to own or even occupy the Upper Missouri. But it remains to be seen whether Euro-America, after two hundred years of residency in the Upper Missouri, will establish a sustainable world across the region. Some of the Missouri River tribes appear to have accomplished that very difficult objective. The Mandan, who lived in the Upper Missouri since at least A.D. 900, found the proper balance between their own lifeway and the ecosystem. As a matter of fact, the semisedentary lifestyle of the Mandan and other tribes in the region may have fostered biological diversity rather than impinge upon it. The superabundance of life in the Upper Missouri at the time of the Lewis and Clark expedition attests to that possibility. Biological diversity in turn enabled the Indians to sustain their economy and social order for a thousand years. It appears that the Teton Sioux attempted to accomplish a sustainable economy by establishing a monopoly over the bison herds, but they achieved that objective too late to provide a clear understanding of that economy's workings. Today, Euro-American geography is far from secure. Ecology is mercurial, sometimes violently reminding humanity that the universe does not exist for human purposes.

Obviously, the Upper Missouri's contemporary geography reflects the Euro-American annexation of the region, its biggest river, and its indigenes. Conversely, that geography is a physical representation of Indian subservience to the dominant culture. Indian geography, with its reliance on bison roads, river valleys, and timbered bottoms, along with its absence of firm political boundaries, was supplanted by a geography of railroads, reservations, fences, roads, towns, cities, dams, and oceanic reservoirs. For all intents and purposes, the construction of the geography of extraction came to an end in the 1960s, by which time the large reservoirs across the Missouri main stem filled with water, drowning the final remnants of the old order. By 1964, an imperial geography sat firmly atop the Upper Missouri, and its heavy fingers squeezed the life out of the region's land, water, and human occupants.

Those six earthen dams bestride the Upper Missouri main stem speak volumes about Euro-America—its values, its dreams, and its relationship to the Missouri River and nature at large. To a significant segment of the American populace, the main-stem dams built between 1933 and 1966 symbolize the perceived control by Euro-America (its institutions, beliefs, and technologies) over the Missouri. According to this perception, white America took this formerly useless river and remade it into a tool of Western civilization. For some, the size and sophistication of the dams, especially the enormous Garrison and Oahe Dams, instill a sense of pride, awe, and patriotism. People might look at these structures and recognize the supposed power of the state and culture that constructed them. Dams purportedly proclaim American supremacy over nature.

Dams can be interpreted as something different. They represent imperialism, hierarchy, and political centralization. Dams also remind people of the Euro-American attempt at self-control. The structures are physical representations of an inner, psychological conflict, a war to manipulate humanity for purely industrial, agricultural, or consumptive ends. If nature is a looking glass into the human mind, dams are the tools humans deployed to repress and reroute nomadic and mysterious propensities.

Euro-Americans, like other peoples at other times and in different places, displayed a will to power in their relationship to the Upper Missouri river and region. That will to power manifested itself in the Euro-American attempt to control all facets of the Upper Missouri basin environment to serve human ends. Euro-Americans long viewed the relationship between themselves and the Upper Missouri in a hierarchical fashion, with themselves on top and the river supine at their feet. This perception has been and remains delusional. Euro-Americans never once controlled the Upper Missouri. Even today, after the placement of the big dams across the Upper Missouri and eighty-three hundred wing dams and revetments (what the Corps of Engineers refers to as "control" structures) along a portion of the Upper Missouri and the entire length of the Lower Missouri, the Corps of Engineers and its backers still do not have the river under wraps. It has not been "tamed," as the engineers are so ready to claim.

The Upper Missouri is not submissive. Humanity cannot do with it what it wills. For every human action within the ecosystem, there is a response. When humanity built dams and channelization structures, the system bounced back with the 1993 superflood. The more force humanity applies within the Upper Missouri, the greater the response it can expect. The

Upper Missouri challenges its current residents to learn how to interact with the system without causing or exacerbating ecological oscillations.

A large percentage of the Euro-American public, the Corps of Engineers, and the federal government undertook the monumental engineering projects of the twentieth century to reengineer the Missouri River for an array of social, economic, and political objectives. The army engineers and their civilian cronies, especially the wealthy business elite of Kansas City, remade the river to serve agriculture, industry, urbanism, and consumerism. Billions of dollars and millions of labor hours were spent, and thousands of men and some women shed blood, sweat, and tears to domesticate the river for those ends. Yet, ironically, by attempting to tie the river down behind dams and riprap, humans shackled themselves. Every person engaged in the construction projects, those persons presently involved with the management of the completed projects, and all those who continue to prop up the system of dams and channelization structures served, and continue to serve, the same objectives relegated to the Missouri. By keeping the river dammed, channelized, and directed toward industrial, urban, and consumptive ends, humanity keeps itself dammed, channelized, and directed toward those same purposes.

The engineering projects simultaneously limited both humanity's and the river's creative potential. The Missouri once was, and could be again, far more than energy for agriculture, industry, urbanism, and consumerism. The Missouri and humanity—both creative forces on a grand scale—are waiting to be released onto the land. When humans remove the dams and riprap and allow the Missouri to flow through numerous channels, they will remove the blocks to their own creativity, spontaneity, and freedom. When humans let the river go, they let themselves go. Humans will no longer be imprisoned within a grid system and industrial matrix, automatons preprogrammed to produce and consume. A freer river equals a freer humanity.

In the nineteenth century, prior to the arrival of the railroad in the Missouri Valley, and still decades before the channelization and damming of the stream by the Corps of Engineers, the Missouri served a multitude of purposes. The majestic Missouri provided humanity with everything from drinking water to ice, slough grass to cottonwood timber, daubing clay to shingles, and a navigation route for pirogues, canoes, keels, and steamboats. That previous multiple-purpose river provided such a vast assemblage of resources because it flowed, flooded, and wandered in, around, and over its valley. Free-flowing water connected the Missouri proper with its floodplain and the land on all sides. That nomadic water also connected the river to the life that flourished from riverbed to valley floor to the unfolding plains above. Missouri River water reached outward, touching the land with nourishment.

Since the nineteenth century, Euro-Americans have separated the Missouri main stem from its watershed. As mentioned earlier, whites saw the Missouri first and foremost as a navigation route, water not as life force but as inanimate object to carry commodities and people. Euro-America separated the Missouri from the Upper Missouri territory, first perceptually and later physically. Viewing the river as merely a route to riches and empire and the means of dominating peoples and places, Euro-Americans vastly simplified the Missouri and ignored its fantastic complexity. In perceiving the river in one-dimensional terms, Euro-Americans began the actual physical simplification of the Upper Missouri. Throughout the late nineteenth and twentieth centuries, Euro-Americans made the river into what they had always perceived it to be, nothing more than water to carry passengers and cargo. Euro-America rent the Missouri from its floodplain. The riprap and wing dams south of Sioux City placed a rock barrier between the river and its valley, while the dams in the Dakotas and Montana curtailed the lower river's ability to flood and pour over into its lowlands each spring and summer. Those same dams drowned the Upper Missouri Valley, making it impossible for terrestrial species to reside in the river's trench. The Pick-Sloan dams completed Euro-America's effort at disconnecting the river from its land area and divorcing it from the biotic community. Wing dams and earthen dams and reservoirs keep life away from the valley. All the quarried rock across or along the Missouri acts as a barrier to interaction, connection, ecological intimacy, creativity, and human spirituality. Spirituality is achieved through connection and community, not disconnection.

The engineers and their backers so completely remade the Missouri, and human perception of it, that few individuals in the twenty-first century perceive the river as anything other than water: water to control, drink out of a faucet, cool machinery, moisten crops, power vacuums, and float barges. But the separation of the river from the land and biotic community is a reminder that the Corps of Engineers also separated people from the river. The river represented something to be partitioned, fought over, apportioned, and managed. Americans also found it difficult to link the river with their own lives. By 2003, the human perceptual and physical distance from the Missouri had never been greater. Americans can reestablish their bonds to the Missouri, and succeed in mystifying the river, when they decide to let it flow. Until that is done, interest groups will continue to fight over the Missouri's water as an object with no more significance than how it can be used for greater production and consumption—the Missouri River will continue to be water as commodity.

From the later nineteenth century through the twentieth century, the dominant social discourse argued that dams, reservoirs, and channelization structures would contribute to society's material prosperity. A dammed and channelized Missouri would lift the people of the northern Great Plains, Midwest, and Missouri Valley out of the Great Depression, prevent a post–World War II economic downturn, and halt the effects of drought and flood on the Missouri basin's economy. A regulated Missouri would even out the perturbations in the Upper Missouri system. The river's energies would turn turbines and machines and carry barges, thereby contributing to material prosperity. The reengineered river would enrich the United States, making food, fiber, and manufactured products cheaper and readily available to all. According to this frame of reference, the remade Missouri would put more money into the wallets or purses of the American citizenry. Those dollars, yanked out of the bowels of the Missouri, would engender a higher degree of individual mobility, material comfort, and individual influence within the American sociopolitical order.

Yet the engineering projects have not led to greater freedom or influence for the majority of the residents of the Missouri Valley, especially in the Dakotas or Montana. Euro-Americans have long associated freedom with cash. More cash means more freedom. But cash only ties the Upper Missouri's people closer to the established sociopolitical order. Cash, as well as the desire to spend it, save it, or make more of it, aligns Upper Missourians with a hierarchical, exploitative system. During the construction of the Missouri River dams, federal officials understood the ties between cash and the dominant order. One of the primary reasons the Corps of Engineers and the Bureau of Indian Affairs worked so diligently to inundate Indian lands along the Missouri Valley in the 1950s and 1960s was that these two government entities wanted to destroy the last vestiges of Indian self-sufficiency and autonomy. The army and the Bureau of Indian Affairs admitted that the undammed Upper Missouri, with its "free produce" (natural products such as fish, berries, timber, and game), fostered traditionalism, regionalism, independence, and autonomy among the Indian tribes of the valley. Dam the river, flood the "free produce," and the Indians would lose their freedom and be forced into the cash economy dominated by Euro-Americans. More cash does not necessarily mean more freedom; independence and cash are in no way the same thing. A free-flowing river, with its "free produce," equals freedom—the federal government knew this fact in the 1940s, 1950s, and 1960s and still knows it today. This explains why the Corps of Engineers and its backers are so reluctant to let the river go. To let the reins fall from the shoulders of the Upper Missouri River means letting that same yoke fall from the backs of Upper Missouri residents, especially the colonists in the Dakotas and Montana.

There is no doubt that dam construction and channelization benefitted a few individuals and interest groups, particularly farmers in the valley south of Sioux City, real estate brokers, bankers, and the Corps of Engineers. The projects led to a concentration of political influence in the hands of the Corps of Engineers, a federal entity long interested in securing its own imperial domain. Removing the dams and channelization structures would mean the establishment of a locally based, nonimperial relationship with the river. Dam removal and channel restoration will take the Missouri out of the hands of its federal overseers. A free-flowing Missouri River would enhance democracy, regionalism, and economic autonomy; all valley residents would become less dependent on federal institutions and global, corporate-dominated markets. Additionally, Upper Missourians would once more enjoy the free produce offered up by the river, including timber, organic silt deposits to fertilize cropland, fish, and eventually bison and elk. Such native produce would decrease dependence on centralized political and economic institutions and foster the emergence of a bioregional economy and culture. People in northern Nebraska, western Iowa, South Dakota, North Dakota, and Montana would rightfully claim a past and an identity long dominated by the imperial United States and its mass, media-driven culture. Removing the dams and riprap is a major step toward rejecting the geography of extraction and establishing a new geography. It is also the first step in acknowledging the Upper Missouri as a distinct bioregion. Bioregionalism entails a rejection of mass culture, a redrawing of borders, and the organization of society along the contours of a watershed. River restoration and bioregionalism are the ultimate reassertion of localism and grassroots democracy.

Obviously, in some quarters, the breaching of the dams and the destruction of the pile dikes and revetments sound absolutely preposterous, outrageous, even sacrilegious. Such a proposition scares those who believe devoutly in the American dream of ever-rising levels of material abundance, gadgetry, and convenience. Breaching dams will throw us back into the

Stone Age, according to certain elements within society. An unimpeded Missouri River will flood farms, dislodge bridges, sink cities, and wash away our cherished civilization. This perspective holds that the river is a beast on a short, tenuous chain. The chain has only six links, each one an earthen dam across the main stem. Remove one link in the chain, or the chain altogether, and the beast will trounce upon society.

This view of the Missouri as a monster waiting to rampage, which is promoted by the established sociopolitical order and its elitist members, has its roots among the early nineteenth-century navigators of the stream. The Corps of Engineers, valley farmers, and property owners in the valley south of Yankton believe, or at least want everyone else to believe, in this tenet. These same interests continue to perpetuate the image of the Missouri as a mad dog on a rusty chain. Those who want the status quo often harken back to the Great Flood of 1952. According to their logic, the 1952 flood justified all ecologically harmful actions against the Missouri in the past five decades. Of course, the Missouri-as-beast analogy is a self-serving perception and a justification for the continued damming and channelization of the river.

Each of these elite interest groups extends support to the others. They are in alliance, working in concert to keep the river bound tightly behind dams and rock. Since 1952 and the closure of Fort Randall Dam, the army engineers have aggressively supported industrial, agricultural, and housing construction in the valley lowlands south of Yankton. Each expensive home built on the river's riprapped bank line, every road cut through valley alluvium, each factory constructed in a former timbered bottom, each coal-burning power plant on the river's edge, and every riverside city that leaves the bluffs and spills down into the valley represent a prop to the Corps of Engineers and its system of dams and channelization structures. The army engineers understand that the more construction that takes place in the valley, the less likely their dams will be removed in the future. Predictably, the Corps of Engineers, by encouraging construction in the river valley, is able to gain the allegiance of very influential groups, particularly bankers, energy companies, real estate brokers, politicians, and farmers. All these individuals and groups benefited from the dam and channelization projects. Farmers advanced their fields to the river's banks, industry and the power companies followed farmers down to the water, real estate brokers bought the valley lands cheap and sold them high, and all the while bankers fattened their wallets as valley development proceeded apace.

What exists today is a situation in which the Corps of Engineers is the bedfellow of society's most wealthy members. The real estate broker who sells sandlots at Dakota Dunes, South Dakota, for tens of thousands of dollars is also a strong supporter of keeping the Missouri River inside its riprapped banks. The farmer who plants, plows, and sprays his crops only inches from the Missouri River is an advocate for holding the Missouri back behind those dams. These interests do not want a free-flowing river. They make money from the damming and channelizing of the stream, and they use the river to remain on top of the socioeconomic hierarchy. These same interests denounce dam removal and changes in the flow regime. Their opposition is strong because they stand to lose the most. The middle and lower classes will gain from dam removal and a free-flowing Missouri, which will empower most and disempower few. This is why the big interests, the Corps of Engineers, Mid-American Energy, the Farm Bureau, and the barge industry all stand against dam removal and work furiously to keep the river dammed and channelized. They resist change because breaching dams means divesting them of the river's energies and the political influence that flows from water.

Establishing a sustainable economy across the Upper Missouri requires the reopening of ancient migratory routes through the removal of dams and reservoirs and the elimination or modification of other human constructs that block species migration, such as roads, towns, or cities in the Missouri Valley bottoms. Deconstruction of the geography of extraction is not designed to save one or two species. Rather, it will ensure the survival of a multitude of species, including *Homo sapiens*. As this book has repeatedly asserted, the Missouri River once pulsed with life; its main stem served as the heart of a vast region. Dams and reservoirs sharply curtailed its pulse (fig. 10.2). The species entourage of the northern plains and Midwest, including *Homo sapiens*, relied on the resources found in the Missouri River trench to survive and prosper. *Homo sapiens* lived adjacent to a free-flowing, wandering, and flooding Missouri for at least eleven thousand years, until the arrival of Euro-Americans. It is questionable, considering the current ecological condition of the Upper Missouri bioregion and Missouri River, whether humanity will sustain a presence there for another century, let alone a thousand years, and another eleven thousand years at current extractive levels appears absolutely preposterous. The environmental doubts surrounding Upper Missouri society and the uncertainties about its future sustainability will be partially alleviated through dam removal.

Breaching dams does not have to be as frightening or catastrophic as the dominant discourse portrays it. The dams cannot come down all at once;

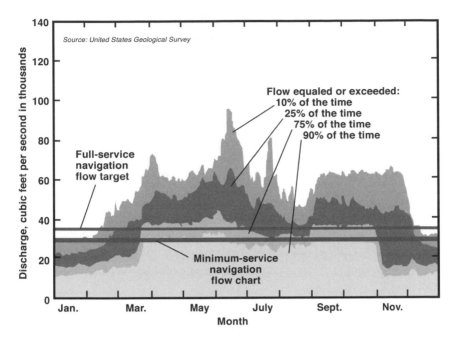

Figure 10.2. The Missouri River's pre- and post-dam hydrograph, which, like the one of the Yellowstone, illustrates how the Missouri rose in April and again in June, only to fall in August. The Missouri, in a manner similar to the Yellowstone, witnessed a rise later in the fall, before once more dropping to its lowest level in the winter months. The six main-stem dams built in the twentieth century eliminated the river's pulsation. The flatter lines across the hydrograph indicate severe ecological disturbance and the death of innumerable species that relied on fluctuating flow volumes to survive and thrive. (Courtesy of the United States Geological Survey)

that would be impractical and dangerous. Immediate and simultaneous re-moval of all six main-stem dams would result in deadly flooding in the valley south of Yankton and would also have disastrous consequences for the strug-gling species still found there. However, the dams can be breached in a se-quence that restores the Missouri and protects human life. Gavin's Point Dam at Yankton, South Dakota, which is the least useful structure of the Big Six across the main stem and is rapidly filling in with silt, should be removed first. Breach Gavin's Point Dam, and the nutrients, sediment, and sporadic flows from the Niobrara River (a stream largely left alone because of the na-ture of its watershed and the rugged terrain through which it flows) will enter the Lower Missouri and begin to resurrect its disappearing species. The dams at Fort Peck, Garrison, and Big Bend could also be removed with very little effect on flood heights in the lower valley. Big Bend Dam is a single-purpose structure. The Corps of Engineers did not even want it in the 1950s but nevertheless built it because of South Dakota's incessant lobbying efforts. Big Bend Dam provides hydropower to mostly off-reservation residents of the upper Midwest. Big Bend does not provide flood control to the Lower Missouri, nor aid the navigation channel, and it provides only a marginal amount of water for irrigation. As for the hydropower lost from the dam's decommissioning, Upper Missourians can build windmills and solar power units to meet local needs, and the urbanites who use most of the river's energy can do the same. The drained reservoir area behind the Big Bend Dam could be revived by introducing species from elsewhere and by inflows from the Bad River. Fort Peck Dam should also come down. The corps built it to offer work relief to the unemployed of eastern Montana during the Dirty Thirties and to deliver water to the navigation channel south of Sioux City. The depression era is long gone, and so is the usefulness of the barge channel. Remove Fort Peck, and restore the far Upper Missouri. Additionally, Garrison Dam should be bulldozed away. The lands under Lake Sakakawea will be restored by the creatures parading down the semiwild and still biologically diverse Yellowstone River. Both nature and humanity preserved the Yellowstone River and Yellowstone National Park from the dam builders. Now is the time to reap the ecological rewards of that preservation. The Yellowstone River can be far more than scenery or a recreational resource. The species found in Yellowstone National Park, if allowed, could move down the Yellowstone and jump-start the Missouri's ecology. The park could be the incubator, the Yellowstone River the line of transfusion, and the Missouri Valley the recipient. The Yellowstone River could once more serve as a key ecological corridor in the Upper Missouri bioregion.

Only Oahe and Fort Randall Dams need to stand into the foreseeable future. Both structures protect the lower valley from superfloods. However, once humanity pulls back from the Missouri River, those structures can be punctured full of holes. A moratorium on building in the Missouri Valley should be put in place immediately to stop expensive construction there. The present buildings would be allowed to remain until humans have evacuated the old floodplain. At that point, Oahe and then Fort Randall could be decomissioned. Fort Randall should be the last structure taken out of the Missouri because it takes four feet off any superflood south of Sioux City. It is the key dam in the entire Upper Missouri hydraulic system.

Coevolution is vital to life on this planet. If humanity arrests the evolution of other creatures, has it not then arrested its own evolution? *Homo sapiens* evolved within a biotic community. We cannot evolve outside of it. *Homo sapiens* came out of sand, savanna, gravel, free-flowing rivers, timber, prairies, bison, and mosquitoes. Can we evolve without those entities that originally gave our species life? Is it possible for us to break our connections to our evolutionary past and still survive? Is it admissible to radically alter the very environments and habitat that spawned us, shaped our minds, and sculpted our limbs? Will we meet the same fate as the pallid sturgeon, the least tern, the bison, the grizzly bear? To think we will not, to think we are savvy enough to avoid decline, is to perpetuate the myth of our separation from nature. Humans are as much a product of wild rivers and grasslands as the pallid sturgeon and the bison. Neither we nor they flourish in a dammed, fenced, flooded, bulldozed, planted, and paved ecosystem. To say we do not need the ancient Upper Missouri any longer is to reject our evolutionary past, to reject our earthly connections, and to utterly ignore from whence we came. Can we afford to go it alone?

Dam removal is only a first step in creating a sustainable, ecologically based, grassroots, democratic, anti-imperial bioregion in the territory once known as the Upper Missouri. The Upper Missouri was a bison world, and any future, sustainable socioeconomic order there must consider bison. The bison needs to be reintroduced all across the Upper Missouri, not just in several isolated and widely dispersed national parks or private enclaves. Many groups and individuals are working to restore the bison world and assemble the Big Open and the Buffalo Commons, including the Inter-Tribal Bison Cooperative, the Nature Conservancy, and billionaire Ted Turner. Free-flowing rivers are essential to bison reintroduction. Bison need to be reconnected to the Missouri and Yellowstone main stems. The reservoirs need to be drained, the fences taken down, city landscapes situated in the bottoms altered to accommodate large mammals, old migratory routes reopened, and the bison, bears, mountain lions, birds, and fish allowed to move once more between river and interior. Bison ought to become the American equivalent of India's sacred cow, allowed to roam unmolested over plain, across valley, and through urban areas that now sit atop the animal's former bottomland sanctuaries. After the animals reach maturity, humans could hunt some on a sustainable basis to meet human needs.

Additionally, we need to be willing to die by natural causes. Each human death is a tragedy, but it is also an ecological necessity. Society cannot re-

spond to every death by forest fire, flood, bear, or bison with massive retalia-
tion. Mutually Assured Destruction as a policy may have worked during the
cold war, but it is no way to relate to nature. Such a retaliatory approach
has only contributed to the further diminishment of species variety and
human quality of life. Every flood does not deserve a flood control structure,
and every bison that gores a person to death does not deserve to be shot
dead. In a wilder Upper Missouri, Grandpa may be swept up by a fast-
moving bison herd, little Johnny may go missing with the mountain lions,
and drunk Uncle Bubba may be mauled by a grizzly at the family barbecue.
We need to acknowledge those possibilities and take sound ecological steps
to prevent them; and if they happen, which they likely will, we need to accept them.

Reconnecting the Missouri River to its drainage basin and to bison and
other life-forms does not mean a complete abandonment of our cultural system, but it does mean learning for the first time how to live with a pulsating
Upper Missouri and its migrating fauna. We could learn much from the Indians of the bioregion, whose deep history there could teach us how to retain
villages and farms in the bottomlands alongside bison and a nomadic river.
Indian peoples could also teach us, through their oral histories, how they
established and maintained a sustainable bison population. We could recap-
ture the opportunities for cultural exchange lost since the Lewis and Clark
expedition. What is more, the experience of the Teton Sioux in the Yellowstone basin between the mid-1850s and mid-1870s can teach us about the
conservation of herd numbers.

To rename the region, its rivers, and its landmarks is another means of
rebuking imperial geography. Renaming is reclaiming. Through renaming we
begin to identify ourselves with the land and rivers, making the region and its
wonders our own, not something that belongs to Washington D.C., the Corps
of Engineers; or long-dead white conquerors. We can start by renaming the
Heart River in North Dakota its original Mandan name, the Natke Passaha,
which will be an admittance of the ecological integrity of Indian geography.
We can also refer to the region north and west of the Platte as the Upper
Missouri, instead of the northern plains, or as the separate states of Montana,
Wyoming, North Dakota, South Dakota, Nebraska, and Iowa. State boundaries trespass against ecological systems. The term "Upper Missouri" admits
a past ecological and geographic reality, while rejecting later imperial names
and political borders. The name also recognizes the connectedness between
river and land, river and ecology, and river and ancient geography. Because

personal names are a powerful method of connecting with the environment, we might also begin to name ourselves after one of the creatures that live in the Upper Missouri. With so many white people now living in the Upper Missouri, perhaps White Bull or White Bear could become popular names that would serve as constant reminders of humanity's links to the bioregion and the other members of the biotic community.

The modern geography of the Upper Missouri has a quality of rock-hard permanence. The limestone wing dams and revetments from Ponca, Nebraska, to the river's mouth do not appear to be going anywhere anytime soon. The dams across the main stem have life expectancies ranging from one hundred to nine hundred years. They appear as immovable, gigantic lumps of earth that proclaim the permanence of the Euro-American presence along the Missouri. The concrete roads, the steel rails, the Victorian-style brick homes in river towns from Omaha to Great Falls all exude an age-defying confidence in the future, a sense of security, a presence on the land that is irreversible. It is as if the size of the cultural constructs and the materials used in their construction (reinforced concrete, stone, and steel) represent an attempt on Euro-America's part to rid of any doubts it may have about the firmness of its hold upon the environment. Did Euro-Americans overcompensate for their fears by erecting excessively large structures upon the land and across the waterscape? Has the construction of a heavy steel and concrete geography atop the earth and its rivers calmed some of Euro-America's environmental fears, especially that deep-seated, biblical fear of the wilderness within and without? Contemporary geography proclaims the wish that wilderness never again break loose and bare its claws.

Imperial Euro-American geography has laid over the Upper Missouri a tightfisted grasp. It is as if modern geography, with its strands of roads and dams, placed a rope around the neck of the Upper Missouri and is attempting to turn the region and its watercourses into a beast of burden. It is no wonder that dam advocates in the 1940s and 1950s used the word "harness" to describe the human effort to capture the Missouri behind earthen barriers. "Harnessing the Big Muddy" was a popular phrase at the time. A harness implies that humanity intended on riding the Missouri like a plow horse into a future of agricultural and industrial prosperity. But by the early twenty-first century, Americans understand, especially after the superflood of 1993, that the Upper Missouri is a bucking bronco.

The Euro-American geography of extraction has had a tremendous influence on Euro-American thought and inaction. It has thoroughly convinced Euro-Americans of its permanence; it is a geography that is supposedly here to stay. That is the very perception the federal dam builders wanted to imbue in the American people and the United States' communist enemies abroad. Big dams were designed to quash domestic and foreign doubts about the strength and long-term durability of the American system. The perception of permanence is self-perpetuating. By believing in the irreversibility of contemporary geography, humanity does not act to deconstruct it. Instead, inaction is a tacit acceptance of it. All of us prop it up and reinforce it by continuing to travel, work, and live within its parameters. By continuing to reside within the grid system, we bolster the cage holding back the Upper Missouri and ourselves (fig. 10.3).

Everyone's daily actions within the grid system continue to draw energy from ecologically insensitive constructs, harming the bioregion and ultimately society. By believing in the permanence of roads, rails, cities, and big dams, Americans become participants in the geography of extraction. We uphold the established sociopolitical and geographic order.

Extractive geography has distanced us from the living systems that we draw upon to sustain our lives. Euro-American geography routes people away from ancient ley lines; distorting our view of ecological boundaries and blinding us to ecological processes. The separation from ecology is acute and constant—thanks to roads and rails that do not follow ecological or hydrologic contours. A person shooting west through North Dakota on Interstate 94 has a hard time seeing even a hint of the old bison geography from the comfort of his or her speeding car. The walleye fisher, in a sparkly blue bass boat on Lake Oahe, has no idea that he or she is fishing two hundred feet above a former timbered bottom. The passenger in a jet at thirty-five thousand feet is over six miles removed from the ground below. We are distant from ecology because our geography holds us back. That separation is present in every bioregion within the United States, and it is chronic in the Columbia, Snake, Colorado, and Rio Grande basins.

If we are going to restore the Upper Missouri and its ecological processes, foster a democratic polity, create a sustainable economy, and wed our destiny to that of the biotic community, we need to begin by stepping out of our cars and walking across the land. We need to get down inside a worn and weathered gully and envelop ourselves in the bison world of long ago. We literally need to get close to the land and water, step away from the concrete, get off the reservoirs, paddle a wild, undammed plains river, or hike an Indian trail. In those places and on those rivers, we will understand what needs to be done.

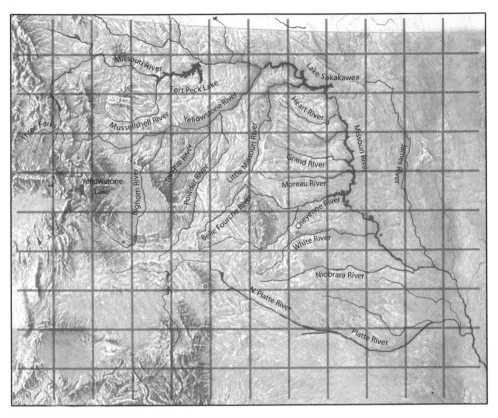

Figure 10.3. The grid system of roads, rails, dams, and fences. The Euro-American grid system places the Upper Missouri bioregion and its inhabitants (including *Homo sapiens*) inside a series of disjointed and isolated cages that impede human ecological awareness while also diminishing the creative capacity of the biotic community. (Paul Davidson, South Plains College, Levelland, Texas)

Notes

Introduction

1. George E. Hyde, *Red Cloud's Folk: A History of the Oglala Sioux Indians* (Norman: University of Oklahoma Press, 1937; reprint, Norman: University of Oklahoma Press, 1975), 21, 23, 31.

2. Reuben Gold Thwaites, ed., *Early Western Travels, 1748–1846, vol. 5, Bradbury's Travels in the Interior of America 1809–1811* (New York: AMS Press, 1966) [hereafter cited as Bradbury, *Early Western Travels*], 73, 74.

3. Paul Wilhelm, "First Journey to North America in the Years 1822 to 1824 by Paul Wilhelm, Duke of Wuerttemberg," trans. Wm. G. Bek, *South Dakota Historical Collections,* vol. 19 (Pierre, S.D.: Hipple Printing Company, 1938), 443–444.

4. Reuben Gold Thwaites, ed., *Early Western Travels, 1748–1846*, vols. 22–24, *Maximilian, Prince of Wied's Travels in the Interior of North America, 1832–1834* (New York: AMS Press, 1966) [hereafter cited as Maximilian, *Early Western Travels*], 271.

5. James Harkness, "My Montana Journal, 1862" manuscript, SC 792, James Harkness Papers, Montana Historical Society Archives, Helena, Mont., 5.

1. The Upper Missouri

1. Annie Heloise Abel, ed., *Tabeau's Narrative of Loisel's Expedition to the Upper Missouri* (Norman: University of Oklahoma Press, 1939), 67, 69.

2. Gary E. Moulton, ed., *The Journals of the Lewis and Clark Expedition,* 12 vols. (Lincoln: University of Nebraska Press, 1983–1999) [hereafter cited as Moulton, *JLC*], 10:21.

3. Donald Jackson, ed., *Letters of the Lewis and Clark Expedition with Related Documents, 1783–1854,* 2d ed., 2 vols. (Urbana: University of Illinois Press, 1978) [hereafter cited as Jackson, *Letters of LCE*], 1:223.

4. Reuben Gold Thwaites, ed., *Early Western Travels, 1748–1846*, vol. 6, *Brackenridge's Journal up the Missouri, 1811* (New York: AMS Press, 1966) [hereafter cited as Brackenridge, *Early Western Travels*], 76, 77.

5. John C. Fremont, *A Report on an Exploration of the Country Lying between the Missouri River and the Rocky Mountains, on the Line of the Kansas and Great Platte Rivers* (Fairfield, Wash.: Ye Galleon Press, 1996), 25.

6. Missouri River Journal, unknown title and author, manuscript, Montana Historical Society Archives, Helena, Mont., 2.

7. John Francis McDermott, ed., *Up the Missouri with Audubon: The Journal of Edward Harris* (Norman: University of Oklahoma Press, 1951), 23.

8. Thaddeus Culbertson, *Journal of an Expedition to the Mauvaises Terres and the Upper Missouri in 1850,* ed. John Francis McDermott, Smithsonian Institute, Bureau of American Ethnology, Bulletin 147, (Washington, D.C.: GPO, 1952), 17.

9. Maximilian, *Early Western Travels,* 23:290.

10. Daniel H. Weston, "Diary, on Board Steamer 'Colorado,' Missouri River, above St. Joseph, Mo, 1866," manuscript, Montana Historical Society Archives, Helena, Mont., 16.

11. Elias J. Marsh, "Journal of Dr. Elias J. Marsh: Account of a Steamboat Trip on the Missouri River, May–August, 1859," *South Dakota Historical Review* 1, no. 2 (January 1936): 79–127.

12. Maximilian, *Early Western Travels,* 22:386.

13. Edmund C. Bray and Martha Coleman Bray, eds., *Joseph N. Nicollet on the Plains and Prairies: The Expeditions of 1838–39 with Journals, Letters, and Notes on the Dakota Indians* (St. Paul: Minnesota Historical Society Press, 1976), 151.

14. John C. Luttig, *Journal of a Fur-Trading Expedition on the Upper Missouri, 1812–1813,* ed. Stella M. Drumm (1920; reprint, New York: Argosy-Antiquarian, 1964), 46–47.

15. Brackenridge, *Early Western Travels,* 81.

16. Moulton, *JLC,* 9:36.

17. Culbertson, *Expedition to the Mauvaises Terres,* 37.

18. Wilhelm, "First Journey to North America," 341.

19. Ibid., 59.

20. Henry A. Boller, *Among the Indians: Four Years on the Upper Missouri, 1858–1862,* ed. Milo Milton Quaife (Lincoln: University of Nebraska Press, 1972), 73, 74.

21. Moulton, *JLC,* 8:310–311.

22. Roger L. Nichols, ed., *The Missouri Expedition, 1818–1820: The Journal of Surgeon John Gale with Related Documents* (Norman: University of Oklahoma Press, 1969), 86.

23. Marsh, "Account of a Steamboat Trip," 82.

24. Culbertson, *Expedition to the Mauvaises Terres,* 37.

25. Charles Larpenteur, *Forty Years a Fur Trader on the Upper Missouri: The Personal Narrative of Charles Larpenteur, 1833–1872* (1933; reprint, Lincoln: University of Nebraska Press, 1989), 250.

26. Boller, *Among the Indians,* 297.

27. Annie Heloise Abel, ed., *Chardon's Journal at Fort Clark: 1834–1839, Description of Life on the Upper Missouri; of a Fur Trader's Experiences among the Mandans, Gros Ventres, and Their Neighbors; of the Ravages of the Smallpox*

Epidemic of 1837 (1932; reprint, Lincoln: University of Nebraska Press, 1997), 107.

28. Ibid., 62–63.

29. Luttig, *Journal of a Fur-Trading Expedition,* 118.

30. Maximilian, *Early Western Travels,* 24:78

31. Abel, *Chardon's Journal,* 153.

32. Maximilian, *Early Western Travels,* 24:66.

33. Rudolph Friederich Kurz, *Journal of Rudolph Friederich Kurz: An Account of His Experiences among Fur Traders and American Indians on the Mississippi and Upper Missouri Rivers during the Years 1846 to 1852,* ed. J. N. B. Hewitt, trans. Myrtis Jarrell (Lincoln: University of Nebraska Press, 1970), 332.

34. Maximilian, *Early Western Travels,* 23:28.

35. Larpenteur, *Forty Years a Fur Trader,* 119.

36. Abel, *Chardon's Journal,* 153.

37. Maria R. Audubon, *The Missouri River Journals, 1843,* in *Audubon and His Journals,* ed. Elliot Coues (1897; reprint, New York: Dover, 1960), 2:10.

38. Maximilian, *Early Western Travels,* 24:78.

39. Ibid., 299.

40. Bray, *Nicollet on the Plains,* 159.

41. Emma S. Dickinson, "The Diary of Emma Slack Dickinson, Written before and during Her Journey up the Missouri to Fort Benton and Overland to Missoula in 1869," manuscript, Montana Historical Society Archives, Helena, Mont., 1–6.

42. Bradbury, *Early Western Travels,* 92–93.

43. Maximilian, *Early Western Travels,* 22:338–339.

44. Abel, *Chardon's Journal,* 34–35.

45. Boller, *Among the Indians,* 324.

46. Maximilian, *Early Western Travels,* 23:188.

47. Bradbury, *Early Western Travels,* 122.

48. Abel, *Chardon's Journal,* 113–115.

49. U.S. Congress, Senate, *Explorations in the Dacota Country in the Year 1855 by Lieut. G. K. Warren, Topographical Engineer of the "Sioux Expedition,"* 34th Cong., 1st sess., 1856, Senate Ex. Doc. 76, [hereafter cited as *Warren, Explorations in the Dacota Country*], 70.

50. Maximilian, *Early Western Travels,* 23:47–48.

51. Maximilian, *Early Western Travels;* Harkness, "My Montana Journal"; Warren, *Explorations in the Dacota Country;* Audubon, *Missouri River Journals;* Culbertson, *Expedition to the Mauvaises Terres;* Bray, *Nicollet on the Plains.*

52. Bray, *Nicollet on the Plains,* 151.

53. Harkness, "My Montana Journal," 17.

54. Culbertson, *Expedition to the Mauvaises Terres,* 88.

55. Marsh, "Account of a Steamboat Trip," 81–82.

56. Bray, *Nicollet on the Plains,* 157.

57. Abel, *Tabeau's Narrative of Loisel's Expedition,* 65.

58. Maximilian, *Early Western Travels,* 22:296–297.

59. Bradbury, *Early Western Travels,* 100–101.

60. Ibid., 184.

61. Weston, "Diary, on Board Steamer 'Colorado,'" 6.

62. Harris, *Up the Missouri with Audubon,* 93.

63. Ibid., 60, 62.

64. Maximilian, *Early Western Travels,* 22:281–282.

65. Wilhelm, "First Journey to North America," 381.

66. Moulton, *JLC,* 3:76–77.

67. Brackenridge, *Early Western Travels,* 108.

68. Maximilian, *Early Western Travels,* 23:216.

69. Ibid., 22:373.

70. Weston, "Diary, on Board Steamer 'Colorado,'" 16.

71. Moulton, *JLC,* 8:255.

72. U.S. Congress, Senate, *Report on the Exploration of the Yellowstone River by Bvt. Brig. Gen. W. F. Raynolds,* 40th Cong., 1st sess., 1868, Senate Ex. Doc. 77 [hereafter cited as *Raynolds, Report on the Exploration of the Yellowstone River*], 58.

73. A. H. Wilcox, "Up the Missouri River to Montana in the Spring of 1862," manuscript, Montana Historical Society Archives, Helena, Mont., 1.

74. Audubon, *Missouri River Journals,* 1:462.

75. Jackson, *Letters of LCE,* 1:223.

76. Culbertson, *Expedition to the Mauvaises Terres,* 121.

77. Brackenridge, *Early Western Travels,* 151.

78. Mary E. Cook, "Diary of Mrs. Mary E. Cook, Written While Coming up the Mo. River in 1868," manuscript, Montana Historical Society Archives, Helena, Mont., 10.

79. Abel, *Tabeau's Narrative of Loisel's Expedition,* 60.

80. Audubon, *Missouri River Journals,* 1:491.

81. Ibid., 496.

82. Moulton, *JLC,* 10:31.

83. Brackenridge, *Early Western Travels,* 86.

84. Maximilian, *Early Western Travels,* 22:279.

85. Bray, *Nicollet on the Plains,* 168.

86. Harris, *Up the Missouri with Audubon,* 26.

87. Ibid., 56–57.

88. Luttig, *Journal of a Fur-Trading Expedition,* 64.

89. Cook, "Diary of Mrs. Mary E. Cook," 6.

90. Maximilian, *Early Western Travels,* 22:368.

91. Bradbury, *Early Western Travels,* 188.

92. Brackenridge, *Early Western Travels,* 151.

93. Lewis Henry Morgan, *The Indian Journals, 1859–62* (New York: Dover, 1993), 202.

2. Bison World

1. Kurz, *Journal of Rudolph Friederich Kurz,* 28; Brackenridge, *Early Western Travels,* 152; Harris, *Up the Missouri with Audubon,* 19.

2. Brackenridge, *Early Western Travels,* 109–110.

3. Ibid., 92.

4. Maximilian, *Early Western Travels,* 23:42.

5. Culbertson, *Expedition to the Mauvaises Terres,* 31.

6. Cook, "Diary of Mrs. Mary E. Cook," 3.

7. Brackenridge, *Early Western Travels,* 84.

8. Weston, "Diary, on Board steamer 'Colorado,'" 9.

9. Andrew C. Isenberg, *The Destruction of the Bison, An Environmental History, 1750–1920* (New York: Cambridge University Press, 2000), 25–30.

10. Bradbury, *Early Western Travels,* 125.

11. Brackenridge, *Early Western Travels,* 90.

12. Moulton, *JLC,* 3:7.

13. Wilhelm, "First Journey to North America," 390.

14. Moulton, *JLC,* 3:81.

15. Ibid., 96.

16. Bradbury, *Early Western Travels,* 184.

17. Abel, *Chardon's Journal,* 134.

18. Raynolds, *Report on the Exploration of the Yellowstone River,* 165.

19. Moulton, *JLC,* 4:67.

20. Ibid., 8:219.

21. Ibid., 237.

22. Wilhelm, "First Journey to North America," 392–393.

23. Moulton, *JLC,* 10:95.

24. Ibid., 8:226.

25. Ibid., 258.

26. Ibid., 273.

27. Audubon, *Missouri River Journals,* 1:107.

28. Brackenridge, *Early Western Travels,* 105–106.

29. Moulton, *JLC,* 10:95.

30. Harris, *Up the Missouri with Audubon,* 21.

31. Maximilian, *Early Western Travels,* 22:332.

32. Raynolds, *Report on the Exploration of the Yellowstone River,* 153.

33. Ibid., 142; Moulton, *JLC,* 8:185.

34. Kurz, *Journal of Rudolph Friederich Kurz,* 105.

35. Raynolds, *Report on the Exploration of the Yellowstone River,* 140.

36. Ibid., 134.

37. "White Pigeon Journal," Montana Historical Society Archives, Helena, Mont., 3.

38. Maximilian, *Early Western Travels,* 23:181.

39. Lawrence A. Frost, ed., *Some Observations on the Yellowstone Expedition of 1873* (Glendale, Calif.: Arthur H. Clark, 1981), 96–97.

40. In Raynolds, *Report on the Exploration of the Yellowstone*, 128.

41. Gary E. Eichorn, *Peter Jackson, Nimrod and Scout* (Miles City, Mont.: Star Printing Company, 1959), 10.

42. James H. Chambers, "Original Journal of James H. Chambers, Fort Sarpy, 1855–1856," *Contributions to the Historical Society of Montana*, vol. 10 (Helena, Mont.: Naegele Printing, 1940), 137.

43. Raynolds, *Report on the Exploration of the Yellowstone River*, 128.

44. Ibid., 42, 145.

45. Moulton, *JLC*, 8:252.

46. Culbertson, *Expedition to the Mauvaises Terres*, 114.

47. Raynolds, *Report on the Exploration of the Yellowstone River*, 38.

48. Gouverneur K. Warren, *Explorer of the Northern Plains: Lieutenant Gouverneur K. Warren's Preliminary Report of Explorations in Nebraska and Dakota, in the Years 1855-'56,-'57*, introduction by Frank N. Schubert (Washington, D.C.: GPO, 1981), 74.

49. Ibid., 39–41.

50. Maximilian, *Early Western Travels*, 22:366.

51. Ibid., 23:214.

52. Ibid., 51.

53. Ibid., 63.

54. Brackenridge, *Early Western Travels*, 109.

55. Moulton, *JLC*, 9:62.

56. Wilhelm, "First Journey to North America," 393.

57. Ibid., 394.

58. Bradbury, *Early Western Travels*, 99.

59. Warren, *Explorer of the Northern Plains*, 43.

60. Boller, *Among the Indians*, 275.

61. Jerry N. McDonald, *North American Bison: Their Classification and Evolution* (Berkeley: University of California Press, 1981), 245–248.

62. Quoted in Maximilian, *Early Western Travels*, 23:307.

63. Ibid., 51.

64. Ibid., 185.

65. Edwin T. Denig, *Five Indian Tribes of the Upper Missouri: Sioux, Arickaras, Assiniboines, Crees, Crows*, ed. John C. Ewers (Norman: University of Oklahoma Press, 1961), 118.

66. Maximilian, *Early Western Travels*, 23:245–246.

67. Abel, *Chardon's Journal*, 25.

68. Joel Berger and Carol Cunningham, *Bison: Mating and Conservation in Small Populations* (New York: Columbia University Press, 1994), 165.

69. Abel, *Chardon's Journal*, 17.

70. Abel, *Tabeau's Narrative of Loisel's Expedition*, 64–65.

71. M. M. Quaife, *Yellowstone Kelly: The Memoirs of Luther S. Kelley* (1926; reprint, Lincoln: University of Nebraska Press, 1973), 187.

72. Boller, *Among the Indians*, 145.

73. Raynolds, *Report on the Exploration of the Yellowstone River,* 34.

74. Bradbury, *Early Western Travels,* 188, 189.

75. Harris, *Up the Missouri with Audubon,* 171.

76. Berger and Cunningham, *Bison,* 188.

77. Ibid., 187.

78. Abel, *Tabeau's Narrative of Loisel's Expedition,* 71.

79. Maximilian, *Early Western Travels,* 23:186.

80. Abel, *Chardon's Journal,* 10–11.

81. Maximilian, *Early Western Travels,* 23:213.

82. Abel, *Chardon's Journal,* 15, 99.

83. Luttig, *Journal of a Fur-Trading Expedition,* 97; Maximilian, *Early Western Travels,* 22:390.

84. Peter deMenocal et al., "Cultural Responses to Climate Change during the Late Holocene," page 2 of 14, http://doherty.ldgo.columbia.edu/~peter/Resources/CultureClimate.html.

85. Bradbury, *Early Western Travels,* 124.

86. Harris, *Up the Missouri with Audubon,* 22.

87. Abel, *Tabeau's Narrative of Loisel's Expedition,* 71; Oscar Brackett, "Oscar Brackett Reminiscence," manuscript, SC 29, folder 1/1, Montana Historical Society Archives, Helena, Mont., 0B7; F. S. Grant, "Report of Observations on His Trip up the Yellowstone River, 1875," manuscript, U.S. Army Engineer Department, Public Library, Glendive, Mont., 10.

88. Brackett, "Reminiscence," 0B5.

89. Eichhorn, *Peter Jackson, Nimrod and Scout,* 11.

90. Chambers, "Original Journal of James H. Chambers," 152.

91. Warren, *Explorer of the Northern Plains,* 33.

92. Quoted in Frost, *Yellowstone Expedition of 1873,* 112.

93. Brackenridge, *Early Western Travels,* 91.

94. Luttig, *Journal of a Fur-Trading Expedition,* 92.

95. Bradbury, *Early Western Travels,* 186.

96. Wilhelm, "First Journey to North America," 403.

97. Abel, *Chardon's Journey,* 71.

98. Ibid., 79.

99. Ibid., 112.

100. Maximilian, *Early Western Travels,* 23:194.

3. Buffalo People

1. Moulton, *JLC,* 3:22.

2. Abel, *Tabeau's Narrative of Loisel's Expedition,* 72.

3. Ibid., 102.

4. Maximilian, *Early Western Travels,* 22:342.

5. Luttig, *Journal of a Fur-Trading Expedition,* 50, 82.

6. Ernest Callenbach, *Bring Back the Buffalo! A Sustainable Future for America's Great Plains* (Berkeley: University of California Press, 1996), 28.

7. Denig, *Five Indian Tribes,* 159.

8. Brackenridge, *Early Western Travels,* 108.

9. Maximilian, *Early Western Travels,* 23:89.

10. Brackenridge, *Early Western Travels,* 135.

11. Bradbury, *Early Western Travels,* 149.

12. Maximilian, *Early Western Travels,* 24:27.

13. Abel, *Chardon's Journal,* 102.

14. Moulton, *JLC,* 3:268.

15. Maximilian, *Early Western Travels,* 22:383.

16. Boller, *Among the Indians,* 225.

17. Bradbury, *Early Western Travels,* 140–141.

18. Brackenridge, *Early Western Travels,* 109.

19. Maximilian, *Early Western Travels,* 22:318.

20. Ibid., 23:35.

21. Hyde, *Red Cloud's Folk,* 66.

22. Moulton, *JLC,* 8:324.

23. Ibid., 329; italics added.

24. U.S. Congress, House, *Upper Missouri Agency,* House Doc. 4 (Washington, D.C.: GPO, 1846), 293.

25. Kurz, *Journal of Rudolph Friederich Kurz,* 295.

26. Ibid., 350.

27. Warren, *Explorer of the Northern Plains,* 51.

28. Wilhelm, "First Journey to North America," 403.

29. Kurz, *Journal of Rudolph Friederich Kurz,* 174.

30. Maximilian, *Early Western Travels,* 24:64.

31. Denig, *Five Indian Tribes,* 24.

32. Warren, *Explorer of the Northern Plains,* 19.

33. Kurz, *Journal of Rudolph Friederich Kurz,* 173.

34. Denig, *Five Indian Tribes,* 182.

35. Hyde, *Red Cloud's Folk,* 82.

36. Brackenridge, *Early Western Travels,* 119.

37. Ibid., 177; Denig, *Five Indian Tribes,* 95.

38. Raynolds, *Report on the Exploration of the Yellowstone River,* 51; italics added.

39. Bradbury, *Early Western Travels,* 108.

40. Maximilian, *Early Western Travels,* 22:267.

41. Denig, *Five Indian Tribes,* 200–201, 202.

42. Kurz, *Journal of Rudolph Friederich Kurz,* 119.

43. Ibid., 119; Abel, *Chardon's Journal,* 165; James Henry Morley, "Diary of James Henry Morley in Montana, 1862, 1865," Manuscript, Montana Historical Society Archives, Helena, Mont., 5.

44. Denig, *Five Indian Tribes,* 60, 184.

45. Luttig, *Journal of a Fur-Trading Expedition,* 90.

46. Bradbury, *Early Western Travels,* 132; Maximilian, *Early Western Travels,* 23:73; Denig, *Five Indian Tribes,* 34.

47. Bradbury, *Early Western Travels,* 114.

48. Maximilian, *Early Western Travels,* 23:133.

49. Boller, *Among the Indians,* 143; Frank Raymond Secoy, *Changing Military Patterns of the Great Plains Indians* (1953; reprint, Lincoln: University of Nebraska Press, 1992), 55–57.

50. Barton H. Barbour, *Fort Union and the Upper Missouri Fur Trade* (Norman: University of Oklahoma Press, 2001), 27.

51. Maximilian, *Early Western Travels,* 23:202.

52. Boller, *Among the Indians,* 146, 216; Abel, *Tabeau's Narrative of Loisel's Expedition,* 72–73.

53. Secoy, *Changing Military Patterns,* 75–77; Denig, *Five Indian Tribes,* 93–94.

54. Luttig, *Journal of a Fur-Trading Expedition,* 104; R. Eli Paul, *Autobiography of Red Cloud: War Leader of the Oglalas* (Helena: Montana Historical Society Press, 1997), 46.

55. Denig, *Five Indian Tribes,* 96.

56. Abel, *Chardon's Journal,* 51.

57. Wilhelm, "First Journey to North America," 407.

58. Denig, *Five Indian Tribes,* 35.

59. Ibid., 102.

60. Ibid., 47.

61. Ibid., 81.

62. Ibid., 93.

63. Brckenridge, *Early Western Travels,* 128.

4. Explorers beyond the Platte

1. Jackson, *Letters of LCE,* 3–4, 32–33.

2. Moulton, *JLC,* 3:373.

3. Jackson, *Letters of LCE,* 1:47.

4. Ibid., 26.

5. Ibid., 54.

6. Ibid., 109–110.

7. Ibid., 33.

8. Ibid., 23.

9. Ibid., 19–20.

10. Ibid., 26.

11. Ibid., 27.

12. Ibid., 63.

13. Anthony F. C. Wallace, *Jefferson and the Indians: The Tragic Fate of the First Americans* (Cambridge, Mass.: Belknap Press, 1999), 15, 223.

14. Jackson, *Letters of LCE,* 1:35.

15. Ibid., 61.

16. Ibid., 61–66.

17. Ibid., 63.

18. Ibid., 65.

19. Moulton, *JLC,* 8:97.

20. Ibid., 219.

21. Ibid., 362.

22. Jackson, *Letters of LCE,* 2:704–707. Many of the interpretations in this chapter are derived from a number of sources, including John Logan Allen, *Lewis and Clark and the Image of the American Northwest* (1975; reprint, New York: Dover, 1991); Stephen Ambrose, *Undaunted Courage: Meriwether Lewis, Thomas Jefferson, and the Opening of the American West* (New York: Simon and Schuster, 1996); Elliot Coues, ed., *The History of the Lewis and Clark Expedition by Meriwether Lewis and William Clark,* 3 vols. (1893; reprint, New York: Dover, n.d.); James Ronda, *Voyages of Discovery: Essays on the Lewis and Clark Expedition* (Helena: Montana Historical Society Press, 1998); Ronda, *Lewis and Clark among the Indians* (Lincoln: University of Nebraska Press, 1984); Wallace, *Jefferson and the Indians;* Moulton, *JLC;* and Jackson, ed., *Letters of LCE.*

5. In Search of Place

1. Hyde, *Red Cloud's Folk,* 15; Secoy, *Changing Military Patterns,* 67.

2. Joseph White Bull, *Lakota Warrior,* trans. and ed. James H. Howard (Lincoln: University of Nebraska Press, 1968), 6.

3. Moulton, *JLC,* 4:77.

4. Don C. Miller and Stan B. Cohen, *Military and Trading Posts of Montana* (Missoula, Mont.: Pictorial Histories Publishing Company, 1979), 85; Abel, *Chardon's Journal,* ix; Frederick T. Wilson, "Fort Pierre and Its Neighbors," *South Dakota Historical Collections,* vol. 1 (Aberdeen, S.D.: News Printing Company, 1902): 270; Barbour, *Fort Union and the Upper Missouri Fur Trade,* 39.

5. Wilson, "Fort Pierre and Its Neighbors," 270.

6. Luttig, *Journal of a Fur-Trading Expedition,* 56.

7. Culbertson, *Expedition to the Mauvaises Terres,* 91.

8. Luttig, *Journal of a Fur-Trading Expedition,* 100.

9. Abel, *Chardon's Journal,* 6.

10. Chambers, "Original Journal of James H. Chambers," 104.

11. Harris, *Up the Missouri with Audubon,* 149.

12. Ibid., 166.

13. Moulton, *JLC,* 8:206.

14. Ibid., 219.

15. Ibid., 226.

16. Cook, "Diary of Mrs. Mary E. Cook," 8.

17. Weston, "Diary, on Board Steamer 'Colorado,'" 13.

18. John Napton, "My Trip on the 'Imperial'" in 1867," manuscript, Montana Historical Society Archives, Helena, Mont., 4–5.

19. Audubon, *Missouri River Journals,* 2:5–6.

20. Nichols, *The Missouri Expedition,* 60.

21. Maximilian, *Early Western Travels,* 22:258.

22. Wilhelm, "First Journey to North America," 342–343.

23. Quoted in Frost, *Yellowstone Expedition of 1873,* 78.

24. Kurz, *Journal of Rudolph Friederich Kurz,* 139.

25. Maximilian, *Early Western Travels,* 22:268.

26. Ibid., 334.

27. Ibid., 366.

28. Audubon, *Missouri River Journals,* 1:503–504.

29. William E. Lass, *A History of Steamboating on the Upper Missouri River* (Lincoln: University of Nebraska Press, 1962), 41.

30. Bradbury, *Early Western Travels,* 190.

31. Maximilian, *Early Western Travels,* 22:317.

32. Culbertson, *Expedition to the Mauvaises Terres,* 88.

33. Ibid., 87.

34. Cook, "Diary of Mrs. Mary E. Cook," 10.

35. Ibid., 8.

36. J. A. Wells, "First Connected Account of the Warfare Waged by the Sioux Indians against Wood Choppers, Missouri River between Ft. Buford & Ft. Benton, 1866–1870," manuscript, Montana Historical Society Archives, Helena, Mont., 2.

37. Wilcox, "Up the Missouri River to Montana," 5.

38. Warren, *Explorations in the Dacota Country,* 36.

39. Harris, *Up the Missouri with Audubon,* 115, 145.

40. Wilhelm, "First Journey to North America," 369–370.

41. Warren, *Explorations in the Dacota Country,* 79.

42. Denig, *Five Indian Tribes,* 25, 30.

43. Kurz, *Journal of Rudolph Friederich Kurz,* 72, 271.

6. To the Horizon

1. U.S. Congress, House, *Report of Superintendent of Indian Affairs, D. D. Mitchell,* House Doc. 2 (Washington, D.C.: GPO, 1851), 324.

2. U.S. Congress, House, *Report of the Upper Missouri Agency, No. 43, Alfred D. Vaughn,* House Doc. 1 (Washington, D.C.: GPO, 1853), 354; Maximilian, *Early Western Travels,* 22:380.

3. U.S. Congress, House, *Report of the Upper Missouri Agency,* 354.

4. U.S. Congress, House, *Council with the Sioux Indians at Fort Pierre,* 34th Cong., 1st sess., Ex. Doc. 130, 1856, 34.

5. Ibid., 20–21.

6. Denig, *Five Indian Tribes,* 93–94.

7. Ibid., 203.

8. Lass, *Steamboating on the Upper Missouri River,* 41.

9. U.S. Congress, House, *Report of Upper Missouri Agency,* 368–369; Morgan, *The Indian Journals,* 228–229.

10. Robert G. Athearn, *Forts of the Upper Missouri* (Lincoln: University of Nebraska Press, 1967), map.

11. Dickinson, "The Diary of Emma Slack Dickinson, 1869," 6, 12.

12. "Fort Laramie Treaty, April 29, 1868," manuscript, Institute of American Indian Studies, University of South Dakota, 7 of 17 http://www.usd.edu/iais/siouxnation/treaty1868.html.

13. Robert M. Utley, *Frontier Regulars: The United States Army and the Indian, 1866–1891* (1973; reprint, Lincoln: University of Nebraska Press, 1984), 245–247.

14. Ibid., 254, 259.

15. Ibid., 254–260.

16. White Bull, *Lakota Warrior,* 51–56.

17. Charles E. Rankin, ed., *Legacy: New Perspectives on the Battle of the Little Bighorn* (Helena: Montana Historical Society Press, 1996), illustration between pages 230 and 231.

18. *The Yellowstone Journal, Illustrated and Historical Edition,* Miles City, Montana, September 27, 1900, 3.

19. Brackett, "Reminiscence," 0B5.

20. Eichhorn, *Peter Jackson, Nimrod and Scout,* 11.

21. *Yellowstone Journal,* 3.

22. Eichhorn, *Peter Jackson, Nimrod and Scout,* 11.

23. John M. Peterson, "Buffalo Hunting in Montana in 1886: The Diary of W. Harvey Brown," *Montana: The Magazine of Western History* 31, no. 4 (October 1981): 5, 8.

7. A Hydraulic Empire

1. Department of the Army, U.S. Army Corps of Engineers, *Annual Report of the Chief of Engineers, U.S. Army, Survey of the Yellowstone River* (Washington, D.C.: GPO, 1879–1912) [hereafter cited as *ARCE*], 128.

2. Ibid., 1881–1882, 231, 1674–1676.

3. Ibid., 1883–1884, 1366.

4. Ibid., 1366.

5. Ibid., 1879, 1097.

6. Ibid., 1900, 451.

7. U.S. Congress, House, *Yellowstone River, Mont.*, 62d Cong., 1st sess., H. Doc. 83, 1911, 22.

8. Lass, *Steamboating on the Upper Missouri*, 41.

9. *ARCE*, 1881–1882, 1675; *ARCE*, 1882–1883, 1746; *ARCE*, 1883–1884, 1366; *ARCE*, 1884–1885, 1543.

8. Try and Try Again

1. Yellowstone Irrigation Association, *Report on Proposed Project for Flood Control and Irrigation in the Yellowstone River Valley, Wyoming, Montana, North Dakota* (Livingston, Mont.: Yellowstone Irrigation Association, 1921), 12.

2. Ibid., 10.

3. Ibid., 12.

4. Department of the Interior, National Park Service, *Statement on Diversion Proposal Affecting Yellowstone Lake, Yellowstone National Park, as Embodied in S. 3925 and H.R. 10489,* 75th Cong., manuscript, National Archives, Mammoth Hot Springs, YNP, 1938, 4.

5. Department of the Interior, National Park Service, *Division of the Waters of the Yellowstone River and Tributaries by the States of Wyoming and Montana,* manuscript, National Archives, Mammoth Hot Springs, 1933, YNP: 15–16; Department of the Interior, National Park Service, *Statement on Diversion Proposal Affecting Yellowstone Lake,* 7–9.

6. U.S. Congress, House, *Yellowstone River, Wyo., Mont., and N. Dak.,* 73d Cong., 2d. sess., House Doc. 256, 1934, 135; House Doc. 256, Appendix V, *Yellowstone River Basin, Data on Potential Power Projects,* manuscript, Montana Historical Society Archives, Helena, Mont., 1934, 4, 8.

7. http://muextension.missouri.edu/xplor/agguides/agecon/g00404.htm.

8. U.S. Congress, House, *Yellowstone River, Wyo., Mont., and N. Dak.,* 112.

9. Ibid., 126.

10. Ibid., 121.

9. Vanishing Act

1. Jean Prior, *Landforms of Iowa* (Iowa City: University of Iowa Press, 1991), 105.

2. U.S. Congress, House, *Yellowstone River, Wyo., Mont., and N. Dak.,* 174.

3. U.S. Congress, House, *Missouri River Basin,* 78th Cong., 2d sess., House Doc. 475, 1944, 3–4.

4. U.S. Congress, Senate, *Missouri River Basin,* 78th Cong., 2d sess., Senate Doc. 191, 1944, 47.

5. USGS, Water Resources, Daily Streamflow for USA, USGS 06185500, Missouri River near Culbertson, Mont., March 1, 1943, to August 1, 1943;

USGS, Water Resources, Daily Streamflow for USA, USGS 06329500, Yellowstone River near Sidney, Mont., March 1, 1943, to August 1, 1943, http://water.-usgs.gov/nwis/discharge.

6. U.S. Army Corps of Engineers, Omaha District, Public Relations Office, phone interview, 25 July 2001.

7. John R. Ferrel, *Big Dam Era: A Legislative and Institutional History of the Pick-Sloan Missouri Basin Program* (Omaha, Nebr.: Missouri River Division, U.S. Army Corps of Engineers, 1993), 29.

8. "Overview of the Missouri River Basin," http://www.joss.ucar.edu/gcip/map_99_lsa_nw/section2.html, 2.

9. Kurz, *Journal of Rudolph Friederich Kurz,* 178.

10. U.S. Congress, House, *Council with the Sioux Indians at Fort Pierre,* 3, 33–35.

11. Department of the Interior, Bureau of Indian Affairs, *Damage to Indians of Five Reservations from Three Missouri River Reservoirs in North and South Dakota, Missouri River Basin Investigations Project, Report No. 138* (Billings: Department of the Interior, Bureau of Indian Affairs, 1954), 85.

12. U.S. Congress, Senate, Subcommittee of the Committee on Public Works, *Plans for Big Bend Dam, South Dakota: Hearing before the Subcommittee of the Committee on Public Works,* 86th Cong., 1st sess., 1959, 18.

Bibliography

On-Line Sources

"06185500, Missouri River Near Culbertson, MT, Missouri River Main Stem, National Stream Quality Accounting Network Station." http://nd.water. usgs.gov/index/d.06185500wq99.html.

"06186500, Yellowstone River at Yellowstone Lake Outlet, YNP." U.S. Geological Survey. http://montana.usgs.gov/rt-cgi/gen_stn_pg?station = 06186500.

"06214500, Yellowstone River at Billings, MT." U.S. Geological Survey. http:// montana.usgs.gov/rt-cgi/gen_stn_pg?station = 06214500.

Abel, Heather. "Yellowstone Mine Swap Is in a Very Deep Pit." *High Country News*, April 28, 1997. http://www.hcn.org/servlets/hen.Article?article_ id = 3401.

"Acts of Forty-fourth Congress—Second Session, 1877, Feb. 28, 1877, 19 Stat., 254." http://www.usd.edu/iais/siouxnation/1877act.html.

"Annual Peak Streamflow for Station 06186500." U.S. Geological Survey. http:// 136.177.224.7/rt-cgi/gen_peak_pg?station = 06186500.

"Annual Peak Streamflow for Station 06192500." U.S. Geological Survey. http:// 136.177.224.7/rt-cgi/gen_peak_pg?station = 06192500.

"Annual Peak Streamflow for Station 06214500." U.S. Geological Survey. http:// 136.177.224.7/rt-cgi/gen_peak_pg?station = 06214500.

"Calendar Year Streamflow Statistics for USA, USGS 06192500 Yellowstone River Near Livingston, MT." U.S. Geological Survey. http://water.usgs.gov/ nwis/annual/?site_no = 06192500&agency_cd = USGS.

"Calendar Year Streamflow Statistics for Wyoming, USGS 06190500 Gardner River at Mammoth, YNP." http://water.usgs.gov/wy/.../calendar_year? site_no = 06190500&agency_cd = USGS&format = htm.

"Canyon Ferry Dam," "Historic Development of the Canyon Ferry Unit," "Authorization of the Canyon Ferry Unit," "Construction History of the Canyon Ferry Unit," "Canyon Ferry Powerplant," and "Project Features of the Canyon Ferry Unit." Bureau of Reclamation, DataWeb.

"Chorus of Concern Growing: Eight New Voices Call for Immediate Halt to Yellowstone River Destruction." *GYC News Releases*, September 18, 1998. http://www.greateryellowstone.org/yellowstone_river6_ nr.html.

"Clarks Fork of the Yellowstone River (1996)." http://www.americanrivers.org/ mostendangered/clarksfork1996.html.

"Daily Streamflow for Nebraska, USGS 06805500 Platte River at Louisville,

NE." U.S. Geological Survey. http://water.usgs.gov/ne/nwis/discharge/?si-te_no=06805500.

"Daily Streamflow for USA, USGS 06185500 Missouri River Near Culbertson MT, March 1, 1943 to August 1, 1943." http://water.usgs.gov/nwis/dis charge.

"Daily Streamflow for USA, USGS 06329500 Yellowstone River Near Sidney MT, March 1, 1943 to August 1, 1943." http://water.usgs.gov/nwis/dis charge.

DeMenocal, Peter, et al. "Cultural Responses to Climate Change during the Late Holocene." http://doherty.ldgo.columbia.edu/~peter/Resources/Culture Climate.html.

"Division Spans Nation, Top to Bottom." http://www.hq.usace.army.mil/cepa/pubs/feb00/story8.htm.

"Events That Shaped Yellowstone." The Yellowstone Association. Winter 1999–2000. http://yellowstoneassociation.org/membership/ydautumn99.htm.

"Fort Laramie Treaty, April 29, 1868." Manuscript. Institute of American Indian Studies, University of South Dakota. http://www.usd.edu/iais/siouxnation/treaty1868.html.

"Free Flowing River or Rip-Rapped Channels?" GYC Newsletter. August 1997. http://www.greateryellowstone.org/yellowstone_r_sum97nl.html.

Gourley, Bruce. "Yesteryear in Yellowstone." http://www.yellowstone.net/news paper/1999/news051999.htm.

"The Great Flood of 1993 Post-Flood Report." http://www.mvr.usace.army.mil/PublicAffairsOffice/HistoricArchives/Floodof1993/fl-1.htm.

Helfrich, Louis A., et al. "Influence of Low-Head Diversion Dams on Fish Passage, Community Composition, and Abundance in the Yellowstone River, Montana." Abstract. http://www.cnr.vt.edu/fisheries/helfrich_influence_of_lowhead_diversion_dams_abstract.htm."

"Is This Any Way to Treat the Last Best River?" Summer 1998. http://www.greateryellowstone.org/yellowstone_r_sum98nl.html.

Kesselheim, Alan S. "The Last Wild River." High Country News, March 27, 2000. http://www.hcn.org/servlets/hcn.Article?article_id=5648.

"Mississippi Valley Division Spans Nation." The Lower Mississippi River Conservation Committee. http://www.lmrcc.org/2000fallstories/MVD.htm.

"The Missouri River Story." http://infolink.cr.usgs.gov/The%20River/descrip tion.htm.

"Montana Spring Creek Flooding." http://www.geocities.com/Yosemite/5696/fn0896.htm.

"New Restoration Plan Keep Spring Creeks Open to Public." February 6, 1998. http://www.flyshop.com/Centers/RMWest/02–98Depuy/.

"New World Gold Mine Dead." August 20, 1998. http://www.flyshop.com/centers/rmwest/08–98bear/.

"Overview of the Missouri Basin." http://www.joss.ucar.edu/gcip/map_99_lsa_nw/section2.html.

Reuss, Martin, and Charles Hendricks. "U.S. Army Corps of Engineers, Brief History." http://www.usace.army.mil/htm.

"Rivers Systems of the World." http://www.rev.net/~aloe/river/.

Ryckman, Fred. "Cross the Wide Missouri, Sakakawea Headwaters Area. http://www.npwrc.usgs.gov/resource/2000/cwmiss/sakakawe.htm.

"Significant Characteristics of the LSA-NW." http://www.joss.ucar.edu/gcip/map_99_lsa_nw/section2.html.

"This Step Back Is Giant Leap Forward." *GYC Newsletter*, fall 1999. http://www.greateryellowstone.org/yellowstone_r_fall99nl.html.

"Treaty of Fort Laramie with Sioux, Etc., 1851, Sept. 17, 1851, 11 Stats., p.749." http://www.usd.edu/iais/siouxnation/treaty1851.html.

"Treaty with the Sioux, Brule, Oglala, Miniconjou, Yanktonai, Hunkpapa, Blackfeet, Cuthead, Two Kettle, Sans Arcs, and Santee, and Arapaho, Apr. 29, 1868, 15 Stats., 635, Ratified, Feb. 16, 1869, Proclaimed, Feb. 24, 1869." http://www.usd.edu/iais/siouxnation/treaty1851.html.

"Treaty with the Sioux, etc., August 19, 1825, Proclaimed February 6, 1826." http://www.ukans.edu/~kansite/pbp/books/treaties/t_1825.html.

"Treaty with the Yankton Sioux, 1858, Apr. 19, 1858, 11 Stat., 743, Ratified Feb. 16, 1859, Proclaimed Feb. 26, 1859." http://www.usd.edu/iais/siouxnation/treaty1858.html.

USGS, Water Resources, Daily Streamflow for USA, USGS 06185500, Missouri River near Culbertson, Mont., March 1, 1943, to August 1, 1943; USGS, Water Resources, Daily Streamflow for USA, USGS 06329500, Yellowstone River near Sidney, Mont., March 1, 1943, to August 1, 1943. http://water.usgs.gov/nwis/discharge.

"Yellowstone Geology, Lake, Bridge Bay & Fishing Bridge Area." http://www.us-parks.com/US_National_Parks/yellowstonc/yellowstone_lakc.shtml.

"Yellowstone Lake." *GYC Newsletter*, summer 1998. http.//www.yellowstone parknet.com/geninfo/attr_yellowstone_lake.htm.

Printed Sources and Archival Materials

Abbey, Edward. *Desert Solitaire: A Season in the Wilderness*. New York: Simon and Schuster, 1990.

Abel, Annie Heloise. "Trudeau's Description of the Upper Missouri." *Mississippi Valley Historical Review* 8, nos. 1/2 (1921): 149–179.

———, ed. *Chardon's Journal at Fort Clark: 1834–1839, Descriptive of Life on the Upper Missouri; of a Fur Trader's Experiences among the Mandans, Gros Ventres, and Their Neighbors; of the Ravages of the Smallpox Epidemic of 1837*. 1932. Reprint, Lincoln: University of Nebraska Press, 1997.

———. *Tabeau's Narrative of Loisel's Expedition to the Upper Missouri*. Norman: University of Oklahoma Press, 1939.

Algier, Keith. "Robert Meldrum and the Crow Peltry Trade." *Montana: The Magazine of Western History* 36, no. 3 (summer 1986): 36–47.

Allen, Joel A. *The American Bison, Living and Extinct.* 1876. Reprint. New York: Arno Press, 1974.

Allen, John Logan. *Lewis and Clark and the Image of the American Northwest.* 1975. Reprint, New York: Dover, 1991.

Ambrose, Stephen. *Undaunted Courage: Meriwether Lewis, Thomas Jefferson, and the Opening of the American West.* New York: Simon and Schuster, 1996.

Anderson, Gary Clayton. "Early Dakota Migration and Intertribal War: A Revision." *Western Historical Quarterly* 11 (January 1980): 17–36.

Anderson, Robert, and the Committee to Save the Upper Yellowstone. *The Challenge of Allenspur: A Report on Allenspur Dam.* Livingston, Mont.: Livingston Enterprise, 1974.

Armstrong, Moses Kimball. "History and Resources of Dakota, Montana, and Idaho." *South Dakota Historical Collections* 14 (1928): 9–70.

Ashby, S. C. "Journey from St. Louis to Fort Benton, M.T. on Steamboat 'Nile' in 1867." Manuscript. Montana Historical Society Archives, Helena, Mont.

Athearn, Robert G. *Forts of the Upper Missouri.* Lincoln: University of Nebraska Press, 1967.

———. *High Country Empire: The High Plains and Rockies.* Lincoln: University of Nebraska Press, 1960.

Atherton, Lewis. *The Cattle Kings.* 1961. Reprint. Lincoln: University of Nebraska Press, 1972.

Audubon, Maria R. *The Missouri River Journals, 1843.* In *Audubon and His Journals*, edited by Elliot Coues. 2 vols. 1897. Reprint, New York: Dover, 1960.

Bakeless, John. *America as Seen by Its First Explorers: The Eyes of Discovery.* 1950. Reprint, New York: Dover, 1961.

Baker, Charles W. "Diary of Charles W. Baker, Trip to Montana, Idaho, Year 1867." Manuscript. Montana Historical Society Archives, Helena, Mont.

Baker, Eugene M. "Reports of Eugene Baker (October 18, October 28, 1872), Stanley Expedition of 1872, War Department, Department of Dakota." Manuscript. SC 919, Folder 1/1. Montana Historical Society Archives, Helena, Mont.

Barbour, Barton H. *Fort Union and the Upper Missouri Fur Trade.* Norman: University of Oklahoma Press, 2001.

Barks, Coleman, translator, with John Moyne, A. J. Arberry, and Reynold Nicholson. *The Essential Rumi.* San Francisco: HarperSanFrancisco, 1995.

Barnett, LeRoy. "The Ghastly Harvest: Montana's Buffalo Bone Trade." *Montana: The Magazine of Western History* 25, no. 3 (summer 1975): 2–25.

Barrett, Jim. "River of Paradise: Death Throes of the Mighty Yellowstone." *Fly Fisherman* 30, no. 3 (March 1999): 10–14.

Barry, John M. *Rising Tide: The Great Mississippi Flood of 1927 and How It Changed America.* New York: Simon and Schuster, 1998.

Berger, Joel, and Carol Cunningham. *Bison: Mating and Conservation in Small Populations.* New York: Columbia University Press, 1994.

Billings Gazette. Billings, Montana, 1903–1906, 1960–1963, 1972–1977.

Blouet, Brian W., and Merlin P. Lawson, eds. *Images of the Plains: The Role of Human Nature in Settlement.* Lincoln: University of Nebraska Press, 1975.

Boller, Henry A. *Among the Indians: Four Years on the Upper Missouri, 1858–1862.* Edited by Milo Milton Quaife. Lincoln: University of Nebraska Press, 1972.

Bonney, Orrin H., and Lorraine Bonney. *Battle Drums and Geysers: The Life and Journals of Lt. Gustavus Cheyney Doane, Soldier and Explorer of the Yellowstone and Snake River Regions.* Chicago: Swallow Press, 1970.

Botkin, Daniel B. *Our Natural History: The Lessons of Lewis and Clark.* 1995. Reprint, New York: Berkley Publishing Group, 1996.

Brackett, Oscar. "Oscar Brackett Reminiscence." Manuscript. SC 29, Folder 1/1. Montana Historical Society Archives, Helena, Mont.

Bradley, James H. *The March of the Montana Column: A Prelude to the Custer Disaster.* Edited by Edgar I. Stewart. Norman: University of Oklahoma Press, 1991.

Bray, Edmund C., and Martha Coleman Bray, eds. *Joseph N. Nicollet on the Plains and Prairies: The Expeditions of 1838–39 with Journals, Letters, and Notes on the Dakota Indians.* St. Paul: Minnesota Historical Society Press, 1976.

Brown, Joseph Epes, ed. *The Sacred Pipe: Black Elk's Account of the Seven Rites of the Oglala Sioux.* Norman: University of Oklahoma Press, 1953.

Brown, Mark H. *The Plainsmen of the Yellowstone: A History of the Yellowstone Basin.* 1961. Reprint, Lincoln: University of Nebraska Press, 1969.

Brown, W. C., and Charles King. "Map Showing Many Battlefields of the Indian Wars and Trail of the Big Horn and Yellowstone Expedition of 1876." Map adapted from *Western Sheet, Map of Yellowstone and Missouri Rivers,* from Capt. Raynolds' Exploration 1859–60, with additions by Major Gillespie. Washington, D.C.: Office of the Chief of Engineers, U.S. Army, 1877.

Brundage, T. J. "Diary of Mr. T. J. Brundage, Narrating Certain Experiences on His Trip across the Plains in 1864 with the Townsend Expedition." Manuscript. Montana Historical Society Archives, Helena, Mont.

Bryan, Charles W., Jr. "Aboard the Western in 1879." *Missouri Historical Review* 59, no. 1 (October 1964): 46–63.

———. "Dr. Lamme's Gallant Sidewheeler 'Yellowstone.'" *Montana: The Magazine of Western History* 15, no. 3 (July 1965): 24–43.

Burks, David Clarke, ed. *Place of the Wild: A Wildlands Anthology.* Washington D.C.: Island Press, 1994.

Callenbach, Ernest. *Bring Back the Buffalo! A Sustainable Future for America's Great Plains.* Berkeley: University of California Press, 1996.

Cameron, Julia. *The Vein of Gold: A Journey to Your Creative Heart.* New York: Putnam, 1996.

Cameron, Walter A. "Montana Episodes: Building the Northern Pacific in 1881. A Memoir of Building the Northern Pacific in the Yellowstone River Valley over a Century Ago and How They Blasted the Big Horn Tunnel." *Montana: The Magazine of Western History* 33, no. 3 (summer 1983): 70–76.

Canfield, Andrew N. "Diary of Andrew Nahum Canfield, January 1 to December 2, 1868." Manuscript. Montana Historical Society Archives, Helena, Mont.

Capra, Fritjof. *The Web of Life: A New Scientific Understanding of Living Systems.* New York: Doubleday, 1996.

Carrels, Peter. *Uphill against Water: The Great Dakota Water War.* Lincoln: University of Nebraska Press, 1999.

Catlin, George. *Letters and Notes on the North American Indians.* 2 vols. North Dighton, Mass.: J.G. Press, 1995.

Chambers, James H. "Original Journal of James H. Chambers, Fort Sarpy, 1855–1856." *Contributions to the Historical Society of Montana.* Vol. 10. Helena: Naegele Printing, 1940.

Chapple, Steve. *Kayaking the Full Moon: A Journey down the Yellowstone River to the Soul of Montana.* New York: Harper Perennial, 1994.

———. "The Yellowstone: The Last Best River." *National Geographic* 191, no. 4 (April 1997): 56–77.

Chittenden, Hiram. *History of Early Steamboat Navigation on the Missouri River.* 2 vols. New York: F. P. Harper, 1903.

Clark, Robert. *River of the West: A Chronicle of the Columbia.* New York: Picador, 1995.

Clark, William P. "Memo: Of a Voyage from Benson's Landing on the Yellowstone, 27 Miles from Fort Ellis, to the Mouth of Powder River." Manuscript. SC 538, William P. Clark Diary. Montana Historical Society Archives, Helena, Mont.

Clarke, Richard W. "Reminiscences." Manuscript. MC 64, Box. 1, Folder 3, Montana Historical Society Pioneer Reminiscences. Montana Historical Society Archives, Helena, Mont.

Clifford, W. "Diary of Captain W. Clifford, Company E., 7th Infantry, United States Army, June 28 to August 10, 1876, Sioux Campaign, from the files of the Bureau of American Ethnology, Smithsonian Institution." Manuscript. Montana Historical Society Archives, Helena, Mont.

Cobbans, Roy M. "Roy M. Cobbans Diaries, 1880." Manuscript. SC 348. Montana Historical Society Archives, Helena, Mont.

Collier, Michael, Robert H. Webb, and John C. Schmidt. *Dams and Rivers: A Primer on the Downstream Effects of Dams, U.S. Geological Survey Circular 1126.* Denver: U.S. Geological Survey, Branch of Information Services, 2000.

Cone, Carl B. "Steamboat Trip from New Orleans to Montana, 1869." Manuscript. Montana Historical Society Archives, Helena, Mont.

Conner, Stuart W. "Prehistoric Man in the Yellowstone Valley." *Montana: The Magazine of Western History* 14, no. 2 (April 1964): 14–21.

Cook, Mary E. "Diary of Mrs. Mary E. Cook, Written While Coming up the Mo. River in 1868." Manuscript. Montana Historical Society Archives, Helena, Mont.

Corbin, Annalies. "Shifting Sand and Muddy Water: Historical Cartography and River Migration as Factors in Locating Steamboat Wrecks on the Far Upper Missouri River." *Historical Archaeology* 32, no. 4, (1998): 86–94.

Coues, Elliot, ed. *The History of the Lewis and Clark Expedition by Meriwether Lewis and William Clark*. 3 vols. 1893. Reprint, New York: Dover, n.d.

Cramer, Joseph L. "The Lean Site: An Historic Log Structure in Yellowstone County, Montana." *Plains Anthropologist* 6, no. 14 (1961): 267–270.

Culbertson, Thaddeus A. *Journal of an Expedition to the Mauvaises Terres and the Upper Missouri in 1850*. Edited by John Francis McDermott. Smithsonian Institute, Bureau of American Ethnology, Bulletin 147. Washington D.C.: GPO, 1952.

Curry, Thomas. "Early Settlers and Pioneers of Montana." Manuscript. MC 64, Box 1, Folder 33, Montana Historical Society Pioneers Reminiscences. Montana Historical Society Archives, Helena, Mont.

Cutright, Paul Russell. *Lewis and Clark: Pioneering Naturalists*. Lincoln: University of Nebraska Press, 1969.

DeLorme Mapping. *Montana Atlas and Gazetteer*. 3d ed. Yarmouth, Maine: DeLorme Mapping, 1999.

———. *North Dakota Atlas and Gazetteer*. Yarmouth, Maine: DeLorme Mapping, 1999.

———. *South Dakota Atlas and Gazetteer*. 3d ed. Yarmouth, Maine: DeLorme Mapping, 1997.

———. *Wyoming Atlas and Gazetteer*. 2d ed. Yarmouth, Maine: DeLorme Mapping, 1998.

Denig, Edwin T. *Five Indian Tribes of the Upper Missouri: Sioux, Arickaras, Assiniboines, Crees, Crows*. Edited by John C. Ewers. Norman: University of Oklahoma Press, 1961.

Department of the Army. District of the Yellowstone. Correspondence, Nelson Miles to Assistant Adjutant General, Department of Dakota, December 27, 1877. Manuscript. Montana Historical Society Archives, Helena, Mont.

Department of the Army. "Report of Col. O. M. Poe, U.S. Engineers, Aide-de-Camp to General W. T. Sherman, 1877." Washington, D.C.: GPO, 1878.

Department of the Army, U.S. Army Corps of Engineers. *Annual Report of the Chief of Engineers*. Washington, D.C.: GPO, 1880–1913.

———. *Annual Report of the Chief of Engineers, U.S. Army, 1879, Survey of the Yellowstone River*. Washington, D.C.: GPO, 1880.

———. *Annual Report of the Chief of Engineers, U.S. Army, 1884–85, Appendix W, Report of Captain Quinn, Improvement of Yellowstone River, Montana and Dakota*. Washington, D.C.: GPO, 1886.

———. *Annual Report of the Chief of Engineers, U.S. Army, 1891, Preliminary Examination of the Yellowstone River, Montana, from Its Mouth to the Mouth of the Tongue River*. Washington, D.C.: GPO, 1892.

———. *Appendix V, Yellowstone River Basin: Data on Potential Power Projects.* Appendix to House Document 238. Manuscript. Montana Historical Society Archives, Helena, Mont., 1934.

———. *Fort Peck Dam and Lake, Montana.* Washington, D.C.: GPO, 1997.

Department of the Army, U.S. Army Corps of Engineers, Missouri River Division. *Master Water Control Manual, Missouri River, Review and Update, Draft Environmental Impact Statement.* Omaha, Nebr.: U.S. Army Corps of Engineers, MRD, July 1994.

Department of the Army, U.S. Army Corps of Engineers, Omaha District. *Yellowstone River Navigability Study, Fort Union Historic Site, North Dakota, to Gardiner, Montana.* Omaha, Nebr.: U.S. Army Corps of Engineers, 1974.

Department of the Interior, *F. V. Hayden, Geological Survey of the Territories.* Fifth Annual Report. Washington, D.C.: GPO, 1872.

———. *Report of the Surveyor General of Montana Made to the Secretary of the Interior for the Year 1879.* Washington, D.C.: GPO, 1879.

Department of the Interior, Bureau of Indian Affairs. *Damage to Indians of Five Reservations from Three Missouri River Reservoirs in North and South Dakota, Missouri River Basin Investigations Project, Report No. 138.* Billings, Mont.: Department of the Interior, Bureau of Indian Affairs, 1954.

Department of the Interior, Bureau of Reclamation. *A Half Century of Irrigation, Lower Yellowstone Project, Montana–North Dakota, December 1958.* Billings, Mont.: Bureau of Reclamation, Division of Irrigation, Region 6, 1958.

———. *Opportunities for Farm Ownership on the Lower Yellowstone Project, Montana–North Dakota.* Washington, D.C.: GPO, 1927.

———. *Reconnaissance Report of Recreation Use and Development, Allenspur Reservoir, Yellowstone Division, Montana.* Billings, Mont.: Bureau of Reclamation, 1962.

Department of the Interior, National Park Service. *Division of the Waters of the Yellowstone River and Tributaries by the States of Wyoming and Montana.* Manuscript. National Archives, Mammoth Hot Springs, YNP, 1933.

———. Fort Union Trading Post, Official Map and Guide. Washington, D.C.: GPO, 1995.

———. *Lewis and Clark Trail.* Washington, D.C.: GPO, 1997.

———. *Statement on Diversion Proposal Affecting Yellowstone Lake, Yellowstone National Park, as Embodied in S. 3925 and H.R. 10489.* 75th Cong. National Archives, Mammoth Hot Springs, YNP, 1938.

———. *Yellowstone, Official Map and Guide.* Washington, D.C.: GPO, 1995.

Department of the Interior, National Park Service, Midwest Region, Missouri River Basin Survey Resource Planning. *Reconnaissance Report of Recreation Use and Development, Allenspur Reservoir, Yellowstone Division, Montana.* Omaha, Nebr.: National Park Service, Midwest Region, 1962.

Department of the Interior, U.S. Geological Survey. Annual Reports, 1872–1905.

———. *Biohydrology of Mountain Fluvial Systems: The Yellowstone, Part I, Re-*

port No. 147. A. J. Silverman and W. D. Tomlinsen. Reston, Va.: United States Geological Survey, 1984.

———. *Field Record File, Field Notes and Diary from Permanent Camp to Yellowstone Lake, 1871, Index No. P-1.* A. C. Peale. Manuscript. Field Records Library, USGS, Geological Division, Denver, Colo.

———. *Field Record File, Livingston, 1885, Index No. P-22.* A. C. Peale. Manuscript. Field Records Library, USGS, Geological Division, Denver, Colo.

———. *Field Record File, Livingston, Three Forks & Vicinity, 1891, Index No. P-39.* A. C. Peale. Manuscript. Field Records Library, USGS, Geological Division, Denver, Colo.

———. *Huntley Irrigation Project, Montana.* Denver: U.S. Reclamation Service, 1911.

———. *Huntley Project, Montana, 1 March 1910.* Vol. 1. Record Group 115, Project Histories—Huntley, Box 204, Entry 10. National Archives and Records Center, Denver, Colo..

———. *Lower Yellowstone Irrigation Project, Montana, North Dakota.* Billings, Mont. (?): Pellen Publishers, 1913.

———. *Lower Yellowstone Project.* Washington, D.C.: GPO, 1961.

———. "Report of the Surveyor-General of Montana Made to the Secretary of the Interior for the Year 1879." Washington, D.C.: GPO, 1880.

———. *Report, United States Geological Survey.* Washington, D.C.: GPO, 1883.

Department of the Interior, U.S. Reclamation Service. *Fifth Annual Reclamation Service Report, 1907, Dams across Yellowstone River, Montana.* Washington, D.C.: GPO, 1907.

Department of the Interior, U.S. Reclamation Service. *Second Annual Report of the Reclamation Service, 1902–03.* Washington, D.C.: GPO, 1904.

DeVoto, Bernard. *The Course of Empire.* 1952. Reprint, Magnolia, Mass.: Peter Smith Publications, 1990.

Dickinson, Emma S. "The Diary of Emma Slack Dickinson, Written before and during Her Journey up the Missouri to Fort Benton and Overland to Missoula in 1869." Manuscript. Montana Historical Society Archives, Helena, Mont.

Dickson, Frank H. "Hard on the Heels of Lewis and Clark." *Montana: The Magazine of Western History* 26, no. 1 (January 1976): 14–25.

Dietrich, William. *Northwest Passage: The Great Columbia River.* New York: Simon and Schuster, 1995.

Ehrenberg, Ralph E. "Sketch of Part of the Missouri & Yellowstone Rivers with a Description of the Country & C." *Journal of the National Archives* fall 1971.

Eichhorn, Gary E. *Peter Jackson, Nimrod and Scout.* Miles City, Mont.: Star Printing Company, 1959.

Evans, Howard Ensign. *The Natural History of the Long Expedition to the Rocky Mountains, 1819–1820.* New York: Oxford University Press, 1997.

Federal Power Commission, Bureau of Engineering, Denver Regional Office. *Preliminary Report on Yellowstone River Basin: Compilation of Factual*

Data Relating to the Basin for Use of the Yellowstone River Compact Commission, Copy No. 60. Denver, Colo.: Federal Power Commission, 1940.

Ferrell, John R. Big Dam Era: A Legislative and Institutional History of the Pick-Sloan Missouri Basin Program. Omaha, Nebr.: Missouri River Division, U.S. Army Corps of Engineers, 1993.

———. Heartland Engineers: U.S. Army Corps of Engineers, Kansas City District, a History. Kansas City: U.S. Army Corps of Engineers, Kansas City District, 1993.

———. Soundings: 100 Years of the Missouri River Navigation Project. Omaha: Missouri River Division, U.S. Army Corps of Engineers, 1995.

Flores, Dan. Horizontal Yellow: Nature and History in the Near Southwest. Albuquerque: University of New Mexico Press, 1999.

———. The Natural West: Environmental History in the Great Plains and Rocky Mountains. Norman: University of Oklahoma Press, 2001.

Fradkin, Philip L. A River No More: The Colorado River and the West. 1981. Reprint, Berkeley: University of California Press, 1995.

Freedom, Gary S. "Moving Men and Supplies: Military Transportation on the Northern Great Plains, 1866–1891." South Dakota History 14, no. 2 (1984): 114–133.

Freeman, Lewis R. Down the Yellowstone. New York: Dodd, Mead, 1922.

Fremont, John C. A Report on an Exploration of the Country Lying between the Missouri River and the Rocky Mountains, on the Line of the Kansas and Great Platte Rivers. Fairfield, Wash.: Ye Galleon Press, 1996.

Frey, Rodney. The World of the Crow Indians: As Driftwood Lodges. Norman: University of Oklahoma Press, 1987.

Frost, Lawrence A., ed. Some Observations on the Yellowstone Expedition of 1873. Glendale, Calif.: Arthur H. Clark, 1981.

Funk, John L., and John W. Robinson. Changes in the Channel of the Lower Missouri River and Effects on Fish and Wildlife. Aquatic Series No. 11. Jefferson City, Mo.: Missouri Department of Conservation, 1974.

Furtwangler, Albert. Acts of Discovery: Visions of America in the Lewis and Clark Journals. Urbana: University of Illinois Press, 1993.

Gardner, E. M. "From the Diary of E. M. Gardner, Telling of the Breaking Up of the Farm Home in Missouri, the Sale, and the Trip up the Missouri." Manuscript. Montana Historical Society Archives, Helena, Mont.

"General Crook's Second Expedition to the Big Horn, 1876." Manuscript. Montana Historical Society Archives, Helena, Mont.

Gerber, Max E. "The Steamboat and Indians of the Upper Missouri." South Dakota History 4, no. 2 (Spring 1974): 139–160.

Gilmore, Melvin Randolph. Uses of Plants by the Indians of the Missouri River Region. 1919. Reprint, Lincoln: University of Nebraska Press, 1991.

Gilpatrick, Stephen Collins. "Journal of Trip up the Missouri, 1862." Manuscript. Montana Historical Society Archives, Helena, Mont.

Goetzmann, William H. Exploration and Empire: The Explorer and the Scientist *in the Winning of the American West.* 1966. Reprint, Austin: Texas State Historical Association, 1994.

Goudie, Andrew. *The Human Impact on the Natural Environment.* 4th ed. Oxford: Blackwell, 1993.

Grant, F. S. "Report of Observations on His Trip up the Yellowstone River, 1875." Manuscript, U.S. Army Engineer Department, Public Library, Glendive, Mont.

Greene, Jerome A. *Yellowstone Command: Colonel Nelson A. Miles and the Great Sioux War, 1876–1877.* Lincoln: University of Nebraska Press, 1991.

Haig-Brown, Roderick L. *A River Never Sleeps.* 1946. Reprint, New York: Lyons Press, 1991.

Haines, Aubrey L., ed. *Osborne Russell's Journal of a Trapper.* 1955. Reprint, Lincoln: University of Nebraska Press, 1965.

Hampton, Duane H, ed. "Promise of the West: The Letters of Isaac Schultz, 1884–1887." *Montana: The Magazine of Western History* 36, no. 4 (autumn 1986): 52–63.

Hanh, Thich Nhat. *Living Buddha, Living Christ.* New York: Riverhead Books, 1995.

Hanson, Joseph M. *The Conquest of the Missouri: Being the Story of the Life and Exploits of Captain Grant Marsh.* 1909. Reprint, New York: Murray Hill Books, 1946.

Hardorff, Richard G. *Lakota Recollections of the Custer Fight.* Spokane, Wash.: Arthur H. Clark, 1991.

Harkness, James. "My Montana Journal, 1862." Manuscript. SC 792, James Harkness Papers. Montana Historical Society Archives, Helena, Mont.

Harris, Charles L. *The Crow Reservation, Homeseekers' Advisor, A Pictorial and Descriptive Book of the Famous Yellowstone Valley and the Ceded Portion of the Crow Indian Reservation.* Helena, Mont.: State Publishing Company, 1906.

Hart, Henry C. *The Dark Missouri.* Madison: University of Wisconsin Press, 1957.

Hart, Jeff. *Montana Native Plants and Early Peoples.* 1976. Reprint, Helena: Montana Historical Society Press, 1992.

Haynes, F. J. Photograph Collection, Photographs H-312, H-702, H-704, H-705, H-729, H-730, H-736, H-740, H-746, H-819, H-863, H-1407, H-1677, H-3112, H-3126, H-3127, H-3128, H-3131, H-3132, H-3135, H-3138, H-4817. Montana State Historical Archives, Helena, Mont.

Hazlitt, Ruth, ed. "The Journal of Francois Antoine Larocque." *Sources of Northwest History,* no. 20. Reprint, Missoula: University of Montana, 1934.

Hedges, James Blaine. *Henry Villard and the Railways of the Northwest.* 1930. Reprint, New York: Russell and Russell, 1967.

Heidenreich, Adrian C. "The Native Americans' Yellowstone." *Montana: The Magazine of Western History* 35, no. 4 (autumn 1985): 2–17.

Herring, Hal. "Confining the Yellowstone: One of the Greatest American Trout

Rivers Is Becoming a Victim of Its Own Wildness." *Field & Stream*, June 1999, 8.

Hildebrand, John. *Reading the River: A Voyage down the Yukon.* 1988. Reprint, Madison: University of Wisconsin Press, 1997.

Hosmer, Allen J. "A Trip to the States in 1865, by the Way of the Yellowstone and Missouri." Edited by Edith M. Duncan. 1867. Reprint, *Sources of Northwest History*, no. 17. Missoula: University of Montana, 1932.

Howard, Joseph Kinsey. *Montana: High, Wide, and Handsome.* 1943. Reprint, Lincoln: University of Nebraska Press, 1983.

Hoxie, Frederick E. *Parading through History: The Making of the Crow Nation in America, 1805–1935.* Cambridge: Cambridge University Press, 1997.

Hudson, John C. "Main Streets of the Yellowstone Valley: Town-Building along the Northern Pacific in Montana." *Montana: The Magazine of Western History* 35, no. 4 (autumn 1985): 56–67.

Hundley, Norris, Jr. *The Great Thirst: Californians and Water, 1770–1990s.* Berkeley: University of California Press, 1992.

Hyde, George E. *Red Cloud's Folk: A History of the Oglala Sioux Indians.* Norman: University of Oklahoma Press, 1937. Reprint, Norman: University of Oklahoma Press, 1975.

Isenberg, Andrew C. *The Destruction of the Bison: An Environmental History, 1750–1920.* New York: Cambridge University Press, 2000.

Jackson, Donald. *Among the Sleeping Giants: Occasional Pieces on Lewis and Clark.* Urbana: University of Illinois Press, 1987.

———. *Thomas Jefferson and the Stony Mountains: Exploring the West from Monticello.* Urbana: University of Illinois Press, 1981. Reprint, Norman: University of Oklahoma Press, 1993.

———. *Voyages of the Steamboat Yellow Stone.* New York: Ticknor and Fields, 1985.

———, ed. *Letters of the Lewis and Clark Expedition with Related Documents, 1783–1854.* 2d ed., 2 vols. Urbana: University of Illinois Press, 1978.

Jensen, Richard E. *The Fontenelle and Cabanne Trading Posts: The History and Archeology of Two Missouri River Sites, 1822–1838.* Lincoln: Nebraska State Historical Society, 1998.

Jensen, Richard E., and James S. Hutchins, eds. *Wheelboats on the Missouri: The Journals and Documents of the Atkinson-O'Fallon Expedition, 1824–26.* Lincoln: Nebraska State Historical Society, 2001.

Jones, Stephen R. *The Last Prairie: A Sandhills Journal.* Camden, Maine: Ragged Mountain Press, 2000.

Joslyn Art Museum and the University of Nebraska Press. *Karl Bodmer's America.* Omaha, Nebr.: Joslyn Art Museum, 1984.

Kahrl, William L. *Water and Power: The Conflict over Los Angeles' Water Supply in the Owens Valley.* 1982. Reprint, Berkeley: University of California Press, 1983.

Kelley, Robert. *Battling the Inland Sea: Floods, Public Policy, and the Sacramento Valley.* Berkeley: University of California Press, 1998.

Kellogg, Mark. "Notes of the Little Big Horn Expedition." Manuscript. Montana Historical Society Archives, Helena, Mont.

Kirkpatrick, Mrs. James. "Early Life in Beaverhead County, in Which She Describes Her Trip up the Missouri River to Montana, in 1878, the Early Mining Camp of Glendale, and Early Religious, Educational, and Social Life in the Beaverhead Valley, Etc., Etc." Manuscript. SC 940. Montana Historical Society Archives, Helena, Mont.

Koch, Peter. "Life at Muscleshell in 1869 and 1870." Manuscript. Montana Historical Society Archives, Helena, Mont.

Krakel, Dean. *Downriver: A Yellowstone Journey.* San Francisco: Sierra Club Books, 1987.

Kurz, Rudolph Friederich. *Journal of Rudolph Friederich Kurz: An Account of His Experiences among Fur Traders and American Indians on the Mississippi and Upper Missouri Rivers during the Years 1846 to 1852.* Edited by J. N. B. Hewitt. Translated by Myrtis Jarrell. Lincoln: University of Nebraska Press, 1970.

LaBarge, Joseph(?). "Yellowstone Guide from the Mouth to Big Horn River for the Guidance of Pilots." Manuscript. Montana Historical Society Archives, Helena, Mont.

Ladner, Mildred D. *William de la Montagne Cary: Artist on the Missouri.* Norman: University of Oklahoma Press, 1984.

Lang, William L. "Saving the Yellowstone." *Montana: The Magazine of Western History* 35, no. 4 (autumn 1985): 87–90.

———, ed. *Stories from an Open Country: Essays on the Yellowstone River Valley.* Billings, Mont.: Western Heritage Press, 1995.

Lang, William L., and Robert C. Carriker, eds. *Great River of the West: Essays on the Columbia River.* Seattle: University of Washington Press, 1999.

Lannoo, Michael J. *Okoboji Wetlands: A Lesson in Natural History.* Iowa City: University of Iowa Press, 1996.

Larpenteur, Charles. *Forty Years a Fur Trader on the Upper Missouri: The Personal Narrative of Charles Larpenteur, 1833–1872.* 1933. Reprint, Lincoln: University of Nebraska Press, 1989.

Lass, William E. *A History of Steamboating on the Upper Missouri River.* Lincoln: University of Nebraska Press, 1962.

———. "Steamboats on the Yellowstone." *Montana: The Magazine of Western History* 35, no. 4 (autumn 1985): 26–41.

Leach, Samuel. "Samuel Leach Reminiscence, 1865–1870." Manuscript. SC 369, Folder 1/1. Montana Historical Society Archives, Helena, Mont.

Lehmer, Donald J. *Introduction to Middle Missouri Archeology.* Anthropological Papers 1. Washington, D.C.: National Park Service, U.S. Department of the Interior, 1971.

Lemann, Nicholas. "Atlas Shrugs: The New Geography Argues That Maps Have Shaped the World." *New Yorker*, April 9, 2001, 131–134.

LeMay, Ray. "Buffalo Hunting." Manuscript. SC 2082, Ray LeMay Papers, Buffalo Hunting in Montana. Montana Historical Society Archives, Helena, Mont.

Linderman, Frank B. *Pretty-shield: Medicine Woman of the Crows.* 1932. Reprint, Lincoln: University of Nebraska Press, 1974.

Lowie, Robert H. *The Crow Indians.* 1935. Reprint, Lincoln: University of Nebraska Press, 1983.

Luttig, John C. *Journal of a Fur-Trading Expedition on the Upper Missouri, 1812–1813.* Edited by Stella M. Drumm. 1920. Reprint, New York: Argosy-Antiquarian, 1964.

MacDonald, John. "A History of Steamboat Navigation on the Yellowstone River." Master's thesis, Montana State University, 1950.

Maguire, Horatio N. *The Coming Empire: A Complete and Reliable Treatise on the Black Hills, Yellowstone, and Big Horn Regions.* Sioux City, Iowa: Watkins and Smead, 1878.

Malone, Michael P. *The Battle for Butte: Mining and Politics on the Northern Frontier, 1864–1906.* 1981. Reprint, Helena: Montana Historical Society Press, 1995.

Malone, Michael P., Richard B. Roeder, and William L. Lang, *Montana: A History of Two Centuries.* Rev. ed. Seattle: University of Washington Press, 1991.

Marsh, Elias J. "Journal of Dr. Elias J. Marsh: Account of a Steamboat Trip on the Missouri River, May–August, 1859." *South Dakota Historical Review* 1, no. 2 (January 1936): 79–127.

Marshall, Mark C. *Yellowstone Trails: A Hiking Guide.* 5th ed. Yellowstone National Park: Yellowstone Association, 1995.

Martin, Russell. *A Story That Stands Like a Dam: Glen Canyon and the Struggle for the Soul of the West.* Salt Lake City: University of Utah Press, 1989.

Mattison, Ray H. "The Indian Frontier on the Upper Missouri to 1865." *Nebraska History* 39, no. 3 (1958): 241–266.

McCullough, David. *The Path between the Seas: The Creation of the Panama Canal, 1870–1914.* New York: Simon and Schuster, 1977.

McDermott, John Francis, ed. *Up the Missouri with Audubon: The Journal of Edward Harris.* Norman: University of Oklahoma Press, 1951.

McDonald, Jerry N. *North American Bison: Their Classification and Evolution.* Berkeley: University of California Press, 1981.

McElrath, Thomson P. *The Yellowstone Valley. What It Is, Where It Is, and How to Get to It. A Hand-Book for Tourists and Settlers.* St. Paul, Minn.: Pioneer Press, 1880.

McGinnis, Michael V. ed. *Bioregionalism.* London: Routledge, 1999.

McLemore, Clyde. "Fort Pease, The First Attempted Settlement in Yellowstone Valley." *The Montana Magazine of History* 2, no. 1 (January 1952): 17–31.

McNamee, Gregory. *Gila: The Life and Death of an American River.* Albuquerque: University of New Mexico Press, 1994.

Meinig, Donald W. *The Great Columbia Plain: A Historical Geography, 1805–1910.* 1968. Reprint, Seattle: University of Washington Press, 1995.

Mercier, Laurie K. "Montana Episodes, Memories of Sidney, Montana, and the Lower Yellowstone Valley, 1919–1939." *Montana: The Magazine of Western History* 35, no. 4 (autumn 1985): 78–83.

Miller, Don C., and Stan B. Cohen. *Military and Trading Posts of Montana.* Missoula, Mont.: Pictorial Histories Publishing Company, 1979.

Missouri River Commission. *Missouri River, Mouth to Three Forks.* Washington, D.C.: GPO, 1894.

Missouri River Journal. Unknown title and author. Manuscript. Montana Historical Society Archives, Helena, Mont.

Montana Department of Fish and Game. *The Ecological Implications of Yellowstone River Flow Reservations.* Helena, Mont.: Montana Department of Fish and Game, 1979.

Montana Department of Fish, Wildlife, and Parks, Ecological Services Division. *The Yellowstone River: An Instream Flow Allocation for the Warm Water Portion.* Helena, Mont.: Montana Department of Fish, Wildlife, and Parks, 1980.

Morgan, Lewis Henry. *The Indian Journals, 1859–62.* New York: Dover, 1993.

———. "Lewis Henry Morgan Diary, 1862." Manuscript. SC 525. Montana Historical Society Archives, Helena, Mont.

Morley, James, Henry. "Diary of James Henry Morley in Montana, 1862, 1865." Manuscript. Montana Historical Society Archives, Helena, Mont.

Morrow, Delores. "Forsyth's Booster: Walter B. Dean, Jr." *Montana: The Magazine of Western History* 35, no. 4 (autumn 1985): 68–77.

Moulton, Gary E., ed. *The Journals of the Lewis and Clark Expedition.* 12 vols. Lincoln: University of Nebraska Press, 1983–1999.

Mount, Jeffrey F. *California Rivers and Streams: The Conflict between Fluvial Process and Land Use.* Berkeley: University of California Press, 1995.

Mulloy, William. "An Indian Village Near Pompey's Pillar Creek, Montana." *Plains Anthropologist* 14, no. 4 (1969): 95–102.

Murray, John A. *The River Reader.* New York: Lyons Press, 1998.

Napton, John. "My Trip on the 'Imperial' in 1867." Manuscript. Montana Historical Society Archives, Helena, Mont.

Nasatir, A. P., ed. *Before Lewis and Clark: Documents Illustrating the History of the Missouri, 1785–1804.* 2 vols. Lincoln: University of Nebraska Press, 1990.

National Geographic Maps, Trails Illustrated. *Yellowstone National Park, Wyoming/Montana.* Rev. ed. Evergreen, Colo.: Trails Illustrated, a division of National Geographic Maps, 1994.

Neihardt, John G. *The River and I.* Reprint, Lincoln: University of Nebraska Press, 1968.

Newman, O. N. "Diary 1879." Manuscript. SC 146, Folder 1/1. Montana Historical Society Archives, Helena, Mont.

———. "O. N. Newman Diary, 1884." Manuscript, Montana Historical Society Archives, Helena, Mont.

Nichols, Roger L., ed. *The Missouri Expedition, 1818–1820: The Journal of Surgeon John Gale with Related Documents*. Norman: University of Oklahoma Press, 1969.

Norall, Frank. *Bourgmont, Explorer of the Missouri, 1698–1725*. Lincoln: University of Nebraska Press, 1988.

Norris, Kathleen. *Dakota: A Spiritual Geography*. New York: Houghton Mifflin, 1993.

North Dakota Department of Transportation, Planning Division. *North Dakota, Official Highway Map, 1997–1998*. Bismarck: North Dakota Department of Transportation, 1997.

Northern Pacific Railroad. *Irrigation in Montana*. St. Paul, Minn.: Northern Pacific Railroad, 1904(?).

Oglesby, Richard E. *Manuel Lisa and the Opening of the Missouri Fur Trade*. Norman: University of Oklahoma Press, 1963.

Osgood, Ernest S. "The Return Journey in 1806: William Clark on the Yellowstone." *Montana: The Magazine of Western History* 28, no. 3 (July 1968): 9–29.

Outwater, Alice. *Water: A Natural History*. New York: Basic Books, 1996.

Owen, Richard. "Diary of the Travels of Richard Owen from Omaha, Nebraska, to the Gold Regions of Idaho." Manuscript. Montana Historical Society Archives, Helena, Mont.

Palmer, Tim. *Endangered Rivers and the Conservation Movement*. Berkeley: University of California Press, 1986.

Parker, Donald D. "Expeditions up the Missouri, 1818–1825." *South Dakota Historical Collections* 33 (1966): 458–487.

Paul, R. Eli, ed. *Autobiography of Red Cloud: War Leader of the Oglalas*. Helena: Montana Historical Society Press, 1997.

Peterson, John M. "Buffalo Hunting in Montana in 1886: The Diary of W. Harvey Brown." *Montana: The Magazine of Western History* 31, no. 4 (October 1981): 2–13.

Pfaller, Louis L. "Eli Washington John Lindesmith: Fort Keogh's Chaplain in Buckskin." *Montana: The Magazine of Western History* 27, no. 1 (January 1977): 14–25.

Pickett, William D. "William D. Pickett Diaries, 1876." Manuscript. SC 1436, Folder 1/7. Montana Historical Society Archives, Helena, Mont.

"Pierre Chouteau, Jr. & Company Collection." MC 4, Box 1, Folder 1–3. Correspondence, J.A.H. to Kenneth McKenzie. Montana Historical Society Archives, Helena, Mont.

"Pierre Chouteau, Jr. & Company Collection. Fort Union Letterbook." MC 4, Box 1, Folder 1–3. Correspondence, Kenneth McKenzie to Samuel Tulloch. Montana Historical Society Archives, Helena, Mont.

"Pierre Chouteau, Jr. & Company Collection. Statements of Furs & Robes Shipped & on Hand." MC 4, Box 1, Folder 1–10. Montana Historical Society Archives, Helena, Mont.

Pisani, Donald J. *To Reclaim a Divided West: Water, Law, and Public Policy, 1848–1902*. Albuquerque: University of New Mexico Press, 1992.

Pitzer, Paul C. *Grand Coulee: Harnessing a Dream*. Pullman: Washington State University Press, 1994.

Powell, John Wesley. *The Exploration of the Colorado River and Its Canyons*. 1895. Reprint, New York: Dover, 1961.

Prior, Jean C. *Landforms of Iowa*. Iowa City: University of Iowa Press, 1991.

Prodgers, Jeanette, ed. *The Champion Buffalo Hunter: The Frontier Memoirs of Yellowstone Vic Smith, by Victor Grant Smith*. Helena: Falcon Publishing, 1997.

Quaife, Milo Milton. *Yellowstone Kelley: The Memoirs of Luther S. Kelley*. 1926. Reprint, Lincoln: University of Nebraska Press, 1973.

Quivey, Addison M. "The Yellowstone Expedition of 1874." *Contributions to the Historical Society of Montana*. Vol. 1. Helena, Mont.: Rocky Mountain Publishing Company, 1876.

Raban, Jonathan. *Bad Land: An American Romance*. New York: Pantheon, 1996.

Rankin, Charles E., ed. *Legacy: New Perspectives on the Battle of the Little Bighorn*. Helena: Montana Historical Society Press, 1996.

Rapp, Valerie. *What the River Reveals: Understanding and Restoring Healthy Watersheds*. Seattle: The Mountaineers, 1997.

Reed, Irving. "Letter to the Editor of the White Pigeon Journal, June 28, 1879." Manuscript. Helena: Montana Historical Society Archives.

Reuss, Martin. *Designing the Bayous: The Control of Water in the Atchafalaya Basin, 1800–1995*. Alexandria, Va.: Office of History, U.S. Army Corps of Engineers, 1998.

Richards, Bill. "The Untamed Yellowstone." *National Geographic*, August 1981, 257–278.

Robinson, Michael C. *Water for the West: The Bureau of Reclamation, 1902–1977*. Chicago: Public Works Historical Society, 1979.

Rodman, Paul W. *The Far West and the Great Plains in Transition, 1859–1900*. New York: Harper and Row, 1988.

Ronda, James P. *Lewis and Clark among the Indians*. Lincoln: University of Nebraska Press, 1984.

———. *Voyages of Discovery: Essays on the Lewis and Clark Expedition*. Helena: Montana Historical Society Press, 1998.

Rothman, Hal K. *Devil's Bargains: Tourism in the Twentieth-Century American West*. Lawrence: University Press of Kansas, 1998.

Runte, Alfred. *National Parks: The American Experience*. Lincoln: University of Nebraska Press, 1989.

Russell, Don, ed. *Trails of the Iron Horse: An Informal History by the Western Writers of America*. Garden City, N.Y.: Doubleday, 1975.

Schneider, Bill. *Montana's Yellowstone River*. Helena: Montana Magazine, 1985.

Schneiders, Robert Kelley. *Unruly River: Two Centuries of Change along the Missouri*. Lawrence: University Press of Kansas, 1999.

Schullery, Paul. *Searching for Yellowstone: Ecology and Wonder in the Last Wilderness.* New York: Houghton Mifflin, 1997.

Schuyler, James Dix. *Reservoirs for Irrigation, Water-Power, and Domestic Water-Supply.* New York: Wiley, 1902.

Secoy, Frank Raymond. *Changing Military Patterns of the Great Plains Indians.* 1953. Reprint, Lincoln: University of Nebraska Press, 1992.

Shallat, Todd. *Structures in the Stream: Water, Science, and the Rise of the U.S. Army Corps of Engineers.* Austin: University of Texas Press, 1994.

Sherow, James Earl. *Watering the Valley: Development along the High Plains Arkansas River, 1870–1950.* Lawrence: University Press of Kansas, 1990.

Sidney, Montana, Chamber of Commerce. *Our Jubilee, 1911–1961, Sidney, Mont., Lower Yellowstone Valley.* Sidney, Mont.: Chamber of Commerce, 1961.

Smalley, Eugene V. *History of the Northern Pacific Railroad.* New York: Putnam's, 1883.

Smith, Burton M. "Business, Politics and Indian Land Settlements in Montana, 1882–1904." *Canadian Journal of History* 20 (April 1985): 45–64.

———. "Politics and the Crow Indian Land Cessions, 1851–1904." *Montana: The Magazine of Western History* 36, no. 4 (autumn 1986): 24–37.

Snell, George Ellsworth. *George Ellsworth Snell Diary.* SC 1864, Folder 1/2. Montana Historical Society Archives, Helena, Mont.

Spitzley, Stephen A. "Stephen A. Spitzley Journal, 1867." Manuscript. Montana Historical Society Archives, Helena, Mont.

Stanley, D. S. "Transcribed Copy of Colonel Stanley's 1872 Yellowstone Expedition, Escorted a Surveying Party of the N.P.R.R., Original Addendum to Report Is Attached." Manuscript. SC 919. Montana Historical Society Archives, Helena, Mont.

Stegner, Wallace. *Beyond the Hundredth Meridian: John Wesley Powell and the Second Opening of the West.* 1954. Reprint, New York: Penguin, 1992.

Steinberg, Theodore. *Nature Incorporated: Industrialization and the Waters of New England.* 1991. Reprint, Amherst: University of Massachusetts Press, 1994.

Stevens, Joseph E. *Hoover Dam: An American Adventure.* Norman: University of Oklahoma Press, 1988.

Stine, Jeffrey K. *Mixing the Waters: Environment, Politics, and the Building of the Tennessee-Tombigbee Waterway.* Akron, Ohio: University of Akron Press, 1993.

Stuart, James. "The Yellowstone Expedition of 1863, from the Journal of Captain James Stuart, with notes by Samuel T. Hauser and Granville Stuart, Active Members of the Historical Society of Montana." *Contributions to the Historical Society of Montana.* Vol. 1. Helena: Rocky Mountain Publishing Company, 1876.

Sunder, John E. *The Fur Trade on the Upper Missouri, 1840–1865.* Norman: University of Oklahoma Press, 1965.

Thwaites, Reuben Gold, ed. *Early Western Travels, 1748–1846*. Vol. 5, *Bradbury's Travels in the Interior of America 1809–1811*. New York: AMS Press, 1966.

———. *Early Western Travels, 1748–1846. Vol. 6, Brackenridge's Journal up the Missouri, 1811*. New York: AMS Press, 1966.

———. *Early Western Travels, 1748–1846*. Vols. 22–24, *Maximilian, Prince of Wied's Travels in the Interior of North America, 1832–1834*, New York: AMS Press, 1966.

Travel Montana, Department of Commerce, and Montana Department of Transportation. *Montana, 1998–99 Official State Highway Map*. Helena: Montana Department of Transportation, 1998.

Trulsson, Nora Burba. "A Flood Expert Makes Waves." *Nature Conservancy*, September/October 1999, 10–11.

U.S. Congress, House. *Additional Improvements of the Yellowstone and Missouri Rivers*. 45th Cong., 3d sess., 1879. House Misc. Doc. 27.

———. *Council with the Sioux Indians at Fort Pierre*. 34th Cong., 1st sess., 1856. House Ex. Doc. 130.

———. *Destitution of Sioux Indians*. 40th Cong., 2d sess., 1868. House Ex. Doc. 76.

———. *Improvement of Missouri and Yellowstone Rivers*. 44th Cong., 1st sess., 1876. House Misc. Doc. 90.

———. *Indians of the Upper Missouri*. Message of the President of the United States. 34th Cong., 1st sess, 1856. Ex. Doc. 65.

———. *Irrigation Easements in the Yellowstone National Park*. 66th Cong., 2d sess., 1920. House Report 767.

———. *Military Expedition against the Sioux Indians*. 44th Cong., 1st sess., 1876. House Ex. Doc. 184.

———. *Missouri River Basin*. 78th Cong., 2d sess., 1944. House Doc. 475.

———. *Missouri River*. 60th Cong., 2d sess., 1908. House Doc. 1120.

———. *Missouri River*. 73d Cong., 2d sess., 1935. House Doc. 238.

———. *Report of Superintendent of Indian Affairs, D. D. Mitchell*. House Doc. 2. Washington, D.C.: GPO, 1851.

———. *Report of the Upper Missouri Agency, No. 43, Alfred D. Vaughn*. House Doc. 1. Washington, D.C.: GPO, 1853.

———. *Sioux Indians*. 43d Cong., 2d sess., 1875. House Ex. Doc. 144.

———. *Surveys and Reconnaissances*. 43d Cong., 2d sess., 1875. House Ex. Doc. 145.

———. *Teton-Sioux Indians*. 42d Cong., 3d sess., 1873. House Ex. Doc. 96.

———. *Upper Missouri Agency*. House Doc. 4. Washington, D.C.: GPO, 1846.

———. *Yellowstone River, Mont.* 62d Cong., 1st sess., 1911. House Doc. 83.

———. *Yellowstone River, Wyo., Mont., and N. Dak.* 73d Cong., 2d sess., 1934. House Doc. 256.

U.S. Congress, Senate. *A Copy of the Report of Brevet Major General Harney upon the Sioux Indians on the Upper Missouri*. 40th Cong., 3d sess., 1869. Senate Ex. Doc. 11.

————. *Explorations in the Dacota Country in the Year 1855 by Lieut. G. K. Warren, Topographical Engineer of the "Sioux Expedition."* 34th Cong., 1st sess., 1856. Senate Ex. Doc. 76.

————. *Hearing before the Committee on Irrigation and Reclamation.* 67th Cong., 2d sess., 1922. Senate Bill 274.

————. *Hearing before the Committee on Irrigation.* 66th Cong., 3d sess., 1921. Senate Bill 4529.

————. *Missouri River Basin.* 78th Cong., 2d sess., 1944. Senate Doc. 191.

————. *Missouri River Basin.* 78th Cong., 2d sess., 1944. Senate Doc. 247.

————. *Report on the Exploration of the Yellowstone River by Bvt. Brig. Gen. W. F. Raynolds.* 40th Cong., 1st sess., 1868. Senate Ex. Doc. 77.

————. Subcommittee of the Committee on Public Works. *Plans for Big Bend Dam, South Dakota, Hearing before the Subcommittee of the Committee on Public Works.* 86th Cong., 1st sess., 1959.

United States Geological Survey. *Eleventh Annual Report, 1889–1890.* Part 2, *Irrigation Survey.* Washington, D.C.: GPO, 1891.

————. *Fifth Annual Report, 1883–1884, Report of Mr. Arnold Hague, United States Geological Survey, Yellowstone National Park Survey.* Washington, D.C.: GPO, 1885.

————. *Nineteenth Annual Report, 1897–1898.* Part 4, *Hydrography, Yellowstone Basin.* Washington, D.C.: GPO, 1899.

————. *Ninth Annual Report, 1887–1888, Report of Mr. Arnold Hague, United States Geological Survey, Yellowstone National Park Survey.* Washington, D.C.: GPO, 1889.

————. *Tenth Annual Report, 1888–1889.* Part 2, *Irrigation Survey.* Washington, D.C.: GPO, 1890.

————. *Thirteenth Annual Report, 1891–1892.* Part 3, *Irrigation.* Washington, D.C.: GPO, 1893.

————. *Twentieth Annual Report, 1898–1899.* Part 4, *Hydrography, Yellowstone Drainage Basin.* Washington, D.C.: GPO, 1900.

————. *Twenty-fifth Annual Report, 1903–1904.* Washington D.C.: GPO, 1905.

————. *Twenty-first Annual Report, 1899–1900,* Part 4, *Hydrography, Yellowstone Drainage Basin.* Washington, D.C.: GPO, 1901.

————. *Twenty-sixth Annual Report, 1904–1905.* Washington, D.C.: GPO, 1906.

Utley, Robert M. *Cavalier in Buckskin: George Armstrong Custer and the Western Military Frontier.* Norman: University of Oklahoma Press, 1988.

————. *Frontier Regulars: The United States Army and the Indian, 1866–1891.* 1973. Reprint, Lincoln: University of Nebraska Press, 1984.

————. *Frontiersmen in Blue: The United States Army and the Indian, 1848–1865.* 1967. Reprint, Lincoln: University of Nebraska Press, 1981.

————. *The Lance and the Shield: The Life and Times of Sitting Bull.* New York: Ballantine, 1993.

————. "Origins of the Great Sioux War: The Brown-Anderson Controversy Revisited." *Montana: The Magazine of Western History,* 42, no. 4 (autumn 1992): 48–52.

———. "War Houses in the Sioux Country: The Military Occupation of the Lower Yellowstone." *Montana: The Magazine of Western History* 35, no. 4 (autumn 1985): 18–25.

Van West, Carroll. *Capitalism on the Frontier: Billings and the Yellowstone Valley in the Nineteenth Century.* Lincoln: University of Nebraska Press, 1993.

———. "Coulson and the Clark's Fork Bottom: The Economic Structure of a Pre-railroad Community, 1874–1881." *Montana: The Magazine of Western History* 35, no. 4 (autumn 1985): 42–55.

———. "Roughing It Up the Yellowstone to Wonderland: An Account of a Trip through the Yellowstone Valley in 1878, by Colgate Hoyt." *Montana: The Magazine of Western History* 36, no. 2 (spring 1986): 22–35.

Varley, John D., and Paul Schullery. *Yellowstone Fishes: Ecology, History, and Angling in the Park.* Mechanicsburg, Pa.: Stackpole Books, 1998.

Vileisis, Ann. *Discovering the Unknown Landscape: A History of America's Wetlands.* Washington, D.C.: Island Press, 1997.

Viola, Herman J. *Little Bighorn Remembered: The Untold Indian Story of Custer's Last Stand.* New York: Times Books, 1999.

Walcheck, Ken. *Treasure of Gold: The Lower Yellowstone River.* Helena: Montana Department of Fish, Wildlife, and Parks, 1979.

Wallace, Anthony F. C. *Jefferson and the Indians: The Tragic Fate of the First Americans.* Cambridge, Mass.: Harvard University Press, 1999.

Walton, John. *Western Times and Water Wars: State, Culture, and Rebellion in California.* Berkeley: University of California Press, 1992.

Warren, Gouverneur K. *Explorer of the Northern Plains: Lieutenant Gouverneur K. Warren's Preliminary Report of Explorations in Nebraska and Dakota, in the Years 1855–'56–'57.* Introduction by Frank N. Schubert. Washington, D.C.: GPO, 1981.

Water Resources Division, Montana Department of Natural Resources and Conservation. *Aquatic Invertebrates of the Yellowstone River Basin, Montana, Technical Report No. 5, Yellowstone Impact Study.* Helena, Mont.: Montana Department of Natural Resources and Conservation, 1977.

———. *The Effect of Altered Streamflow on Existing Municipal and Agricultural Users of the Yellowstone River Basin, Montana, Technical Report No. 9, Yellowstone Impact Study.* Helena, Mont.: Montana Department of Natural Resources and Conservation, 1977.

———. *The Effect of Altered Streamflow on Fish of the Yellowstone and Tongue Rivers, Montana, Technical Report No. 8, Yellowstone Impact Study.* Helena, Mont.: Montana Department of Natural Resources and Conservation, 1977.

———. *The Effect of Altered Streamflow on Furbearing Mammals of the Yellowstone River Basin, Montana, Technical Report No. 6, Yellowstone Impact Study.* Helena, Mont.: Montana Department of Natural Resources and Conservation, 1977.

———. *The Effect of Altered Streamflow on the Hydrology and Geomorphology of the Yellowstone River Basin, Montana, Technical Report No. 2, Yellowstone*

Impact Study. Helena, Mont.: Montana Department of Natural Resources and Conservation, 1977.

———. *The Effect of Altered Streamflow on Migratory Birds of the Yellowstone River Basin, Montana, Technical Report No. 7, Yellowstone Impact Study.* Helena, Mont.: Montana Department of Natural Resources and Conservation, 1977.

———. *The Effect of Altered Streamflow on Water-Based Recreation in the Yellowstone River Basin, Montana, Technical Report No. 10, Yellowstone Impact Study.* Helena, Mont.: Montana Department of Natural Resources and Conservation, 1977.

———. *How the River Runs: A Study of Potential Changes in the Yellowstone River Basin, Yellowstone Impact Study, Final Report.* Helena, Mont.: Montana Department of Natural Resources and Conservation, 1981.

Webb, Walter Prescott. *The Great Plains.* 1931. Reprint, Lincoln: University of Nebraska Press, 1981.

Wells, J. A. "First Connected Account of the Warfare Waged by the Sioux Indians against Wood Choppers, Missouri River between Ft. Buford & Ft. Benton, 1866–1870." Manuscript. Montana Historical Society Archives, Helena, Mont.

Werden, Francis H. "Journal Kept by F. H. Werden While on His Way to the Mines, 1864." Manuscript. Montana Historical Society Archives, Helena, Mont.

Weston, Daniel H. "Diary, on Board Steamer 'Colorado,' Missouri River, above St. Joseph, Mo, 1866." Manuscript. Montana Historical Society Archives, Helena, Mont.

White Bull, Joseph. *Lakota Warrior.* Translated and edited by James H. Howard. Lincoln: University of Nebraska Press, 1968.

White, Richard. *The Organic Machine: The Remaking of the Columbia River.* New York: Hill and Wang, 1995.

———. "The Winning of the West: The Expansion of the Western Sioux in the Eighteenth and Nineteenth Centuries." *Journal of American History*, 125, no. 2 (September 1978): 319–343.

"White Pigeon Journal." Montana Historical Society Archives, Helena, Mont.

White, William H. "Diary Kept by William H. White in 1876." Manuscript. Montana Historical Society Archives, Helena, Mont.

Wilcox, A. H. "Up the Missouri River to Montana in the Spring of 1862." Manuscript. Montana Historical Society Archives, Helena, Mont.

Wilhelm, Paul. "First Journey to North America in the Years 1822 to 1824 by Paul Wilhelm, Duke of Wuerttemberg." Translated by Wm. G. Bek. *South Dakota Historical Collections.* Vol. 19, Pierre, S.D.: Hipple Printing Company, 1938.

Williams, Terry Tempest. *Red: Passion and Patience in the Desert.* New York: Pantheon, 2001.

Wilson, Frederick T. "Fort Pierre and Its Neighbors." *South Dakota Historical Collections.* Vol. 1. Aberdeen, S.D.: News Printing Company, 1902.

Wilson, Gilbert L. *Buffalo Bird Woman's Garden.* St. Paul: Minnesota Historical Society Press, 1987.

Wishart, David J. *The Fur Trade of the American West 1807–1840: A Geographical Synthesis.* Lincoln: University of Nebraska Press, 1979.

Wood, Raymond W. "An Introduction to the History of the Fur Trade on the Northern Plains." *North Dakota History, Journal of the Northern Plains* 61, no. 3 (summer 1994): 2–6.

Wood, Raymond W., and Gary E. Moulton. "Prince Maximilian and New Maps of the Missouri and Yellowstone Rivers by William Clark." *Western Historical Quarterly* 12, no. 4 (October 1981): 372–386.

Worster, Donald. *Rivers of Empire: Water, Aridity, and the Growth of the American West.* New York: Pantheon, 1985.

Wright, John W. "Diary of Sergeant John W. Wright, 1840–1884." Manuscript. Montana Historical Society Archives, Helena, Mont.

Wyckoff, William, and Lary M. Dilsaver, eds. *The Mountainous West: Explorations in Historical Geography.* Lincoln: University of Nebraska Press, 1995.

Yellowstone Association and the National Park Service. *Canyon.* Yellowstone National Park, Wyo.: Yellowstone Association, 1999.

Yellowstone Irrigation Association. *Report on Proposed Project for Flood Control and Irrigation in the Yellowstone River Valley, Wyoming, Montana, and North Dakota.* Livingston, Mont.: Yellowstone Irrigation Association, 1921.

The Yellowstone Journal. Illustrated and Historical Edition. Miles City, Montana. September 27, 1900.

Yellowstone Lake Papers. Correspondence. National Archives, Mammoth Hot Springs, Yellowstone National Park, Wyo.

Zinn, Howard. *On History.* New York: Seven Stories Press, 2001.

———. *On War.* New York: Seven Stories Press, 2001.

Index